CAMBRIDGE
UNIVERSITY PRESS

Success
International English Skills
for Cambridge IGCSE™

TEACHER'S RESOURCE

Frances Reynolds, Ingrid Wisniewska & Marian Barry

CAMBRIDGE
UNIVERSITY PRESS

University Printing House, Cambridge CB2 8BS, United Kingdom

One Liberty Plaza, 20th Floor, New York, NY 10006, USA

477 Williamstown Road, Port Melbourne, VIC 3207, Australia

314–321, 3rd Floor, Plot 3, Splendor Forum, Jasola District Centre, New Delhi – 110025, India

103 Penang Road, #05–06/07, Visioncrest Commercial, Singapore 238467

Cambridge University Press is part of the University of Cambridge.

It furthers the University's mission by disseminating knowledge in the pursuit of education, learning and research at the highest international levels of excellence.

www.cambridge.org
Information on this title: www.cambridge.org/9781009122733

© Cambridge University Press 2022

First published by Georgian Press (Jersey) Limited 1998
Second edition 2005
Reprinted and published by Cambridge University Press, Cambridge 2010
Third edition 2015
Fourth edition 2017
Fifth edition 2022

20 19 18 17 16 15 14 13 12 11 10 9 8 7 6 5 4 3 2

Printed in Great Britain by CPI Group (UK) Ltd, Croydon CR0 4YY

A catalogue record for this publication is available from the British Library

ISBN 978-1-009-12273-3 Paperback with Digital Access (2 Years)

DEDICATED TEACHER AWARDS

Teachers play an important part in shaping futures. Our Dedicated Teacher Awards recognise the hard work that teachers put in every day.

Thank you to everyone who nominated this year; we have been inspired and moved by all of your stories. Well done to all of our nominees for your dedication to learning and for inspiring the next generation of thinkers, leaders and innovators.

Congratulations to our incredible winners!

WINNER

Regional Winner Middle East & North Africa	Regional Winner Europe	Regional Winner North & South America	Regional Winner Central & Southern Africa	Regional Winner Australia, New Zealand & South-East Asia	Regional Winner East & South Asia
Annamma Lucy GEMS Our Own English High School, Sharjah - Boys' Branch, UAE	Anna Murray British Council, France	Melissa Crosby Frankfort High School, USA	Nonhlanhla Masina African School for Excellence, South Africa	Peggy Pesik Sekolah Buin Batu, Indonesia	Raminder Kaur Mac Choithram School, India

For more information about our dedicated teachers and their stories, go to
dedicatedteacher.cambridge.org

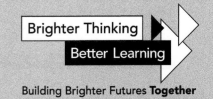

> Contents

Assessment criteria for writing and speaking		vi
How to use this series		x
How to use this Teacher's Resource		xi
Introduction		xiii
Approaches to learning and teaching		xxiii
The Cambridge Learner Corpus		xxv

Teaching notes

1	Goals and achievements	1
2	Fitness and well-being	23
3	Where we live	43
4	Our impact on the planet	63
5	Entertainment	84
6	Travel and the outdoor life	105
7	Student life	126
8	The search for adventure	148
9	Animals and our world	172
10	The world of work	194
	Answers to Workbook questions	216
	Workbook audioscripts	243
	Acknowledgements	252

Digital resources

The following items are available on Cambridge GO. For more information on how to access and use your digital resource, please see inside front cover.

Approaches to teaching and learning:

- Active learning
- Assessment for learning
- Developing learning language skills
- Differentiation
- Improving learning through questioning
- Language awareness
- Metacognition
- Skills for life

Sample answers for extended writing tasks

Unit tests and mark schemes

Writing and speaking marking criteria

Practice exam-style papers and mark schemes

Coursebook answers

Workbook answers

Coursebook audioscripts

Workbook audioscripts

Audio for the Coursebook

Audio for the Workbook

> Assessment criteria for writing and speaking

These marking criteria were written by the authors. In the examination, the way marks would be awarded to answers like these may be different.

The information in this section is based on the 0510 / 0511 / 0991 / 0993 syllabuses for examination from 2024. You should always refer to the appropriate syllabus document for the year of your students' examination to confirm the details and for more information. The syllabus document is available on the Cambridge International website at www.cambridgeinternational.org

Writing

Award up to 6 marks for content and 9 marks for language according to the guidelines below.

[Total: 15]

Content

Description	Marks
The answer: • addresses the task completely • only includes content that is relevant to the task • uses an appropriate format and register throughout • shows an excellent understanding of purpose and audience • is very well developed • meets the word-count requirement.	5–6
The answer: • mainly addresses the task • mainly includes content that is relevant to the task • uses mainly appropriate format and register • shows a good understanding of purpose and audience • is mainly well developed • meets the word-count requirement.	3–4

Description	Marks
The answer: • partially addresses the task • includes some content that is not relevant to the task • produces text with an inconsistent or inappropriate format and register • shows a lack of understanding of purpose and audience • shows minimal development • is below the required word count.	1–2
No creditable content	0

Language

Description	Marks
The answer: • uses a broad range of both common and uncommon vocabulary • uses a broad range of simple and complex structures • uses language that is almost always accurate; any errors are in less common vocabulary or complex structures, and do not affect the reader's comprehension • is organised effectively • uses a broad range of linking words and devices.	7–9
The answer: • uses a range of common vocabulary, with some examples of less common vocabulary • uses a broad range of simple structures, and tries to use some complex structures • uses language that is mainly accurate; errors are mostly in less common vocabulary or complex structures, and do not affect the reader's comprehension • is reasonably well organised • uses a range of a range of linking words and devices.	4–6
The answer: • uses only common vocabulary • uses only simple structures • uses language that is sometimes difficult to understand, due to errors in common vocabulary and simple structures • shows only a basic attempt at organisation • uses a small range of linking words and devices.	1–3
No creditable content	0

Speaking

When using the marking criteria below for the unit tests, consider the student's responses to all parts of the speaking exercise. Select a mark from 0–10 for each of grammar, vocabulary, development and pronunciation.

Grammar	Vocabulary	Development	Pronunciation	Marks
• Student uses a range of simple and complex structures. • Student makes minimal errors in both simple and complex structures. • Meaning is always clear.	• Student can talk about and express opinions on a range of facts and ideas. • Student uses a wide range of vocabulary. • Student can use some vocabulary with precision.	• Student always responds relevantly and develops their ideas. • Student needs no or very little support to maintain communication.	• Student's pronunciation is always clear. • Student often uses intonation effectively to communicate intended meaning	9–10
• Student uses a range of simple structures and attempts to use some complex structures. • Student makes minimal errors in simple structures, but more frequent errors in complex structures. • The meaning is always clear despite errors.	• Student can talk about and express opinions on a range of facts and ideas. • Student uses a reasonable range of vocabulary. • Student uses vocabulary correctly.	• Student responds relevantly and develops most of their ideas. • Student needs occasional support to maintain communication.	• Student can be understood despite some pronunciation issues. • Student sometimes uses intonation effectively to communicate intended meaning.	7–8
• Student uses a range of simple structures, but rarely uses complex structures. • Student makes some errors in the structures used. • Meaning may sometimes be ambiguous because of errors.	• Student can talk about and express opinions on simple facts and ideas. • Student uses a range of vocabulary. • Student uses most vocabulary correctly.	• Student responds relevantly and develops some of their ideas. • Student needs frequent support to maintain communication.	• Student can mostly be understood, but some effort is needed because of pronunciation issues. • Student rarely uses intonation effectively to communicate intended meaning.	5–6

Grammar	Vocabulary	Development	Pronunciation	Marks
• Student uses a very limited range of simple structures. • Student makes frequent errors. • Meaning is often ambiguous because of the errors.	• Student can only talk about and express opinions on basic facts. • Student uses a limited range of vocabulary.	• Student provides some irrelevant responses and rarely develops their ideas. • Student has difficulty maintaining communication despite frequent support.	• Student can rarely be understood, effort is needed because of pronunciation issues. • Student does not use intonation effectively to communicate the intended meaning.	3–4
• Student only uses isolated words or simple short phrases. • Meaning is ambiguous throughout.	• Student has difficulty talking about and expressing opinions on even basic facts. • Student only uses extremely limited and repetitive vocabulary.	• Student only provides very short isolated responses. • Student cannot maintain communication despite frequent support.	• Student has serious pronunciation issues, which lead to a break-down in communication. • Student does not use any intonation patterns.	1–2
No answer given	No answer given	No answer given	No answer given	0

[Unit test speaking exercise total: 10]

› How to use this series

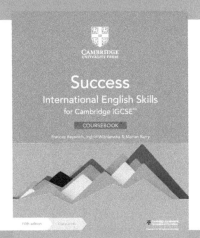

The Coursebook is designed for students to use in class with guidance from the teacher. It offers complete coverage of the Cambridge IGCSE and IGCSE (9–1) English as a Second Language syllabuses (0510/0511/0991/0993) for examination from 2024. Ten topic-based units engage students and help them to develop the necessary reading, writing, speaking, listening and grammar skills. Each unit contains opportunities to check progress with exam-style questions and self-assessment features.

A digital version of the Coursebook is included with the print version and available separately. It includes videos and audio as well as simple tools for students to use in class or for self-study.

The Teacher's Resource provides everything teachers need to deliver the course, including suggestions for differentiation and common misconceptions, audioscripts, answers, sample writing answers, a word list, unit tests and a full practice exam-style test.

Each Teacher's Resource includes:

- a **print book** with detailed teaching notes for each unit
- **digital access** with all the material from the book in digital form plus extra downloadable resources and audio.

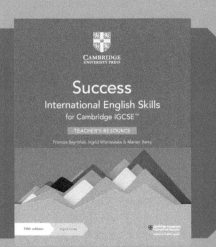

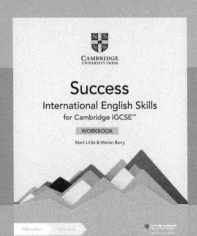

The write-in Workbook provides further reading, writing and listening practice and is ideal for use in class or as homework.

A digital version of the Workbook is included with the print version.

⟩ How to use this Teacher's Resource

This Teacher's Resource contains both general guidance and teaching notes that help you to deliver the content in our Cambridge resources.

There are **teaching notes** for each unit of the coursebook. Each set of teaching notes contains the following features to help you deliver the topic.

At the start of each unit there is a **learning plan**. This specifies which syllabus assessment objectives (AOs) are covered in the unit and also summarises key learning intentions and success criteria.

Learning plan

AOs	Key learning intentions	Success criteria
S1, S2, S3, S4, R2, R3, R4	Explore the topic of goals, achievements and qualities we admire	• Students can join in a discussion about the topic using appropriate vocabulary • Students can express opinions about the issues • Students can use appropriate language to express their own future goals

This is followed by an **overview** of what is covered in the unit, including details about the **theme** and **language work** that will the focus of the unit.

Overview

The main aims of this unit are to introduce students to some of the key skills they will need for the course, which they will then revisit throughout the units. They will participate in discussions, where critical thinking skills will be important; they will read and begin to explore the key features of a range of text types while working on their inference skills; they will listen to understand people's attitudes and opinions; and they will begin to think about the content and style of their writing, building an awareness of audience and purpose. There are also activities to help them use a dictionary more effectively, and to give them strategies for spelling and learning new words.

There is also guidance on **common misconceptions** that students may have about the topic and how you can overcome them – these have been compiled using research from the **Cambridge Learner Corpus**. The topic is then introduced, with a section on how to use the **topic** video for each unit, followed by guidance on how to deliver the content of the unit.

Common misconceptions

Misconception	How to identify	How to overcome
Students often omit the **possessive apostrophe** or put it in the wrong position. Examples:	Display some correct and incorrect examples. Ask students to identify the correct ones and to discuss the rules. For example: *my sister*	If possible, practise translating sentences containing possessive forms from students' first language. Often possessive forms

Differentiation support gives advice and ideas on how to support and challenge learners according to their confidence levels. **Wider practice** boxes give suggestions for further way to develop and extend themes, enabling students to make meaningful connections with the material and cross-curricular links, building their skills for life.

WIDER PRACTICE

1   Look out for English-language interviews with well-known people (or people with an interesting story) online, in magazines or on the radio/television. Where they describe key stages in the person's development, this can make an interesting follow-up to the work on goals and life's challenges, especially if the interview is with a personality students can identify with. Reading/listening to a particular style of article can help students become more aware of the distinctive features and language of different genres.

Each unit also contains **audioscripts** for all listening activities in the Coursebook and **answers** to all activities.

For each unit there are downloadable unit tests covering a full range of question types to help students feel confident about assessment. Guidance is given for **exam-style questions**, including an example answer for a writing question in each unit. There are also two downloadable full **sample answers** with commentaries written by the authors for one writing exam-style question from each unit.

Audioscript track 1.1

Listen to the five speakers talking about how they react to challenges.

Speaker 1:   I used to bite my nails all the time, and I'd tried several times to give up, without success. I just didn't seem to have the mental strength to quit. But when I was about 12, my mum promised she'd buy me a phone I

DIFFERENTIATION

Provide more **support** by writing these words on the board and checking their meaning: *marine life, ecosystem, coastline, destruction, accommodation.* Encourage students to use monolingual dictionaries, if available, or use context clues. To provide more **challenge**, ask students to write definitions for each of these words.

Answers

1   Website (Home, Contact tabs, etc.); it's a blog post (blogger's name – which may not be real – and photo, 'strapline' (*Make every day count*), date of entry).

Example answer

I want to describe Joseph Lister. He was a surgeon who was born in England in 1827. In those days, many patients died after operations because their wounds became badly infected. Lister wondered if (the) bacteria in the air which made meat decay also made wounds septic.

Lister decided to clean everything that touched (the) patients' wounds with carbolic acid. The carbolic acid destroyed all the germs. / Carbolic acid destroys all germs. As a result of these precautions, patients recovered quickly after/ from (their) operations. The rate of infection fell dramatically.

> Introduction

This Teacher's Resource fully supports the *Success International English Skills for Cambridge IGCSE™* Coursebook. Together with the Workbook, the course components provide detailed support for Cambridge IGCSE and IGCSE (9–1) English as a Second Language. The Coursebook has been fully updated to bring it in line with the syllabuses for examination from 2024. Changes or additions to the course include:

* a range of new reading and listening texts, reflecting interesting contemporary themes and topics aligned to the syllabus

* many new or revised speaking and writing activities

* a 'Before you start' photo and questions for each unit to stimulate interest in the unit topic

* new exam-style questions, to support the updated syllabus, at the end of each unit, with sample answers and commentary written by the authors for selected writing tasks

* a self-assessment section at the end of each unit

* questions and tasks to encourage the use of critical thinking skills, with support in this resource to help you to exploit these

* a new 'Common misconceptions' feature in this resource, with advice on identifying and overcoming common learner language errors at this level.

The Workbook consolidates and tests understanding of reading, writing and listening skills, using the language and themes in the Coursebook, with a range of exercises suitable for classroom use or homework. The Workbook has also been revised and extended to include several new exercises reflecting the developments in the syllabus. The final section of this resource contains the answers to the Workbook exercises.

How the course supports the syllabus

The course reflects the integrated skills nature of the syllabus. For example, a listening exercise may also be exploited to develop topic and vocabulary knowledge, and to practise functional language and intonation.

The holistic nature of the course is based on the expectation that students are receiving their education through the medium of English or living in a country where English is widely spoken. Students will therefore be more comfortable with English than will 'pure' EFL students at a similar level. Unlike other language courses for non-native speakers, there is no isolated assessment of freestanding language structures.

Care has been taken in the course to highlight the structures and vocabulary that would be useful for a particular topic. In addition, the Grammar spotlight at the end of each unit clarifies the purpose of a key structure, although the emphasis throughout is on how grammar can be applied in natural English.

Writing activities in this course develop students' understanding of how the purpose and audience for a piece of writing affect the language required. The course gives students plenty of practice with identifying, understanding and using various styles of spoken and written language. This includes quite informal language (such as might be used on social media posts) and language used in a more formal context (such as in a written report for an authority figure or in a speech).

Educational aims and objectives

The material is intended to develop students both intellectually and linguistically, to increase personal awareness and to encourage an understanding of the world. An investigative approach is taken, and students are encouraged to use critical-thinking skills to analyse and solve problems. They apply skills, knowledge and understanding, and are encouraged both to undertake individual tasks and to work as part of a team. It is important that you develop these broader skills if the material is to work as intended. The educational aims and objectives of this course also make it suitable for syllabuses other than Cambridge IGCSE English as a Second Language.

Age range

The course is designed to be used by young people in the age range 14–18. Unit themes reflect the interests of teenagers and aim to promote maturity of thought and outlook. This approach reflects the aims of the syllabus.

Time allocation

The course can be used over a period of up to two years, which is the recommended period of time suggested to prepare for Cambridge IGCSE English as a Second Language. This takes into account young people's rate of intellectual and emotional development. Alternatively, the material can be adapted to be covered in one year if this is the time available. The progression of language work, and the selection and treatment of topics, have been carefully chosen to reflect these factors.

Course structure

The course is organised into ten topic-based units, each systematically and gradually developing the four skills. Longer writing tasks tend to come at the end of a unit, enabling students to build relevant skills and vocabulary throughout the unit and then apply them in their writing.

The units offer in-depth topic coverage. Units are divided into Sections A–D or A–E, with a shift of focus indicated by the section headings. By studying a topic from many perspectives, students can answer questions with new angles on familiar topics and demonstrate depth of thought.

As well as building specific skills in reading, writing, speaking and listening, each unit includes vocabulary building, spelling and pronunciation work, functions such as showing enthusiasm or interrupting, and an International overview (see How to use the Coursebook units below). The unit offers both a Grammar spotlight and a Language study feature, which grows out of the texts that are being studied, to maximise relevance, accessibility and practical application.

Exam-style questions are placed at the end of each unit. This means that work students have done throughout the course of the unit will help them as they tackle these tasks, which are linked thematically to the unit where possible.

How to use the Coursebook units

Lead-in

Each unit starts with a set of questions based on a stimulating photo thematically linked to the unit topic. This serves to introduce the topic, drawing on any existing knowledge that students may have and allowing them to share their experience and acquire new insights. Teachers should use the lead-in to discover gaps in students' knowledge, such as key vocabulary needed for later work in the unit. The Teachers' Resources always provide a full backup to support the lead-in. This lead-in provides an opportunity to engage students across the ability range.

Developing reading skills

Most units have two substantial reading texts from (or closely based on) a variety of authentic sources, representing a wide range of styles but staying within what teenagers could be expected to experience or imagine. Texts are chosen specifically to practise skills such as skimming, scanning and detailed reading and matching.

Texts are introduced through a range of structured exercises, including speculation and prediction, and vocabulary and language checks. They are often enhanced by a visual image to help students focus fully on the topic.

Developing writing skills

Writing skills receive particular treatment. The overall aim is to develop a more mature writing style necessary both for a wide range of real-life situations and for examinations, while stimulating individuality of style and expression.

Developing listening skills

The units provide listening texts in a variety of styles, including speeches, announcements, interviews and both informal and more formal conversations. There are also recordings addressing phonology and focusing on functions such as expressing disappointment. Young voices have been used in some of the recordings for greater authenticity, and a few voices are very lightly accented with non-British accents, including Australian and American.

Listening texts are multi-purpose. Not only do they build specific skills, such as listening for a specific point or listening for attitude, but they also demonstrate a range of linguistic strategies, including functional language (e.g. interrupting, expressing disagreement, blaming) and phonological features (pronunciation, stress and intonation). These can be used to help build students' own speaking skills.

Developing speaking skills

Oral work is encouraged at every opportunity through whole-class interaction, pairwork, group work and delivering speeches. There is a strong emphasis on discussion activities, but there are also more structured exercises that develop understanding of functions, pronunciation, intonation and stress, for example. The exercises will work at different levels and with less outgoing students if you give credibility to oral work by making time for it in the classroom. The oral work leads up to exam-style speaking exercises at the end of every unit.

Language study and grammar

The language work in the units is based on a combination of deductive and inductive reasoning. With deductive reasoning, students are presented with rules and encouraged to find examples and explore how to apply the rules. With inductive reasoning, students study examples and work out patterns and rules for themselves. They can build on their prior knowledge and experience, with prompting from you as necessary. It is useful to apply the principle of inductive reasoning wherever possible when students are working on spelling, grammar or punctuation, or building vocabulary.

The space given to grammar teaching in the course is balanced against the need to develop a range of skills. For example, a grammatically correct letter of welcome that sounds unwelcoming in tone might be considered less acceptable than a letter that is slightly flawed grammatically, but which is warm and inviting, on the grounds that the first letter does not communicate effectively. Similarly, a letter packed with spelling errors might create a poor impression on the person receiving it, even if the grammar is perfect.

The Grammar spotlight highlights one or two key grammatical structures encountered during the unit. It provides clear, concise explanations and examples, and directs students to look back in the unit for further examples to consolidate their knowledge.

Developing an awareness of register

If students are to be successful communicators, it is important for them to be able to use language appropriately in a variety of contexts. They need to build an awareness of how language varies depending on the degree of formality involved, for example, or the medium of communication (texting is very different from writing a letter or posting in an online forum, and chatting with your best friend differs greatly from delivering a formal talk to a roomful of people). The units provide a range of texts and tasks that cover some of these different contexts – including some examples of very colloquial language. It is important to draw students' attention to the features of each, and the teacher's notes provide support with this.

International overview

This feature of each unit provides information and provokes discussion on a range of issues of global interest and concern. It includes data carefully researched from respected sources and presented via charts, tables and quizzes. It is a device to raise international awareness, as well as allowing students to use their language skills in the context of interpreting simple but authentic data sources. The teacher's notes provide detailed backup, and you can use the material in a way that is sensitive to your particular context.

Self-assessment

At the end of a unit, it is helpful to pause to allow students to reflect on the progress they have made, what they have learnt and what they need to focus on as they move on. The self-assessment checklist, with its list of *I can* statements, is a tool to help students do this. You can encourage them to keep their own self-assessment scores in mind when they move on to look at the 'Advice for success' section (see below), prioritising the tips that will help them with any areas where they feel less confident.

Advice for success

The 'Advice for success' section at the end of each unit provides tips to help students extend and showcase their skills. These tips build student independence by helping them develop learning strategies and allowing them to overcome any individual learning weaknesses they may have identified (see the 'Self-assessment' section above). It is important to discuss the key advice fully in class and to ask students to highlight or underline points of special relevance.

The advice also contains suggestions for language development beyond the classroom to further strengthen learner autonomy and responsibility.

Exam-style questions

The exam-style questions at the end of each unit are intended to help familiarise students with the style and format of questions they will encounter in their examinations, and to practise some of the skills they will need. They are closely aligned to the unit topics and provide valuable opportunities for students to gain confidence by using knowledge, vocabulary and ideas they have learnt doing the unit activities. ESQs exemplify question types that may appear in examinations. Please see the syllabus for details of the number of questions and exercises that will appear in examinations.

Differentiation

The Cambridge IGCSE English as a Second Language syllabus is no longer structured into two levels, Core and Extended. However, the material in this course has built-in flexibility to cater for a range of confidence levels. While the emphasis overall is on the more challenging aspects of the syllabus, there are plenty of suggestions in this resource for supporting all your students.

There are many ideas throughout this resource to help students develop their English, whatever their current skills level. These are outlined in the 'Differentiation' sections. However, as every class will vary, care needs to be taken to ensure that all students benefit from the work that is done. The following suggestions offer some general ways of supporting a class with a broad range of confidence levels.

- Use your knowledge of your students when setting a word limit for writing tasks and, where appropriate, give students shorter tasks that can then be gradually increased in length.

- Simpler words can be added to replace some of the more difficult words on the spelling lists.

- When setting a problem-solving exercise for the class, include an extra element of challenge for those who would benefit from this (e.g. something extra, or harder, to do in the same time frame) and, for those who need more support, make the task simpler with more scaffolding, fewer actions to carry out, and so on.

- At the start of a lesson, differentiate your recapping of key points from the previous lesson. To support students, do a quick run-through of an exercise that is the same or very similar to one from last time. To challenge students, on the other hand, offer a new and more challenging context for the same language.

- Some of the more challenging questions on reading and listening texts can be answered by a pair or group of students working together under your direction, rather than individually.

- An exercise can simply be divided in half and allocated to two groups in the class so there is less for each group to do.

- Students can be encouraged to learn a few selected items on a list of words, for example, rather than trying to learn the complete list.

- The 'jigsaw technique' can be used to break a whole task down into component parts. The class is put into groups, and each group is assigned a component to complete, with groups of students who require more support being given easier tasks. New groups are then formed, consisting of one representative from each of the original groups. Each representative is responsible for reporting the answers for their component part of the task. In the end, all students have a complete set of answers.

Throughout this book, a range of ideas for prompting students is given. The extent to which the prompts are used can be adjusted to suit the level of students.

Teaching support

Throughout this resource, you will find ideas for how to approach challenging tasks and make them more accessible, as well as information about the language and factual content of the Coursebook. In addition, you may find the general advice in the following sections helpful, and you may like to refer back to it as necessary.

A general approach to teaching reading skills

Preparing to read

- Establish the topic (use pictures and headings to encourage students to make predictions about the subject matter).

- Focus on the type of text that students are going to read. Is it an article, an advertisement, a report?

Reading the text

- Ask students to read the text quietly to themselves and, as they progress through the course, ask them to read within a given time limit to give them practice of reading in exam-style conditions

- Encourage students to skim read a text to get its general meaning and scan it to find specific information.

- Tell students to read the easiest parts of the text quickly and to take their time over the more complex parts.

- Encourage students to either use context to work out the meaning of new words or look them up in a dictionary.

Dealing with the exercises

- Tell students to both identify the key words in a text and think about how those words relate to questions in comprehension exercises. This means understanding paraphrase, which means saying the same thing in a different way.

- Support students by telling them in which paragraph an answer can be found or reduce the number of questions they have to answer.

- Encourage students to move on if they don't know an answer to a question; they can come back to it at the end.

- Challenge students to give fuller answers to questions about the text.

Discussing the text

- Analyse the style of the text: Is the language formal or informal? How does the way a text is written affect a reading of it?

- Examine the way that information has been ordered into paragraphs and how one paragraph flows into another. This means that students must understand how words and phrases connect one part of a text to another – for example, *However, Although, Having said that, In addition.*

- Focus on the intention of the writer. Ask students: *'What is the angle of the piece?' 'Who is the target audience?'*

Encourage students to look for what is *not being said:* students need to develop their ability to infer meaning. You can help them to do this by drawing their attention to things the writer has left out and the bias they might show against something.

A general approach to teaching writing skills

Preparing to write

- Ask students to think about the type of text they are going to write. For example, if it is a report, focus on its distinctive features: the neutral tone, its use of headings, and so on.

- Elicit the vocabulary that students will need.

- Examine ways of beginning and ending the piece of writing.

- Discuss the way information can be arranged into paragraphs which follow a logical sequence of ideas.

- Discuss style, formality, tone, register and target audience. Who is the piece of writing for?

- Study an example of the writing type from the unit.

- Encourage students to make notes before they begin writing. Support students by giving them more guidance with the content of their writing. It may sometimes be helpful to allow students to talk through their ideas for the writing with a partner before they begin.

Writing the first draft

- Encourage students to refer to the model texts in the unit. Writing is imitative – everyone learns by copying from someone who knows what they are doing.

- Encourage students to get their ideas down on the page – that is what matters most at the first draft stage.

- Tell students they should aim to capture the reader's imagination.

- As writing is a complex skill, and one that students can feel nervous and unsure about, support them when they are planning their ideas and help with any vocabulary they may require.

Rewriting the composition

- Tell students to think about how they can improve the organisation of information on the page.

- Support students by giving them more guidance with the form of their writing.

- Tell students that their aim is to be clear in their writing – remind them that they are trying to communicate a particular message.

- Encourage students to read aloud what they have written: they should concentrate on the rhythm and flow of their sentences.

- Tell students to check the grammar, punctuation and spelling of their work before they finish it.

- Encourage peer review of the first draft. Pair students with another student they trust and provide a checklist for each student to use when assessing their partner's work. The checklist could consist of general points (e.g. Are there any spelling mistakes? Have they used verb tenses correctly?) or could specify particular issues that the class has been working on (e.g. Have they included a rhetorical question / some interesting adjectives? Does the email sound friendly and welcoming? Is there a conclusion?) Emphasise the importance of constructive feedback.

A general approach to teaching listening skills

Preparing to listen

- Focus on the type of recording that students are going to hear. For example, is it a conversation, an announcement, a discussion?

- Elicit vocabulary that will feature in the recording, especially if you think it will be new to students. Put this vocabulary into context and make sure students are clear about its meaning.

- Encourage students to think about how we listen for key words – nobody listens to every single word that someone says.

Listening to a recording

- Play a recording several times, if necessary.

- Tell students to listen first to get the general meaning.

- Tell students to listen again to make notes or answer questions.

- In the early stages of the course and with particularly demanding listening tasks, give students the typescript to read while they listen, or do so after they have already listened once or twice.

Dealing with the exercises

- Encourage students to identify the key words in a recording and to think about how these relate to questions in comprehension exercises. This means understanding inference and paraphrase.

- Help support students by replaying the part of a recording that contains the answer to a particular question.

- With the most demanding listening tasks, do the exercise with the whole class, pausing the recording as necessary and asking students specific questions to guide them to the answers to a question.

Discussing the listening

- Analyse the recording with the class. How did the person or people speak? What was easy to understand; what was more difficult? Are there any particular accents that students found hard to understand?

- Suggest sources for further practice: listening to a variety of radio or online programmes and podcasts offers excellent general practice. The 'Advice for success' section provides ideas.

A general approach to teaching speaking skills

Preparing to do a speaking exercise

- Make sure that students understand what they are going to talk about (or which part they are going to play, if they are doing a role play).

- Elicit vocabulary needed for the speaking exercise. Put this up on the board and encourage students to refer to it.

- Remind students that it doesn't matter if they make a few mistakes with grammar and vocabulary in a speaking exercise as long as they communicate clearly and are easy to understand. Many discussion activities in the course are content-based: emphasise that the ideas students have (and their ability to convey those ideas) is often more important than the accuracy of the language they use.

- Give students a couple of minutes to prepare beforehand. They can make a few notes and ask you any questions they may have.

- Remind students to listen to each other, bring others into the discussion as necessary and make sure all group members are involved. You could briefly recap suitable language for asking others their opinion and interrupting politely.

Doing a speaking exercise

- Support students by giving them prompts so that they are not lost for something to say. For example, in a conversation about happiness, you could give one student a piece of paper with the statement *'Nobody can be happy all the time.'* Students can then make use of this statement in their discussion.

- Encourage critical thinking by prompting students, if necessary, to give reasons or examples to support points that they make in a discussion or to consider another angle or point of view. This resource provides support with this.

- You could agree beforehand to make a recording of students. If so, record unobtrusively.

- Don't let any speaking exercise go on too long – five to ten minutes is fine.

- Monitor while students are doing the speaking exercise and make a note of common errors. You can go through these with the class at the end.

Analysing a speaking exercise

- When the speaking exercise is over, ask students to analyse their own performance and that of their peers. What did they do well? What did they do less well? What did they find easy or difficult? How could they improve?

- Congratulate students on the ideas they conveyed in their discussion rather than focusing only on any weaknesses in language.

- If you made a recording, listen back to it with the class as a whole and then discuss what went well and what could be improved.

- Discuss group dynamics. Did everyone participate? Did anyone dominate the conversation? How might they improve the situation in a future discussion?

A general approach to teaching vocabulary

Presenting vocabulary

- Put the word into context, then ask students to think of a context of their own.

- Drill the pronunciation of the word – make sure that students are familiar with the sound of the word right at the beginning.

- Focus on the spelling. Does it contain any silent letters or double consonants? (See Unit 1, Section B12, where students are encouraged to consider what kind of misspelling they might make and why.)

- Make sure that students understand the social and cultural context of new words.

- Encourage students to learn complete phrases rather than words in isolation. This helps them to learn and remember the context in which words can be used. For example, rather than trying to remember *breathtaking*, they might note and remember *breathtaking scenery*.

- Ask students to translate the word into their own language.

Recording vocabulary

- Encourage students to keep a vocabulary notebook in which they write example sentences using new words. At the end of a lesson, encourage students to test each other on the meanings of the words they have written down.

- Ask students to make cards. On one side is a word; on the other, its meaning and pronunciation. These cards can then be used in vocabulary games that can be played at the end of a lesson.

- There is a range of electronic means for storing (and testing yourself on) vocabulary. Provide suggestions or ask students to share any that they know about with their classmates.

Using vocabulary

- Make sure that students feel comfortable with new language by giving them an opportunity to use new words as soon as possible. This can be in the form of simple conversation, debate or games.

- When new vocabulary reappears in later exercises or units, test students' understanding of its spelling, pronunciation and meaning. How much do they remember?

A general approach to teaching grammar

Presenting grammar

- Elicit ideas from students with regard to the form and use of the structure you want to focus on. Build on what they already know and take account of any misconceptions they may have.

- Encourage students to learn grammatical terms – knowing how to talk about language will help them to master it.

- Set each exercise in turn, giving a time limit for the completion of the exercises if you find it helps. Students can work on exercises in pairs, in small groups or alone – vary your approach here.

- If students have to complete a gap with the correct grammatical structure, tell them to look at the words around the gap to help them decide how to complete it.

Recording grammar

- Encourage students to keep their own grammar reference notebook: they can include the information they think is most important. They can do this electronically if they prefer.

- Encourage students to write a correct example sentence in their grammar notebook for each grammar point learnt.

- Encourage students to compare and contrast the grammar of their own language with English. What is similar? What is completely different?

Using grammar

- Do a speaking activity to practise the grammar, even if it is a basic one. What matters is that you give students the chance both to use the grammar and to see it as something they can make use of.

- Encourage students to revise the grammar they know regularly.

- Tell students to record themselves saying sentences using the new grammar structures. When they listen back to the recording, they can analyse their performance. Did they make any mistakes? How could they improve their sentences?

A general approach to exam-style writing and speaking exercises

Note that the teacher's notes for the exam-style questions give specific information and tips relevant to individual exercises. What follows is applicable to the writing and speaking tasks more generally.

Writing exam-style exercises

The writing exercises draw on themes and language from the unit. Encourage students to draw on the range of vocabulary they have explored and any new ideas they have learnt. Point out, however, that specific factual knowledge is not expected.

Remind students that it is very important to take note of who they are writing for, the *audience*, in each exercise. Encourage them to think about how this will affect what they say and how they say it.

For informal writing exercises (e.g. emails), students should use a friendly tone and register, imaginative vocabulary and details. They should always cover all the bullet points given. Encourage students to look at the picture, if there is one, which may suggest extra details for their email.

For formal writing exercises (e.g. articles, reports or reviews), students should use an objective, formal (or semi-formal) tone and register. It is important that students check that they are clear about the *purpose* of the writing and essential that they reflect this in their writing – especially when more than a description is required. Point out that they do not have to use the comments provided. They can use their own ideas, so recommend that they include at least one different view from those in the comments for the writing exercises.

If you are not asking students to do the formal writing exercise in examination conditions, you could allow them to discuss the topic in pairs or small groups before they tackle the writing. This may help to generate more ideas. Encourage them to make brief notes to organise their ideas before they start writing. Just three or four minutes spent planning can help to improve the quality of content and organisation significantly. They should aim to express their reasons clearly and back up their opinions with examples.

Remind students to read their work carefully when they have finished writing, allowing enough time to check spelling, grammar and punctuation.

Speaking exam-style exercises

The speaking exercises in the Coursebook are divided into three sections: an interview, a short talk and a discussion. Point out the difference between the short talk and the discussion. In the talk, students deliver a short speech, aiming to speak for two or three minutes. The discussion should be a conversation between student and questioner. You could also include a non-assessed warm-up question. Warm-up questions usually relate to students' own interests and are intended to relax the students and make them feel comfortable before starting the assessed questions. The questions are spoken by the interviewer and topics may include friends, family, hobbies, school life, music or food.

If speaking practice in pairs is difficult to arrange in your setting, to help your students perform with greater confidence you could:

- Brainstorm key words or phrases they would use in their answers, first individually and then as a class.

- Have students write out the dialogue with a partner, passing their paper back and forth as they take turns writing questions or answers.

- Ask two of your more confident students to model the task and ask the class to evaluate their performance, encouraging positive feedback and tips for improvement.

- Develop a list of tips and advice for completing these speaking tasks successfully.

Remind students that these exercises are an opportunity to demonstrate the best of their speaking ability, so they should use their English to respond in a natural way and develop their ideas as much as they can. Encourage them to give reasons and examples and to use the range of vocabulary they have already explored as the topics of the speaking exercises draw on themes encountered in the unit. Also emphasise that they are not being tested on content knowledge, so they don't need to worry about giving opinions based on incorrect facts. Instead, they should focus on demonstrating their fluency and range of vocabulary, and on keeping the conversation going.

For the interview and discussion, students could work in pairs, with one leading the questioning and the other answering the questions. They could then swap parts. Emphasise that, if students don't understand something, they can ask for an explanation. Similarly, if they cannot remember a particular word or think of a different way of expressing what they want to say, they can allude to what they want to say (e.g. *the thing that does . . .*).

For the short talk, encourage students to spend one minute thinking about the statements before they begin to speak, concentrating on what points they are going to make rather than thinking of specific words. Remind them that it is important to cover both bullet points rather than just talk about one of them. Also remind them to give two or three reasons for any choice they make and to explain why they did *not* choose other options. Particular language will also be useful – for example, conditionals (*if we did X, then Y would happen*), the language of speculation (*it's possible, I doubt, it's unlikely, might,* etc.) and language for sequencing (*first of all, second, finally*).

For the discussion, students should again aim to give extended answers, including details from personal experience. In this part in particular, students will have to give opinions on a number of related topics. They should aim to demonstrate a wide vocabulary and use a wide range of expressions to give opinions and express agreement or disagreement.

We recommend that students practise these speaking exercises in pairs, taking turns to role-play the interviewer and interviewee. Emphasise that the interviewer should allow their partner to speak as much as possible. Another option is to have groups of three, with one playing the `observer' who can give feedback to the others at the end.

While students are practising, walk around the room and monitor any possible difficulties or misunderstandings, also taking note of things that students are doing well. Once students are familiar with the format of the exercise, you may wish to call one or more students to come to your desk and practise with you individually while the other students are working in pairs.

If there is not enough time to complete all the speaking exercises in every unit, it may be a good idea to focus on just one of the sections (i.e. interview, short talk or discussion).

As an alternative to carrying out speaking tasks in class, students could record themselves (e.g. using their phone) for homework. Encourage them to listen back and assess their own performance against a checklist that you provide (re-recording if they wish). Students could submit the recordings to you for feedback/assessment or to each other for peer review.

Wider practice

Each unit in this resource ends with suggestions for further ways to develop and extend the themes and skills practised. These include suggestions for mini-projects, including internet research on extension topics, ideas for role plays and presentations, writing leaflets or blogs, contributing to online forums, listening to the radio and watching relevant TV programmes, and making posters and videos.

These 'Wider practice' sections are intended to:

- Allow students to follow their own enthusiasms. Many students make better progress when they find a meaningful personal connection to what they are learning.

- Encourage students to take responsibility for what they learn. At university, they will have to manage their own learning, and the 'Wider practice' sections encourage them to take the initiative.

- Develop links with other areas of the curriculum so students understand that what they learn is interconnected.

- Encourage students to see how an idea can be developed.

- Ensure that students do not solely concentrate on their examinations but see the opportunity to use their English for pleasure too (for example, reading novels or watching films).

Answers for exam-style writing questions

The exam-style writing questions provide examples of the style and format of exercise that students will encounter in their examinations. Answers are provided for all listening and reading exercises, and, in addition, example answers are given covering each of the different kinds of writing exercises (e.g. informal email, report, article, review). These sample answers are annotated to draw attention to particular features that students should be trying to include in their own writing.

And finally . . .

We hope you will continue to find this course a helpful aid to teaching and exam preparation.

> Approaches to learning and teaching

The following are short introductions to the key pedagogies that underpin our courses and how we define and use them within this Teacher's Resource. You will find documents within this section that explain these pedagogies further. The activity ideas in our student and teacher resources enable you to make use of these approaches and embed them in your lesson planning.

Active learning

Active learning is a pedagogical practice that places learning at its centre. It focuses on how students learn, not just on what they learn. We as teachers need to encourage students to 'think hard', rather than passively receive information. Active learning encourages students to take responsibility for their learning and supports them in becoming independent and confident students in school and beyond.

Assessment for Learning

Assessment for Learning (AfL) is a teaching approach that generates feedback that can be used to improve students' performance. Students become more involved in the learning process and, from this, gain confidence in what they are expected to learn and to what standard. We as teachers gain insights into a student's level of understanding of a particular concept or topic, which helps to inform how we support their progression.

Metacognition

Metacognition describes the processes involved when students plan, monitor, evaluate and make changes to their own learning behaviours. These processes help students to think about their own learning more explicitly and ensure they are able to meet a learning goal that they have identified themselves or that we, as teachers, have set.

Differentiation

Teachers need to find ways to welcome all students and organise their teaching so that each student gets a learning experience that makes engagement and success possible. We should create a good match between what we teach and how we teach it, and what the student needs and is capable of. We need not only to ensure access but also to make sure each student receives the support and individual attention that result in meaningful learning.

Language awareness

For many students, English is an additional language. It might be their second or perhaps their third language. Depending on the school context, students might be learning all or just some of their subjects through English.

For all students, regardless of whether they are learning through their first language or an additional language, language is a vehicle for learning. It is through language that students access the learning intentions of the lesson and communicate their ideas. It is our responsibility as teachers to ensure that language does not present a barrier to learning.

Skills for Life

How do we prepare students to succeed in a fast-changing world? To collaborate with people from around the globe? To use advanced thinking skills in the face of more complex challenges? At Cambridge we are responding to educators who have asked for a way to understand how all these different approaches to life skills and competencies relate to their teaching. We have grouped these skills into six main Areas of Competency that can be incorporated into teaching, and have examined the different stages of the learning journey, and how these competencies vary across each stage.

These six key areas are:

- Creativity – finding new ways of doing things, and solutions to problems
- Collaboration – the ability to work well with others
- Communication – speaking and presenting confidently and participating effectively in groups
- Critical thinking – evaluating what is heard or read, and linking ideas constructively
- Learning to learn – developing the skills to learn more effectively
- Social responsibilities – contributing to social groups, and being able to talk to and work with people from other cultures.

Excerpts have been taken from the Approaches to learning and teaching series, courtesy of Cambridge University Press and Cambridge Assessment International Education: cambridge.org/approachestolearning

Cambridge learner and teacher attributes

This course helps develop the following Cambridge learner and teacher attributes.

Cambridge learners	Cambridge teachers
Confident in working with information and ideas – their own and those of others.	**Confident** in teaching their subject and engaging each student in learning.
Responsible for themselves, responsive to and respectful of others.	**Responsible** for themselves, responsive to and respectful of others.
Reflective as learners, developing their ability to learn.	**Reflective** as learners themselves, developing their practice.
Innovative and equipped for new and future challenges.	**Innovative** and equipped for new and future challenges.
Engaged intellectually and socially, ready to make a difference.	**Engaged** intellectually, professionally and socially, ready to make a difference.

Reproduced from Developing the Cambridge learner attributes *with permission from Cambridge Assessment International Education.*

The Cambridge Learner Corpus

These resources are informed by the Cambridge English Corpus – a multi-billion word collection of examples of spoken and written English. We use our corpus to answer questions about English vocabulary, grammar and usage. Along with this, we collect and analyse learner writing. This allows us to clearly see how learners from around the world are similar and different in how they acquire and use language. These insights allow us to provide tailored and comprehensive support to learners at all stages of their learning journey.

Where you see this icon, the content has been informed by the Cambridge English Corpus:

> 1 Goals and achievements

Learning plan

AOs	Key learning intentions	Success criteria
S1, S2, S3, S4, R2, R3, R4	Explore the topic of goals, achievements and qualities we admire	• Students can join in a discussion about the topic using appropriate vocabulary • Students can express opinions about the issues • Students can use appropriate language to express their own future goals
R2, R3, R4	Build awareness of audience, purpose and features	• Students can understand the connection between audience/purpose and textual features • Students can identify the writer's opinions and feelings • Students are beginning to understand what writers express indirectly • Students recognise different text types
W3, W4	Learn skills for describing people and their qualities	• Students can use and understand a wider range of vocabulary for describing personality traits • Students can write an interesting and convincing description
L2, L3, L4	Practise listening to understand the speaker's ideas and attitudes	• Students are improving their understanding of speakers' feelings and attitudes • Students are beginning to understand what speakers suggest indirectly • Students can answer questions after listening to a range of audio types
W1, W3, W4	Write a formal email for a specific purpose and audience	• Students can write an email that achieves a specific aim • Students can develop basic statements to make them more convincing • Students can assess a partner's writing and give helpful feedback • Students can improve a first draft

Overview

The main aims of this unit are to introduce students to some of the key skills they will need for the course, which they will then revisit throughout the units. They will participate in discussions, where critical thinking skills will be important; they will read and begin to explore the key features of a range of text types while working on their inference skills; they will listen to understand people's attitudes and opinions; and they will begin to think about the content and style of their writing, building an awareness of audience and purpose. There are also activities to help them use a dictionary more effectively, and to give them strategies for spelling and learning new words.

THEME

The main theme of this unit is goals and achievements. Students will think and talk about their own personal goals and influences (and whether they think goal-setting is a good thing), the kind of challenges that we may face, and what kind of achievements we admire in other people.

The reading items include a quiz exploring our outlook on life (typical of popular magazines, social media feeds, etc.), an interview with a woman who overcame a particular problem, a lifestyle blog and comments about a high-flying young entrepreneur who supports small businesses.

Students will listen to a radio interview about people we look up to, and short clips about a range of challenges the speakers have faced.

There is a particular focus on descriptive language and how we can use it to describe people's personal qualities. Students are encouraged to describe people in a way that reveals personality and character, and they learn to improve their own descriptive writing through analysing models.

LANGUAGE WORK

Students' vocabulary is enlarged through work on homophones, figurative language, adjectives with negative or positive connotations, and the use of prefixes. They revise the rules for using apostrophes both for contracted forms and to show possession. The 'Grammar spotlight' contrasts uses of the present simple and continuous tenses, focusing on examples students have encountered in reading texts in the unit.

Spelling is made easier to understand through consideration of the links between speech sounds and spelling patterns, spelling rules and silent letters. In particular, students are taught the strategy of identifying what might make a word hard to spell in order to avoid misspelling it in the future. The 'look, say, cover, write, check' method is introduced as an approach to learning new spellings quickly.

Common misconceptions

Misconception	How to identify	How to overcome
Students often omit the **possessive apostrophe** or put it in the wrong position. Examples: *I want to make a film about <u>students</u> lives.* *Rules are essential in a <u>childs</u> life.* *We need to get some <u>viewer's</u> opinions.*	Display some correct and incorrect examples. Ask students to identify the correct ones and to discuss the rules. For example: *my sister house (✗); my sisters house (✗); my sister's house (✓); my sisters' house (✓); the childrens bedroom (✗); the children's bedroom (✓).*	If possible, practise translating sentences containing possessive forms from students' first language. Often possessive forms are expressed quite differently in those languages.
Students sometimes omit the **apostrophe with contracted forms.** Examples: *<u>Its</u> really nice to hear from you.* *I <u>dont</u> need it.*	Display several contracted forms with the apostrophe missing (e.g. *she isnt there; thats terrible; theyre not interested*). Ask students to write the full form of each and to identify what letters are missing in each contracted form. Get a student to draw an apostrophe to show where the letters are omitted, using a different coloured pen.	Give students a short text containing only full forms (no contractions). Ask them to identify forms that could be contracted (e.g. in speech) and to rewrite the texts, crossing out letters that could be removed and replacing them with an apostrophe.
Students use **present simple** instead of **present continuous** or vice versa. Examples: *I am going shopping quite often.* *It's a shame you aren't here, but I'm sure you have a good time in England.*	Display a photo/video of a famous person all students will know doing a particular exercise (e.g. accepting an award, waiting on the start line). Ask questions to elicit what the person is doing (i.e. in the photo) and what they are famous for. Write and display some of the students' responses and discuss why they chose the simple or continuous form of the present in each case.	Remind students of the key differences (i.e. present simple for permanent states or regular routines, present continuous for events in progress). Give them some sentence starters and elicit how each sentence might continue and whether the simple or continuous form would be appropriate, and why. For example: *Every Saturday, I . . .* *Look at that crazy man! He . . .* *Most shops . . .* *Tamara usually likes colourful clothes, but today . . .* *We're watching the second half of the match and my team . . .*

Introducing the unit topic (5–10 minutes)

Working with a partner, students look at the photo and discuss the questions.

Make sure students can use *in the background* and *in the foreground* to describe parts of the scene in the photo. The pairwork discussion should draw out some of the themes of the unit: achievements, how and why we set goals for ourselves, how they might affect those around us, and so on. They should note the sense of happiness and pride in the occasion shown, and perhaps be able to identify the occasion as a student graduation ceremony. You could introduce vocabulary such as *gown* and *mortarboard*, and draw out the themes by encouraging students to discuss how the graduate him/herself may be feeling (possibly relieved and excited, but maybe also a little nervous about what comes next or sad that this phase of their life is over). Other possible lines of questioning might include: *Do we put too much pressure on young people to go to university (and similar)? What other achievements of young people can we celebrate, particularly for those who don't go on to higher education?* (Examples might include getting a first job, passing a driving test, winning a sporting award, getting married, etc.) *Why do people dress up in special clothes for such occasions? Or Why did the photographer focus on the face of the parent?*

⟩ **Digital coursebook:** At the start of the lesson, use this video to introduce and review:

- the topic of goals and achievements
- a range of vocabulary related to personal qualities
- present continuous and present simple.

Read the question on the title screen and ask learners what they think they might see. Then play the video all the way through and check learners' predictions.

Play the video a second time, pausing to discuss what is being shown and the questions on the end screen. You can take the opportunity to revise words and phrases associated with the topic of goals and achievements.

Note that there is no 'correct' answer for question 3, rather it is an opportunity for the class to share their ideas of what habits are without revealing personal information. However, if learners do not suggest 'biting finger nails', elicit this by asking them if the reward of a manicure might be important.

You may like to play the video a third time for consolidation.

A Our outlook on life

1 Quiz (10–15 minutes)

The quiz is intended as a light-hearted way of approaching the subject of our personal goals and happiness, and considering how far we make our own decisions or are influenced by those around us. It's not intended that students should take the quiz or results too seriously! Start by asking students whether they have done questionnaires like this before. Where might they find a quiz like this? What is the purpose of quizzes like this? (Perhaps to get us to think about a certain aspect of our life, but often mainly to entertain us.)

Tell students not to worry about each individual word but to try to understand the gist of the language. (You can follow up any key vocabulary of particular interest afterwards.) Ask students not to look at the 'Scores' (at the end of the unit) until they have finished.

DIFFERENTIATION

Ideally, students should work out the meaning of most of the vocabulary in context and by working with a partner, but for more **support** you could provide a glossary covering some of the trickier language, for example, *sign up, scuba diving, split up, plan ahead, cross* (adjective).

2 Discussion (5–10 minutes)

Tell students how long you are allowing for the discussion and whether you will be asking pairs to feed back key ideas to the whole class afterwards.

1   The direction of this discussion may depend on the students' culture and context. Omit these questions if you would prefer.

2   Point out that the questions can refer to short- and medium-term goals, not necessarily life plans. (For example, students could talk about their English-language learning, school learning in general, any out-of-school activities such as sports training or learning a musical instrument, learning to drive, etc.)

3   If students can't think of anything, consider prompting them by giving an example personal to you.

3 New Year resolutions (10 minutes)

> **Critical thinking:** Briefly discuss the concept of New Year resolutions as a class. Students then work in a small group to choose and rank the top five New Year resolutions.

Based on the results of surveys from a range of countries, the most common New Year resolutions are: **1** Do more exercise and improve your fitness; **2** Eat more healthily; **3** Spend less money and save more; **4** Take up a new hobby or learn a new skill; **5** Get more sleep.

Encourage students to think about their answers and give reasons. You could prompt their discussion with questions such as: *Do you think younger and older people might make different resolutions? Why? Why is the beginning of the year a good time to make resolutions? After the Covid-19 pandemic, do you think people's resolutions changed?*

If students are interested, encourage them to use a search engine to try to find out about the most popular New Year's resolutions in their own country (though they may need to do this in their first language).

4 Setting goals for the future (15 minutes)

Follow up the writing task by asking students to share examples with the class. Since their goals may be quite personal, let them choose which example(s) they want to share.

5 Pre-reading tasks (5–10 minutes)

> **Critical thinking:** Use the *plokzack* examples as a way of modelling how to deal with an unfamiliar word in a text. For question 1a, show students how you would 'think aloud' to work out what part of speech it is (noun, verb, adverb, etc.) and to predict its meaning using clues in the surrounding text. For example:

I think it's probably a noun, because it follows the word 'a'. And if we read the rest of the sentence, we know that it's something to do with 'driving the wrong way down a one-way street'. Now, let's think about what happens to people if they do this? They might have an accident, or the police might give them some kind of fine or punishment. Which one of those fits with 'She got a' something? I think plokzack must mean a fine.

Suggested answers

1. a. fine or penalty
    b. run out of battery
    c. thoroughly/carefully

6 Reading for gist (10 minutes)

If students are unfamiliar with the meaning and concept of 'reading for gist', explain that it means looking over a text to get a general idea of what it is about, rather than reading it word for word. It's what you would do instinctively with a text in your first language to find out what it's for, whether it's aimed at you (rather than, for example, a child or a specialist of some kind), and to get an idea of the content.

Answers

1. Website (Home, Contact tabs, etc.); it's a blog post (blogger's name – which may not be real – and photo, 'strapline' (*Make every day count*), date of entry).

2. Anybody who follows this blogger regularly ('Some of you have been asking . . . ').

3. To give helpful 'lifestyle' advice to the reader; perhaps to entertain and make readers feel part of a community of 'followers'; perhaps to gain followers for the blogger (you can discuss the fact that some bloggers are sponsored and make money out of collecting 'followers').

4. Perhaps someone with professional training in counselling, life coaching or psychology – but discuss/point out that anyone can set themselves up as a blogger and offer advice.

Ask whether students have read blogs similar to this before. Do they have any favourite bloggers – or vloggers?

7 Comprehension check (20 minutes)

Discuss how students arrived at each answer and which words from the text helped them. The answers are not given directly in the text and some inference is required.

Support students by asking them to start by underlining key words in each question. Point out that the answers to the questions will be in the same order as the questions, and ask them to identify which part of the text has information corresponding to the words they have just underlined (e.g. for question 1 they'll find 'tick off our progress' and 'when we were five'). The answer will be easier to work out once they have worked out which part of the text it is in.

Answers

1 True ('When we were five . . . and that habit . . . has never really left us!')

2 False ('There's nothing wrong with having aspirations . . . , but the secret is not to make the end goal itself the only thing that matters.')

3 True ('Reward yourself for the small milestones you reach along the way.')

4 False (' . . . move the goalposts. Move them as often as you like!')

8 Style features (10 minutes)

Point out to students that in English, as in their own first language(s), texts written for different purposes and audiences use differing vocabulary and styles, and have different features. It's useful to notice these differences, both to help with comprehension but also so that they can adopt some of them in their own writing.

DIFFERENTIATION

Challenge students to look at two or three similar blog posts (by using a search engine to look for 'blog setting goals' or similar; if you prefer, you could find these yourself in advance and, if necessary, print out the text). Students then check which of these features they find in these other blog posts; they could also try to identify any further features that seem common to all the posts.

Answers

a Direct address to the audience: *Some of you have been asking . . . Don't set . . . Make sure . . . Reward yourself . . .* , and so on.

b Writer making connections with the reader (*we/us*): *when we were five . . . let's talk about . . .* , and so on.

c Writer sharing information about him/herself: *I find it interesting . . . A cousin of mine . . .* , and so on.

d Some informal, conversational language: *Let's talk about . . . top university . . . worked like crazy . . . zero social life . . . OK, so . . .* , and so on.

9 How helpful is your dictionary? (5–10 minutes)

If possible in your setting, use online dictionaries for this exercise (or a mixture of online and print). Some bilingual dictionaries will work, too, but part of the object of the exercise is to help any students who *only* use a basic translation dictionary to wean themselves off the habit by showing them what information they are missing.

If students are not used to working with dictionaries like this, you may need to circulate and help them find the relevant information.

Answers given here are based on the Cambridge Learner Online Dictionary.

DIFFERENTIATION

Some students may be more used to using the various features of a dictionary than others (and this may not necessarily be the more able students). You could pair more experienced users with the less experienced to **support** the less experienced.

Challenge students to investigate other features of better dictionaries not listed in the exercise and to report back on them to the others.

Answers

a **loathe**: /ləʊð/ (There is also a clickable audio file that provides both UK and US pronunciation of the word)

b **stray**: yes – verb, noun, adjective

c **aspiration**: yes – I've never had any political aspirations

d **vision**: both – indicated by [C] (countable) and [U] (uncountable)

e **goalpost**: yes (labelled 'Idiom') *move the goalposts*: to change the rules while someone is trying to do something in order to make it more difficult for them. Note: You could also point out that the dictionary also tells you this expression is 'disapproving' – that is, it is used in a negative sense.

f **beat yourself up**: informal

10 Figurative meanings (10–15 minutes)

You may need to help students understand the difference between literal and figurative meanings of a word. If we use a word or phrase figuratively, we are not using it with its usual (literal) meaning. For example, if we tell someone, *'You're a star!'* we are not suggesting that they are a ball of burning gas in the sky but that they are brilliant or special in some way.

DIFFERENTIATION

Allow students who require **support** to focus initially on just three examples.

To extend students who require more **challenge**, ask them to explore further figurative uses of *jump* and *break*. They could then choose some examples to teach to the rest of the class.

B Facing challenges

1 Discussion (10 minutes)

> **Critical thinking**: Check understanding and pronunciation of *overcoming obstacles*, as well as *heights* and *procrastinating*. *Obstacles* can refer to anything that blocks someone's path and stops them

making progress, whether an actual object (e.g. a fallen tree trunk on a road) or something abstract (e.g. lack of confidence might stop someone applying for a particular job). Challenge students to name a phrasal verb with *put* which means the same as *procrastinate* (= to put off doing something).

After the discussion, feed back as a class.

Allow conversations to run naturally as far as possible, but prompt students with questions if you need to encourage deeper thinking. For example, why do they think some people have fears like these? What might have caused the fear to develop?

2 Expressing fears and reassuring someone (10–15 minutes)

Check understanding of *reassure* (help someone to stop feeling worried).

Students study and practise the functional language in pairs.

You might like to elicit other phrases students may know to express fear, **e.g.** *I really dread . . . , I panic when I think about it.*

Students can use their own situations for the practice, if they prefer. You could ask a pair of students who have done particularly well to perform an example to the whole class.

DIFFERENTIATION

While more confident students can be **challenged** to expand their dialogues into mini-conversations, students who require additional **support** could focus on one (or two) simpler dialogues. They could then swap partners with another pair so they have a further opportunity to practise the language.

3 Pre-listening task (5 minutes)

Answers
a 2; b 5; c 3; d 6; e 1; f 4

4 Listening: How people react to challenges (15–20 minutes)

This exercise provides a relatively gentle introduction to multiple matching tasks, in which students listen to several short monologues and match the speakers with a set of statements. The task requires students to show an understanding of the connections between ideas, opinions and attitudes, and to understand what is implied but not directly stated.

Explain to students that they are going to practise listening for information about how each experience made the speaker feel, and any opinions the speaker expresses. The answer to the questions will not necessarily use the same words as the question – for example, if the question says, *'Which speaker felt sad . . . ?'*, they may not hear the word *'sad'* in the audio recording; instead, they will need to listen out for different words that express the same thing.

Encourage students to read the questions carefully before they listen, and to underline words they think are important. Tell them it can be useful to make very brief notes as they listen.

 After the exercise, if students are still unsure, let them look at the audioscripts and underline the key words and phrases that provide the answers to the questions.

DIFFERENTIATION

If students need extra **support** (or are simply unfamiliar with this kind of task), it may be useful to pause the audio recording after the first two or three speakers and allow students to compare what they understood with a partner before repeating those two/three speakers.

Answers
a Speaker 3; b Speaker 4; c Speaker 5; d Speaker 1; e Speaker 2

Audioscript track 1.1

Listen to the five speakers talking about how they react to challenges.

Speaker 1: I used to bite my nails all the time, and I'd tried several times to give up, without success. I just didn't seem to have the mental strength to quit. But when I was about 12, my mum promised she'd buy me a phone I really wanted if she didn't have to see those horrible bitten nails anymore – and I stopped the habit within two days! So, unfortunately, that experience made me realise I'm much more likely to succeed at things when I'm promised some kind of reward.

Speaker 2: I've always been the kind of person who likes to look like everyone else and not draw attention to herself. So when a friend decided to shave off all the hair on her head to raise money for a cancer charity event, she thought I was joking when I agreed to take on the same challenge myself. Surprisingly, I didn't mind having my hair shaved – but walking into school next day was one of the hardest things I've ever done, as I was expecting people to laugh and stare at me. Everyone was really nice about it though.

Speaker 3: In my head, there's one of those photos that you see on social media of me screaming with terror and laughter as I throw myself off a very high platform with a rope tied around my feet. You know, those bungee jump things that people do to impress their friends, and then they buy the photo to prove they did it. What actually happened, sadly, is that I froze as I was standing on the platform, and I had to admit to myself that I just wasn't brave enough to do it.

Speaker 4: I'd always dreamed of walking the whole of the 450-kilometre King's Trail in Sweden, north of the Arctic Circle. But when I finally did it, it was tougher than I'd imagined: I was exhausted from the long distances carrying a heavy backpack, wet from the constant rain showers and covered in mosquito bites! So you'd think that I would have been quite pleased when I finished it, wouldn't you? But it was quite the opposite: there's something magical about that place, and I wanted the trail to go on for ever.

Speaker 5: It might be hard to believe this now, but as a kid I was really shy. Something that helped me to get over this was a trip to the UK to do a language course when I could speak hardly any English. One day, our teacher sent us out into the street to find some native English speakers to practise interviewing. You can imagine how nervous I was, approaching strangers, but I found myself talking to some lovely people – and that experience took away much of my fear and helped me believe in myself.

5 Pre-reading discussion (5–10 minutes)

> **Critical thinking:** This is intended to be a brief discussion on the themes of the reading text, since there will be an opportunity for further discussion with the 'International overview'. However, if students are engaged with the discussion, you could jump straight on to the 'International overview' after Section B9 at this point before returning to exercises 6–9.

Possible answers may include:
1   Not being able to understand food labels, bills, letters, street signs or warnings, labels on medicine, instructions, among others; not being able to fill in forms, text people, leave messages for people, and so on.

2   Not being able to find out where to go for help, being too embarrassed, scared or proud to ask for help, not having time to attend lessons or living too far away, and so on.

3   It might make them afraid to mix with other people to avoid being found out; it would probably make it extremely hard to get a decently paid job; it would probably make them feel generally isolated through being unable to access the internet, news, and so on.

6 Vocabulary check (2–3 minutes)

Answers
stomach ache: pain in your stomach

bully (verb): hurt someone physically or emotionally, often over a period of time

illiterate: unable to read or write (Point out the prefix *il-*, used to make a word negative: *literate/illiterate*, like *legal/illegal*)

fool (verb): trick someone, make them believe something that isn't true

volunteer: person who works without pay, often for a charity

Encourage students to use context clues in paragraph 3 to understand that *let on* means *tell someone that you know a secret.*

7 Reading: Textual organisation (10 minutes)

Before students start reading, you could ask them to predict something about the content of the article from the title.

The aim of this exercise is to provide practice in skim-reading the text – reading for gist – in order to match the general meaning of each paragraph with one of the seven headings.

If you think your students will try to read every word, rather than skimming, try the following. (They will, of course, be able to study the text more closely afterwards.) Close books, display the list of paragraph headers and tell students to read them carefully. Then, alongside the headers, display only one or two paragraphs of text at a time. Explain that you are going to give them only a short time (e.g. 15 seconds per paragraph) to skim the paragraph, looking out for key words which give them a general idea of what the paragraph is about. After the fixed time, hide the paragraph(s) and get students to write down the letter of the corresponding header. Repeat for the remaining paragraphs.

> **DIFFERENTIATION**
>
> **Support** students by allowing them a little longer and reducing the number of possible headers to match for the first couple of paragraphs.

Answers
a 7; **b** 2; **c** 1; **d** 5; **e** 3; **f** 6; **g** 4

8 Comprehension check (20 minutes)

Point out that some of the questions require students to use inference, the skill of using clues in the text to draw conclusions. If students are worried about this, tell them they will have plenty of opportunities to practise the skill in reading and listening throughout the course. Go through the answers as a class, especially any wrong ones, identifying how students were able to use clues to arrive at the answers.

DIFFERENTIATION

To **support** students with the concept of inference, you could give a very simple illustrative example, such as the following: *Serena left her house carrying a suitcase and a passport, as her sister shouted, 'Have a great flight!' Is Serena going to the cinema, the office or the airport? The text doesn't tell us, so how do we know?*

Answers
1 A; 2 B; 3 B; 4 C; 5 B; 6 C

Students may also argue that answer C could be true for question 5. Accept this if they can justify their view.

9 Text style and features (10 minutes)

Before students begin, briefly check understanding of key words from the exercise:

setting: (the place where something happens)

format: (in this case, the way something is arranged on the page or screen)

anecdote: a short, true story about a person or an event

quote: the words that someone says (usually shown with speech punctuation)

angle: a particular way of looking at something

helpline: a phone number that you can call for help or information on a particular topic (e.g. advice if you're being bullied)

Clarify the difference between *interview/interviewer/ interviewee*.

Students could work individually and compare answers afterwards.

Answers
The following are correct: a, b, d, e, f, h

International overview (10–15 minutes)

〉 **Critical thinking:** This exercise involves a very basic understanding of a simple graph, followed by a discussion. Guide and organise the discussion according to the time available and your students' level of interest. Note that this topic provides an excellent opportunity to encourage students to do further research themselves: you can research suitable English-language websites ahead of the lesson and recommend them for students to either refer to in class or for homework. It's also an opportunity, if appropriate, to teach some basic skills with using a search engine (through the medium of English), assessing the suitability of sources, and so on.

If students don't know how to reply to question 3, prompt them to think about specific areas: for example, will people be more or less likely to have skilled jobs, good health, to need state benefits; how will their literacy affect their children's education and futures?

Answers
1 Males: 9–10%; females: 17% (Note that different sources may give different figures, depending on the measurement criteria). Possible reasons may include the fact that, in many countries, girls are (or have been) expected to devote a lot of time to very basic household and family duties, for example, fetching water and fuel to cook with, thus robbing them of time to go to school. Also, in some countries, schooling is very expensive and the opportunity has traditionally been given to the male members of the household. As always, encourage students to relate the information to the situation in their own countries. You could point out that in many of the world's affluent nations, it was the custom to give priority to boys' education until relatively recently.

2 Older adults. Literacy rates have been steadily improving because of greater access to education; therefore, literacy rates are much better among younger people worldwide than for older people.

3 Examples of the effects of better literacy on a community/country include: stronger economic development (more highly trained workforce), better health, lower child mortality, lower rates of crime, more gender equality.

4 Answers will vary.

10 Pronunciation and spelling (10 minutes)

The exercise focuses on the sound of schwa /ə/ – the most common sound in English – to help students with their own pronunciation but mainly to help with recognition of the sound and awareness of the range of spelling patterns that feature the sound.

Use the audio recording to help students hear and practise reproducing the sound.

(You could also draw attention to the fact that, in fluent speech, words like *desperate* and *separate* become almost two syllables as the middle one (*per/par*) tends to disappear.)

DIFFERENTIATION

Challenge students to think of more adjectives ending in *-ate* or *-ite* containing the schwa sound. For further challenge, provide them with a short list of *-ate* words which can have two different pronunciations (one with *schwa* and one with /eɪ/ to rhyme with *eight*), asking them to come up with a rule for the two pronunciations: *separate, graduate, delegate, estimate, duplicate.* (Answer: the verb form is pronounced /eɪt/ while the adjective/noun is /ət/.)

Audioscript track 1.2

Listen to each word carefully. Then practise saying it.

accurate

appropriate

desperate

separate

delicate

fortunate

considerate

definite

11 Approaches to spelling (5 minutes)

The aim here is to elicit students' previous knowledge of spelling patterns and to encourage them to consider a wider range of ways of remembering spelling.

12 Why do we misspell words? (10 minutes)

Students are more likely to avoid spelling errors if they consider what spelling 'traps' they might fall into when they look at new words.

Example answers
cupboard: silent *p* (and unstressed *schwa* pronunciation of *oard*)

responsible: confusion with more common *-able* ending

beautiful: omitting one of the three vowels, or adding an extra *l* to *ful*

accommodation: wrong number of *c*s or *m*s

autumn: silent *n*

receipt: silent *p*, and *ie* instead of *ei* (Note the rule '*i* before *e* except after *c*' may be useful, although there are exceptions to the rule)

exhausted: silent *h*

definitely: *ate* instead of *ite*

wrist: silent *w*

batteries: forgetting the rule that a *-y* ending changes to *-ies* if the preceding letter is a consonant

13 Look, say, cover, write, check (15 minutes)

This is an uncomplicated method of memorising spellings. There is a similar exercise in every unit. It's a good idea to emphasise the simplicity of the method. When they get the hang of it, students can learn spellings effectively and with a lower failure rate than with many other methods.

Of course, they'll also be using other methods, such as spelling rules and how speech sounds are linked to spelling patterns.

C Personal qualities

1 Vocabulary practice: Describing people's qualities (10 minutes)

Encourage students to make effective use of their dictionaries for this exercise (see Section A9). For example, they should carefully check any example sentences that the dictionary provides and note where the dictionary points out that we use a word in a 'disapproving' way (e.g. obstinate, judgemental).

Some words could, arguably, belong to more than one category – encourage discussion about how we perceive certain qualities.

Draw students' attention to the photo of the girl. Which adjectives from the lists might they use to describe her?

DIFFERENTIATION

Support students with a limited vocabulary range (who may be unfamiliar with most of the words) by allowing them to check the meanings of words ahead of the lesson. They can then do the categorisation task in class.

Challenge faster finishers to think of more words to add to the lists.

Suggested answers
Positive: outgoing, confident, considerate, open-minded, trustworthy, reliable, has a good sense of humour, generous, cheerful, imaginative, calm, friendly, practical

Negative: absent-minded, over-confident, obstinate, narrow-minded, untidy, argumentative, judgemental, grumpy, highly strung

Neutral/It depends: sensitive, shy, quiet, ambitious, keeps himself to himself / herself to herself, laid back

---

2 Vocabulary practice (10 minutes)

The main purpose of this exercise is to get students to engage with and therefore better remember the long list of (potentially new to them) vocabulary from the previous exercise.

Check understanding of *flatmate* (someone you share a flat with – not usually a family member). You could also mention the similar words *housemate* and *roommate*.

3 Negative prefixes (10 minutes)

Ask students to think back to the reading text about Monica Chand (Section B7) and remember which prefix was used to form the opposite of *literate and literacy (illiterate and illiteracy B6)*.

Point out how a dictionary can, once again, help with words beginning with prefixes. A good online dictionary will direct you towards the correct

version if you enter a word with the wrong prefix (i.e. 'No exact match – did you mean . . . ?'). Students should also check how the opposite version of the words are used – for example, the opposite of *mature (immature) is used in a critical sense, rather than simply meaning 'young'*.

Answers
irresponsible, insecure, inefficient, disloyal, untrustworthy, inconsiderate, immature, unreliable, dishonest

---

4 What are they like? (5–10 minutes)

Point out that just giving a description of someone's physical appearance can be uninteresting if you don't also give an impression of their personality; so using 'S/he looks . . .' is a useful way to speculate about personal traits when we're talking or writing about a stranger.

Ask (referring to the photo): *What do you think he is like?* Check students are clear about the difference in meaning between *What's he like?* (asking about personality), *What does he like?* (asking about preferences) and *How is he?* (asking about his health).

5 Demonstrating personal qualities through actions (15 minutes)

This reading exercise will help students practise the skill of inference (drawing conclusions based on available evidence and clues). They won't find the answers by looking for the same wording in the comments that is used in the conclusions **a–j**.

DIFFERENTIATION

To give **support**, tell students to read just the first three comments and to decide which of the conclusions can be drawn from those comments.

For a **challenge**, students could try making up another two-sentence comment to illustrate another (imaginary) aspect of Alex's work or behaviour. They could then display their comment for other students to draw conclusions about him.

Answers
a yes; **b** yes; **c** no; **d** yes; **e** yes; **f** no; **g** yes; **h** yes; **i** yes; **j** no

---

6 Criticising negative qualities (10 minutes)

Suggested answers

- He can be rather naïve / a bit too idealistic / a bit reckless / a bit over-optimistic.

- He's not always very practical.

- He doesn't always listen to advice from his colleagues.

Accept any answers that students can justify with reference to the comments.

7 Discussion (5–10 minutes)

> **Critical thinking:** Make sure students give reasons for any opinions they offer.

8 Improving a description (10 minutes)

The exercise provides an example of a piece of description with accurate grammar and some higher-level adjectives, but which is otherwise unimpressive. It is intended to stimulate ideas about how to write a better one. (The next exercise, in Section C9, serves as a contrast.)

Possible criticisms of the description:

- It consists of a number of short, simple sentences – it would sound more interesting if they could be linked together. (Reading the passage aloud to students would make it easier for them to recognise this.)

- There are some interesting adjectives, but putting them in a long list is stylistically odd and uninteresting.

- The adjectives don't really give us a picture of what Shannon is like as they are not developed at all (there are no examples of what she does or how she behaves).

- 'She used to be shy but now she's more confident' – it might have been interesting to find out *why*.

- We learn that the writer admires Shannon but we're not told why (not developed).

- 'She loves spiders. She wants to be an architect . . . ' – there are no examples, not developed in any way.

DIFFERENTIATION

For more **support**, provide a checklist of features for students to compare with the sample description. For example:

- Is there a variety of sentence structures or mainly short, simple sentences?

- Are there some interesting adjectives? Do you think there are enough / too many?

- Are there any examples of the person's behaviour or actions?

- Do we learn what the writer thinks about the person – with reasons?

Focus tightly on specific areas of improvement. For example, demonstrate (by eliciting ideas from students) how to connect the first two sentences into one – for example, *I met my friend Shannon at primary school six years ago.* Choose a couple of the descriptive adjectives, and invite students to make up possible behaviours or anecdotes to demonstrate them. Similarly, choose one of the last two sentences and elicit ideas for expanding upon it (e.g. *One unusual thing about Shannon is that she loves spiders, and she keeps one in a special tank in her bedroom / she draws little sketches of them on her school books, etc.*)

For more **challenge**, invite students to rewrite all/ part of the description and read their improved version to the class.

9 Comparing style (10–15 minutes)

Ask students to look at the notes they made in Section C8 for what needed improving. How does this next text compare? Have the kind of improvements they suggested been made?

Students will (hopefully) comment on some of the better features in this description. Draw attention to the features if they don't mention them. For example:

- better variety of sentence structure/length (including use of connectives *but, so, although* and clauses with *which*)

- examples of behaviour/anecdotes (as well as just adjectives)

- we learn *why* people admire Hassan

- the description of his looks also helps us understand his personality
- we learn one negative personality trait, which gives balance.

DIFFERENTIATION

Challenge more ambitious writers by focusing on the non-defining relative clause in the second sentence (*he was wearing . . . a bright-yellow woolly hat, <u>which he never wanted to take off</u>*) and asking them to find two further examples of this in the description. Relative clauses will be covered in more detail in Unit 8, but this is a useful feature to include in descriptions, so you could challenge these writers to include such a clause in their writing in Section C10.

10 Writing your own description (20 minutes)

Students may find it helpful to describe the person orally with a partner before they start working on their writing. This often helps ideas to flow better.

Ask students to refer to the checklist as they complete their own writing.

Share some of the completed examples with the class and invite (positive) feedback about any features that students find effective.

11 Spelling homophones (10 minutes)

It is helpful if students read the sentences aloud, so they can hear the correct meaning without being distracted by the misspelt word.

Answers

1   **a** peace; **b** whole; **c** allowed; **d** site; **e** their; **f** you're; **g** whether; **h** bear; **i** brakes; **j** heal

2   The photos represent the homophones *paw* and *pour*

If you wish to and have time, ask students to write a sentence for each of the forms used incorrectly, but this time with the correct meaning.

D People we look up to

1 Vocabulary practice: Multi-word verbs for relationships and attitudes to people (10 minutes)

Tell students that when they come across a new multi-word verb and want to record it for future reference, it is particularly useful to write down an example of how it is used, rather than just the verb, as a reminder. There are a large number of multi-word verbs in English and they often sound confusingly similar – and students also tend to make errors with the position of the object in relation to the parts of the verb.

As a follow-up, ask students to make up new sentences containing each multi-word verb.

Answers
a 2; **b** 4; **c** 6; **d** 5; **e** 1; **f** 3

2 Discussion (10 minutes)

The main purpose of the discussion is to activate ideas about people we admire (and why) in preparation for the activities that follow.

3 Pre-listening tasks (5–10 minutes)

This exercise pre-teaches key concepts and vocabulary for the listening task in Section D4.

1   Note that the pronunciation of Zhejiang is jeh-jang.

2   *People with special needs* refers to people who are unable to do some things in the same way as the majority of the population due to a range of mental or physical issues.

3   If you are *named after* a parent, you have the same name as them. (This normally refers to a given name, rather than surname / family name.)

4 Listening: Podcast (20 minutes)

Draw attention to the photos. What can students infer about these images?

Tell students they are going to listen to a podcast. (Ask for a volunteer to explain what that is, in case there are others who don't know.) Remind them to read the questions carefully before they listen, and to underline/highlight any key words. Once again, as with reading activities that they have done in this unit, the answers may not be provided directly in the same words as used in the questions; students will need to use inference skills.

If students have any wrong answers, after listening, allow them to study the audioscript to work out why their answers are incorrect.

DIFFERENTIATION

Support students who found the task hard by allowing them to listen to the podcast again while following the audioscript.

Answers
1 B; 2 B; 3 A; 4 C; 5 A

Audioscript track 1.3

Listen to a podcast recorded for a student radio station. Choose the best answer for each question.

Interviewer: OK, Yasmin, so we're here to conduct the next in our series of podcasts on people we look up to. Yesterday we had an interesting discussion on the architect Zaha Hadid and her groundbreaking designs . . . Can you tell us whose achievements you'd like to talk about today?

Yasmin: Well, I'm going to break the rules a little bit, if you don't mind, because I couldn't decide on a single person to focus on. It was really hard to narrow it down!

Interviewer: Yes, I'm sure it was! Well, I think we can let you do that. So how did you choose in the end?

Yasmin: You know, I got to thinking about why we admire people, and I realised it's complicated. We can admire someone's achievements without necessarily liking the *way* they went about doing what they did – or, on the other hand, we may admire a person's courage or their originality,

for example, without agreeing with their beliefs. And society changes, too – so we name a street or building after someone, and then a hundred years later, our values have changed and we're questioning whether those people really deserve to be remembered in that way.

Interviewer: I hadn't really thought of it like that; that's a good point. But you've decided on someone you feel you actually can look up to?

Yasmin: OK, yes I have, two people, actually, who a lot of our listeners may not have heard of. I'd like to start off with a man from Dubai called Jalal Bin Thaneya – I heard about him from my mother, who comes from that part of the world. He's completed some incredible physical challenges, including cycling 5000 kilometres from Oman to Jeddah in Saudi Arabia, and twice walking across all seven of the United Arab Emirates alone – that's a distance of around 800 kilometres.

Interviewer: Quite a long way, then!

Yasmin: And you have to bear in mind that he would have been walking in extreme heat, on dusty, unpaved desert and mountain roads where there's hardly anything to see, and with little food. As a long-distance walker myself, I can imagine how mentally tough that must have been. But what impresses me most actually, is that he's raised huge amounts of money for various charities supporting people with special needs in the UAE, and generally he's done a lot to make people more aware of the issues around disability. Now, it's interesting that people often support a charity that has a particular connection with their own family, and that's great . . . but Jalal Bin Thaneya has no reason to support those particular charities other than just wanting to help. He feels quite strongly that people don't talk enough about some of the difficulties in society until those difficulties affect them personally.

Interviewer: And you say you're going to tell us about another person who impresses you as well?

Yasmin: Yes, but for completely different reasons this time. For my own medical studies, I'd been finding out about how to look after patients suffering from malaria—

Interviewer: The tropical disease spread by mosquitoes, right?

Yasmin: Yes, exactly. Well, I was learning about that, and I found out about the Chinese scientist Tu Youyou, who discovered a very important anti-malaria drug called artemisinin, which comes from a tree. The work she did has helped save millions of people's lives in China and South-East Asia generally, so I had to choose her.

Interviewer: She won the Nobel Prize, didn't she?

Yasmin: Yes, that's right, she did. Well, Tu Youyou was born in Zhejiang province in eastern China in 1930, and she trained as a pharmaceutical scientist during China's Cultural Revolution, at a time when it really wasn't easy to be a scientist.

Interviewer: No, I can imagine.

Yasmin: Thousands of people were dying of malaria, and there was a lot of pressure to find a treatment for it. She eventually found a clue to an effective cure by reading about ancient Chinese medicine in a text hundreds of years old. So she tried it out on herself and her team, which must have been pretty brave. Then she and the team had to create the drug, using some toxic chemicals which damaged their health. She didn't get to see her family during this period, either,

so she had to make quite a lot of personal sacrifices. And she got very little thanks or recognition for her work at the time – it wasn't until she was in her seventies that people heard about her awards and began to take an interest.

Interviewer: It sounds as if Tu Youyou deserves to be more well-known than she actually is – and it's good that you've told us about her today.

Yasmin: Yes, it's not always the most famous people who most deserve our admiration, is it?

Interviewer: No, I'd agree.

5 Discussion (10 minutes)

> **Critical thinking:** Challenge students to justify any opinions they offer with explanations or examples. Tell students how long you wish to spend on the discussion. If you wish (and have time), put each pair with another pair so that they can compare views as a group of four.

With these questions, it may be helpful to refer to examples relevant to your setting, which will be familiar to students, if you can think of any. For example, for question 1 you may be able to draw attention to a sportsperson, artist, musician, or another well-known person in your country who is not only very talented but also known in the news / on social media for some kind of bad behaviour or a rather outrageous lifestyle.

6 Writing from notes (15 minutes)

Begin by activating any knowledge students may have about Joseph Lister: encourage any students who know about him (e.g. from science classes) to share their knowledge with the class.

Focus on the photo: what does it show? Discuss the fact that everything is extremely clean and sterilised, and that the people are wearing masks and protective clothing. Students may not have specific knowledge of the period mentioned (the 1840s), but they may well be aware that cleanliness in hospitals and understanding of infection hasn't always been as good as it is today. Tell them that in the 1840s, approximately half of all patients died after having surgery.

The writing from notes task helps students to focus on grammar (especially use of tenses, definite and indefinite articles, prepositions, etc.), since the content and structure are provided for them. It may be best done as a homework task.

Example answer

I want to describe Joseph Lister. He was a surgeon who was born in England in 1827. In those days, many patients died after operations because their wounds became badly infected. Lister wondered if (the) bacteria in the air which made meat decay also made wounds septic.

Lister decided to clean everything that touched (the) patients' wounds with carbolic acid. The carbolic acid destroyed all the germs. / Carbolic acid destroys all germs. As a result of these precautions, patients recovered quickly after/ from (their) operations. The rate of infection fell dramatically.

Lister developed safe, antiseptic operations, which was a major medical advance. He received many awards for his work, and today he is known as 'the father of modern surgery'. I admire him because he was dedicated and unselfish. He took great personal risks to make this discovery. Surgery used to be highly dangerous. People were terrified of the surgeon's knife. Lister changed all that. Modern surgery is a lifesaver.

7 Looking for a 'local hero' (10 minutes)

This task gives students an opportunity to put into practice some of the learning from the unit about describing people and their qualities. It also gives a gentle introduction to writing a report (a piece of structured formal writing presenting information).

As a class, briefly discuss the kind of things you might expect to find on a forum of the type where the 'Local hero of the year' notice appears. (This might include information about local events and services, details of local businesses, things for sale, lost or found, etc.)

Ask students to read the 'Wanted' notice carefully. Check understanding. Draw out the meaning of

nomination, asking students if they have come across the word in relation to prizes or awards such as the Oscars in the USA or Golden Rooster awards in China. What does the notice ask you to do? Who do you write to? What information do you need to provide in the email?

Put students in pairs (or small groups) to discuss who they might write about and what they might say. (Accept a broad interpretation of what a 'hero' might be – students may even want to write about a family member or friend.) Briefly ask for suggestions from a few pairs to support any students who are short of ideas.

8 Drafting your nomination (20–25 minutes)

Establish that students are writing something that will be read by the forum administrator (and probably a group of adults who will choose the best nomination) who they don't know. Briefly review the meaning of register and tone if necessary. Register refers to the vocabulary, grammar and level of formality we use depending on who we are communicating with or the situation we are in. Tone refers to the mood or attitude we convey. Make sure that students understand why register and tone are important – if we get them wrong, we might upset or offend someone. The tone should be fairly formal and respectful (although there is no need to be extremely formal).

Since students may not have carried out a task like this before, a basic framework is provided, with guidance.

Don't focus too much on word length for the moment: it's more important that students carry out the task effectively.

9 Giving feedback (10 minutes)

If necessary (if students are not familiar with drafting, receiving feedback and redrafting), explain to students the usefulness of having their writing read by another person, i.e. other than the teacher. Point out that if we want to improve our writing, we should expect to write a 'first draft' and then rewrite parts of it to make improvements.

Make sure that, when assessing their partner's draft, students are focusing on the questions provided. Correction of spelling, punctuation, etc., should not be the *main* focus, unless they happen to notice any obvious errors.

DIFFERENTIATION

Give **support** by asking students to focus only on the first question in the checklist. This is the most important one.

Example answer

I am writing to nominate Eleni Borakis for the award of 'Local hero of the year'.

As a post-office employee, Eleni has been cheerfully and reliably delivering our letters for 40 years now. However, she not only brings us our mail but she also keeps an eye on everyone, knocking on the doors of elderly or disabled people who are stuck at home to check they are alright and to have a quick chat. Last month, she saved the life of a neighbour of ours who had collapsed, because she noticed he had not opened his shutters as usual and called the police.

In her free time, Eleni is a keen gardener, and she generously gives away packages of carrots or courgettes to local people along with their post. She wants to share her enthusiasm for growing vegetables with the next generation, too, so she runs a weekly children's gardening club with our local primary school.

Our community could not do without the amazingly kind and considerate Eleni Borakis, who does so much for us. I really hope you will consider her for the award.

10 Language study: Using apostrophes (20 minutes)

It is assumed that students will already be fairly familiar with apostrophes, so this is intended as revision. Ask students to collaborate to work out the two main uses of apostrophes in the example sentences.

Answers

a   To show where letters have been omitted ('contractions / contracted forms') – *Someone <u>has</u> put a lot of effort . . .*

b   To indicate possession – *the phone of someone*

Practice

As far as possible, allow students to work out rules on their own. You could also encourage some peer teaching (e.g. invite a student who feels confident with contractions, or the rules for using an apostrophe for possession with singular and plural nouns, to do a mini-presentation for others).

Note that even when students are able to hear contractions, they may have difficulty incorporating them in their own speech. Remind them that using a non-contracted form (e.g. *She would not come*) conveys meaning accurately, but it sounds much less fluent than the use of a contracted form.

DIFFERENTIATION

For **support**, provide a brief presentation of the rules for contracted forms (with a few examples) before students do Question 1.

For **challenge**, ask students how you might substitute a phrase using apostrophes for the following tricky examples:

The cat belonging to Min and Cheng (= Min and Cheng's cat)

The flat belonging to my sister-in-law (= My sister-in-law's flat)

The car belonging to the Russian girl with the broken laptop (= The Russian girl with the broken laptop's car – but note that we tend to avoid forms like this as they sound awkward!)

The bag belonging to James (James's bag – pronounced James-iz – although James' bag is also possible)

Answers

1   a   You are going . . .

    b   . . . he has lived . . .

    c   Do not set . . .

    d   You will be . . .

    e   I would ask . . .

    f   I had left . . .

    g   He is always . . .

2 With a singular noun, the apostrophe comes
   before the *s*. With a plural noun, it comes after
   the *s*. With an irregular plural, the apostrophe
   comes before the *s*.

3 **a** No apostrophe is needed in *trolleys*.
      It's a plural form, not a contraction or
      possessive. (Note that the *y* follows a
      vowel here, so it doesn't change to *ies* as
      a plural.)

   b An apostrophe is needed in *Women's*.
      (Possessive form)

   c No apostrophe is needed in *its*. It's a
      possessive adjective (like *his*, *her*, *our*, etc.)
      not a contraction.

You could extend the exercise by writing up
a few phrases which show possession without
apostrophes, for example:

• a field belonging to a farmer

• a dining room for students

• a library for children

• the coat belonging to Mary.

Then ask students to substitute phrases that use
apostrophes – for example, *a students' dining room*.

GRAMMAR SPOTLIGHT (10 MINUTES)

This section provides a brief review of the use
of present simple and continuous forms, which
should be very familiar to students by now. It also
lists some common stative verbs (which are not
generally used in the continuous form).

Answers

1 Any five of: they say, you love, you think, you
   don't want, do you watch ...?, I choose, things
   that interest me, I limit, etc. they are feeling

2 Any one of: She is sitting, (She is) listening

3 **a** is arguing; argues; **b** seem; **c** makes

WIDER PRACTICE

1 Look out for English-language interviews
   with well-known people (or people with an
   interesting story) online, in magazines or on
   the radio/television. Where they describe key
   stages in the person's development, this can
   make an interesting follow-up to the work on
   goals and life's challenges, especially if the
   interview is with a personality students can
   identify with. Reading/listening to a particular
   style of article can help students become more
   aware of the distinctive features and language
   of different genres.

   Students could be set this work as a project to
   research in their own language and present a
   translation to the class if they don't have easy
   access to English-speaking media.

2 To help students develop their ability to link
   character with appearance, you could select
   and display photographs from the internet
   showing interesting-looking people with a
   variety of facial expressions and clothing
   styles in different settings. Alternatively, you
   could freeze a frame of a character on a

video clip. You could then ask students to study
all the details of the person's appearance: facial
expression, body language, clothing, shoes,
accessories, hairstyle, and so on. You could ask
questions like: *What do you think they are like?
What clues do we have from their appearance?
What are they thinking? What do you think
their home life is like? What kind of job do you
think they might do?*

Encourage students to be as speculative
as possible, as there are no right answers.
Students could follow up this exercise with
some creative writing in which they build a
situation around the character.

3 If students were intrigued by the fact that Alex
   Garcia became a multimillionaire by the age
   of 21, they may like to find out more about
   teenage millionaires who have made use of
   the internet or modern technology to build
   successful businesses. They could develop
   the project in interesting ways, support their
   findings with facts and statistics, and present
   them to the class.

CONTINUED

4 You could ask pairs of students to research another well-known person that they admire, from a particular field of interest (scientific research, sport, art, literature, computing, etc.), using online sources in either English or their first language. They could then put together a short, interesting presentation in English to present this person to the rest of the class.

5 Find out if there is any local/national (i.e. local to you) equivalent of the 'community hero award' from Section D of the unit (for example, 'young volunteer of the year' or similar) or use a search engine to look for examples in English-speaking countries. Often it's possible to read information about 'Previous winners', which might be interesting for students to read before they draft their emails.

Exam-style questions

Reading and writing

Reading and Writing: open response

This exercise provides practice with answering open comprehension questions.

Remind students to take their time and pay attention to the detail in order to find the correct answers. Point out that they do not need to write their answers in full sentences and that a brief answer is sufficient in this exercise. It is also fine to use words from the text (students don't need to paraphrase) but, as always, they need to take care with spelling. Point out that the questions follow the order of the text, except for the last question, which covers the whole text.

Students will encounter some scientific words in this text that are probably unknown to them (e.g. *ornithophobia*), but the meaning is given within the text where understanding is crucial to answering the questions. If students find other unfamiliar words, remind them to use the strategies they studied within the unit (Section A5) to predict the meanings.

Remind students that it is very important to note whether they will be writing to a friend or to the headteacher. Encourage them to think about how this will affect what they say and how they say it.

Point out that they can use their imagination in the informal exercises – there is no need to base their writing on an actual visit to their school (or to consider who might realistically be invited to give a talk). If you wish, to generate ideas, you could have a brief pre-writing discussion about the kind of person who might come and why (e.g. an ex-student of the school, real or not, who has become famous or successful for some reason).

Example answer

Informal writing

Hi Kevin

Let me tell you a story. Last Sunday our cat, Tom, went missing. I thought he might be in the woods behind our house. And I was right. I could hear him crying, but I couldn't see him anywhere. Then I realised he had climbed up a tree but was too scared to come down. I am terrified of heights, but I had to rescue him. I was so frightened! My ladder wasn't high enough to reach Tom, so I had to climb the tree. It was horrible. I didn't dare look down, but I had to save him. I was sweating, but I finally reached him. As soon as I went to grab him, he climbed down. I couldn't believe it. Now I was stuck up the tree. Very slowly and fearfully I managed to get back to the ground, although I was shaking. I will never put my life at risk for an animal again.

Sarah

(160 words)

Answers
1 In childhood
2 Fight or flight response
3 Her (over-anxious) parents
4 To distract themselves from negative thoughts
5 The birds are harmless
6 Doing the shopping; using a lift; going for a walk

Reading and Writing: informal and formal

You will find advice on general approaches to exam-style writing exercises at the end of the 'Teaching support' section in the Introduction.

Listening

Listening: interview

Students answer multiple-choice questions based on an interview.

Make sure students read through the questions before they listen to the recording. They should use the second listening to check their answers.

The recording reflects some of the themes from the unit.

Answers
1 B; 2 C; 3 A; 4 C; 5 A; 6 B; 7 A; 8 B

Audioscript track 1.4

You will hear Victor, a radio presenter, asking Carlos Gomez, a teenage blogger, some questions about his hobby as part of a radio feature on developing potential in young people. For each question, choose the correct answer, A, B or C, and put a tick in the appropriate box.

You will hear the interview twice.

Now look at questions 1–8.

Presenter: Today we have an exciting guest, teenage blogger Carlos Gomez. Welcome to the show, Carlos.

Carlos: Thank you, Victor. Pleased to be here.

Presenter: Our listeners would love to hear about your amazing blog, *boyzownzone*, which is one of the most successful in the blogosphere. What do you blog about?

Carlos: Anything! Well, that's not strictly true. I'm very selective about what I blog about. A blog – it says a lot about you as a person.

Presenter: That's a good point. I suppose blogging gives everyone the opportunity to give their opinions and, well, just be yourself. And there are certainly some amazing blogs on the internet.

Carlos: There are some fabulous blogs for teenagers, but they are mainly for teenage girls. If I'm honest, the motive for doing my blog in the first place was that I thought it was something I could achieve. I said to myself, 'Carlos, come on, start your own blog. It can't be all that hard.' I wanted to achieve a blog that would be interesting to read.

Presenter: So you blog about your daily life, what you're doing at the moment, with a focus on activities boys like?

Carlos: That is absolutely correct. I love blogging about scientific inventions . . . that is one of my favourite things. I used to focus on teenage boy inventors, but now I write about anyone who deserves recognition even if many people haven't heard of them or their work.

Presenter: You have sections dedicated to different topics: music, art, football. It's not all about inventions.

Carlos: And don't forget my book review section! I am a reading fanatic and have reviewed some amazing books. People say boys only want to watch action movies or play on the PlayStation, but now I get loads of hits from boys about books I recommend. I also get comments from little kids, mums, dads and grandparents who want to buy books for their grandchildren. One lady asked her local bookseller for one of the books I'd recommended and he said that the book became his bestselling book overnight.

Presenter: Sounds like you have made reading cool. That is not bad.

Carlos: I got a brilliant post from a boy who said that he used to be anti-reading unless it was social media, and he wasn't very interested in that. He used to play computer games all the time. Then he started reading *The Dark in Their Eyes*, which is the horror series I blog about. I guarantee these books are as thrilling as any action movie. He says he's now a reading addict, just as I am. His friends can't believe it! He's a total bookworm!

Presenter:	I hear you are interested in the *Wonderworld* series of comic books. They have very unusual drawings, don't they?
Carlos:	*Wonderworld* is laugh-out-loud funny. Comic books with a difference! My family say the illustrations are strange and they would prefer pictures of flowers or sunsets, but that kind of art leaves me unimpressed. I look up to those artists who create the artwork – they are so talented. If I ever win the lottery, I'm going to buy the original artworks and put them on my bedroom wall. The *Wonderworld* books are expensive but they are definitely worth it. I persuaded my school library to buy a set of *Wonderworld* and now almost everyone at school is on the waiting list!
Presenter:	How do you find time for all this?
Carlos:	Blogging makes me happy and is a priority. Some bloggers communicate almost constantly but, although I love sharing my news, I think quite carefully before I update my blog. However, people visit my site almost daily so I do not want to let them down by not updating. I post up a page when I get a free evening or when there is a quiet lunchtime at school.
Presenter:	Any tips for would-be bloggers who might be listening now?
Carlos:	Just go for it. Don't let your spelling or anything hold you back. People don't judge you. My grammar and spelling used to be rubbish but blogging has made my literacy better. What matters most is the people who are going to read your blog, so think about what they would like. Using appealing pictures makes a big difference to the blog as well.
Presenter:	What are your future goals?
Carlos:	If I have a future goal, it's to meet one of the wonderfully talented people I have blogged about. Just to get a post from one of them would be a dream come true.
Presenter:	Thank you, Carlos. We've had lots of texts coming in from listeners while we've been talking. Here is one from . . .

Speaking

You will find advice on general approaches to speaking exercises at the end of the 'Teaching support' section in the Introduction.

If students are doing this exercise under examination conditions, warm-up questions may help to put them at ease. These are included in the corresponding Coursebook unit.

>2 Fitness and well-being

Learning plan

AOs	Key learning intentions	Success criteria
S1, S3, W1, W3	Explore the topic of fitness, health, sport and well-being	• Students can maintain a conversation relating to the topic • Students can express personal opinions about the issues • Students can use appropriate vocabulary to talk and write about the topic
R1, R2, R3, W2, W3	Focus on how to take notes effectively	• Students can identify the main point in a reading text or audio recording • Students can write concise notes • Students can write notes under appropriate sub-headings
R1, R2, R3, R4	Read and understand a more formal text, exploring its features	• Students understand the ideas conveyed • Students understand the writer's intentions • Students are able to make notes that accurately reflect key points and how they interrelate • Students can compare the features and language with other types of text
L1, L2	Extract information from short audio clips without knowing the context in advance	• Students can isolate key factual information while listening without prior knowledge of context • Students can work out what is or is not relevant
L2, S4	Explore how sentence stress conveys meaning in speech	• Students understand why particular words or syllables are stressed • Students begin to make use of sentence stress appropriately in their own speech

Overview

The unit focuses on the theme of fitness and well-being, providing related vocabulary practice as well as skills work, including reading a more formal text and exploring its features. There is also a strong focus on writing notes, including discussion of why they are useful and tips on how best to write them. Students also look at ways of keeping a discussion with a partner going through use of appropriate questioning and practise using intonation to make their meaning clearer when they speak.

THEME

The theme is a broad one and it allows you and your students to carry out related discussion and research appropriate to your students' interests and experience, as well as your setting.

In recent years, there has been much greater awareness internationally of issues around mental as well as physical health, particularly with regard to young people, so the unit covers well-being generally. It begins with an opportunity for students to define for themselves what they understand by 'a healthy lifestyle'. It moves on to look at small changes that people can make to improve their health on a day-to-day basis through reading a magazine article about a young woman who decides to take control of her own health. Other sub-themes include competitive sport and whether it is good or bad for young people, whether you can improve your health through activities such as cold-water swimming or laughter, and the effects on young people of spending long periods of time looking at screens. There is also an opportunity to discuss technology in sport, and to read a typical review comparing different kinds of gadgets that people might want to buy.

LANGUAGE WORK

The language work in this unit includes functional language for making suggestions and giving warnings. Spelling work looks at spelling patterns when adding suffixes to words ending in –e, and there is an opportunity to look at word building and word families to consider how they can help to expand vocabulary and predict the meanings of unfamiliar words. Students explore words associated with particular sports and consider collocations such as *go swimming* but *do* judo. They learn how to form adjectives from expressions of measurement (e.g. a 30-minute run) and they look at different uses of the conditional in *if*-clauses. In looking at a model for their writing, they consider ways of linking shorter sentences into longer ones using suitable linking words.

Common misconceptions

Misconception	How to identify	How to overcome
Students use a plural form and/or omit the hyphen when forming compound adjectives with numbers. Example: *I could barely move my legs during the <u>eight hours</u> trip.*	Display some correct and incorrect examples. Ask students to identify the correct ones and to discuss the rules. For example: *a **15** storeys building* (✗); *a 10-seconds pause* (✗); *my 18-year-old cousin* (✓); *a six-course meal* (✓)); *a three-star review* (✓).	After establishing the rules, have students form compound adjectives based on example sentences. For example: *a TV series with six parts* (= a six-part TV series) *an exam lasting 45 minutes* (= a 45-minute exam) *a prison sentence lasting 5 years* (= a 5-year prison sentence).

Misconception	How to identify	How to overcome
Students use the wrong tense after *if* in first and second conditional sentences. Examples: *I will call you if I <u>will come</u> to your town!* *I would stay with you a bit longer if I <u>would have</u> more time.*	Display and discuss incorrect examples from students' writing. (Depending on students' confidence and knowledge, it may be better to deal with first and second conditionals on separate occasions.) In pairs, have them discuss what is incorrect and work out the rules for correct formation of conditional sentences. Check, then display some correct examples.	Practise forming conditional chains (with either first or second conditionals) in groups or as a class. Provide a starter clause (e.g. *If I won a plane ticket in a competition . . .*) and students continue the chain. For example: *If I won a plane ticket in a competition, I would fly to Canada. If I flew to Canada, I would go to see the Rocky Mountains. If I went to the Rocky Mountains, I would learn to ski. If . . .*

Introducing the unit topic (5–10 minutes)

Working with a partner, students look at the photo and discuss the questions:

The questions will draw out students' ideas about what fitness and well-being consist of. Some of them may think of fitness in terms of traditional team sports or activities such as running, going to the gym, and so on, so it is useful for them to consider whether there are other ways for people to improve their physical health. It is also helpful to explore the concept of mental health, especially among young people, and to consider whether activities that make you happy may also be healthy.

Students will note that the skateboarder in the photo appears to be doing a skateboard trick. When skateboarding first became popular in the 1970s, some people regarded it as being part of a dangerous subculture for rebellious teenagers and it had quite negative associations. However, it was accepted as an Olympic sport for the first time ahead of the 2020 Olympics, and (depending on where they live) your students may regard it as a sport just like any other. Positive benefits that some people have claimed for skateboarding include teaching 'life skills' (patience, turn-taking, concentration, picking yourself up after a fall, socialising, courage), physical skills like hand–eye–feet coordination, building muscle strength, improving balance, reducing stress and keeping some young people from getting into trouble.

〉 **Digital coursebook:** At the start of the lesson, use this video to introduce and review:

- the topic of fitness, health, sport and well-being
- a range of vocabulary related to fitness and well-being
- zero, first and second conditional forms.

Read the question on the title screen and ask learners what they think they might see. Then play the video all the way through and check learners' predictions.

Play the video a second time, pausing to discuss what is being shown and the questions on the end screen. You can take the opportunity to revise words and phrases associated with the topic of fitness and well-being. Note that the end-screen contains some differentiated two-part questions. The first part can be answered by using the content of the video. The second part requires learners to develop their thinking. More confident learners will be able to offer more extensive reasons for their ideas.

You may like to play the video a third time for consolidation.

A What is a healthy lifestyle?

1 Top tips (10–15 minutes)

〉 **Critical thinking:** The purpose of the exercise is to introduce vocabulary relevant to the topic and to get students to consider what a 'healthy lifestyle' means so that they are able to talk about it. If necessary, prompt students to consider how issues around mental health (such as spending time with friends and family, or avoiding stress) might be just as important to your health as diet and exercise.

Support students by going through the list as a class or group, eliciting suitable verbs to go with each noun or noun phrase before they start writing their top tips. They will also need to use words like 'a' or 'your', or words denoting quantity such as 'some', 'plenty of' or 'too much'. Alternatively, you could supply a list of useful verbs from which they could choose (e.g. *get, check, do, play, spend, avoid, cut down on, look after*, etc.).

2 Keeping the conversation going (10–15 minutes)

This exercise will be more useful for some students than others, depending on their speaking ability with English as well as their personality and confidence. Encourage them to use the listed techniques in future discussions.

It is useful to give a demonstration to the class first where you talk to one student, showing how to follow the suggested techniques.

If you prefer, you can set up the exercise as an interview rather than a discussion, with students taking it in turns to be A the interviewer (asking questions and giving prompts) and B the interviewee (answering A's questions).

3 Pre-reading (2–3 minutes)

The purpose of the exercise is to encourage students to get as much information as possible about an article before they read it in detail. Give them a very brief time to look at the title, photo and first line before discussing the questions as a class. Ask students to explain what clues tell them the correct answers. Do students know, or can they guess, what the idiom *feeling on top of the world* means? (= feeling extremely happy).

Answers
1 C; 2 A

4 Read and make notes (15–20 minutes)

It is assumed that students will have some previous experience of making notes, even if they have not yet done it in English. In Section B, they will be looking in more detail at how to make notes (see Sections B1–B3), so for the moment don't focus

too much on how they do it. They will be looking back on the notes they make in this exercise and discussing what was tricky and how to improve their note-taking.

Point out that only one line (and bullet point) is provided for the first heading. In other words, they need to consider what the *main* point is – they don't need lots of detail.

Support students by displaying a copy of the text. Read it aloud, asking students to tell you when they think you have come to something that is relevant to the note-taking task. Use two different colours to highlight/underline parts of the text that relate to the two headings in the task.

Example answers
Students' notes should reflect an accurate understanding of the text.

Why Shalimar became unfit
* Too busy setting up her company

Examples of Shalimar's unhealthy lifestyle
* Never took a meal break
* Worked long hours
* Bad diet – high-energy drinks and biscuits
* Didn't cook a proper meal
* Didn't sleep well

5 Making suggestions (10 minutes)

Note that conditional sentences (including the second conditional, which is required here) are covered in the 'Grammar spotlight' at the end of this unit. Model one or two examples as a class before asking students to continue doing the exercise in pairs.

Reduce the number of suggestions required by students who need **support**, or **challenge** others to come up with more.

6 Read and compare (15 minutes)

This is an exercise in scanning. Remind students that scanning consists of running your eye over a text to pick out particular information.

DIFFERENTIATION

Support students who need it by providing a list of straightforward comprehension questions on Part 2.

You could **challenge** more confident readers to create a specific number of comprehension questions on Part 2 and exchange them with another confident reader to answer them. Creating their own comprehension questions requires gaining a deep understanding of the text.

Example answers (from text)
Students' coding S or D will vary depending on their own suggestions in Section A5.

What Shalimar did to improve her health

- Give the [fitness] programme a try
- Getting off the bus a stop earlier
- Making time to shop for fresh ingredients
- I make up my packed lunch every day and leave the office to eat it in a park down the road
- She now uses the stairs as much as possible instead of the lift
- Avoids fizzy drinks and drinks tea or water instead

---

7 Post-reading discussion (5–10 minutes)

> **Critical thinking:** Ask students to discuss the questions in small groups while you circulate, prompting deeper critical thinking skills through appropriate questioning. You could ask one student in each group to take notes, and have a class feedback session after the group discussions.

Issues to consider might include the economic cost to a country if people miss work or need hospital treatment because of poor health, the links between health and education, and between health and income. You could also specifically talk about mental health, which has been described as a 'forgotten crisis'. Encourage students to discuss ways of encouraging people (of all ages) to look after their health better.

Depending on what you consider suitable in your culture or country (and school setting), you could prompt students to include wider health issues such as problems with physical or mental health, or bullying at school, etc., as well as issues with diet and lack of exercise.

8 Words in context (10 minutes)

Answers
1   **a** 8; **b** 10; **c** 3; **d** 6; **e** 5; **f** 7; **g** 4; **h** 9; **i** 1; **j** 2

2   **a** thrilled, going from strength to strength; **b** sped up; **c** sipped, pluck up the courage; **d** boosted; **e** immersed; **f** inconceivable

International overview (10 minutes)

> **Critical thinking:** Use the exercise to encourage students to think about the implications of improved worldwide health leading to longer lifespans, while at the same time birth rates are falling. Discuss the fact that many countries have raised their retirement age.

You could also widen the discussion to look at varying life expectancies in different countries and what the reasons might be.

Answers
1   **a** 9.3%; **b** 22.6%

2   **a** 5–14 year age group (although 'under 5s' should also be accepted as an answer if students have calculated it differently); **b** 65 and over age group

3   People living for longer (better health care, greater awareness of lifestyle issues, etc.) while birth rates fall.

4   Issues may include: fewer people of working age paying taxes, but more money needed to pay for medical care for the elderly; possible housing shortages (if older people are living alone); the need for people to save up for their retirement; more healthy older people available for voluntary work and childcare; the need for more facilities for older people, and so on.

Audioscript track 2.1

John and Ella are watching an international football match on TV. Poland are playing against Finland. Listen to the dialogue while you read, and notice which words or syllables the speakers emphasise. Why are these words or syllables emphasised?

Ella: Is Poland playing in the blue and green?

John: No, Poland's playing in the yellow and green.

Ella: Did you say Finland was in the yellow and green?

John: No, I said Poland was in the yellow and green.

Ella: Is Poland playing France this season?

John: Poland plays France every season.

Ella: Did Poland win a few of their matches last season?

John: They won all their matches last season!

9   Sentence stress (10 minutes)

Point out that the stressed words are not only louder in volume, but are also a little longer and the intonation may change (the voice may rise).

You could demonstrate and practise with some examples before students listen to the dialogue. For example:

Did you leave your football shorts at school?

No, I left my <u>boots</u>.

No, I left them on the <u>bus</u>.

No, I left my <u>running</u> shorts at school.

No, <u>Ali</u> left them at school.

DIFFERENTIATION

Students whose first language does not use sentence stress in a similar way to English may need more **support** for this and the following exercise. An understanding of sentence stress helps both with listening (the words most important to the meaning are emphasised) and

CONTINUED

with speaking (it can be harder to understand a speaker who speaks in a very 'flat' way with little use of stress or one who uses it wrongly). *All* English sentences use patterns of stressed and unstressed words, but when we are correcting another speaker or emphasising a point, we use stress more strongly. To give more support, it can be useful to practise clapping the rhythm of sentences, with stronger and longer beats for the stressed words.

10   Practising sentence stress to convey meaning (10 minutes)

Point out that there will be other stresses within the sentences but you are asking students to identify the *main* stress(es) that speaker B uses to correct speaker A's misunderstanding.

Answers
a Everybody; **b** never; **c** any; **d** No one;
e Union, last; **f** think, know, saw

Encourage students to practise listening for and using stress in any discussion they have in English.

11   Spelling: Adding suffixes to words ending in –e (10 minutes)

English is said to have one of the most inconsistent spelling systems of any language due to the wide variety of language influences that formed it, but there are rules which can help with certain aspects of spelling. This exercise helps students work out certain rules for themselves, which makes it more likely they will understand and remember them.

DIFFERENTIATION

Support students by giving the 'sums' to practise adding suffixes. For example:

adore + able =

postpone + ment =

Alternatively, **challenge** them to make up their own 'sums'.

Answers

1   The *e* disappears in group A, but remains in group B. Students may be able to work out that the suffixes in A start with a vowel while those in B start with a consonant.

2   Examples (others may be possible):
    a   exciting, excitable, excitement
    b   caring, careful, careless
    c   advising, advisable
    d   creating, creative
    e   expensive
    f   achieving, achievable, achievement
    g   hoping, hopeful, hopeless

3   Help students to realise that -*e* is required in cases where, without it, the word could be wrongly pronounced.

4   Looking up the words will make students more likely to remember them. Note that likeable is mainly used to describe people rather than things.

12 Spelling practice (15 minutes)

Answers

1 a increasing; **b** replacing; **c** having; **d** exciting; **e** creativity; **f** moving; **g** improvement; **h** noticeable; **i** motivation; **j** dancing/dance; **k** stimulating; **l** participating/participation; **m** encouragement; **n** sizeable; **o** participating; **p** celebration; **q** stylish; **r** diversity; **s** imaginative; **t** memorable

13 Word families (10 minutes)

Remind students of the prefixes they studied in Unit 1, Section C3.

This exercise allows students to explore the connections between words with a common base word, and (where relevant) to apply spelling rules they have learnt.

Suggested answers

a   hoping, hoped, hopeful, hopeless, hopefully, hopelessly, hopefulness, hopelessness

b   changed, changing, changeable, unchanged, unchangeable, unchanging

c   achieved, achieving, achievable, achievability, achievement

d   impatient, patiently, impatiently, patience, impatience

e   competed, competing, competition, competitor, competitive

f   decided, decision, decisive, indecisive, undecided, indecision, indecisive

B Note-taking and sports

1 Discussion (3–5 minutes)

Points to include in the discussion: We identify the key points, and write a small number of words – to help us remember, so that we have something to look back to, to help us make sense of what we are reading/listening to.

The scope of the discussion for question 2 will vary depending on what technology your students have access to. At a basic level, differences may include: handwriting notes is slower, they can be lost, it can be easier to draw arrows, shapes, diagrams, and so on, while digital notes can be searched, cross-referenced, shared. Research on university students' lecture notes suggests that students who write their notes manually are more likely to be focusing on the meaning (and therefore learning) than those who try to key in every word they hear on their laptop. However, it is possible your students may have accessed a range of digital tools which make note-taking very different from simply typing words on a laptop.

2 How to make notes (10 minutes)

The purpose of this exercise and Section B3 is to take students through the steps required to make notes effectively.

In the short text about Jonas Hornik, students need to be able to ignore unnecessary details or repetitions.

DIFFERENTIATION

If students need **support** to move away from copying large chunks of text, display sentences and ask for suggestions as to what is not relevant or necessary. For example:

the other members of his ~~morning~~ yoga group, ~~none of them musicians,~~ soon became ~~very close and supportive~~ friends

~~the whole experience~~ provided ~~him with~~ a ~~much-needed~~ new focus in life outside ~~of~~ music

Answers

1   'Not only did the yoga classes teach him to relax'; 'The other members . . . became very close and supportive friends'; 'a much-needed new focus in life outside of music'

2 and 3   The notes are too long; there is no need to include 'The first/second point is that'. The student copied word for word and didn't adapt the verb tense or cut out repetition or irrelevant detail.

Suggested 'correct' notes:

*   (It) taught him to relax
*   (It) helped him make friends / Other group members became friends
*   (It) provided a new focus outside music

3   Note-taking practice (5–10 minutes)

DIFFERENTIATION

Break down the task into steps for those who need **support**. Tell them to first identify and highlight key points, and check with a partner. Then they should work out which words are not relevant. Finally, they should write the notes, keeping them brief but ensuring they make sense.

Suggested answer

*   (They) provide 20 times more vitamin C – boosts immunity
*   (They) provide folic acid – helps produce healthy red blood cells

4   Sports vocabulary (10–15 minutes)

Tell students to copy the table in their notebooks, replacing badminton and running with their chosen activities.

Encourage students to think about any aspects of their chosen activities that they might need vocabulary for to discuss that sport with someone. This may apply either to activities students take part in themselves or ones they follow on TV, read about, and so on.

It may also be useful to teach and drill phrases for asking about specialised terms that you don't know

the word for, for example *What is the name of the thing you use for –ing . . . ? What do you call it when you . . . ?*

Talk about collocation – the way that certain words go together in a language. We say that we go swimming, but *we play hockey* and *we do weightlifting*, for example.

DIFFERENTIATION

Challenge students to look at the words in the lists that they *didn't* include in their columns and work out what sport/activity those words might apply to. They will need a good (online or print) dictionary. You could also show them how to create a spider diagram for a sport they are particularly interested in. For example, if the sport is football, the spider diagram might have sub-sections for playing positions, equipment, rules, skills, and so on, and they could expand the diagram as much as they like.

5   Is sport always fun? (10 minutes)

> **Critical thinking:** Challenge students to think through the implications of their opinions and to suggest possible solutions or alternatives. Encourage them to challenge each other too.

DIFFERENTIATION

Challenge students to use a wider variety of expressions than simply 'I agree' or 'I disagree'. Suggest some examples, if necessary.

6   Pre-reading (3–5 minutes)

Explain that 'primary school' means a school for younger children, usually up to the age of 11.

Point out that predicting the content of a text is a good way of preparing for reading tasks because it makes the task a little easier. Students should think about what information they would expect a text to include based on such things as the summary in the rubric, its title, the photo accompanying it, and so on.

7   Reading for gist (10 minutes)

If you think your students will be tempted to read the text too slowly, focusing on every word, give them a time limit for the task.

Answers

Points covered from Section B6: the competitive aspect of the day, the bad effects of sports day on some children, possible alternatives to traditional sports day.

8 Comprehension check (10 minutes)

Support students by offering alternative article titles from which they can choose, and get them to justify their choice. For example:

- Sports day is much too competitive
- Sports day misery
- Mum criticises sports day
- No more!
- School criticised for sports day disaster.

Answers
1 a 4; b 3; c 5; d 2; e 1

9 Note-taking practice (20 minutes)

Students should try to present their notes in their own words where possible. Note-taking tasks may be slanted in a particular way (e.g. asking students to list the advantages and disadvantages of something), so students need to have practised adapting their wording to the question.

Support students by asking them to highlight (or underline) the points in the text relevant to each of the three headings in three different colours.

Alternative approaches (depending on what is causing them particular problems) might include: providing notes under each heading including one extra point not mentioned in the text, which students have to eliminate; or giving them a set of notes that are unnecessarily long and detailed, asking them to cut them down to the key points.

Suggested answers

Reasons for having a sports day

- competition is character-building
- taking part is important, not winning
- school tradition.

The negative effects of sports day

Any two of:

- stomach ache / being sick / not sleeping the night before
- children who are overweight / not good at sport are upset/embarrassed
- children who fall over in front of everyone are shamed.

Sports day: possible improvements

- team games
- a few races (for those who want them).

10 Language study: Compound adjectives with numbers (10 minutes)

Answers

a   50-minute fitness video

b   six-number code

c   10-million-dollar mansion

d   five-course meal

e   one-euro coin

f   two-kilogram bag of sugar

g   12-hour shift

h   three-star hotel

11 Listening for specific information (10 minutes)

Students will be practising two key skills in this exercise: orientating themselves quickly when they have to listen to something without background knowledge of the situation or the speakers, and picking out key information while ignoring what is not relevant.

Point out to students that words from the *wrong* options will often be mentioned in the audio recording too, so they need to check the surrounding information. For example, in question 1, they may hear the names of all three sports a–c, but if they have carefully read the question, they should be able to identify the correct answer.

DIFFERENTIATION

If students get answers wrong after listening at least twice, **support** them by allowing them to follow on the audioscript as they listen an extra time. This will help them to identify where they went wrong.

Answers

1 b; **2** b; **3** c; **4** c;

5 **a** Yes; **b** Yes; **c** No; **d** Yes

Audioscript track 2.2

Listen to two short conversations and one recorded message. Listen carefully for the information to answer the questions.

Extract 1

Man: So I heard about your new hobby from your mum. That's quite an unusual sport for someone your age, isn't it? What made you decide to take it up?

Girl: Well, I used to really like hockey, but I've never been particularly good at it so I wanted to try something else. My school sports teacher told me about a free try-out session that our local golf course was offering, but unfortunately I missed the deadline for signing up, so for a while I tried out tennis with a cousin of mine. But then another opportunity came up to play golf, and I fell in love with it! Since then, I've been playing three times a week with a friend.

Man: Well, it's great that you're enjoying it. Have you had some lessons?

Girl: Yes. I've had 2 paid lessons so far.

Extract 2

News reporter: Here's Hailey Donovan, who's going to tell us about wild swimming in lakes and rivers. Hailey, I know lots of people are huge fans of this kind of swimming and believe it's really good for you. But is there anything we need to know, from a safety point of view?

Hailey: Thanks, Ivan. Yes, it's getting really popular, and I'm seeing loads of new swimmers and that's great! But bear in mind, firstly, that rivers and lakes can be very cold, so be careful to allow your body to get used to the temperature by only swimming for a short period at first, especially if you haven't done it much before. Summer's probably the nicest time to get started – and you can wear a wetsuit if you want to. When you enter the water, do it slowly and watch out for rocks or strong currents – if you jump in, you'll risk getting cold-water shock, which can be really dangerous. And make sure there's a safe and easy place to exit the water – you'd be surprised how tricky it can be to pull yourself up a slippery, muddy riverbank. Have a towel and warm clothes ready for when you get out. Your body temperature will continue to drop after you leave the water and you'll be shivering, so you should quickly strip off your wet swimming costume, wrap up well and sip a hot drink. But most vital of all, never swim by yourself in case you get into difficulties. If you follow my safety tips, you'll have a wonderful experience!

Extract 3

Hello, you're through to Sandmarsh Leisure Club. We're open to the public from 8 a.m. till 10 p.m. Wednesday to Saturday, Sunday 9 a.m. till 1 p.m., and closed Monday and Tuesday except for private bookings. Our three badminton courts are available by calling us in advance to reserve a half-hour slot. Rackets and shuttlecocks can be borrowed if required, free of charge, by paying a refundable deposit of $10 per person. Indoor shoes with rubber soles are to be worn on the courts, please.

Our 20-metre heated swimming pool has the same public opening hours as the leisure club, apart from Wednesdays and Thursdays from 2 p.m. till 5 p.m., when it is reserved for under-11s' swimming lessons. Please remember to bring your own towel as well as a $1 coin if you want to store valuables in a locker while you swim. Note that if you swim regularly, discount rates are available at our reception desk.

We currently have yoga for the over-70s on Fridays from 11 a.m. till noon, followed by a keep fit class, which is held in the small dance room by the pool. This is a drop-in session, costing $12 per session, with no need to book. Please wear loose, comfortable clothing and bring a drink.

12 Expressing warnings (10–15 minutes)

DIFFERENTIATION

For **support**, reduce the number of mini-conversations that students need to create.

For **challenge**, invite students to create a lengthier dialogue incorporating at least three different warnings.

C Fitness and technology

1 Discussion (5–10 minutes)

The scope of this discussion will very much depend on your students' experience and interest. Those who watch sport on TV will probably be familiar with goal-line technology (football) or hawk-eye technology (e.g. tennis), and may be able to explain to classmates what it does and what the possible problems with it can be. Ask students if they can think of any other ways that sports rely on technology.

2 Pre-reading vocabulary (5–10 minutes)

If students are unfamiliar with the more technology-related vocabulary, invite other members of the class to try to explain what it means.

3 Reading for gist (5–10 minutes)

Note that the text consists of reviews of different kinds of fitness trackers, but students don't need to have used one to be able to follow the texts and do the exercise.

The purpose of the questions is to remind students to use clues to help them understand a text. They should not need long to work out the answers to the questions (skimming just the first of the four texts should be enough), so you may wish to impose a time limit.

Answers
1 To give people information to help them choose the most suitable fitness tracker for their needs.

2 In a print or online magazine (or website) about technology and gadgets. Or in a sports/fitness magazine/website?

3 Members of the public (adults or teenagers) who are interested in healthy living or keeping fit, and who are also fairly confident with technology. (The article seems to assume that the reader is familiar with terms like app, mode, manually, and it refers to 'the usual data'.)

4 Scanning to match information (15–20 minutes)

This is quite a tricky exercise, which relies on students being able both to scan for information and to recognise synonyms and different ways of expressing the same thing.

DIFFERENTIATION

To provide more **support**, you could demonstrate one or two of the examples with the whole class before students continue on their own. Or, for more practice with synonyms before they start on the main exercise, you could get students to do a matching exercise based only on the first text (GoZone 24/7). Display the following and get students to match them with phrases from the text (given in brackets) with the same meaning but expressed differently:

- very many features (= *wealth of features*)
- to allow you to be more relaxed (= *to help you reduce that stress*)
- you might wonder if it's worth it (= *you might question the value of*)
- more important for everybody (= *more universally important*)
- is able to notice differences (= *can spot any changes*)
- could save your life (= *potentially a lifesaver*).

CONTINUED

An extension exercise to provide **challenge** would be to set up a 'Dragon's Den' scenario (based on the TV format popular in many countries, where entrepreneurs present their business ideas to a panel of wealthy investors, who choose whether or not to invest in each entrepreneur's idea). Pairs of students could come up with ideas for a new fitness tracker or app, and write a description of it using similar language to that in the text they have been reading. Other students could vote for the most convincing.

Answers

a   GoZone 24/7

b   Vivace Pro

c   Kilston Sportwatch

d   FitterGogo 5

e   Kilston Sportwatch

f   FitterGogo 5

g   GoZone 24/7

h   Vivace Pro

i   Vivace Pro

j   FitterGogo 5

5   The writer's opinion (10 minutes)

This exercise gives further practice in matching ideas expressed with different words.

Answers

GoZone 24/7: **a** 'you might question the value of the latter'; **b** 'surely more universally important'; **c** 'cleverly designed screen layout'

Kilston Sportwatch: **d** 'What is particularly appealing in these challenges'

FitterGogo 5: **e** 'a unique range of exciting workouts'; **f** 'FitterGogo's many fans don't find this an issue'

Vivace Pro: **g** 'would undoubtedly be the winner if we were to judge trackers purely by their ability to look good on your wrist'; **h** 'looks likely to be a big hit'

6   Post-reading discussion (10 minutes)

> **Critical thinking:** The questions explore the psychology of exercising and motivation. Encourage students to explain and justify their thinking.

7   Pre-listening prediction (3–5 minutes)

This exercise assumes that students are familiar with some of the issues around computers and mobile phones (and their overuse). If not (and especially if some of your students don't have access to these), you could have this discussion as a class, inviting those who do have computers and mobile phones to explain some of the issues to their classmates.

8   Listening to check predictions (10 minutes)

Explain, if necessary, the meaning of *hormones, teens* and, in a sensitive way, *cyberbullying*.

Ask students whether their predictions were correct, and also ask a few questions to check general understanding of the content of the audio. (For example: *Who is being interviewed? Why have they invited her to speak on the radio? Is she saying that computers and phones are dangerous or is she saying some positive things? What sort of problems does she mention?*)

Audioscript track 2.3

Listen to an interview on a radio programme. Two worried parents contacted the show to talk about their 14-year-old children's use of computers and mobile phones at home. The radio programme has invited an expert to reply to the parents.

Jeremy: This afternoon, we're going to talk about teenagers and their habits with regard to computers and mobile phones.

And we have with us Manal Osman, who, as many of you will know, is head of student well-being services. Hello, Manal.

Manal: Hello, Jeremy!

Jeremy: So, just to remind our listeners, this morning we talked to the parents of 14-year-old twins about their son and daughter's use of their PC and the other devices they have at home. It was a lively discussion and, like many parents of teens, they had some slight concerns about the large amounts of time that their son and daughter spend staring at a screen. So, Manal, what would you say to them?

Manal: Well, I'd like to start by trying to reassure them that the time we spend on computers, phones and so on is not necessarily problematic. It's not as if screen time is some dangerous medicine where you can have too much. In fact, research suggests that even those people who spend the most time hunched over their PC don't automatically have more mental health problems than anyone else.

Jeremy: Well, that's good to hear. So are you saying, then, that we should just shut our teenagers' bedroom door and let them stay on their screens 24 hours a day, if that's what they want?

Manal: No, not exactly, it's not quite that simple. You could argue that it's not so much what they're doing with that screen as what they're *not* doing – for example, they might be missing out on time spent hanging out with friends or doing physical activity, or even getting their school work done. And that could be worrying. But on the other hand, a lot of what teenagers do online is extremely sociable – online gaming, for example, is very much a shared activity, for boys in particular, and social media is all about connecting with other people.

Jeremy: So if they're on their phones at 3 in the morning but socialising safely with people they know, that's ok?

Manal: (Laughing) Ah, well, I didn't say that . . . no, that's an example of screen time getting in the way of something more important, and in this case, it's sleep. Teenagers in particular are affected quite badly if they don't get enough. For example, it can alter their moods and lower their self-confidence so they are less able to cope with challenges during the daytime. They ought to be getting eight to ten hours' sleep at night, in fact, and it's best for them to shut down any screens an hour before their agreed bedtime . . .

Jeremy: They shouldn't look at phones just before they go to bed?

Manal: That's right, because the screens give out blue light similar to sunlight. It tricks our body into thinking it's still daytime, and stops it producing melatonin – that's the hormone that makes us feel sleepy.

Jeremy: Ah, I see. So maybe this is where the parent steps in and takes away the phone or tablet until the next morning.

Manal: Well, maybe, although I'd argue that it normally works better to respect the teenager's maturity and discuss these things rather than making it seem like a punishment. Most teenagers are extremely sensible, generally. And, by the way, let's not forget that this applies to many adults as well – overuse of screens late at night is a problem for people of any age, and parents can be equally guilty. You need to lead by example!

Jeremy: Well, yes, absolutely! So, just to come back to Jin and Sheena Patel, our parents from this morning's interview . . . as well as feeling that their children had become prisoners of their own computers, they felt very suspicious about what their kids were looking at online. Can you relate to that at all?

Manal: Oh one hundred percent, yes I can – obviously, that has to be a worry for any parent, what with the dangers of cyberbullying, violent games, inappropriate advertising, and so on:

I could talk about that all day! But the simplest advice I can give is to keep the communication open, talk to your teens about what they're doing online but without making them feel you're invading their privacy – because that would not encourage an open, honest relationship. Make sure they trust you enough to come to you if they ever feel uncomfortable with anything they see on their screen.

Jeremy: Great advice – thanks, Manal!

Manal: My pleasure.

9 Listening for detail and attitude (10–15 minutes)

Point out to students that the interviewer's questions are a useful guide to what Manal is talking about. Remind them that the answer will probably be given in different words from the question. They should read the questions carefully before listening again.

DIFFERENTIATION

For extra **support**, break the recording into perhaps three sections, each with two main question-and-answer dialogues. Tell students which questions will be answered in the section you are about to play. After listening to a section, pause the recording and get students to tell you (or, in groups, to tell their groups) as much as they can about what Jeremy asked and what Manal said in reply. Then play that section again and see if students are better able to answer the relevant questions.

Answers
1 B; 2 C; 3 B; 4 C; 5 B; 6 C

10 Post-listening discussion (5–10 minutes)

> **Critical thinking:** This may be a useful way for students to discuss issues around mobile phone and computer use without feeling that they themselves are being judged or criticised. If you wish, you could broaden out the discussion to cover issues of safe and unsafe use of phones and the internet more generally. Present the relevant vocabulary as necessary.

Note that conditional sentences (including the second conditional, which students are likely to be using in this discussion) are covered in the 'Grammar spotlight' at the end of this unit. You could point out briefly that we would normally say 'If I *were* (rather than *was*) the parent, I would . . .' because this is an unreal situation (the person speaking is not the parent). This is an example of the subjunctive form, which is not often used in English.

D Different approaches to well-being

1 Sayings (10 minutes)

Students could discuss the sayings in pairs, and you could then round off with a brief whole-class discussion of equivalent phrases in students' own language.

DIFFERENTIATION

Challenge students to think of any other sayings they have heard in English.

2 Pre-reading: Predicting audience and purpose (5 minutes)

Answers
1 B; 2 A; 3 B

3 Reading strategy: Using word families to predict meaning (10 minutes)

The main purpose of the exercise is to help students realise that they can often predict the meaning of new words in a text by linking them with other words that they already know. This is particularly useful when reading more academic texts, which tend to use more complex language and more noun-based phrases (e.g. the building site was abandoned *due to its inaccessibility* rather than *because it was difficult to access it*).

Rather than scanning the text for the listed words before reading it, ask students to refer back to the list as they read the text for the activities that follow.

Related words in the text
to measure: *measurable*
energy: *energetically*
to row (a boat): *rowing machine*
comfort: *discomfort*
different: *differ*
to vary, various: *invariably*
infection: *infectious*
cooperate (with someone): *cooperative*
horror: *horrendous*
tense (adjective): *tension*
to prove: *disprove*

4 Reading (20 minutes)

Students read the text carefully and answer the questions individually, referring to the glossary as necessary.

DIFFERENTIATION

Support students by drawing attention to the topic sentence at the start of each paragraph. In more formal writing especially, this first sentence tends to sum up what you will read about in the rest of the paragraph, so it is helpful when you are looking for the answers to specific questions. You could display a copy of the text for the class, highlighting the topic sentences, and check that students understand the meaning of each topic sentence in simpler English.

Answers
1 C; 2 A; 3 A; 4 B; 5 C

Discuss why the writer does not offer a personal opinion about laughter therapy. (In this kind of article, the writer is interested in facts rather than opinions, and points out that there has not been much research to prove whether the therapy is effective or not.)

In paragraph 3, there is a reference to radio programmes being broadcast 'during the Covid-19 lockdown'. Explain, if necessary, that in many countries during the pandemic of 2020–21, people were not allowed to leave their houses or meet indoors with other people. This meant that radio programmes that are normally recorded with a studio audience had to be recorded in an empty studio with no audience and hence no background laughter.

5 Vocabulary practice (10 minutes)

DIFFERENTIATION

Challenge students who finish quickly to write further definitions for tricky words in the text. They can then exchange these with a partner or you could collect these definitions and display them for the whole class to find the answers.

Answers
a boost; b monitored; c associated with; d fellow; e release; f wards; g fake

6 Making notes (10 minutes)

This exercise provides more practice with note-taking and is a further way of checking comprehension of the text. Encourage students to consider how they would organise their notes (what sub-headings they would use, etc.).

As an extension exercise, some students could deliver the talk, using their notes as a prop. You could encourage further research on the topic to include more detail.

7 Style and features (10 minutes)

Students work individually to answer the questions, which focus on the features of more formal or academic texts.

Answers
1   a   The purpose is different. The article in Section D4 is aimed at readers who want facts, while the newspaper article here is more for entertainment. (We don't see the rest of the article, but it is possible that it is also trying to persuade readers to take part in laughter therapy classes, etc.)

   b   The language in the newspaper article is less serious and aims to grab the reader's attention through expressions like 'a good giggle', 'can do wonders', and so on. While the earlier text is careful not to give opinions, this one contains adjectives like 'amazing', exclamation marks to make it sound exciting, and exaggeration such as 'If everyone did this, doctors would be out of work'.

2   'The exercises are the same as working out at the gym' – *are* rather than *could be* considered (the Section D4 text avoids stating things that cannot be proved). There is more factual detail and more formal language in the Section D4 text, while the audience for the newspaper text does not need detail.

3   True statements: **a, c, d, e, f, h**

8 Describing and recommending an activity (15 minutes)

Mel's article and writing plan could serve as a possible model for students' own writing (see Section D10), and the exercise provides a further example of the usefulness of note-taking.

1 Mel swapped the order of 'How I started' and 'Why I recommend it'. A possible reason is that he realised this was a more logical order. By first explaining that Go helps you to focus and calm down, he shows why his grandfather felt it was a good activity for a lively and hyperactive child.

If you think it appropriate, you could discuss what 'hyperactive' means. ADHD (attention deficit hyperactivity disorder) is now a widely recognised condition, which affects many young people.

9 Writing style: sentence structure (5–10 minutes)

You could ask students to underline the sentences and highlight the linking words.

Example answers

I've never been interested . . . , <u>but</u> I'm passionate about . . .

<u>In case</u> you haven't heard of it, Go is . . . , <u>which</u> was invented . . .

Go can be played . . . , <u>but</u> I prefer . . .

This is <u>partly because</u> . . . <u>so</u> a change of focus suits me, <u>but also</u> because . . .

I recommend Go <u>because</u> . . . <u>but</u> if you . . .

It improves your ability to . . . , <u>as well as</u> making you forget . . .

It can even be . . . <u>if</u> you . . .

I started playing . . . <u>when</u> I was . . . , <u>who</u> has . . .

<u>As</u> I was a . . . , he realised . . .

10 Planning and drafting your own article (20–25 minutes)

Students write their own article for 'I recommend'.

Decide whether you want to provide restrictions or guidelines on what they can write about. Insist that students write a plan first – they should all be aware of the need to organise their writing, even if ultimately some prefer to plan in their head.

DIFFERENTIATION

Some students find it helpful to talk through their writing with a partner first. Encourage students who need this kind of **support** to make a plan first and then work with a partner to explain their plan and what they will say for each section. Their partner may have suggestions for improvements or alternative ideas at this stage.

11 Feedback and redrafting (10–20 minutes)

Point out that students' feedback to each other should be focused around the questions provided, rather than a list of errors such as spelling or grammar. It may be helpful to display a copy of one student's writing anonymously and make (or invite from the class) some feedback suggestions to model how to deliver feedback positively and sensitively.

Encourage students to alter or redraft their writing as necessary and to finish by doing a separate proofread for errors.

12 Look, say, cover, write, check (10–15 minutes)

These words are included in the list either because they involve adding suffixes to words ending in –*e* (see Section A11) or because they come up elsewhere in the unit and are words that tend to be misspelt. See Unit 1, Section B12 for a reminder of the 'Look, say, cover, write, check' method for learning vocabulary.

GRAMMAR SPOTLIGHT (15 MINUTES)

This section provides an overview of three of the main kinds of conditional sentences (with 'if'): the so-called zero, first and second conditionals. At the end, there is a short practice section. Some students may benefit from further practice with conditionals.

Answers

Zero conditional: Box 1 (to talk about facts or rules that are always or generally true); **First conditional:** Box 2 (to talk about future situations we believe to be real or likely); **Second conditional:** Box 1 (to imagine situations that are unlikely or not real)

1   a   '. . . if you want to play skilfully, it challenges . . . ' 'It can be quite a sociable game if you join a club.'

b   '. . . if you miss . . . your daily target... it will be lowered . . .'

c   'Most people would happily wear the Vivace Pro . . . if it had nothing further to offer'; 'if you used the active mode continuously . . . it would last a week'

2   **a** second conditional; lived; would/could swim; **b** zero conditional; aren't; advise; **c** first conditional; stand; will get

WIDER PRACTICE

1   Students could develop the sports theme further by researching a sports personality of their choice and presenting a profile. Or they could research a topical issue in sport and fitness: for example, sport sponsorship, improving opportunities for women in sports such as football, the history of a particular sport or, if their interests are more scientific, they could find out more about the effects of sport on our bodies (including reading some more formal academic-style texts or viewing videos). You could ask students to take notes in English when they read or watch something interesting for further note-taking practice.

2   Students might enjoy visiting their local sports centre or swimming pool and finding out about its day-to-day operations, its role in the community, the facilities it offers, etc. They could then report back to the class.

3   You could ask students to research other topics associated with health and well-being, such as whether certain diets are better for us than others or ways of improving our mental health. Students may also be interested in following up the 'International overview' topic about an ageing population – for example, reading articles about the 'secret' of living longer, or about new kinds of facilities or retirement villages for older people.

4   There are also many magazine and online articles giving opinions about whether and how prolonged periods using phones and PCs can affect teenagers. This is another area students may be interested in reading more about.

5   Students could get further practice with expressing warnings in English by reading (and/or writing) about the risks and necessary safety measures for sports or other physical activities that interest them.

6   Help students improve their ability to recognise, use and spell words within word families by encouraging them to think of related words when you encounter suitable vocabulary in shared texts. When they record new words in their vocabulary books, suggest that they also record the related words (having checked the spelling).

Exam-style questions

Reading and writing

Reading and Writing: note-taking

This exercise provides practice with answering comprehension questions that require note-taking.

As well as covering the topic of health and exercise, which students explored in this unit, this exercise gives students the opportunity to practise what they have learnt about making notes. Remind them, if necessary, that notes should be brief and there is no need for full sentences (see Section B in this unit). You might wish to recommend these simple steps for successful note-taking:

1 Read the question carefully and underline the key words as you read.

2 Look carefully at the heading and any pictures to pick up clues about the content before you begin to read the text.

3 Read the text fairly quickly, with as much concentration as possible. Then reread more slowly any parts you found confusing. Don't worry if you don't understand bits of the text – you may need to read through the complete text before you understand it all properly. Reread the text again if necessary.

4 Underline key parts of the text that are relevant to the question as soon as you notice them.

5 Write short notes by copying short, relevant words and phrases from the text, or by using words of your own. You do not need to write complete sentences. Be selective, and remember that you are making notes not writing paragraphs. Your notes should be brief, relevant and easy to understand.

Answers

1 Any four of: helps fight cancer; reduces risk of heart attacks or strokes; boosts our mood; exposes us to sun's rays so we absorb vitamin D (good for bones, teeth, muscles); lowers stress

2 • Stresses muscles and joints, causing injury
  • Leads to expensive treatment for injuries
  • Makes you sweat and need a shower

Reading and Writing: informal and formal

You will find advice on general approaches to exam-style writing exercises at the end of the 'Teaching support' section in the Introduction.

With the email exercise, point out that it is important to address any of the so-called 'wh- questions' in the task (*what, when, where, why, how, who*). Students may find it helpful to underline them and/or tick them off as they write.

For the article exercise, students may find it helpful to have a brief discussion about the topic before they write, particularly if any of them don't actually use social media themselves. The language work on giving warnings (Section B12 in this unit) may be useful for this exercise.

Example answer

> **Informal writing**
>
> Hi Jo
>
> How are you keeping, well, I hope? I'm fine, I must tell you about how lucky I was last week. My neighbour had two tickets for the World Tennis Championship, but his wife was ill, and he invited me to join him in her place. I love tennis, although I'm not very good at it, so I was really thrilled. We saw two matches, first a doubles, which was very exciting with some amazing shots at the net, then a singles between two of the top five players in the world. It is remarkable to see the level of fitness achieved by top athletes, and their speed around the court. It was such a great experience that I'm planning to go again next year. Do you fancy coming with me? I'm sure you'd enjoy it.
>
> Jackie
>
> **(138 words)**

Listening

Listening: multiple matching

Students match a list of opinions with six audio extracts.

This is a challenging exercise, so you may like to let students listen more than twice. Remind them that they should listen for genuine understanding. If they simply match words on the recording with words in the statements, they might choose an incorrect answer, so it is useful to draw attention to the way paraphrasing is used.

You may like to pause the recording when checking the answers in order to focus on a particular expression or individual word. Encourage students to discuss why this particular word or phrase is important in making the right answer correct.

Answers
1 H; **2** D; **3** C; **4** G; **5** B; **6** A

Audioscript track 2.4

You will hear six people talking about sport.

For questions 1–6, choose from the list (A–H) which idea each speaker expresses. For each speaker, write the correct letter (A–H) on the answer line. Use each letter only once. There are two extra letters, which you do not need to use.

You will hear the recordings twice.

Now look at the information A–H.

Speaker 1: My favourite football star, George Razak, is only 17 – the same age as me – but he is amazing. I've watched him mature in the last 12 months, and now he plays a great all-round game and is improving at a spectacular rate. He's won all his matches this season. Young sports stars show so much determination to succeed and get ahead, no matter what the effort. They make me more aware of my potential and desire to achieve. My friends say the same. We are inspired to put more into everything we do. We feel we can win if we try hard enough.

Speaker 2: To get to the top of my game as a professional tennis player, I have needed to be quite single-minded. I got interested in tennis around the age of ten, I suppose, and my dad used to drive me to my coaching sessions and to play in matches. I spent hours and hours on it every week of my childhood and as a teenager, building up strength and stamina. But no one can develop skills and potential without putting in the time. It would have been no good at all if I had waited until I was an adult before going into tennis. I would not be where I am today if I had done that.

Speaker 3: I just love sport. There's so much excitement. On a Saturday morning, we play matches, and I can't wait to get out on the sports field with my team. We all run around, trying to get the ball, trying to win. Sure, we're focused on concentrating on our technique, but we all care about winning too. Winning is great! That's what sport is about. I have never heard anyone say they want to lose a game.

Speaker 4: My grandson is ten years old, and I get so much pleasure seeing him and the other young kids run out into the playground when school is over for the day. They kick a ball, and some can run like the wind too. When I was my grandson's age, we had hours of sports lessons every week – we called it PE and, if you ask me, it's what's lacking these days. 'Put more sport into the school timetable' is what I say. When you are young, you need exercise and fresh air, not to sit still in a classroom all day, every day.

Speaker 5: I understand what people mean when they say sport is a lesson for life. At school, we are often told that losing a game is good because it can help us cope with disappointment in everyday life. But I don't think life is just about losing and disappointment, it's about fun too. Sport is brilliant for me – I love it – and I think we should be encouraged to see it as fun and an amusement, not as something serious. Sports lessons in the school curriculum can reflect that.

Speaker 6: Teenagers are giving up sport at school and say they don't care who wins or loses. If you ask me, that attitude isn't going to help them at all. Kids need to do sport at school and experience winning or losing because it's such a great way to learn what life will be like later on. Dealing with disappointment and accepting luck isn't always on your side are important lessons best learned when you're young. Teenagers need to understand this before they leave school and get a job. There will be setbacks sometimes, and they will have to cope in a grown-up way, taking responsibility for their actions.

Speaking

You will find advice on general approaches to speaking exercises at the end of the 'Teaching support' section in the Introduction.

If students are doing this exercise under examination conditions, warm-up questions may help to put them at ease. These are included in the corresponding Coursebook unit.

> 3 Where we live

Learning plan

AOs	Key learning intentions	Success criteria
S1, S2, S3, S4, W1, W3	Explore the topic of home, neighbourhood and places to live	• Students can discuss issues relating to the topic using appropriate vocabulary • Students can express opinions about the issues • Students can express personal feelings about the issues • Students can use descriptive language relating to the topic
R2, R3, R4	Continue exploring a range of text types and their features	• Students can recognise the target audience and purpose for a text • Students can understand and use vocabulary appropriate for the audience and purpose • Students understand tone and register
W1, W2, W3, W4	Learn skills for writing an email to someone your age	• Students can follow instructions to complete a task • Students can use tone and register appropriate to the audience and purpose • Students can check their grammar, punctuation and spelling for accuracy
L1, L2, L4	Listen for gist and then detail in a conversation and a formal talk	• Students can identify the topics covered in a talk and its intended audience • Students can understand detail in a more formal talk • Students can complete notes while listening
S1, S3, S4	Use stress and intonation appropriately to persuade others or to express a reaction	• Students can express opinions • Students can develop an argument, responding to another person's viewpoint • Students are aware of the effect of intonation and are beginning to use it in their own speech

Overview

The main aim of this unit is to develop students' ability to talk and write about where they live, and to explore issues around other places where people live. Students will continue to look at texts of differing levels of formality, considering tone and register, and they will focus on reviewing their own writing both for appropriate tone and register, and for accuracy of spelling, grammar and punctuation.

THEME

Students will consider their home and local neighbourhood in terms of the facilities it offers the community and how they might describe it to someone who is coming to stay.

In Unit 1, students focused on describing people, and in this unit there is further work on building vocabulary and techniques for description (oral and written), but this time in the context of describing places.

Students will read a range of texts, including informal online forum-style posts on the topic of living away from home, a magazine-style article discussing the practicalities of life on a remote island, and a more formal academic-style text which presents the history and features of two unusual towns. They will listen to a discussion about whether to convert a disused warehouse into a study centre or youth club, and a more formal description of a well-known landscape painting in an art gallery.

There will be plenty of discussion activities to help students to improve their ability to keep a conversation going on a range of subjects connected to the reading texts and the broader unit topic. Often these will provide opportunities for critical thinking skills and the possibility of further research to expand on the topics covered. More specifically, there will be a focus on the use of appropriate intonation, both to express interest and enthusiasm and to convey a point of view more emphatically. Students will be able to put this into practice during a discussion arguing in favour of a new facility for their community.

Students will write descriptions both of an object that is important to them and a favourite place, and will draw together skills they have learnt throughout the unit to write an informal email welcoming a cousin to stay in their home.

LANGUAGE WORK

Students continue to examine the language features of different text types and, specifically, how the language they use shapes the impression they make on others. They learn some of the features of very informal language, in particular.

Students' understanding of spelling is improved through studying the rules for doubling the consonant in one- and two-syllable words. Vocabulary development focuses on words for describing places, colloquial language in context, and expressions using *home* and *house*.

The 'Grammar spotlight' examines key uses of the passive voice and summarises how passive verbs are formed. Elsewhere in the unit, students look at the use of the gerund and infinitive after various verbs, as encountered in texts in the unit, and learn basic rules for the order of multiple adjectives before a noun.

Common misconceptions

Misconception	How to identify	How to overcome
Students may form the passive incorrectly (e.g. they may omit the auxiliary *be* or use the present participle, or past or infinitive form instead of the past participle). Examples: *I applied for the job which <u>advertised</u> on the noticeboard.*	Display some incorrect examples and ask students to correct them and explain what was wrong. Examples: *The <u>building made</u> of stone and glass.* *You will <u>be give</u> 30 minutes for the exam.* *He <u>was saw</u> outside the bank at midnight.*	Revise and display rules for the correct formation of the passive (i.e. verb *be* + past participle). Give students some verbs (e.g. make, write, send, win) and ask them to create passive sentences using those verbs. Display some of their correct sentences alongside the rules for future reference.

Misconception	How to identify	How to overcome
The email <u>was writing</u> by my friend. *At the bottom <u>was wrote</u> that Jose Rodríguez was coming.* *Training will be <u>give</u>.*		
Students may use the **infinitive** (with or without *to*) after verbs that take a **gerund**, or the gerund after verbs that take the infinitive. Examples: *I <u>suggested to go</u> by train.* *I <u>decided going on</u> holiday with my parents.*	Display some correct and some incorrect examples, asking students to identify which is which. For example: *We enjoyed to stay with you (✗); He admitted stealing the car (✓); Would you like going skating with us? (✗)*	Provide or elicit lists of verbs that are followed by either the infinitive or gerund. Practise by doing a warm-up or filler activity in which you say one of the verbs and students have to quickly write (or say) a sentence using that verb followed by the correct form.

Introducing the unit topic (5–10 minutes)

Working with a partner, students look at the photo and discuss the questions.

Before moving on to questions 2–4, check that students recognise that the houses are very close together and built of cheap materials on a steep mountainside. They are the type of poor, crowded housing know as a slum, shantytown or *favela*. There is no need to identify the geographical location in order to hold the discussion, but if you have students who recognise it as a *favela* on the edge of Rio de Janeiro, Brazil (perhaps because they have studied the area in geography lessons), encourage them to tell others what they know about it.

Difficulties that students might mention could include noise and disease caused by people living so close together. Often such houses are built illegally, so they may not have access to electricity, rubbish collection, running water or plumbing, and so on, and there may not be proper roads, public transport or hospitals. Tropical storms may lead to problems (e.g. leaking roofs). There may be a high level of crime, making the area dangerous at night. It might be difficult for people who live in such places to get jobs. Advantages might include a strong community spirit – people get to know each other well and help and support each other, sharing skills to build or improve their homes. Students may have opinions as to whether improving the look of your home makes you feel happier living there. In fact, in Rio de Janeiro, the *favela* painting was part of a project to improve the well-being of people living there but also to make other people look at the areas differently instead of ignoring them. There are now 'slum tours', which are popular with tourists. (There are some similar schemes in other parts of the world.)

If you wish, you could broaden the discussion to ask students for their ideas on how best to help people who live in slums.

⟩ **Digital coursebook:** At the start of the lesson, use this video to introduce and review:

* the topic of home, neighbourhood and places to live
* *-ing* form (gerund)
* passives.

Read the question on the title screen and ask learners what they think they might see. Then play the video all the way through and check learners' predictions.

Play the video a second time, pausing to discuss what is being shown and the questions on the end-screen. You can take the opportunity to revise words and phrases associated with the topic of home, neighbourhood and places to live. Note that the end-screen contains some differentiated two-part questions. The first part can be answered by using the content of the video. The second part requires learners to develop their thinking. More confident learners will be able to offer more extensive reasons for their ideas. The 20-minute neighbourhoods are for everyone, so city planners need to consider access for all, including the elderly and wheelchair users, safety and play areas for children, and so on. Two serious challenges are public health (especially fitness-related issues like obesity), and the environment.

You may like to play the video a third time for consolidation.

A Our neighbourhood

1 Discussion (10 minutes)

The discussion aims to give students practice in talking about the familiar topic of where they live. If there is no risk of the topic being sensitive, you could also get students to say more about their homes, feeding in or revising relevant vocabulary (e.g. what type of building, how many rooms, what their bedroom looks like). You could teach the phrase 'I'd rather not say' in case a particular question feels too intrusive.

Check correct use of verb tense for describing how long you have lived somewhere (e.g. I have lived . . . for/since . . . / I used to live . . . , etc.).

Check understanding of *look out for each other*. In this context, it means to think about the needs of / care for each other.

Review students' lists for question 3 as a class, using the opportunity to check or feed in vocabulary. (Note that the term *amenity* tends to mean something that provides pleasure or comfort, such as a restaurant or swimming pool, while *facility* means something necessary for a particular function, such as medical facilities or facilities for changing money. However, the terms have a similar meaning and native speakers tend to use them interchangeably, so students shouldn't worry about the distinction.)

2 Homesickness (2–3 minutes)

Check understanding of what a 'forum' is (a place where people can discuss a topic by writing comments that others can see and respond to). Have any students used one?

If students have not spent much time away from home, ask them to use their imagination. Point out that it might not necessarily be the most obvious things that they would miss (e.g. their family, their room). They could share their list with a partner before moving to the next exercise.

3 Reading comments on a forum (10–15 minutes)

Before reading the text, draw attention to the starter post by Anil861 and the wording 'you guys'

(an informal way of referring to a group of people, both male and female). Have they come across this expression before? Why is Anil861 using it here? (It's an informal expression for use with friends or people your own age, and he sees the forum users as a group of friends.) Check understanding of the terms *tone* and *register*, asking why it is important to use them correctly.

4 Colloquial language (5–10 minutes)

Answers

1   **a** 6; **b** 3; **c** 1; **d** 7; **e** 4; **f** 5; **g** 8; **h** 2

2   We would use colloquial language of this type with people we know well. It is useful for students to recognise and understand it, but it is best avoided in more formal contexts (e.g. with work colleagues, unless you know them well socially, or with older relatives) and in school work or exams.

3   **> Critical thinking:** Check understanding of the terms *tone* and *register*, asking why it is important to be aware of the context in which we are speaking or writing. You could discuss this with reference to students' first language.

Students discuss the questions in pairs. They can think of examples in their own language if they prefer.

You could point out that sometimes wrong use of register is used as a deliberate comic device. (Can they think of any examples in their own language?)

5 Language study: Using the gerund (15 minutes)

1   Some examples in the forum posts:

a   *I miss having my laundry done for me; I miss hanging out with my mates; I love having control over my own life; I don't mind doing without some of the home comforts*

b   *I can't stand being told what to do*

c   *. . . without my mum telling me what time . . .*

d   *Living in beautiful surroundings is fab . . .*

2   Examples in the forum posts:

Gerund: *She never stops talking!*

Infinitive: *Stopping to chat*

We use *stop* + gerund form to mean that an activity or habit ceases (e.g. she stopped playing tennis because she broke her arm). Note that the example in the forum includes the word *never* (She never stops talking) so the meaning is effectively the opposite: she never ceases, so in other words she keeps doing it.

We use *stop* + infinitive form to mean that we stop one activity in order to start another (e.g. the builders stopped to have lunch - i.e. they stopped working so that they could have lunch).

3   Monitor to make sure students correctly use gerund forms after *enjoy* and *miss*.

DIFFERENTIATION

If some students need extra **support** with grammar, provide targeted follow-up practice exercises with using gerund forms, dealing separately with the various uses listed (a–d). You could also get them to write their own example sentences for each category (a–d) or to find examples from their dictionary.

6   Pre-listening task (5–10 minutes)

Prepare students by asking if they have ever helped with any improvements at their school or in their community. How did they feel about it (e.g. pride or frustration)?

Check understanding of *official* (somebody who has a position of responsibility within an organisation).

Students could work in pairs to discuss the meaning of the words listed (or look up half the words each).

DIFFERENTIATION

As a separate follow-up, **challenge** students with a wider vocabulary to investigate 'binomials' such as *wear and tear*. English contains many binomials: pairs of words separated by *and*, in a fixed order, and sometimes rhyming or alliterative (e.g. *peace and quiet, sooner or later, pros and cons*). Students can start by finding one in the text in Section A3 (= *hustle and bustle*), then think of more, with the help of a dictionary or search engine.

7   Listening for gist (10 minutes)

Answers

a   She wants a study centre.

b   He wants a youth club.

c   'When you put it like that, maybe . . .'

Audioscript track 3.1

Listen to a discussion between two officials, John and Pamela, about creating a new facility for local teenagers. Money is available to convert a disused warehouse, and local young people were asked to give their views about how it should be used. Pamela starts by identifying the two main ideas they received from teenagers.

Pamela: Right, John – two ideas really stood out. The idea of converting the warehouse into a study centre for after-school studies was very popular. Also very popular was the request for a social club, a sort of youth club.

John: What do you want to go for?

Pamela: I'm all in favour of converting it into a study centre. It would be very cheap to run because it wouldn't need much maintenance. Students could come after school and at weekends to do homework or research school projects. As a lot of them are sharing bedrooms at home, they have nowhere suitable to study.

John: But Pamela, do you really think it's a good idea to develop it as a study centre? After all, we already have an excellent public library, only five minutes away. What's wrong with that?

Pamela: But it's always crowded! The staff are rushed off their feet with all they have to do, and they aren't very helpful to students.

John: A study centre sounds all right in theory, but in practice it's not going to solve the very real problem of the lack of leisure facilities for teenagers.

Pamela: I take your point, John, but qualifications are very important if they're to do well in the future. Isn't it up to us to help them?

John:	Oh, talking about the future is all very well, but what about the present? Teenagers who aren't interested in studying don't want a study centre. Having a youth club would be fun for everyone. They all deserve a place where they can unwind after a long day at school or work.
Pamela:	Well, I'm not absolutely convinced. I think parents would prefer a study centre much more than they want a rowdy and undisciplined youth club.
John:	We can't know what parents want because they haven't been asked. I don't think young people will be rowdy. Most of them are well behaved. Just think of how hard local teenagers work to raise money for disabled people in the town.
Pamela:	Well, I think it's rather unrealistic to expect no noise or litter or wear and tear. In my view, a youth club is going to be expensive to maintain. It'll be a drain on resources.
John:	Well, I accept that a youth club will be more expensive to maintain than a study centre. We could reduce maintenance costs and control misbehaviour by having a supervisor in charge.
Pamela:	Can we afford a supervisor?
John:	I've had a look at the budget and it would stretch to paying a small wage for the first year of the club's operation. After that, we'd have to review it. Even consider voluntary help.
Pamela:	Hmmm. Not many people want to work for nothing.
John:	And we shouldn't forget that the premises are next to a sports field, so there's no worry about a lot of noise late at night. Well, it's not as if it's in a residential street.
Pamela:	That's true, but you never know, do you? I still say a study centre is the better bet.

John:	Well, look at it this way: what's worse – a youth club or the situation of young people hanging around the streets at night? Do you remember that awful case in the papers recently?
Pamela:	Oh, that was a tragedy!
John:	It was said those teenagers would be alive today if they'd had a decent place to spend their free time.
Pamela:	Yes, I remember that.
John:	I know we both feel the safety of young people comes first.
Pamela:	I agree with you there.
John:	A well-run youth club could put many people's minds at rest.
Pamela:	Hmmm. When you put it like that, maybe a youth club isn't such a bad idea after all.
John:	So you're willing to give it a try?
Pamela:	Only if a proper supervisor is taken on.
John:	Oh great! I'll let the Social Committee know. Let's keep our fingers crossed they give the idea the go-ahead.

8 Detailed listening (10 minutes)

DIFFERENTIATION

Pair students who need **support**. One from each pair should listen out for the answers about Pamela (questions 1, 3, 6 and 8), while the other should focus on John (questions 2, 4, 5 and 7). They can compare answers after listening and swap roles for a further listening.

Answers
1 A; 2 C; 3 A; 4 B; 5 C; 6 B; 7 C; 8 B

9 Post-listening discussion (2–3 minutes)

Remind students that inference involves listening for clues to get the answers.

Answer

2   **C**: John tries to persuade Pamela, rather than give orders, and she is confident about rejecting his views without apologising or showing embarrassment. This suggests they are on equal terms.

10 Persuading: Stress and intonation (10 minutes))

Point out that word stress means not only that the stressed word is slightly louder, but also that it is also slightly *longer* and more clearly pronounced.

Once students have grasped the word-stress patterns, ask them to focus on the rise and fall of the pitch of the speaker's voice in each phrase. It may be helpful to get students to draw a line above the sentence, which rises as the voice rises and dips as it falls (demonstrate at least one example as a whole class first).

DIFFERENTIATION

English stress and intonation patterns are particularly difficult for students whose first language uses stress and intonation very differently (e.g. Mandarin Chinese). If students find this very hard or haven't done exercises like this before, it may be useful to **support** them by doing some more general practice. For example, you could take a sentence such as: *I didn't buy the red car.* Read it aloud to them, stressing one of the elements (*I, didn't, buy, red,* or *car*) and get the students to identify which word you stressed and how that affects the meaning. For example, *I didn't buy the red car* = *I* didn't, but **somebody else** did. *I didn't buy the red car* = I didn't buy the **car**, but I bought the **red van** instead. Students could then practise reading the sentences in different ways themselves.

Audioscript track 3.2

John and Pamela use polite phrases to persuade each other to listen to their point of view. Listen to the phrases, noticing the intonation (the way the voice rises or falls) and how the words in **bold** letters are stressed.

Practise saying each phrase aloud to each other. How could you complete each one?

Do you **really** think it's a good idea to . . . ?

(That) sounds all right in **theory**, but in **practice** . . .

I take your **point, but** . . .

(That)'s all very well, **but** . . .

That's true, **but** . . .

Look at it **this** way: . . .

11 Arguing for a new facility for your community (15 minutes)

> **Critical thinking:** Remind students to give reasons for the points that they make and to challenge their partners to give reasons too.

If students feel uneasy expressing their own views, emphasise that the discussion is a role play. You could even create role cards – for example, you might have a teenage sports fan, a parent with three young children, and an elderly retired teacher. You may prefer to decide on the three facilities yourself and let students decide which role would support which facility.

An alternative way to practise the language would be to role play members of a family discussing how to spend $30 000 that the family has won in a competition. One family member might want to save it, one to spend it on home improvements, and one to go on the holiday of a lifetime.

DIFFERENTIATION

Support students who would find this challenging by noting down the points they should make before they carry out the role play. Alternatively, put two 'Student As' and two 'Student Bs' together to prepare the arguments they will make before combining an A with a B to hold the discussion. It's easier when you don't have to think about the language and the content points at the same time.

International overview (10 minutes)

> **Critical thinking:** The data and related questions are not challenging, but it is a useful opportunity for

students to find the locations of the various European countries if they are not familiar with them.

The main purpose of this section is to encourage discussion (perhaps as a whole class) about the wider topic of families and whether older and younger generations live together. It is useful for students to be aware of differences between countries or cultures.

Answers

2   a   Italy (30.1); Sweden (17.8)

    b   Possible reasons for moving out: to work in another area; to study at university in another area; a desire for independence; to get married; cultural tradition (in some countries it is considered odd for adult children to remain with parents, while in others the opposite is true).

        Possible reasons for variation between countries: cultural reasons (see above); cost of renting or buying homes; different age of going to university; different traditions about where to study (e.g. in some countries, many students study at a university in a different city).

        Encourage students to think about the situation in their own country – they may have family members or friends in their 20s/30s who have moved away or who still share the family home. If you have time and students are interested, you could broaden the discussion to talk about how different cultures look after much older people (e.g. in China they are much more likely to live with their children than in many European countries).

B Living in different locations

1   Discussion (5–10 minutes)

> **Critical thinking:** The photos show a street crowded with nightlife, tourists and neon signs (Tokyo, Japan) and a small, remote village in a cold climate (Lofoten Islands, Norway).

Possible question prompts: *How might the tourists make people's lives better?* (e.g. more jobs, more money spent in local shops) *or worse?* (e.g. too crowded, car parking problems, litter and noise, putting up prices in food shops, houses turned into tourist accommodation creating a shortage for local

people). *In an isolated place, how easy would it be to travel around – for example, to get to the hospital or to a supermarket? What might it be like in winter? What sort of jobs/entertainment might there be for young or older people?*

Students may have an opinion as to whether people are happiest in the place that they know best and accept for what it is. You could introduce the English saying 'The grass is always greener on the other side' and ask students to discuss it in this context.

Useful language: *it would/might be; to be/get used to something*

2   Jigsaw reading (10 minutes)

Put students in pairs, one reading about Derinkuyu and the other reading about Coober Pedy. The purpose of the exercise is to get students to read a text to get an overall idea of its content, focusing on the questions provided. You may wish to give a time limit for this.

Tell students that their task is to find out the basic facts about their place so that they and their partner can work out what is similar or different about the two places they have read about. They will have a chance to read both texts in more detail later. Remind students to write only notes, not full sentences.

Note that, as with many more academic-style texts, some higher-level language is used, so a glossary is provided.

Answers

Derinkuyu: a on a high volcanic plateau, in Cappadocia, Turkey; **b** for defence and to store food; **c** perhaps 3500 years old; **d** 20 000 Anatolian Hittite or Phrygian people; **e** for tourist visits

Coober Pedy: a in the desert in South Australia; **b** to shelter from the heat by people who came to find opals; **c** just over 100 years old; **d** prospectors/miners; now some local people; **e** for homes for locals and for tourist visits

Round off the exercise by asking students (as a class) to summarise what is similar about the two towns (examples of underground living, made possible by local geology, now used for tourism). Then ask what the most obvious differences are (e.g. age – one is much older than the other – or purpose). Students may also be able to point out the difference in scale (one is a complex, interconnected construction, the other is mainly rooms made by individuals).

3 Comprehension and note-taking (15 minutes)

Students now read the whole text in more detail, answering the comprehension questions. Some of these involve further note-taking practice. Point out to students that the number of bullet points indicates how many points are required.

DIFFERENTIATION

Support students by encouraging them to use highlighter pens to locate key information for the note-taking questions.

Answers

Derinkuyu:

1   Water from wells; stored food; fresh milk and meat from livestock

2   a   Black soot stains on the roof of tunnels show that they were lit by flaming torches.

    b   Huge circular stone doors could only be opened from the inside, proving that they were used to help people defend themselves from intruders.

3   a   The rock was soft, made from volcanic ash, and there were already caves and columns caused by wind and water erosion, so it was easy to develop these to make a complete city underground.

    b   It's difficult for archaeologists to tell whether parts of the city were made by people or formed naturally.

Coober Pedy:

1   a   Opals accidentally discovered by a prospector's son; people came looking for opals; miners needed shelter from hostile environment

    b   Mining opals; tourism

2   It has been suggested that . . .

    Throughout the text, note the use of phrases using passive forms such as *It is believed* and *It has been suggested*. The passive is the focus of the 'Grammar spotlight' at the end of the unit.

4 Style (10 minutes)

Suggested answers

a   You need to know a little about the local geology to understand how it was possible to do this.

b   There is still opal mining here, but the town also makes money from tourism.

c   We think that the local people built the city mainly so that they could defend themselves.

5 Prefixes (5–10 minutes)

Answers

1   a multi- = many; b sub- = under, less than; c self- = of or by yourself

2   a multi-purpose tool = a tool with many different purposes (e.g. like a Swiss army knife); b sub-standard work = work that is below the standard required; c self-catering holiday = holiday where you prepare your own meals

3   Possible examples: a multi-million-dollar business, multimedia, multicoloured; submarine, sub-zero temperatures, subtropical; a self-portrait, self-taught, self-service

---

Note that words formed from these prefixes may or may not be hyphenated, or, in some cases, may be two separate words. Students should check in a reliable dictionary, although sometimes more than one option is acceptable. It is important to be consistent if you use the same word more than once within a text.

6 Promoting a tourist attraction (10–15 minutes)

The purpose of the exercise is to provide practice with identifying relevant points from the text and writing about them within a specific context and for a given purpose and audience.

Discuss the task first as a class. Check students understand the purpose of the description (to persuade tourists to come on a tour) and ask them how they might 'sell' the tour (make it sound interesting, fun and unusual; avoid too much detail). Discuss the kind of things that would make the tour sound appealing but emphasise the need to avoid unnecessary detail. Then either write up the description together as a class, incorporating suggestions from students as you write, or set it as an individual or pairwork task. If students/pairs write this themselves, choose some examples to read aloud and ask for class feedback.

DIFFERENTIATION

To **support** students more fully, provide a simple writing frame for the task (perhaps including the 'useful phrases' listed). For example:

Come and enjoy . . .

You will see . . .

This amazing place was built . . .

Don't miss this fascinating tour!

Challenge more adventurous writers to include more elements. For example, they could consider what kind of people the tour would be suitable/unsuitable for, add practical arrangements (start point, tour length, etc.), or even promote the tour as part of a 'weekend package' including accommodation and other things to do in the area.

7 Spelling: Doubling consonants when adding suffixes (10 minutes)

Doubling the consonant in one-syllable and multi-syllable words presents lots of problems for students and is a very common source of errors. Studying the rules and patterns will deepen students' awareness of language as an orderly system, and is an ideal opportunity to expand their understanding of how affixation (adding prefixes or suffixes) changes word meaning and function.

DIFFERENTIATION

Focus only on one-syllable words if students need more **support** and more opportunity to practise, both in this exercise and in Section B8. If you do include multi-syllable words, students may need practice first in identifying which is the stressed syllable. Practise with a set of two-, three- or four-syllable words, getting students to clap the syllables (with a stronger clap for the stressed syllable).

CONTINUED

Students who do the task easily could be **challenged** to make up sentences including words from the list (focusing on those words they feel they would be most likely to misspell).

Answers

2   One-syllable words: **B**; multi-syllable words: **C**

3   *-w, -x* and *-y* never double

---

8 Spelling practice (10 minutes)

Answers

1   **a** louder; **b** hottest; **c** stopped; **d** grabbed; **e** begging; **f** cooler; **g** banned; **h** greeted; **i** boxing

2   **a** visiting; **b** committing; **c** prohibited; **d** gossiping; **e** preferred; **f** forgetting

---

9 Look, say, cover, write, check (15 minutes)

The words are included in the list because they contain double/single letters, which can lead to misspelling, whether or not this is associated with adding suffixes. See Unit 1, Section B13 for a reminder of the 'Look, say, cover, write, check' method for learning vocabulary.

Note that spelling sometimes differs in American English; for example, traveller is spelt traveler.

10 House or home? (10 minutes)

This exercise includes some further examples of collocation, a concept that was introduced in Unit 2, Section B4. These are fixed expressions: words we always use together.

Broadly speaking, *house* refers to the physical building while *home* refers to the place where you live, which might be an apartment, hut, palace, etc., rather than being a house. *Home* tends to have emotional associations, too. However, there is some overlap in the way the terms are used – for example, we might talk about *houses for sale* or *homes for sale*.

Challenge students who complete this exercise easily to find further expressions using *house* or *home*, or example uses of either word that they find interesting. They will need a good dictionary (online or print) to do this.

Answers
a house – 7; b home – 8; c home – 5; d home –9; e house – 3; f home – 4; g house – 10; h house – 1; i home – 6; j home – 2

C Describing places and belongings

1 Order of adjectives (10 minutes)

Note that in descriptive writing, we often use pairs of adjectives that don't easily conform to these categories and where there is flexibility about order. For example, in the description in Section B2 the 'stony, treeless desert' could equally well be a 'treeless, stony desert'. (See Section C2 for information on use of commas with pairs of adjectives.)

Answers
a red canvas sports bag; b beautiful three-bedroomed Swedish house; c unusual eight-sided copper coin; d friendly middle-aged Egyptian woman; e good-quality black leather jacket; f warm woollen winter coat; g priceless Moroccan silver teapot

2 Developing your writing style (10–15 minutes)

The techniques demonstrated here will help to make students' writing more interesting and sophisticated.

Point out the use of a comma before 'which' in the third example (which demonstrates the use of a non-defining relative clause – see Unit 8, Section C11).

The issue of whether to use commas between adjectives is not straightforward and it may be better to avoid discussing it in detail here. If you do decide to focus on this area, the basic rules are as follows. Use a comma between *coordinate* adjectives (e.g. *a dangerous, badly lit road*). Adjectives are *coordinate* if they describe the noun equally and the sentence would still make sense if the adjectives were separated by *and* and the order was changed (e.g. *a badly lit and dangerous road*). Don't use a comma between *cumulative* adjectives, which build upon each other and it would not make sense to change the order or add *and* (e.g. *a dangerous main road* could not be rewritten as *a main and dangerous road*).

If students require extra **support**, ask them to underline or highlight the adjectives or adjective phrases, crossing out words that won't be needed (e.g. *He gave her a box. ~~The box was made of wood~~. ~~It had~~ a picture of a famous story on the lid. ~~It was~~ Russian. ~~It was an~~ unusual box.*) Ask them whether any changes need to be made to create the adjectives, prompting the use of a dictionary as necessary (e.g. *wood* to *wooden*). Once they have done this, they may find it helpful to write the separate parts of the description on slips of paper so they can move them around to find the best order.

Suggested answers
a   He gave her an unusual Russian box made of wood with a picture of a famous story on the lid (*or . . .* an unusual Russian wooden box).

b   He keeps his granddaughter's photo in a small, diamond-shaped photo frame, which used to belong to his mother.

c   She bought herself an expensive set of high-quality, noise-cancelling headphones, which work really well.

d   It's a heavy, French, copper frying pan with a lid.

e   Someone's taken my blue ceramic coffee mug with my name on it.

f   Rosanna decided to wear a long green and white silk dress, which she had bought in America.

3 Describing a personal object (20 minutes)

Students could read aloud their completed descriptions (perhaps in a group), but if you're planning to do this, warn students before they start writing as some descriptions may be quite personal.

If students can't think of their own object to describe, allow them to describe something belonging to a family member.

DIFFERENTIATION

Confident writers could be **challenged** to expand their description; for example, you could ask them to write a whole paragraph, or they might want to tell the story (real or imagined) of how they came to have the object. You could also give them a brief list of specific (more challenging) language or content to include – for example, at least two new (to them) adjectives, a 'which' clause and a reference to more than one of the five senses (e.g. say what the object feels/smells/sounds like, as appropriate).

4 Using all the senses in describing a place (10 minutes)

Point out that the writer has described not only what they can see, but also what can be heard and smelt. What effect does this have? (Check that students know what is meant by 'the five senses' and can say what they are.) What do students like or dislike about the description?

5 Writing about a favourite place (20–25 minutes)

Students could do the visualisation activity at home before they start their writing, or you could read the instructions to the whole class as they close their eyes. If you do the activity in class, you could ask students afterwards to explain to a partner what they were visualising.

Emphasise that the place they choose to think and write about doesn't need to be a 'picture postcard' location – it can be any place they feel enthusiastic about (e.g. a sports stadium, a shopping street they love, etc.).

DIFFERENTIATION

Support students by encouraging them to talk through what they are going to write about before they actually do the writing. This is a helpful strategy to help students who may otherwise experience a 'mental block' before starting a writing task.

Some students may also benefit from a framework for writing their description. Offer the following, encouraging students to go back and expand their description after the first draft.

One of my favourite places is . . .
When I'm there, I can see . . .
I can hear the sounds of . . .
I can smell . . .
This place makes me feel . . .

6 Pre-listening tasks (10 minutes)

Check understanding of the vocabulary.

If any students are familiar with the painting (perhaps because they have studied art), encourage them to tell the class what they know about either this specific painting or the artist. (Note that they don't need to know anything about it to answer the questions in Section C7.)

Looking carefully at the picture and describing it will help students follow the podcast more easily.

7 Listening for gist (10 minutes)

Tell students that they are going to hear someone talking about the painting shown in Section C6. Once students have listened a first time for gist, discuss who the talk was aimed at and why they think so. (The speaker explains the term *genre painting*, suggesting that he doesn't think his audience know, so the talk isn't aimed at experts; the words he uses would be too hard for younger children to understand; and the tone is quite serious and full of factual information, so it is not aiming to be fun.)

Answers
1 B; 2 A, B, D

Audioscript track 3.3

Listen to a podcast about the painting called *The Hunters in the Snow*, which was painted by Pieter Bruegel the Elder in the 16th century.

In today's podcast, we're taking a look at the painting *The Hunters in the Snow* by the Dutch artist Pieter Bruegel – it's one of the most famous images in the art of western Europe.

Bruegel completed the work in 1565, after it was commissioned by the wealthy banker and art collector Nicolaes Jonghelinck. It was actually part of a series of six paintings, of which all but one survive, showing the seasons of the year with their changing weather patterns and their effects on human activities. As some of you may know, illustrating the seasons is an artistic tradition stretching right back to medieval times, when calendars were decorated with small images representing farming tasks for the different months of the year.

If we look at the work, we'll see that the artist invites us to gaze down into the wintry scene from the viewpoint of the hunters, which is why they're shown with their backs to us. The line of trees dominating the image leads our eye down the slope towards the frozen ponds and deeper into the picture, where the countryside is laid out almost like a map.

Our first impression on glancing at the picture might be of a cheerful scene with the group of hunters returning home to the comfort of their village but, if you examine it more closely, you'll observe that the hunters are carrying just one small fox despite their large spears, which are clearly intended for larger prey such as a deer. Their backs are bent, the dogs' ears and tails are down, and the whole group looks tired and disappointed. The sky seems to reflect their mood, threatening to drop more snow on them, making life even harder – it's as if we're being reminded through this painting that man has no control over his natural surroundings.

Bruegel painted familiar landscapes from his native country, but with one crucial difference – the Netherlands is famously very flat! In fact, what Bruegel presents here is an imaginative combination of his homeland with a mountainous scene he must have encountered on his travels in the Italian Alps some years previously. We see people getting on with typical activities for the season – building a fire, carrying firewood, skating and playing hockey on the ice. Bruegel was actually a pioneer of what later came to be called genre painting, which means a focus on the everyday life of ordinary, lower-class people, rather than illustrating scenes from history, for example, or creating portraits of the rich and famous of the time, as most of his contemporaries were doing.

The artist's great skill with this painting is in making us feel the extreme cold of a mid-winter afternoon. He does this through his choice of colour – the green-grey of the sky mirrored in the iced-over ponds, contrasted with the brilliant white of the snow and the bare black trees. Notice the many little details he uses to achieve the same aim – the depth of the footprints where the hunters' feet sink into the snow, and – down to the bottom right – the frozen waterwheel on the side of the mill. At that time, northern Europe was in the grip of what is often referred to as the Little Ice Age, which started in the 14th century but became more extreme at the time Bruegel was painting. People would have experienced winter conditions only too similar to those shown in this painting.

8 Listening comprehension (15 minutes)

Answers
1 B; 2 A; 3 C; 4 C; 5 C; 6 A

9 Post-listening discussion (5–10 minutes)

> **Critical thinking:** Make sure students explain and justify any views they express. Remind them to challenge each other's views as they discuss issues together; even if they agree with what a partner says, it is still useful to ask them to justify it. If students suggest that learning about art is *not* important, you could challenge them to consider whether art can teach us about other cultures, about history, an appreciation of different people's viewpoints, how images can manipulate our emotions (a very relevant modern issue), etc. You could use a search engine to research *why study art history* to find articles posted by many universities and art institutions worldwide.

10 Reading: Scanning for details (20 minutes)

The main purpose of this exercise is to practise scanning a text to locate information (although in some cases, a little inference is needed to judge whether the comment is true, false, etc.).

The wardens in the article work(ed) on the islands of Lundy, Skomer and Skokholm, which are tiny islands close to England and Wales, as shown on the map.

There is a glossary covering higher-level vocabulary (or topic-specific) vocabulary. If there are other words unfamiliar to students, encourage them to use context clues rather than immediately looking up the words.

Note that 'hustly bustly' is a made-up adjective based on 'hustle and bustle', which students may remember from the text in Section A3 (and the exercise in Section A6).

Answers

a Partly true (paragraph 2: Bueche does light fires but feels positive about it)

b False (see paragraph 3)

c False (see paragraph 4)

d True (paragraph 5 'a call to the boatman to see if the weather would permit boats to run' implies that sometimes they can't run)

e False (paragraph 5 'Everyone has got internet and mobile phones')

f False or perhaps partly true (paragraphs 9–10)

g True (paragraph 11)

11 Comprehension check (15 minutes)

The questions in this section focus on the exact meaning of some of the words in the article, and/or give further practice in using inference skills. Tell students to note particularly where a question states 'in your own words' – the questions provide good practice with using synonyms and explaining the same concept with different language.

With question 3, tell students to think carefully about what kind of linking word to use to join the two parts of their sentence (e.g. *while, whereas*).

DIFFERENTIATION

The text is fairly long and, though the questions are in the same order as the answers appear in the text, locating the answers will demand further scanning practice. **Support** students by providing the number of the paragraph where they will find each answer.

Challenge any students who found the task easy to make up some further comprehension questions (and list the answers separately), which they could then exchange with each other. Creating their own questions will make them really get to grips with the language and meaning of the text.

Answers

1 Because they love birds, and there are thousands of them on the island. 'Stubbings and Bueche were drawn to this work through their love of birds.'

2 cacophony (paragraph 3)

3 People think that Skomer is a quiet place where you don't have much contact with other human beings, whereas, in fact, life there is very busy and you are hardly ever on your own.

4 People probably find the idea of a remote, wild island rather romantic, and they may like the idea that there are places where it is possible to escape from phones and the internet.

5 The text doesn't say, but we can infer that he may be trying to put off the people who apply for the job of warden with the wrong expectations, or perhaps he's trying to make us feel less envious of him for living in such a beautiful place.

6 He feels that he has no control at all over the weather but just has to adapt his life to suit it, like a ship's captain steering his ship through the waves.

7 You should keep up good, regular communication with everybody, maintain good relations and deal with any disagreements very quickly.

8 She appreciates it more as a result of being away and doesn't take small luxuries for granted.

12 Post-reading discussion (5–10 minutes)

Make clear that students should find evidence in the text for the qualities they describe.

DIFFERENTIATION

As an extension exercise, **challenge** students to create a written job advertisement for the post of warden on one of the islands. (They can make up practical details that are not provided in the text.)

13 Showing reactions with stress and intonation (10 minutes)

Remind students that appropriate stress and intonation are vital if you are to convince your listener you are genuinely enthusiastic. Point out that the voice jumps to a higher pitch at the beginning of the stressed words and then falls.

Point out to students that they are using:

what + noun or noun phrase

What a great place! I think my friends and I would love the atmosphere there!

What fun! My younger brothers and sisters would love it!

or **how** + *adjective*

How exciting! It would be a fascinating place for my friends and me to go at weekends.

How relaxing! It'd be a wonderful place for me to unwind after studying all day.

For task 3, encourage students to expand their answer with a suitable follow-up comment, if they can. This could be done orally, in pairs or in writing as a homework task.

Suggested answers

3 a How lovely for you! / What a great opportunity! I'm so jealous!

b How strange! I wonder how it got there.

c How annoying/inconsiderate! / What a nuisance! Have you spoken to them about it?

d How exciting! Are you going to take up the offer?

e How kind! / What a generous present! I wish *my* aunt would give me one.

f How scary! Did you find out what it was?

Audioscript track 3.4

Listen to the following descriptions of places. Notice how the most important words are stressed.

a What an **amazing** place! It would make a **great** change from life in the city.

b What a **lovely** place! I'm sure I'd appreciate the special **atmosphere**.

c What **fun**! It would be a **superb** place to relax on holiday.

d How **fascinating**! My friends and I **love** wildlife. We **must** go there.

e How **interesting**! Now I'll see it through **new eyes**!

D Welcoming an exchange visitor

1 Reassuring your guest (10 minutes)

Check first that students understand the concept of an exchange visit. Do they know anyone who has done something like this? Did it work well? The topic presents an excellent opportunity to share cultural information about how guests are normally treated.

Discuss a few specific examples as a class before students write their own notes. They could then compare their ideas in a group or pair.

2 Email beginnings and endings (5–10 minutes)

Beginning and ending emails is not as straightforward as it might seem. It is easy to make the mistake of writing either too formally or too informally. Phrases a–f in the exercise are appropriate for emails between teenagers, even ones who do not know each other that well. Students should work alone to complete the sentences using the words in the box. They can then compare their answers with a partner.

Answers
Beginnings: 1 to; **2** for; **3** to; **Endings: 1** all;
2 from; **3** forget

3 Example email (15 minutes)

The example email aims to show a straightforward way of describing one's home and neighbourhood. One of the biggest challenges for students is getting the tone and register right. You could point out that the email gets to grips with the topic quickly, which students often fail to do.

Where questions ask for examples from the text, consider asking students to underline, highlight or annotate rather than copying out lots of phrases.

Answers

1 a As in paragraphs 1 and 2.

  b *We live in a modern three-bedroomed house with a small front and back garden. It's about ten minutes' walk from . . .*

  c *I'll show you our town museum . . . ,* and as in paragraph 4.

2 *I think you will enjoy sharing family dinners . . . ; I don't think you will mind not having meat.; If you enjoy history . . . ; I heard . . . so I've booked . . .*

3 He immediately mentions the visit. This shows that this is the most important reason for writing and it makes his guest feel welcome.

4 It helps the reader to follow what he is saying, by organising his message into separate topics. Paragraph content: **1** welcome and family; **2** diet; **3** house and local area; **4** plans; **5** ending with good wishes.

5 It's about right (neither formal nor extremely informal).

4 Finding a suitable tone (15 minutes)

Review understanding of register and tone (see Unit 1, Section D8).

Put students in pairs (pairing up students from different cultural backgrounds if that is possible in your setting). Students should consider whether the information is appropriate and, if so, whether it sounds reassuring or should be expressed differently.

Note that the examples in the exercise are based on real examples from emails written by students. (There are no grammatical or spelling errors, etc., although in places the language sounds a little unnatural.)

DIFFERENTIATION

To **support** students before they begin the exercise, you could put some examples of rather inappropriate, negative-sounding sentences on the board and discuss them as a class. For example:

- I live in a small and crowded flat on a noisy street in the city centre.
- We live on a farm and you must help with the farm work.
- My family don't speak your language so they won't speak to you.
- My father is unemployed so we will have to eat at home.

Discuss whether the information needs to be mentioned, and whether it could be written in a more positive way.

Answers

Examples that should (arguably) be reworded or replaced: c, d, e, g, h, j, k, n.

5 Correcting mistakes (20 minutes)

DIFFERENTIATION

To **support** students, highlight some of the errors, rather than requiring students to both find and correct them. Alternatively, reduce the scope of the task by either asking students to check only half the email or by focusing on certain items from the checklist in question 2.

Hi Matt,

I'm back! I just wanted to write to say thank you so much. I had a great time staying with you and your family last week. You were all really kind to me. I've got so many good memories of the trip. Everyone was so friendly – your family, the neighbours, all the students at the college. Tell your mum she is the best cook in the world! Can she come and live with us here? I really liked

> your town, by the way. I think you are lucky to live there. I had such a good time there – we did so many interesting things! I'll send you some photos of our camping trip in my next email.
>
> You really *must* come and stay with us soon! Do you remember I told you that our house is near a lovely big lake? Well, Dad's just fixed the boat, which means we can go out on the lake in it, if you like! The beaches here are great, and now summer is on the way we'll be able to go swimming every day. I know how much you love that. Whenever the weather is not so good, we can go to some of the shops in the town centre – tourists love them!
>
> I can't wait to hear from you. Email soon!
>
> Best wishes,
>
> Zoltan

6 Presenting information positively (10 minutes)

This exercise provides further practice with presenting information positively (and tactfully). It focuses on linking words for concession and contrast; draw attention to the words *but*, *even though*, *despite*, and so on, and help students see how they are used to contrast ideas.

DIFFERENTIATION

Challenge students to rewrite each of their completed sentences using a different linking word in a different position. For example: *Even though he is a nuisance at times, my little brother is very good company.* → *My little brother is a nuisance at times, but he is very good company.*

7 Further practice with tone and register (10 minutes)

Examples a–d are based on examples from students' emails.

Answers

1 c   The others sound aggressive and abrupt in writing; however, in speech, with the right tone of voice and facial expression, they might be acceptable.

2   Possible answers:

a   It was really kind and thoughtful of you to send me such a lovely present, but sadly it was damaged in the post. I'll see if it's possible to mend it, so perhaps we can still use it for dried flowers.

b   What a lovely idea, to go swimming with your friends. Unfortunately, I can't swim so I won't be able to join you, but I'll be happy to watch and then we could all go to the café together afterwards!

8 Reordering an email (10 minutes)

DIFFERENTIATION

You could **support** students by providing the lines of the email on slips of paper, which they can move around and put in order. You could also point out some helpful strategies, such as asking students to look for pronouns and work out what they refer to in a previous sentence (you could highlight/underline the pronouns) – *she* in c, *This* in l and *They* in o. It is also important to look at linking words/phrases, which also show how the sentence links with the rest of the text; for instance, 'Just before the end . . . ' is a clue that this sentence probably comes near the end.

Answers

The order of the email is as follows, although some variation is possible:

1 n; **2** i; **3** e; **4** k; **5** a; **6** o; **7** f; **8** c; **9** j; **10** h; **11** b; **12** l; **13** m; **14** d; **15** g

9 Writing an email to a family member (20–25 minutes)

Students now have an opportunity to put into practice skills they have developed in the unit.

10 Reviewing your email (10–15 minutes)

Remind students that in order to improve their writing skills, it's important to think in terms of a first draft followed by a careful check and revisions to create a second draft.

DIFFERENTIATION

Consider making different versions of the checklist according to your students' needs. **Support** some students by reducing the number of things you are asking them to check – for example, rather than asking them to check for everything on the list in Section D5, you could ask them simply to focus on spelling or specific grammar points.

Challenge others with prompts such as: *Look for any very simple sentences. Can you make them more interesting, perhaps with a linking word? Can you improve your description of where you live by adding an interesting adjective?*

GRAMMAR SPOTLIGHT (15 MINUTES)

This section provides an overview of uses of the passive, with a brief summary of how it is formed and a short practice section. Some students may benefit from further practice, both of the formation of passive forms and their use.

Answers

1   a   The first sentence (using the active form of the verb) is likely to be used in speech, while the second (using the passive form) is likely to appear on a written notice.

    b   There are 21 examples of passive verbs within the text. Encourage students to find as many as they can.

3   a   The scene was painted in the open air. ('by the artist' is probably unnecessary in this case)

    b   I was lent the tools to fix our broken tap by a kind neighbour of mine.

    c   It is believed that these rocks are 200 million years old. / These rocks are believed to be 200 million years old. ('by geologists' is unnecessary)

    d   Ivan was sacked for being late every day. ('by his boss' would probably be avoided – in a case such as this, it is often diplomatic to avoid naming the person responsible)

WIDER PRACTICE

1   Students could interview people in their local area, who have lived there a long time, about how the area has changed. Alternatively, they could interview people who work in a community facility such as a youth club, library, and so on, to find out how the facility benefits groups in the community. They could then write a report of their interview (in English) to share with the class.

2   Students could use a search engine to find articles in English about people who have gone to live in remote or unusual places. Alternatively, if they know people who have lived abroad (or somewhere far from their home town), they could interview them about their experiences, what they missed and what they enjoyed, and so on.

3   There are lots of ways for students to read descriptive writing in English in different contexts, to expand their vocabulary range and see the techniques used, and you could guide them towards suitable sources. For example, they could look at descriptions of homes for sale on estate agents' websites or places to visit on holiday lettings websites (e.g. Airbnb). Alternatively, look for suitable passages in works of literature (using a search engine to find 'passages of descriptive writing in English', or similar, may give you some ideas).

4   Big art galleries often have descriptions of famous scenes in painting, which students may be interested in reading, or even podcast descriptions which they can listen to, for example, look at websites for the Art Gallery of new South Wales in Australia, or the Art Institute of Chicago.

5   Students could also choose a painting they like and practise describing it to the class or a group. They could either do this from a purely personal point of view, or research some facts about the painting and the artists and include those in their presentation.

CONTINUED

6   Take advantage of opportunities for students to practise describing objects – for example, if they have lost or found something, they could write a description to put on the school/ class noticeboard. Students who are interested in history may be able to find descriptions of important historical objects in English on websites for museums.

Exam-style questions

Reading and writing

Reading and Writing: multiple matching

This exercise provides practice with answering multiple-matching comprehension questions.

Encourage students to read the rubric and scan the nine statements so they get a general idea of what the text might be about. Then they should read the texts for general meaning. When they have finished reading, they should tackle the first statement. In this particular exercise, students are asked to decide which person occasionally buys things. Scanning the text again, they will see that both Person A and Person C mention buying, so these two possibilities are close. Person B and Person D do not mention commerce, so these two can be eliminated. Students then need to compare Person A and Person C more carefully to see which one occasionally buys things, as only one answer will be right. Although Person A sells, she does not buy, only customers buy. The correct answer, therefore, is Person C because, although the paintings are too expensive for her to buy, she occasionally buys an artistic card.

Students can then tackle the next statement and repeat the process, and so on. Students' knowledge of vocabulary and topic will be crucial in helping them distinguish between ideas that are similar but not the same. When students have finished the first round of reading and matching, they should return to any problematic matches and refine their choice by checking the detail of the question against the detail of the text.

Answers
a C; b B; c A; d D; e A; f C; g B; h C; i D

Reading and writing

Reading and Writing: informal and formal

You will find advice on general approaches to exam-style writing exercises at the end of the 'Teaching support' section in the Introduction.

For both exercises, students will need to use their imagination to carry out the tasks, unless they have actually been involved in similar community schemes.

With the report exercise in particular, remind students to check they are clear about the *purpose* of the writing. This is a report and they are not simply describing the event but suggesting how it could be improved. It's essential that they reflect this in their writing.

Example answer

> **Formal writing**
> In order to write this report, I interviewed students who participated in the event; the results are described below.
>
> **How did the elderly people benefit?**
> It was gratifying to see how the elderly people benefited from this event. Most arrived with low expectations and didn't expect to be able to learn much. In fact, I think some only came for the tea and cake. But by the end of the evening everyone was happy. Nearly all of them had learned how to email and use video on their phones. We suggested that they practise by emailing each other during the week to help them to remember how to do it, and they happily exchanged their new email addresses.
>
> **How could the event be improved?**
> Personally, I had a good feeling from helping these old people, but next time, we need more computers so we don't have to share, and time afterwards to chat.
>
> **(153 words)**

Listening

Listening: dialogue

Students select the picture that matches what they have heard in each short recording. Note that there are three recordings in this exercise. The number of recordings that may be used in an examination may differ. Please see the details of the assessment section of the syllabus for more information. Each recording is in a different context.

Remind students to read the questions carefully. Encourage them to study the pictures before they listen, noting the differences between them and considering what words they might hear in the recording that distinguish one picture from another. It might be helpful for students to think of a key word for each picture, such as the name of the type of place or activity shown.

Point out that all four options for each question may be mentioned in the recording, but only one of them is the correct answer.

After they have listened, it may be useful to show students the transcript so they can work out why they made any mistakes.

Answers
1 C; 2 A; 3 B

Audioscript track 3.5

You will hear three short recordings. For each question, choose the correct answer, A, B, C or D, and put a tick in the appropriate box.

You will hear each recording twice.

Question 1: Which flat does the man think his daughter Ariane should choose?

Has Ariane managed to find a flat yet?

Well, she thought she'd found the perfect one overlooking a park. I pointed out the rent was unaffordable, though, so she arranged to see one above a bakery. We think it would suit her, even if it's not as nice as the first one, but she's keen on another one on that steep hill in town. The rent's a bargain and it would be ideal, apart from the lack of parking, which is an issue. Anyway, it's up to her.

Question 2: What present has the boy got from his grandmother?

You texted me to say your granny gave you something for your birthday?

Yeah, it was funny . . . she promised me a wooden box of hers that I liked when I was tiny – square with stars on the sides. I opened the present, though, and she'd got confused and given me a round one with birds on instead! She was fine when I explained, and she says she'll give me the right one for my next birthday so I'll have both. I almost wish I'd asked for the one with a star on the lid, which I now know is much more valuable!

Question 3: Where should Ireshi meet the girl and her father?

Hi Ireshi, we're coming to the airport, but we're stuck in traffic and we'll be quite late. Could you meet us by the café? Ignore the first one below the giant clock and carry on to the bigger one with a plastic tree among the tables. Hold on . . . ah, Dad's saying it's a plastic horse now, no idea why! Actually, I'm wondering if the smaller one might be more suitable because it'll be easier to spot you – ok? But get something from the brilliant ice-cream shop while you're waiting.

Speaking

You will find advice on general approaches to speaking exercises at the end of the 'Teaching support' section in the Introduction.

If students are doing this exercise under examination conditions, warm-up questions may help to put them at ease. These are included in the corresponding Coursebook unit.

You could demonstrate how to develop ideas, rather than speak in short sentences, with one or more of the interview questions in Part 1. With the first question, for example, point out that students could simply answer, *I live with my parents, and we usually get on well*, but they would demonstrate their speaking ability much more by saying something like, *I live with my parents. Luckily we have a good relationship most of the time because we spend a lot of time together in a very small flat, but sometimes we do annoy each other a little bit. Then I usually escape by going out with my friends.*

>4 Our impact on the planet

Learning plan

AOs	Key learning intentions	Success criteria
R1, R2, R3, S1, S2, S3, S4	Explore the topic of our environment	• Students can discuss issues relating to environment and climate change • Students can express opinions about the issues • Students can express cause and effect relating to the topic • Students can make predictions relating to the topic
R1, R2, R3	Scan for information in a magazine article	• Students have developed their ability to identify and select relevant information while reading • Students have developed their ability to use information drawn from a text to inform their own opinions
L1, L2	Listen for detailed information in a formal talk	• Students have developed their ability to extract relevant information as they listen to a talk • Students can follow a detailed description of a process as they listen • Students can note down details including numbers • Students can construct a basic, coherent argument • Students can connect sections of their argument with appropriate linking devices • Students can adopt an appropriate tone and be persuasive • Students can take some account of their audience
W1, W2, W3, W4	Use linking devices to organise and present a point of view	• Students can construct a basic, coherent argument • Students can connect sections of their argument with appropriate linking devices • Students can adopt an appropriate tone and be persuasive • Students can take some account of their audience
W1, W2, W3, W4	Write a report giving both sides of an argument	• Students can construct a coherent argument • Students can connect sections of their argument with appropriate linking devices • Students can incorporate prompts but support them with evidence/justifications and use their own words where possible

Overview

The main aim of the unit is to encourage students to use reasoning skills when thinking through real-world issues. They will be challenged to engage with more academic-style material, and they will produce a well-reasoned piece of writing, setting out a strong argument.

THEME

This unit focuses on environmental concerns, including climate change, carbon footprint and transport. If students have specific scientific or geographical knowledge of the topics, that will be very useful, but certainly not necessary, for the discussion activities.

Students will tackle a writing task in which they are given a proposal on which to form an opinion. They can choose to agree with the proposal, disagree with it or be impartial. The skills they will build through doing this will help them with other writing tasks, such as a report on a school visit for the headteacher, saying whether they thought the visit was worthwhile or not, and why.

The most important thing in students' answers is coherence. They should be able to develop the theme clearly, structure their ideas soundly and offer some examples and explanation. They need to present the argument in an appropriate style

depending on the context, and they should show some awareness of their audience.

The reading texts in the unit include a magazine article looking at how businesses and technological innovation can offer alternatives to the environmental problems caused by fast fashion. The article is accompanied by a multiple-matching scanning exercise. A second reading text focuses on the growth in popularity of cycling in Mexico City, with a comprehension task. The exam-style reading comprehension gives students an opportunity to try out the multiple-matching skills practised in the unit.

For listening development, students listen to a formal talk on the links between the global fashion industry and environmental damage, followed by a note-taking exercise. They also listen for specific information in a discussion on the results of a school survey carried out to determine the patterns of car usage among school students.

LANGUAGE WORK

The main focus is on developing reasoning skills. Students extend their understanding of the functions of linking words and their skills for logical sequencing. They improve their writing by practising the appropriate and accurate use of connectives to express reason and consequence, contrast, sequence, and so on.

In addition, spelling and pronunciation are developed by highlighting the contrast between

hard and soft /g/ sounds. Functional skills are practised by listening to talk about favours and asking for a favour. Vocabulary development focuses on euphemisms and words that are often confused.

The 'Grammar spotlight' looks at ways of expressing predictions about the future, using examples students have encountered in the unit.

Common misconceptions

Misconception	How to identify	How to overcome
Instead of using **might** to express **tentative future predictions**, students use *can*, *should* or the simple present. Examples: *Talk it over with your parents – they <u>can accept</u> it.* *You <u>should have</u> problems getting there.* *I think a computer course <u>helps</u>.*	Write examples such as the following: 1 *I think she can do her homework.* 2 *I think she should do her homework.* 3 *I think she does her homework.* 4 *I think she might do her homework.* Have students translate the sentences into their own language and/or explain the difference in meaning between them. Ask which one means the same as: *I think perhaps she will do her homework.* (4)	Ask students to make predictions about an area that interests them, using *might* (e.g. they could predict the results of an upcoming competition, a sports league that they follow or what happens next in an online TV series they are following).
Students use **as a result** as if it were a conjunction like **so**. Examples: *She always met her objectives,<u> as a result </u>she received an award.*	Ask students whether or not the following have the same meaning (yes), and which example has incorrect punctuation (the second): *Eight players were ill so the match was postponed.* *Eight players were ill, as a result, the match was postponed.* Elicit that *Eight players were ill* and *The match was postponed* are two separate clauses. *So* can be used instead of a full stop to connect them, but *as a result* cannot: it needs to be at the beginning of the sentence (unless it is preceded by *and*): *Eight players were ill. As a result, . . .* or *Eight players were ill, <u>and</u> as a result . . .*	Ask students to write a consequence to each of the following, connecting it with either *so* or *as a result*, and using the correct punctuation. *The cook used salt instead of sugar.* *The council banned cars from the city centre.* *The supermarket started charging \$2 per plastic bag.*

Introducing the unit topic (5–10 minutes)

Working with a partner, students look at the photo and discuss the questions.

The photo shows a conventional coal-fired power station and a modern wind turbine. The pairwork discussion should draw out some of the themes of the unit: that our activities are leading to pollution and to climate change, but that new forms of technology are being developed that may help to counteract some of these effects. You can expand the discussion briefly and draw on students' prior knowledge with questions such

as: *What other things that humans do have an impact on our planet? What kind of things are people doing to try to improve the situation?*

› **Digital coursebook:** At the start of the lesson, use this video to introduce and review:

- a range of vocabulary related to the topic of the environment

- using connectives

- making predictions.

Read the questions on the title screen and ask learners what they think they might see. Then play the video all the way through and check learners' predictions.

Play the video a second time, pausing to discuss what is being shown and the questions on the end screen. You can take the opportunity to revise words and phrases associated with the environment. The questions allow for a degree of differentiation. More confident learners will be able to offer more extensive reasons for their ideas.

Take note of the language learners use for the predictions in question 2.

You may like to play the video a third time for consolidation.

A Global warming and industry

1 Global warming vocabulary (5–10 minutes)

This exercise brings together some useful expressions connected with global warming.

If some students are more knowledgeable than others about the topics covered, this exercise (and Section A2) is an excellent opportunity to encourage some peer teaching of the subject matter (e.g. the concept of a carbon footprint). This could be a particularly useful confidence boost for students who are less confident in English but may be able to take a lead in discussions because of their background knowledge. Another approach would be to ask students to do some preparation ahead of the lesson (as homework) by reading/viewing some suitable material in English on the topic of global warming. Some examples of possible sources are provided in the Wider practice section at the end of this unit.

Answers
a global warming; **b** greenhouse gases; **c** fossil fuels; **d** carbon footprint; **e** climate change; **f** carbon emissions

2 Discussion (20 minutes)

Answers
1 The incorrect statement is **c.** (Nuclear energy does not produce greenhouse gases.)

2 › **Critical thinking:** Encourage discussion about the possible benefits and disadvantages of climate change. People might imagine life would be better with warmer winters or less intensely hot summers. However, experts warn us that climate change is generally worrying as a country's economy and way of life is linked to the traditional climate, and change will be disruptive to agriculture, and so on.

Challenge students to justify what they say by giving reasons. Encourage questions such as, 'Why do you think that?', 'What would happen if . . . ?', 'Have you thought about . . . ?'

3 › **Critical thinking:** The activity is a springboard for students to think about actions that they / their family could carry out to lessen their own carbon footprint. If students wish, they can change the examples provided to others that they think are more relevant/realistic to their circumstances. Once the pairs have had time to compare and justify their choices, combine each pair with another pair, and get each student to present their partner's intentions to the other pair ('My partner is going to . . . '). They could then decide as a group which idea might make the most difference to the planet.

3 Pre-listening tasks (2–3 minutes)

Students may well be aware (from the news, social media, etc.) about the environmental impact of their choices in what they eat and how they travel, but they may not have thought about how their carbon footprint is affected by their clothes-shopping habits. This is a topic likely to be of particular relevance to many teenagers.

1 Discuss the meaning of the term 'fast fashion'. In what way is it 'fast'? (Produced quickly and cheaply so we buy it as soon as we see it advertised – we wear it a few times, then quickly move onto the next trend.) Depending on your students' circumstances, you could discuss to what extent they / their family buy only the clothes they need, or whether they have ever bought something they have only worn a couple of times. What influences their choice of clothes? How often do they buy/wear second-hand (or 'pre-loved') garments?

2 Vocabulary check

Garments: items of clothing

Petroleum: oil found under the ground/sea and used to produce petrol

Landfill: area where large amounts of rubbish are buried under the earth

Mattresses: the soft part of a bed that you lie on

4.1

4 Listening for detail (15 minutes)

Students will be listening to a talk delivered by a single speaker in a formal semi-academic style. Their task is to complete a set of notes – point out that only one or two words will be required in each gap. Before listening, ask students to read through these notes and to make the listening task easier for themselves by anticipating what kind of word(s) they are likely to need for each gap. They could discuss this in pairs.

DIFFERENTIATION

For extra **support**, go through some specific examples in the notes that students have to complete to clarify how to use context clues (knowledge of grammar or common sense) to predict what to listen out for. For example, point out that 'about' (question 1) will almost certainly be followed by a number, while 'health risks for' (question 6) will logically be followed by some kind of people.

To provide support with understanding numbers, students could get useful extra practice with number dictations: read out a short list of numbers (small or very large, with or without units such as kilos, dollars, or metres) which the students try to write down correctly. Alternatively, students could write their own list of numbers and dictate them to each other in pairs. Students may need to listen particularly carefully to differentiate between -een and -y – for example, *sixteen* and *sixty*.

For more **challenge**, following on from grammar work in Unit 3, ask students to pick out and write down examples of the passive in the audio recording.

Answers

2 a 107 billion; **b** 52; **c** 160 million; **d** greenhouse gas; **e** fossil fuels; **f** workers; **g** water; **h** burnt; landfill; **i** new clothing

Audioscript track 4.1

Listen to an environmentalist, who is giving a talk to a group of students. He explains the connection between the fast fashion industry and global warming.

Thank you for inviting me to speak to you all today about the fashion industry. Of course, it's a very important industry economically, responsible for employing a great many people worldwide, but the focus of my talk today is its impact on the environment.

I'll start with some figures to give you an idea of the sheer size of the global fashion market. Each year, we buy approximately 107 billion new garments. There is great variation in the spending on clothes in different countries, but if we take the United States as an example, the average consumer buys 52 new items of clothing per year. And the figures are increasing. Over the last 15 years, the size of the clothing industry has doubled – and if we continue at the same rate, it is estimated that by 2050 we'll be buying 160 million tonnes of clothing annually.

So why does this matter? Well, it matters because of the impact of our clothes-buying habits on climate change. Currently, the fashion industry is responsible for more than 8 percent of the world's total greenhouse gas emissions. Its carbon footprint is huge – to give an illustration of this, the carbon footprint of all the new clothes bought in just one minute in Germany is greater than the carbon footprint of driving around the world six times. Furthermore, the industry uses huge quantities of petroleum and other non-renewable fossil fuels in its production processes. And for those who think that natural products are somehow 'cleaner', think again: the cotton grown to supply the fashion industry is responsible for 25 percent of all pesticides used globally; this results in massive pollution to the local environment, and an increased risk from cancer and other health conditions for the workers. Additionally, the industry as a whole uses vast quantities of fresh water – often in countries where that water is in short supply, such as Vietnam.

And what happens to all these tonnes of clothing that we buy? Well, they aren't designed to last, and many of them stay in our wardrobes for just a few months. After this, contrary to what many of us believe, only about 12 percent of clothing is recycled, currently – the rest is burnt, or sent to landfill. And, of course, the burning releases yet more greenhouse gases into the atmosphere. Unfortunately, the process of recycling clothes is harder than most of us think – not only because the clothing is usually made of poor quality synthetic materials, but also because a typical fashion item is made from a blend of different materials that are difficult to separate. As a result, only about 1 percent of used clothing is recycled to create new clothing – most of what we put in the recycling bin becomes industrial cleaning materials or the filling for mattresses.

5 Post-listening discussion (5–10 minutes)

> **Critical thinking:** Encourage students to think of any relevant examples from their own personal experience to back up what they say.

Note that the post-reading discussion that follows the reading text below (Section A8) will investigate and discuss possible solutions to some of the problems raised in the listening topic.

6 Reading: scanning practice (20 minutes)

The reading task encourages students to scan the text to find specific details in it. This is also very good practice of reading and writing multiple-matching exercises.

Answers
a   Growing your own clothes
b   Clothes swapping
c   Recycling marine rubbish
d   Upcycling
e   Fabric from fruit

7 Vocabulary practice (5 minutes)

Encourage students to work out the meaning of the words from the context in the article rather than looking them up in a dictionary.

Answers
a 5; **b** 4; **c** 6; **d** 1; **e** 3; **f** 2

8 Post-reading discussion (5–10 minutes)

> **Critical thinking:** Prompt students to think through the implications of any suggestions they make. (What would happen if: shoppers asked more questions before buying clothes? People kept their clothes for longer? High street retailers put up the prices of their clothes?)

Remind students of the correct verb tenses with second conditional sentences if they are speculating about possible consequences – for example, *if the big high street shops sold only sustainably produced clothes, they would be more expensive.*

9 Language study: Using connectives to guide the reader (10–15 minutes)

The main writing focus for the unit is constructing a formal argument. To do this successfully requires being able to demonstrate the connections between the points made in an argument, using appropriate connective language. Here, the focus is on ways of showing cause and consequence, and adding extra points to support an argument. Later in the unit (Section C), the focus is on ways of showing contrast, and other connectives to help structure an argument (e.g. introducing and concluding an argument) are briefly considered.

You could work through this as a whole-class presentation, with students coming up with examples in pairs.

Expressing reasons and consequences

Students should be able to identify that a link between the two sentences is not clear. We don't know whether the parents bought the shoes because they saw that their son was interested in running, or whether having a new pair of shoes made the son decide to take up running, maybe to please them.

As you look at the examples of connectives, draw attention to the grammatical construction (e.g. *because of / due to* are followed by a noun or a gerund, i.e. *-ing* form). Ask students to try swapping the order of parts of the sentences to check whether that works and to see whether any particular punctuation is required; for example, note the comma in *Because it was raining, they cancelled the open-air concert.* If students don't work it out for themselves, point out that *so* (a conjunction) can connect two parts of the same sentence, while *as a result* and *that's why* cannot be used in the same way. They should be used to begin a separate sentence, with the first sentence ending in a full stop (e.g. *The weather was extremely wet. As a result, many events were cancelled.*) If you wish, you could point out that, alternatively, *as a result* could also follow a semi-colon, though not a comma (*The weather was extremely wet; as a result, many events were cancelled.*).

Suggested answers

2   *The recycling centre was successful so they . . .*

     Because of the success of the (first) recycling centre, they . . .

     The recycling centre was successful. As a result, they . . . and so on.

Adding extra information

Draw attention to the position of the 'signposting' within the sentence and point out where a comma is needed. Point out that you usually need to begin a new sentence with *In addition, Furthermore* and *What's more.* (Note that this is not necessary if you are using it after *and* or a semi-colon.)

> ## DIFFERENTIATION
>
> **Challenge** students who are more ambitious in their writing skills to use the verb phrases *lead to* or *result in* to express connections within sentences. These verbs are common in more formal writing that focuses on cause and effect. Ask students to find one example of each in the article in Section A6 and study how they are used. How might they join the following pairs of sentences, for example?
>
> *Leather manufacturers use large amounts of chemical dyes.*
> *Our rivers become polluted.*
>
> Possible answer: *Leather manufacturers use large amounts of chemical dyes, resulting in pollution in our rivers.*
>
> *Social media 'influencers' are talking about upcycling.*
> *There's a renewed interest in second-hand clothes.*
>
> Possible answer: *Social media 'influencers' are talking about upcycling, leading to a renewed interest in second-hand clothes.*

Suggested answers

3   *A reusable cup is really cheap to buy. Furthermore, it's really good for the environment. / Sometimes, it allows you to get a discount on your coffee as well. / What's more, you can easily carry it in your bag.*

4   *Sustainability is the word on everyone's lips. As a result, . . .*

     Carmen Hijosa developed the product because she became concerned . . .

     Alice was desperate . . . So she created . . .

     The cellulose can grow around a mould . . . What is more . . . when you no longer need it, you can add it to your garden compost heap!

10 Completing a text (10 minutes)

Students practise using some of the linking devices and structures they studied earlier.

Answers

a   because/since/as

b   As a result

c   What's more

d   so

Students may have other possible answers. Note that *so* tends not to be used at the beginning of a sentence or to be followed by a comma, so is a less good alternative for (b).

You could briefly discuss the tone of the leaflet (it's fairly informal). *Therefore* would be a possible alternative answer for (d) but would sound out of place as it's more formal.

International overview (10–15 minutes)

Answer

1   energy use in industry

> **Critical thinking:** Check students are familiar with pie charts and how they are used to present data (percentages of the whole 100%). If necessary, explain where the term *pie chart* comes from (comparison with slices of pie of varying sizes).

Students work in pairs to answer the questions. For questions 2 and 3, challenge them to think through all the processes involved, and therefore all the sectors. For example: *What is chocolate made of? Where does it come from? How did those ingredients get to the factory? What about the wrapper – and what happened to that after you'd eaten the chocolate?*

If appropriate, you could encourage students to follow up this discussion by finding out more detailed information, for example, from the Our World in Data website.

B Transport

1 Discussion (5–10 minutes)

The discussion helps focus students' thoughts on the transport they use in their daily lives. Encourage them to think about alternative methods of transport and answer the question 'If you had a completely free choice of transport, what would you choose and why?' Use this discussion to check that students are familiar with the vocabulary for forms of transport, including those that might be common in cities other than where they live.

2 Pre-listening task (2–3 minutes)

Get a lift from someone: ask someone to drive you free of charge in their car

Exhaust fumes: waste gases coming from a vehicle

EVs: electric vehicles

3 Listening to check information (20 minutes)

This is a variation on the listening and note-taking exercise that students did in Section A4. Here, students listen to check the provided notes for errors (and correct them) rather than completing the notes themselves. Similar skills are involved.

As always, allow students to listen first for general meaning and then to complete the task. Many of the notes paraphrase what is said on the audio recording rather than using the same words.

Answers

a   (Correct)

b   5 per cent (not *9%*)

c   80% (not *80 students*)

d   40% (not *14%*); 33% is correct

e   *expensive* is correct; inconvenient / not available / too far from their houses (not *crowded*)

f   too dangerous (not *too much pollution*)

g   A third (not *two-thirds*)

h   Correct

Audioscript track 4.2

Listen to a discussion between two friends, Zara and Yusuf, on the results of a survey to determine patterns of car usage by students in their school.

Yusuf: Anyway, we've got the results of the survey now.

Zara: Right, well, I can note the main points that come up and then fill in the chart. The school magazine is the best place to publicise the findings, don't you think?

Yusuf: Yes. Erm, well, you know, it's interesting to see the extent of car usage. Usually, students are making between 11 and 20 trips by car a week. Mostly they're, you know... it's what you'd expect, getting lifts from their parents. A small percentage, 5 percent, make over 50 car trips in a week. The results really aren't encouraging.

Zara: Wow, 50 car trips a week! That is a lot, isn't it? They must have a good social life! And understanding parents who don't mind being a taxi service! What was the response like to the question about whether there was an alternative to the journeys they make by car?

Yusuf: Well, an incredible 80 percent said they would get a lift even if they didn't really have to. They're just too lazy to walk anywhere.

Zara: Yes, although having said that, I do think a lot of students at this school do seem to walk to school.

Yusuf: 40 percent said they walked to school regularly but then, well, 33 percent said they always come by car, which is not so good.

Zara: I wonder why, when the school is on a bus route, and there's a train station only five minutes' walk away?

Yusuf: Erm, well, from the survey, it seems that coming to school by bus or train is either too expensive or too inconvenient. Their homes aren't near a bus stop or train station – it's just not available where they live.

Zara:	What did that 33 percent who come by car say about coming to school under their own steam – walking or cycling, for instance?
Yusuf:	A lot of them said their parents wouldn't allow them to walk or cycle because it's just not safe enough. The roads are really dangerous for cycling and some students live over eight miles away, so walking to and from school would just take too long. You can't really expect them to undertake that kind of trek every day.
Zara:	What about wanting a car when they leave school?
Yusuf:	Well, that was pretty encouraging from the point of view of protecting the environment. A third of those who responded were against having their own car when they were adults. One of the main reasons they gave was concern over the environment. They're worried about car exhaust fumes contributing to pollution. And they're also worried about, well, the health issue in general. They think car fumes can cause asthma. But it's interesting to note what several people put in the 'Additional comments' section. They said they would be more likely to get a car if it could be an electric one. They're hoping they'll be cheaper when they're old enough to drive.
Zara:	Well, that's a very good point, and we probably should have mentioned EVs in the survey.
Yusuf:	Yes, because they'll probably be a lot more common in 10 years' time.

4 Post-listening discussion (15 minutes)

> **Critical thinking:** This exercise requires students to think through some of the issues involved in order to form a considered opinion about each statement. Encourage students to justify the numbers they have chosen by giving reasons and evidence if they can.

After the pairwork discussion, round off as a whole class by asking some students to report back on their pair's discussion. Encourage use of language for future predictions from the 'Grammar spotlight'

at the end of the unit: *It will definitely / might / is unlikely to / definitely will not (won't) happen,* and so on.

Depending on your context and students' interests, you could extend the discussion to get their views on other ways of dealing with congestion and car pollution – for example, road tolls, fines for being the sole occupant of a car, and limits to using the car at certain times of the day.

5 Euphemisms (5–10 minutes)

Asking students to offer examples of euphemisms in their first language(s) would be a good way of checking that they have understood the concept.

Drill the pronunciation of *euphēmism* /ˈjuːfəmɪz(ə)m/. Explain that it comes from the Greek *euphēmizein,* a word made up of *eu,* meaning 'well', and *pheme,* which means 'speaking'. Studying the origin of this word is useful because it highlights the main quality of a euphemistic phrase, which aims not to upset anyone.

You could also introduce students to the way euphemisms can be used to disguise the truth. *For example, an ex-politician who is 'spending more time with their family' may actually have been sacked!* Use of euphemisms can vary between countries/cultures. Are they used in the students' own country/culture? Note that *bathroom* is used in the USA while people in the UK would more commonly say *toilet.*

Answers
a 8; b 2; c 5; d 6; e 7; f 1; g 4; h 3

6 Asking for a favour (10–15 minutes)

You might like to ask a couple of students to read the dialogue aloud first to highlight the appropriate intonation patterns.

You could ask *'Does Joe sound tentative or does he sound demanding when he asks a favour? Which approach is more suitable for the situation?'*

Elicit or teach the meaning of the adjective 'tentative'. If someone sounds tentative when they ask a question, it means they are unsure of what they are doing and do it without confidence.

Remind students that *Would you mind . . .* is followed by a gerund *(waiting/giving,* etc.). You could also ask them to identify the more formal / less formal expressions – for example, *put you out/be a nuisance* are more colloquial than *not too inconvenient.*

Where students need **support**, ask them to focus on creating just three of the dialogues. When they are confident with each dialogue, tell them to practise the same dialogue but swapping roles. Check their intonation.

For extra **challenge**, students could think of their own scenario in which they might need to ask for a favour, and act that out (maybe based on a real experience of having to ask for a really big favour!). Or they could consider what to say if they wanted to politely *decline* to carry out the favour.

7 Spelling and pronunciation: The letter *g* (10 minutes)

Recognition

The aim of this exercise is to increase students' awareness of spelling/pronunciation patterns. Note that *gu* pronounced /gw/ is a relatively unusual sound and is often linked with words of Spanish origin, e.g. *guacamole, guava.*

Answers
1 a g; b G; c g; d G; e g; f G; g g; h g; i G; j g; k G; l g

Audioscript track 4.3

Listen to the words. Mark them with a capital letter *G* for a hard *g*, pronounced /g/. Mark them with a lower case *g* for a soft *g*, pronounced /dʒ/.

a	budget	g	oxygen
b	rigorously	h	apology
c	challenge	i	vegan
d	vlogger	j	registered
e	shortage	k	figure
f	guarantee	l	average

Practice

You could ask students to contrast these sounds with voiceless sounds in English, i.e. compare /g/ with /k/ and /dʒ/ with /ch/, where they can feel there is no vibration in the vocal cords. They could

also say sssss and let it gradually become zzzz (a voiced sound).

It would be interesting to contrast voiced and voiceless sounds in English with sounds in students' own language(s), to compare those which are voiced and those which are not.

8 Spelling patterns (2–3 minutes)

Students scan the word list they have just practised and circle the significant spelling features. The soft *g* rule is a fairly trustworthy spelling rule, so it is worth teaching.

Remembering the spelling pattern for soft *g* words will help students spell a wider variety of words and provide some tools for decoding pronunciation. You could follow up this exercise by asking them to make intelligent guesses as to the pronunciation of more unusual words you write on the board, for example *pageant, gym, diagonal, gibberish, extravagant, rigid, geothermal.*

9 Vocabulary (5 minutes)

Students check the meaning of words they met in the earlier exercise. Physically writing out the words will help them remember the spelling patterns.

Answers
a apology; **b** oxygen; **c** vegan; **d** vlogger; **e** challenge; **f** guarantee; **h** budget; **i** figure; **j** rigorously

10 Odd word out (5 minutes)

This exercise introduces some additional common words containing hard and soft *g* sounds.

Answers
a   regard (it has a hard *g* sound)
b   pigeon (it has a soft *g*)

11 Look, say, cover, write, check (15 minutes)

You could ask students to identify why these words pose spelling difficulties, eliciting ideas such as: 'Privilege is often misspelt with a d'; '*ou* is a difficult pattern'; '*ie* words are often misspelt'; 'the *e* in the middle of vegetable is silent and is often left out'.

You could round off this section on spelling by getting students to compose some silly sentences containing as many of the target sounds or problematic spelling words as possible. They then dictate the sentences to each other, for example, *A responsible Egyptian vlogger put Portuguese vegetables in his luggage.*

See Unit 1, Section B13 for a reminder of the 'Look, say, cover, write, check' method for learning vocabulary.

C Looking for solutions

This section develops the theme of transport and environmental issues by focusing on cycling.

1 Pre-reading discussion (5–10 minutes)

> **Critical thinking:** This exercise could be done effectively in small groups as an alternative to pairs. Setting a time limit helps keep students on task and makes the exercise more tightly structured.

More possible advantages of cycling: It's enjoyable / good exercise / relatively cheap (doesn't require petrol, road tax, insurance, etc. – although this may vary by country) / quiet (an environmental benefit) / can be quicker (avoid traffic jams) / no need for a car park / safer for other road users.

More possible disadvantages of cycling: You are exposed to rain and cold / bicycles can easily be stolen / you can't carry much with you on a bike / you need to be fit to cycle, otherwise it's tiring / cycling can be dangerous on busy roads, during bad weather and at night.

Challenge students' views to make them think through their arguments and engage in critical thinking. For example, if they mention the dangers of cycling, ask what might make it less dangerous; if they say cycling is slow, ask if that's necessarily the case during the rush hour.

2 Reading for gist (10 minutes)

The exercise is based on an analysis of three summaries, and encourages students to skim read the article to get a general idea of the content rather than focusing on detail. Discourage them from lingering over individual items of vocabulary at this point; they should be able to answer the question without understanding every word. There will be an opportunity to look more closely at the vocabulary in Section C4.

Answer: C

3 Comprehension check (20 minutes)

Students re-read the article in more detail to answer the questions. They don't need to answer in full sentences.

Answers

1 She didn't have a car – she was waiting for approval for a loan.
2 Commute
3 She turned down the loan – she wanted to cycle instead.
4 Two from the following: It provides a free bike school, it teaches them to ride, cycle safely in the street, make basic repairs.
5 It makes them feel excited and gives them a sense of empowerment.
6 The things that the city has done to help cyclists, like providing bike lanes and safe bike storage.
7 There are no cars.
8 Make motorists take a test to check they can drive skilfully and safely.

4 Vocabulary in context (5–10 minutes)

Students find words in the text that match the given definitions.

DIFFERENTIATION

You may have students who are more confident with vocabulary and want to incorporate more sophisticated terms within their own writing. **Challenge** them to use a good dictionary to investigate the precise context in which some of these words might be used. Many dictionaries provide useful examples of this. For instance, *dealership is mainly used with vehicles and especially with named makes of cars (e.g. a Toyota dealership); thoroughfare is used in formal written contexts to refer to a city route connecting two places; and bureaucrats tends to be used in a negative sense (e.g. faceless bureaucrats). (see Unit 1, Section A9 for further advice on good dictionaries).*

CONTINUED

To provide more **support** with the task, highlight the correct words in the text (plus an extra distractor in paragraphs where there is only one word to find). Then students simply have to match up the highlighted words with the definitions.

Answers

Paragraph 1: advocates, dealership, declined

Paragraph 2: thoroughfare

Paragraph 3: rebel

Paragraph 4: infrastructure, geared towards, metropolis

Paragraph 5: bureaucrats, competence

Note that the term *bureaucrat* is often used in a negative sense. It often implies that the person focuses too much on following rules and procedures, and too little on people's real needs.

5 Reordering an article (10 minutes)

This exercise follows up on the work in Section A9 on 'signposting' within writing, using connectives as appropriate. You could do the first couple of examples as a class, 'thinking aloud' to show students how to follow the flow of the argument by focusing on language that connects one sentence with the next.

Students could work together in pairs or small groups to put the sentences into a logical sequence. Encourage them to copy out the article when they have finished to help them understand the flow of a piece of writing and think about where new paragraphs should begin.

DIFFERENTIATION

You could **support** students who find the task difficult by allowing them to manipulate the sections of text either electronically or on slips of paper. It may also be helpful to point out that the title of the article provides a clue, and ask students to group the sections which refer to 'pros' and those that refer to 'cons'.

Answer

Cycling is an enjoyable, efficient and liberating mode of transport which has many benefits. Followed by:

Paragraph 1: e, i, b, j. **Paragraph 2:** g, d, a, h. **Paragraph 3:** c, f, concluded by:

In conclusion, although there are some drawbacks, I feel that the personal enjoyment and freedom you get from cycling outweigh the disadvantages.

It is important for students to think about how they address the reader in their writing. The writer of the article in Section C5 addresses the reader directly by using the word *you:* 'owning a bike frees you from dependence on your parents'. A writer may also choose to use *we/our/us* to suggest that they share values and assumptions with their readers – for example, *We all enjoy riding bikes. Our bikes are a way to explore the world around us.*

6 What makes a good argument? (10–15 minutes)

The aim is to get students to reflect on what makes a good essay. It should have a formal style, flow, be easy to follow and be persuasive. It should give equal weight to both sides of the issue. Remind students that they should offer their own opinion in the final paragraph of their essay - they shouldn't leave the reader in any doubt as to what they think about the subject.

7 Presenting contrasting ideas in the same paragraph (5 minutes)

This exercise provides a starting point into the style of presenting contrasting ideas in the same paragraph or even the same sentence.

Answers

1   Nevertheless

2   Although I recognise . . . cycling, in my opinion it is essential . . .

I recognise . . . cycling. In my opinion, however, it is essential . . .

I recognise . . . cycling, but/yet in my opinion it is essential . . .

Despite recognising that . . . cycling, in my opinion it is essential.

Point out that *despite / in spite of* is followed by a noun or a gerund (*-ing* form). Sometimes it's difficult to do that so we use *the fact that* (+ clause). Ask students to connect the following sentences with *Despite* and *the fact that*:

Thousands of people use the cycle facilities. The council want to close them. (Despite the fact that thousands of people use . . . , the council . . .)

8 Presenting more contrasting ideas (10–15 minutes)

Encourage students to work in pairs to complete the sentences in a logical way. They could then compare their answers with another pair.

DIFFERENTIATION

To offer more **support**, do the first few examples together as a class, one sentence at a time. Write the sentence starter on the board and give students a short time to complete it. Elicit three or four examples and write these up, sorting out any misunderstandings with grammar as you do. For example, remind students that *despite* and *in spite of* are followed by a noun phrase. Encourage students to read the examples and check that they make sense.

You could **challenge** students/pairs who finish quickly to make up their own sentence(s) using one of the contrast words. They could then write out their sentence with a gap for the contrast word, inviting other students/pairs to work out what the missing contrast word should be.

9 Language study: Further connectives (10 minutes)

Encourage students to add any extra examples they can think of.

DIFFERENTIATION

For more **challenge**, direct students to a suitable short argument text (online or in print) and ask them to identify all the different kinds of linking words used.

Answers
Listing points: secondly, lastly, next, firstly, finally

Summing up: to sum up, taking everything into account, in conclusion

Adding emphasis: above all, undoubtedly, there is no doubt, in particular

10 Group brainstorm (10–15 minutes)

> **Critical thinking:** Allow a fixed time for the brainstorm (e.g. five minutes). Students may work best in small groups, but if they are not used to this type of activity, consider doing it as a whole class for first time. After the time has elapsed, elicit ideas from the groups. Ensure that the groups give reasons and think through the consequences.

Students may or may not be aware of the role of trees in absorbing carbon dioxide and therefore reducing greenhouse gas emissions. If nobody raises the issue, prompt students by asking whether they think trees can help the environment.

Students sometimes say they don't like brainstorming because it gives some students the chance to let others do the work for them. You might think it worth raising this issue in class and making it clear that finding the 'points' for a set topic is a shared responsibility.

Consider allocating roles within each group: for example, one student to note down the points 'for' and one to record the points 'against'. You can change the roles for future brainstorms.

11 Text completion (10–15 minutes)

Answers
a Although; b In the first place; c also;
d Furthermore; e because; f yet; g In addition;
h also; i In my opinion; j On the other hand

12 Discussion (5 minutes)

The email is appropriately formal. This is shown by the absence of colloquial language and the formality of expressions such as *In the first place, Furthermore*. Students may feel that the wording 'stupid, greedy and pointless' is a little too direct.

The writer shows an awareness of his audience by saying that he would be interested in what other readers think.

Roland's argument is convincing because he gives clear reasons for his views – for example, the wood is a habitat for wildlife, the air is cleaner because of the trees, and they help to make a noisy urban area quieter. He also writes that the wood is a beautiful place.

Draw attention to the contrast between the balanced report on the school website (Section C7) and this email. Where does the writer express their opinion in the report? (Right at the end, in the conclusion.) Where does the writer express their opinion in the email? (Right from the start – 'disappointed' – and throughout.)

13 Words often confused (10 minutes)

Note that in British English, there is often a difference in spelling between the noun and the verb – such as practice and practise, or advice and advise – whereas in American English, the words are spelt the same for both noun and verb. Students are working in British English.

Answers

1	a	council	b	counsel
2	a	effect	b	affect
3	a	there; their	b	they're
4	a	lose	b	loose
5	a	alternate	b	alternative
6	a	lightning	b	lightening
7	a	practise	b	practice
8	a	past; passed	b	passed

D The community's views

1 Pre-reading discussion (10–15 minutes)

> Critical thinking: Use the pictures to focus students' thoughts and stimulate an interesting discussion on the advantages and disadvantages of motorways (major roads, which may be known as highways, freeways or expressways in various parts of the world).

Encourage students to consider the relative accident rates, and air pollution levels, caused by motorways as opposed to narrower city roads. They could research this to find evidence.

Brainstorming

Possible advantages

- They can be fast and efficient.
- They are good for businesses, enabling goods to be transported easily across the country.
- They link towns effectively, making business communications easier.
- Building them provides jobs.
- They reduce traffic on local minor roads.
- They can be safer than narrow, winding roads.

Possible disadvantages

- They need a lot of land and destroy countryside.
- They are expensive to build and maintain.
- They pollute the atmosphere.
- They are noisy.
- They can encourage people to drive too fast.
- Serious accidents can happen on a motorway.
- Traffic jams can build up during roadworks or in the rush hour.
- They can encourage car use, especially for long journeys.

2 Reading an email expressing a point of view (10 minutes)

> Critical thinking: Before reading the text, ask students (in pairs or as a class) to think of all the people likely to be for or against the plans for a new motorway at Rosville. Can they think of any people who might be conflicted? (This might include, for example, business people whose business will benefit from more efficient travel but who live near the proposed route, or environmentalists who want to improve air quality in the town yet don't want to see areas of countryside destroyed.)

Tell students to read the email quickly to answer the questions. Remind them that scanning involves quickly looking over the text to pick out information, not studying every word.

3 Comprehension check (10 minutes)

The aim is to make sure that all students understand the factual content of the email.

Answers

1 a newspaper (or online news page)

2 boost to business through improved communications; easier, faster and safer commuting; reduced pollution through tree planting; lorries will bypass town centre

3 The writer gives specific reasons and examples

4 a recession

   b boost

   c motorways

   d commute

   e bypass

4 Analysing the email (5–10 minutes)

These questions focus on the overall structure of the email and reinforce the linking words students have been learning.

You may like to add a little more to earlier discussions about the importance of first and last paragraphs. Perhaps students feel they have no right to try to persuade someone, or perhaps they aren't interested in the topic. Remind them that they need to be clear about what they think, and that they should sound persuasive in their compositions.

DIFFERENTIATION

If students need more **support**, help them to understand the structure of this email (and the purpose of the paragraphing) so they can use it as a model as they move on to the next exercise. Mark up a copy of the email using annotation and different coloured highlighters. Elicit the purpose of the opening and then the closing paragraphs, then mark them 'Introduction' and 'Conclusion'. Explain that each of the other paragraphs makes a different point – highlight and label them points 1–4. Summarise what the four points are and elicit which is which (and annotate the paragraph): less pollution (point 3), better for business (point 1), quicker commuting (point 2), bypass (point 4). Underline words that make the structure clearer: *In the first place*, *Furthermore*, *Finally*.

Answers

1 *delighted, because*. The opening paragraph grabs attention because it focuses immediately and clearly on the topic and uses emotive language such as *delighted*. Ask students to look back to the email in Section C11 where the same device is used. What adjective was used there? (*disappointed*) This is an effective way to begin an email/letter expressing a 'one-sided' (rather than a more balanced) point of view.

2 *Furthermore* and *not only... also*.

3 The opposing point of view is concern over air pollution from the motorway. *On the contrary* is used to introduce a contrasting opinion.

4 *Finally* is used to show that the argument is being rounded off.

5 The last paragraph uses emphatic expressions like *There is no doubt* and *really*, which make the writer's views clear.

5 Putting forward an opposing viewpoint (5 minutes)

Elicit ideas for further relevant points from the class, drawing on those that were raised earlier in the discussion on motorways (e.g. huge cost, noise, accidents, encouraging greater car use). Then ask for ideas to expand upon the other points: What specifically might the motorway construction destroy? (Students can make up an example.) Why might the road not reduce travel time? (Traffic jams, etc.) What problems might be caused by splitting the town in two? (Dividing communities, harder for people to access shops and schools, accidents, etc.)

6 Writing an email expressing your views (15–25 minutes)

Pair students appropriately and allow them to talk through the writing task together, using the writing frame, making notes. Make clear whether (depending on time) you want students to draft out the whole email together or simply make notes that they can fill out later as a homework task. (Note that there are further writing tasks to come in this unit.)

The writing frame encourages students to use clear paragraphs and to consider appropriate linking words to structure the email. However, they don't need to stick to this rigorously – for example, they might want to combine some points together, or use linking devices in other places. The writing frame finishes with a plea to the readers (a common device in this type of email) but, again, students may wish to think of a different way of ending their email.

Example answer

> Dear Editor,
>
> We were horrified to hear of the plans for a new motorway for Rosville, and we are sure our feelings are shared by many of your readers.
>
> Firstly, we believe the scheme would destroy the environment and damage wildlife. The planned route goes through a nature reserve used by several rare bird species.
>
> Secondly, the motorway itself will cost a great deal of money to build. Using this money to improve the rail network would not only help local businesses but city commuters would benefit too.
>
> The idea that the motorway will be more efficient is completely unfounded. The new road will soon attract heavy traffic and become heavily congested.
>
> Furthermore, the suggestion that planting trees alongside the motorway will help eliminate pollution is ludicrous. Trees can never make up for the destruction of wild flowers and wildlife!
>
> Finally, many of us cycle or walk across the road to get to school or work. The new road will split the area into two, making this impossible.
>
> Please, people of Rosville, don't stand by and watch your environment being destroyed! Support the Rosville Nature Society campaign by writing now to your local councillor.
>
> Yours faithfully,
>
> The Rosville Nature Society

Students could read out their emails to the rest of the class and compare the effectiveness of different linking words.

The Nature Society email is – like the Business Group email – one-sided. Both build up an argument in only one direction, so lots of linking words like *furthermore,* moreover are needed rather than several contrast expressions such as *however, on the other hand.* It would be useful to compare the effect of writing a one-sided argument with one that gives more equal weight to both sides (such as Section C5 'The pros and cons of cycling'). You could elicit the fact that a one-sided argument tends to be more emotive.

7 Relating to your target audience (5–10 minutes)

This exercise uses skimming and scanning reading techniques and consolidates earlier work on audience awareness. It provides more examples of typical audience-awareness statements. Once students understand the concept, they shouldn't have too much difficulty with putting the idea into practice in their own writing.

Answers
A music and video-sharing website for internet users; B school magazine for school pupils; C letter to a local newspaper for the general public; D e-newsletter for elderly people; E formal report for the headteacher

---

8 Understanding a balanced report task (5 minutes)

Help students to understand the concept of a report, giving relevant examples if necessary.

Answer
Introduction B is more appropriate (neutral, impersonal and more serious in tone, sets out the facts).

---

9 Writing a balanced report using a framework (25 minutes)

Both this exercise and Section D11 involve writing reports. To reduce the amount of individual writing time (particularly if your students find writing challenging), you may wish to carry out this exercise as a whole-class shared writing task, with you scribing and eliciting suggestions from students as you go.

Before writing the report, discuss the pros and cons of the proposed school facility with students.

The tone of the report is important. It should sound respectful as it is for the headteacher, but should also be direct and honest about the positive and negative points.

Demonstrate or elicit structuring devices as you scribe (e.g. I am writing because . . . Firstly/In addition/Furthermore . . . However/I might suggest one improvement . . . In conclusion, I would recommend . . .). Read back parts of the report as you write, inviting students to decide whether the tone is appropriate, or whether anything could be improved or added.

DIFFERENTIATION

To **support** some students with the structure of this semi-formal report, if they are writing it on their own, provide a pre-prepared writing frame, including some of the structuring language suggested above.

You could **challenge** ambitious writers (once the report has been written) to rewrite this in the form of an email to the school newspaper, either from a parent who thinks the seating area is a waste of the school's money or a younger child who would love one for their age group too.

Example answer
A possible answer could be along the following lines.

This is a report for our headteacher Mr Matuga about the senior school seating area, which we have been using for two months now. We have interviewed all the students to find out what they think of this new facility.

Firstly, the covered area gives us protection when the sun is very hot. Some students have become concerned about sun damage, especially those who have studied climate change and the greenhouse effect in science lessons. In addition, we have had stormy, unpredictable weather recently and the students say they are thankful that they can go under cover in wet weather.

The small tables that are provided are helpful when we want to eat our lunch or do some homework. Furthermore, students are mixing outside their normal friendship circles because

a wide range of students from different ages and classes come to enjoy the protection of the shaded area. It is also peaceful in this part of the grounds as it is further away from the traffic on main roads. We can all enjoy nature and hear birdsong. We go back to our lessons feeling refreshed and in just the right mood to study.

In conclusion, I believe this is a successful facility and very popular with students. I would recommend a similar facility for the younger children, and suggest this is situated in the part of the playground nearest to the water fountains, as young children get very thirsty when they are playing.

10 Preparing points for your own report (10–15 minutes)

Go through the prompts to make sure students understand each one.

> **Critical thinking:** You could ask students to link the comments to personal experiences they have had, for example: *Have they noticed litter being dropped by visitors near rivers (or in another beautiful place) that they visit? Does it matter? Why / Why not? If there was a sudden influx of tourists wanting to fish in a local river, would it cause problems? Why / How?*

Remind students that a report should sound formal and be as objective as possible. Opinions should be supported with clear reasons.

11 Writing your own report (25–30 minutes)

Point out that a report usually has a heading, which sums up what it is about. It should be simple and relevant. (Possible headings in this case might be 'Report on the proposal for a river marina' or 'Should the new river development go ahead?')

Once students have produced a first draft of their report, give them a checklist (appropriate to them) of criteria for assessing what they have written. Then encourage them to make any necessary improvements before they redraft it.

Example checklist:

- ☐ Have I used paragraphs?
- ☐ Is there an introduction and a conclusion?
- ☐ Have I avoided copying any of the comments word for word?
- ☐ Have I given my opinion at the end?

DIFFERENTIATION

Challenge confident writers by asking them to make more ambitious improvements to their first draft. For example, ask them to swap two simple words for more interesting words or phrases.

For more **support**, ask students to find and correct (for example) one spelling and one grammar error – or, if you have looked at their work, put an asterisk in the margin next to a couple of lines where you have found a correctable error, asking them to find it.

Example answer
An answer that selects from the comments and develops them could read as follows. It would be useful to highlight some of the key elements for students.

Should our river be developed for boating?

The council are proposing to develop the local river for tourism and have asked for a report on these plans. I'd like to consider the advantages and disadvantages of the proposed river development, taking into account the views of local residents.

In the first place, the river is in a lovely part of the countryside. People who live and work in the noisy, crowded city will be able to come and enjoy the peaceful atmosphere of the countryside. Furthermore, if people come to the area, they will spend money, which will give a boost to our local economy and lead to many new jobs.

On the other hand, it is likely that oil and rubbish from the boats will be dumped in the river. The blades from boats will tear up plants which feed on pollution, so eventually the water will become dirty and stagnant. In addition, there is a risk of damaging the ecology of our river if too many visitors catch fish.

To sum up, I think it would be wrong to develop the river. Although we need to progress and become more modern, I think this can happen without sacrificing our wonderful river.

GRAMMAR SPOTLIGHT (10 MINUTES)

The 'Grammar spotlight' looks at specific ways to express predictions about the future, using examples drawn from the unit. The examples are selected to show students that they have been handling these structures confidently and the spotlight enables them to consolidate this knowledge. Encourage students to practise writing some predictions about their own town or village 50 years from now.

Answers

1   c, a, b/d

2   (Suggested answer) It makes the Rosville Business Group sound confident and very sure of their facts. It makes their argument much stronger.

3   Students' own answers.

WIDER PRACTICE

1. Inviting a member of a nature conservation or pressure group to class to talk about their aims and projects could be inspiring for students. It's especially good if students can hear about a successful environmental campaign.

2. If students found the 'International overview' interesting, find and direct them to websites that provide interesting data on environmental topics across the globe (presented for a non-specialist). The BBC, National Geographic and WWF (World Wide Fund for Nature) provide clear and readable material (in English) about climate change, which students may find interesting to investigate.

3. Watching a nature documentary online can lead to an increased understanding of ecological issues, which students can make use of in their work in class.

4. Students could write reports on real places they have visited, experiences they have had or products they have bought, so they get practice in developing a calm, measured tone, rather than an emotional one. You could consider asking them to send such reports to appropriate real people: for example, companies/owners of businesses welcome market research of this kind.

5. Local nature conservation areas, country parks and so on may have education officers who can visit and talk to groups of students.

6. As a variation on brainstorming, try brain*writing*. Each student writes an idea about the topic on a slip of paper (anonymously). The slips of paper are collected and each idea is discussed in turn in the group.

Exam-style questions

Reading and writing

Reading and Writing: multiple matching and multiple choice

Two exercises are provided: the first involves multiple matching, the second involves multiple choice.

In the multiple-matching exercise, encourage students to:

- read the rubric carefully for context
- scan the questions to get a general idea of what the texts are likely to be about
- read for general meaning
- match speaker to statement through a process of careful checking and elimination.

It is important that students are patient and proceed logically; when answers appear 'close', students should take extra care to identify the most correct one. If a question is problematic (it seems to match with more than one person), students can pencil in their answer and refine their selection at the end. For example, the first question asks students to decide which person says nature can be harmed but never destroyed. While all the speakers are concerned about environmental damage, only Speaker C mentions the regenerative power of nature.

The text used in the multiple choice exercise is a blog in which the writer (FutureHope) offers a personal view on the climate crisis and how to deal with it. Point out to students that some of the questions require them to use inference skills: using clues in the text to work out what the writer means without saying it directly. They also need to read the text quite carefully. For example, option B in question 6 might *seem* to represent the writer's view (given the content of the blog post as a whole), but does the writer actually say this? It may be particularly useful with this exercise to go through the questions afterwards as a class and highlight/underline the words that provide the answers.

Answers
Exercise 2

a C; b D; c B; d D; e A; f D; g C; h A; i B

Exercise 4

1 B; 2 A; 3 A; 4 C; 5 C; 6 B

Reading and Writing: informal and formal

You will find advice on general approaches to exam-style writing exercises at the end of the 'Teaching support' section in the Introduction.

The article exercise draws on discussion of clothes recycling and the textile industry from texts and activities in the unit, but note that specific factual knowledge is not expected.

Check that students are aware of the audience for their writing. Since the article is for 'their' local newspaper, they will be addressing the readers of that newspaper. So, if students wish, they can address their suggestions in the article to 'you', the newspaper reader.

Example answer

> **Informal writing**
>
> Hi Nicky
>
> You remember we were talking about problems with the environment the other day? Well, I've decided to do my little bit to help. I'm giving up meat. Yes, I know you'll be shocked, because I love meat so much, but when you read all the details about the amount of land and water needed to provide a kilo of beef, you realise the effect that millions of cows all over the world have on our environment. What's more, they affect global warming, because of the methane they produce. I know I'm only one person, but if everyone tries to make a contribution to help the environment it could improve things greatly.
>
> I am sure I will be healthier not eating meat. I will continue to eat fish, but only what I can catch in the sea.
>
> How about you, Nicky, could you do something to help the environment?
>
> Your friend,
> Ali
>
> **(153 words)**

Listening

Listening: sentence completion

Students complete gapped multiple-choice questions based on a talk.

Ask students to look first at the photo and say what clues it gives them about what they are going to hear. Then ask them to read the questions very carefully before listening, underlining key words or phrases that will help them identify the answers.

Point out that answering this type of question often relies on understanding paraphrase. For example, in question 2, students will almost certainly not hear the words 'fairly important', 'extremely important' or 'useful' in the section of the recording that mentions global warming, but they will instead hear a word or

phrase that means the same as one of these options.

Listening out for key words such as place names will help students orientate themselves when listening to a fairly challenging talk like the one they will hear here. (In this particular recording, three place names are mentioned.)

Students should listen twice to the recording. In a class situation, they can listen as often as you think is necessary. It is helpful to check the answers by pausing the recording in the appropriate places. If they find part of the recording tricky and can't answer a particular question on a first listening, they should make sure they move on to the next question, otherwise they may miss the answer to that one too. For this kind of multiple-choice exercise, a useful strategy may be to eliminate the incorrect answers before deciding on the correct answer.

Answers
1 A; 2 C; 3 B; 4 C; 5 A; 6 B; 7 A; 8 C

> **Audioscript track 4.4**
>
> You will hear a conservation volunteer called Chiara Moretti giving a talk about a process called rewilding. For each question, choose the correct answer, A, B, or C, and put a tick in the appropriate box.
>
> You will hear the talk twice.
>
> Now look at questions 1–8.
>
> Hello and welcome. I'm Chiara Moretti and I'm here to tell you a little about rewilding and why it's so important.
>
> The term *rewilding* means that human beings give up their control of an area of land and let natural processes take over instead, returning the land to how it was in the past. Over time, a variety of smaller plants and then trees will grow back by themselves, attracting insect life that, in turn, will draw in birds, animals, and so on.
>
> Rewilding has many benefits, including that trees and plants absorb large amounts of carbon dioxide, which is crucial in fighting global warming. Tree roots also stop soil from being washed away and trees have an important role to play in preventing flooding because rainwater is drawn deep underground by the roots. In fact, perhaps predictably, experiments show that

rainwater is absorbed into soil covered by trees 67 times more efficiently than into soil covered in grass.

In some areas, rewilding involves reintroducing larger animal species. When wolves disappeared from the USA's Yellowstone National Park last century, there was a huge increase in the elk population that they used to feed on – elks are a type of deer. When the wolves were brought back and started to hunt elks again, the elks started to avoid the river valleys where they couldn't hide from the wolves. This allowed the riverside plants to grow back without being constantly eaten, and the resulting healthier plant life provided food and shelter to attract other creatures such as birds, mice and even bears.

There are some challenges to overcome with rewilding. For example, in Abruzzo in Italy, local farmers initially shot or poisoned the brown bears that the conservation workers were trying to protect, fearing the creatures would attack their sheep and cattle. The conservationists approached this problem by providing free electric fencing and, more importantly, by pointing out that the bears are completely harmless – provided you are human, at least. What really gained community support was realising the economic benefits of attracting tourists to the region to view the bears. This support is vital for keeping the bears safe, but another factor almost as important for their survival is to prevent them being hit by cars at night. For this reason, devices have been installed along roads, which make a loud noise when lit up by the beam of a car's headlights, warning the bears to keep away. Over the years, illegal hunting used to be perhaps the greatest risk for the bears; it appears, though, that the staff now employed to stop such criminal activity are working effectively.

You may be imagining that rewilding requires wide, open spaces far from human populations, but this needn't be the case. Urban rewilding can be seen along the side of some of our busiest roads, where wildflowers and long grass have been allowed to grow. As well as providing a healthier environment for motorists, above all, this creates a home for bees and other insects, helping form a wildlife corridor that allows such species to spread more easily. Not having to pay for such frequent grass cutting probably suits the local government as well.

Rewilding came to Barcelona in Spain almost by chance when the Covid pandemic put a stop to the city council's gardening work for several weeks during 2020. While the streets were empty of people, wild flowering plants grew uncontrolled, attracting 74% more butterflies than the previous year and a 28% rise in the number of species. This was positive news in a region that is thought to have lost 71% of its butterfly population over the past 18 years. Thanks to the pandemic, the city's inhabitants came to appreciate nature more because they weren't allowed to go out into the countryside, so they were more willing to tolerate the untidy appearance of their local green spaces. With most residents' approval, Barcelona city council is now creating many more green wild spaces and traffic-free zones, including nesting towers for bats and birds.

Thank you for listening, and I hope I've made you want to find out more about rewilding, a topic I feel passionate about.

Speaking

You will find advice on general approaches to speaking exercises at the end of the 'Teaching support' section in the Introduction.

If students are doing this exercise under examination conditions, warm-up questions may help to put them at ease. These are included in the corresponding Coursebook unit.

〉5 Entertainment

Learning plan

AOs	Key learning intentions	Success criteria
S1, S2, S3, S4, W1, W2, W3, W4	Explore the topic of entertainment, with a focus on the language of reviews	• Students can maintain a conversation relating to the topic • Students can express personal opinions about the issues • Students can identify and describe relevant aspects of films, books, etc., in speech and writing • Students can use a range of appropriate vocabulary to talk and write about the topic
R1, R2, R3, R4	Scan for information and take notes on key concepts	• Students can quickly find required information by scanning • Students can separate main points from detail • Students can write concise, relevant notes
L1, L2, L3	Listen to a formal explanation, first for gist and then for detail	• Students can focus during a long presentation containing some technical content • Students can identify key concepts • Students can make links between key concepts
S1, S2, S3, S4	Prepare and deliver a structured talk	• Students can come up with relevant ideas • Students can organise their ideas • Students can take their audience into account
S3, S4	Learn strategies for interrupting politely	• Students can identify other speakers' strategies for interrupting • Students can identify appropriate points to interrupt another speaker • Students can use appropriate language to interrupt politely

Overview

The main aim of this unit is to develop students' ability to produce a review, suitable for a student audience, of a film, novel or live performance. Students learn how to review something both orally and in writing, with an emphasis on expressing personal opinions clearly. The first half of the unit mainly deals with films (and live performances such as plays), leading up to an oral presentation about a film. The second half mainly develops book-reviewing skills and includes written review tasks.

Conveying exactly why you found a particular film or book so compelling is challenging. In their reviews, students need to demonstrate analytical skills and appropriate use of language. They also need to be able to highlight the aspects of a particular work that make it effective, offering examples so as to make things as clear as possible for the reader.

THEME

The unit includes discussions relating to the role of entertainment in our lives. Obviously, this may cover more than just cinema and books, and will vary enormously for individual students (and across cultures/settings). Try to encourage students to contribute information about any form of entertainment they enjoy, including computer games, music, and so on. This makes the work more stimulating and better prepares students to be able to discuss a wide range of topics linked to the broad 'umbrella' theme of entertainment.

The unit covers or touches on issues such as violence in films / on TV (and whether it affects young people), how to encourage more people to read and why, and whether live entertainment is in decline. It also looks at two aspects of the film industry that students may not have thought about: how soundtracks are created and how audiences choose to access films made in a foreign language. You can develop any of these sub-themes according to the time you have available and your students' interest, knowledge and maturity.

LANGUAGE WORK

The language work focuses on strategies to help students develop analytical skills. These include developing awareness of important aspects such as characterisation, plot, and so on, and providing the means to discuss them. Specific language exercises include use of adjectives and collocations, and the structures *so . . . that* and *such . . . that* to express personal responses to films.

There is an opportunity to explore viewpoint and evaluative adverbs and their function in allowing the writer to express their intention. The 'Grammar spotlight' reviews one aspect of the use of the present perfect tense: talking about experiences at a non-specified time, in contrast to time-specific experiences expressed using the simple past tense.

Spelling and pronunciation focus on the letters *c* and *ch*.

Common misconceptions

Misconception	How to identify	How to overcome
Students use simple past instead of **present perfect tense with** *ever* when talking about experiences in a time frame up to the present. Examples: *It's the best present I ever had.* *These are some friends of mine – I don't think you ever met them.*	Display some correct and incorrect examples. Ask students to identify the correct ones and to discuss the rules. Examples: *Did you ever see the film Jaws? (✗)* *Have you ever eaten insects? (✓)* *Did Muhammad Ali ever lose a boxing match? (✓)* *It's the hardest thing I have ever done. (✓)* *What a great comedy! I don't think I ever laughed so much. (✗)*	Play 'Find someone who . . . '. Students form a series of questions about experiences up to the present, in the present perfect, based on instructions (e.g. Find someone who has met a famous person → *Have you ever met a famous person?*) When someone replies 'yes', they note that person's name next to the question and then ask a follow-up question with a more specific time frame in the simple past (e.g. *Where did you meet them? Did you speak to them?*)

Misconception	How to identify	How to overcome
Students use **so** instead of **such**, or vice versa, or they omit *a/an* with *such* or use it in the wrong position. Examples: *It was so terrible story that John didn't know what to say.* *Everything was such exciting that the time went very fast.* *The land is in such bad state that it will take 40 years to recover.* *I was in a such bad mood that I didn't say anything.*	Display some incorrect examples anonymously from students' own writing. Ask students to correct them and to explain what is wrong.	Create a class poster showing the correct use of *such* and *so*: *so* + adjective *such a/an* + adjective + noun Elicit and write some correct examples below the rules.

Introducing the unit topic (5–10 minutes)

Working with a partner, students look at the photo and discuss the questions.

The photo shows a scared audience focusing on what they are watching. The style of seating, informal clothing, empty spaces and lighting might suggest that they are in a cinema rather than a theatre, though this is debatable. (Clarify, if necessary, that in American English, *a cinema* is referred to as *a movie theater*, while in British English, *a theatre* generally refers only to *a venue for plays and live performances*. You may also need to point out here, or within the unit activities, that British English speakers more often use the word *films* while American English speakers say *movies*.) The people's faces and the varied ages (including children) suggest the audience is most likely to be watching a rather scary family film, not an adult horror film.

Use the questions to explore thoughts about the popularity (or not) of going out to the cinema, or any other entertainment venue, when you can easily watch a wide range of films, live-streamed theatre, and similar, in your own home. Do members of their family go out for entertainment? What is good about going out to the cinema, rather than staying in? What features do they enjoy (e.g. large screen, 3D, popcorn, opportunity to meet up with friends, restaurants nearby) and are there features that could be added to make the experience more appealing to people? What might happen to city centres if cinemas and other public venues closed?

› **Digital coursebook:** At the start of the lesson, use this video to introduce and review:

- the topic of entertainment, specifically films
- the present perfect.

Read the question on the title screen and ask learners what they think they might see. Then play the video all the way through and check learners' predictions.

Play the video a second time, pausing to discuss what is being shown and the questions on the end screen. You can take the opportunity to revise words and phrases associated with the topic of film. Note that the end-screen contains some differentiated two-part questions. The first part can be answered by using the content of the video. The second part requires learners to develop their thinking. More confident learners will be able to offer more extensive reasons for their ideas.

Take note of whether learners use the present perfect in their answers to items 2 and 4.

You may like to play the video a third time for consolidation.

A Cinema and other forms of entertainment

1 Introduction and discussion (5–10 minutes)

Students discuss the questions in small groups.

1 Check understanding of *in the mood* and the rather informal *to be into* (to be keen on

something, perhaps temporarily), and *buskers* (amateur or occasionally professional musicians or groups, who play in the street asking for donations of money).

Encourage discussion of a wide range of forms of entertainment, and of how students' preferences might change in different circumstances. For example, they may love loud music at parties or live concerts but prefer gentle background music while they are studying; or they may enjoy a classic play but also watching TV chat shows or soap operas to unwind after a hard day.

If students have been to see some kind of live performance (e.g. a play, or some kind of live music in a concert or in a public space), encourage them to describe the experience. How was it different/better/less good than watching or listening to something in their own home?

2   Students may have very varying experiences in terms of how and where they watch TV or films. Encourage them to explain their (or their family's) own methods, particularly for the benefit of other students whose experiences may be different. For example, *streaming service* may need explaining.

2   Film vocabulary (10 minutes)

This exercise, which checks film vocabulary, could be set as homework to prepare students for the work of the unit. It's essential that they can use relevant vocabulary when describing a film.

Check understanding of *Oscar* (one of a set of awards given in the USA for acting and other aspects of film production). Do they know of any other film awards specific to their own country? Check pronunciation and understanding of *genre* (a French word now used in English).

Answers
a Oscar; b performance; c heroine; d plot;
e played by; f role; g scene; h cast; i characters;
j directed by; k box office; l film; m genre

3   Film questionnaire (10 minutes)

Students should answer the questions individually. (They will discuss their answers in Section A4.)

Check understanding of the following: *trailer, suspense, twist, sick of*.

4   Asking for information (10 minutes)

Working in pairs, students follow up each other's answers to the film questionnaire.

This exercise builds on skills students learnt in Unit 2, Section A2 for keeping a conversation going by asking for clarification or probing for more detailed answers.

After the pairwork, follow up on any points about which students feel strongly. Develop it into a class discussion if you wish.

5   Following a model discussion about films (10 minutes)

In this exercise, students listen to a conversation about two films (which are not real ones): a futuristic thriller *The Way to the Sea* and a high school drama *You after Me*.

The aim of the exercise is to show students the ways that films can be analysed, not to practise listening skills specifically. Point out to students that the dialogue is *not* aiming to reflect 'natural' conversation. The dialogue is constructed so that the aspects of films (character, plot, etc.) – which the students need to use in reviewing films – are shown as clearly as possible.

Before they listen, ask students what they think the films will be about, based on the titles.

After listening, ask students which aspects of film reviewing would be useful for discussing a novel. (They all would be, except for the special effects and music aspects of films.)

DIFFERENTIATION

As practising listening skills is not the main focus here, you could **support** students by displaying the audioscript to some or all of the class.

Answers
All items should be ticked except *music*.

Audioscript track 5.1

Listen to a model conversation in which two students, Marta and Navid, tell their teacher about two films they have enjoyed. Notice that the teacher asks for information and follows up the students' answers. Which of these aspects of the films are mentioned by Marta and Navid?

Teacher: Navid and Marta, you've each chosen to talk about quite different films. Navid, you've chosen *The Way to the Sea*, and Marta, you've selected *You After Me*. May I ask why you chose these particular films?

Marta: I wanted to talk about a high school drama because that's my favourite genre.

Navid: I wanted to say why I enjoyed a thriller.

Teacher: They sound very interesting! Could you both tell me a bit about the plots?

Navid: *The Way to the Sea* is set in the future. It's about George, a 16-year-old boy, who survives a massive global explosion. His family have disappeared and the population is dead. He believes his family is still alive and living by the coast. He sets out to find them, but law and order have broken down and he often has to hide from gangs.

Marta: In *You after Me*, Ama, a ten-year-old girl makes friends with Betty, a sophisticated teenage girl who comes to Ama's school. Ama admires Betty and is happy when Betty chooses her to be her best friend. Ama doesn't realise that secretly Betty wants to harm her. Betty steals a phone from a classmate, for example, and hides it in Ama's bag so Ama gets into trouble. Betty also encourages Ama to do things Ama knows are wrong.

Teacher: Characters are extremely important in films. Marta, would you mind telling me about how Ama and Betty are portrayed?

Marta: Betty seems sweet and kind, but actually she is very deceitful and is jealous of Ama because she's kind and has a loving family. We see Ama as a trusting child who wants to grow up too quickly.

Teacher: Well, that is very interesting. What's the hero of *The Way to the Sea* like?

Navid: George is strong and brave. His situation is scary and unpredictable but he never panics. The character is played by Julius Mani. He's ideal for the part, because he's a similar age to the character he plays, and his face is very expressive.

Teacher: Can you give me an example of how his character's personal qualities are shown in the film?

Navid: In one scene, he's threatened by a boy who tries to steal his food. I was on the edge of my seat but George keeps calm in the face of danger, and persuades the boy to lay down his knife.

Teacher: *You after Me* is set in a Canadian town. Could you explain why you think the setting is effective, Marta?

Marta: Well, the small town setting is very ordinary. I live in a place like that myself so it felt familiar. Its cosy, ordinary setting is a real contrast to Betty's bad intentions and adds to the tense atmosphere of the film.

Teacher: Navid, you've said that *The Way to the Sea* is set in the future after a major catastrophe. Can you describe the setting?

Navid: It's sinister and shows a world that's desperate. There are burnt-out buildings and dark, scary woods where gangs could be hiding.

Teacher: Something else I'd like to know is whether there are any special effects?

Navid: Yes, quite a lot actually. A powerful special effect is when George finds a poisonous snake in the grass and is able to control it by singing to it.

Teacher: Marta, dramas can have some light-hearted moments. Can you give me an example of humour in *You after Me*?

Marta: There is a hilarious scene when Betty and Ama visit the circus and the clowns play a joke on them. I laughed so much I nearly choked on my popcorn.

Teacher: I'm glad it was so entertaining. Overall, however, it sounds as if the film has a serious theme. Do you think it's right that the film shows Betty setting a bad example?

Marta: Yes, because the underlying message is that evil is overcome by the forces of good. The real interest is waiting to find out how that happens.

Teacher: Navid, did *The Way to the Sea* have a message?

> Navid: I think the message is that courage is essential to achieve a goal.
>
> Teacher: Finally, why do you think other people would enjoy *The Way to the Sea*, Navid?
>
> Navid: It's so full of suspense. I've been working for my exams, and it made a great break from studying.

6 Comprehension and overview (10 minutes)

Answers

1 C

2 C

3 Present tense: it is conventional to talk about the plot/events in a film or novel in the present tense because the plot/events unfold at the same time as you watch/read

4 Students' own answers

The plot of a film, play or book is usually described in the present tense. (Marta and Navid describe their reactions to the film in the past tense because they are now looking back at how they felt at the time.) In practice, native speakers often mix the tenses when they describe films or books. It is of no great importance, as long as the meaning is clear and there is consistency.

Navid and Marta convey the qualities of each film because their reasons and examples are clear and exact. Students tend to generalise quite a lot in their answers, and the dialogue shows the importance of being analytical and succinct.

7 Language study: *So . . . that* and *such . . . that* (5–10 minutes)

Answers

1 I was *so* keen to see the concert *that* I was . . .

2 The death scene was *so* badly acted that the audience . . .

3 The film took *such* a long time to make *that* the director . . .

4 It was *such* a fascinating story *that* the film company . . .

8 Involving your listener (5–10 minutes)

Point out that the completing phrase can begin with 'I' but doesn't have to. For example, the sentences supplied as an example could be completed as follows:

The scene where the monster appears is so frightening that . . . it might give a very small child nightmares.

The scene where the monster appears is so frightening that . . . several members of the audience gasped.

When pairs have finished, elicit some examples as a class and display some of the best.

9 Pre-reading: Sound effects (10 minutes)

1 Students discuss what they know or can guess about sound effects. This prediction exercise will help them during the reading task that follows (see Section A10).

2 Students do a matching exercise which will prepare them for the reading task.

DIFFERENTIATION

The level of the vocabulary in the exercise is challenging. **Support** students who don't have a wide vocabulary by pairing them with another who does. Alternatively, rather than doing the matching exercise, provide the list of words with the definitions beside them and ask pairs to come up with a sentence or a situation when the word might be used.

Challenge students who can do the exercise easily to think of more words that represent noises in English. You could also introduce the term *onomatopoeia*, used to describe words that sound like noises (e.g. *buzz, miaow, quack, tick tock*).

Answers

2 a 4; b 6; c 2; d 10; e 5; f 9; g 8; h 1; i 7; j 3

10 Scanning for information (10 minutes)

The exercise provides another opportunity to focus on the skill of scanning a text for specific information. If you think it will help your students to focus (and to avoid the temptation to translate word for word), set a time limit for the scanning task. Emphasise that answers to the questions can be written as brief notes.

DIFFERENTIATION

Support slower readers by allowing more time. Consider splitting the text into two halves, and ask readers to practise scanning just half the text.

Answers

1   In the 1920s

2   Swords may be made of plastic or wood which don't make the right metallic sound.

3   To add tension to a scene

4   Samples of different surfaces that actors might walk on

5   **a** leather gloves waved up and down; **b** heavy old phone directories dropped onto a cushion

6   Toy Story and Star Wars

---

11   Reading and making notes (20 minutes)

If necessary, review note-taking skills from Unit 2. Remind students that the number of bullet points reflects the number of separate points they should be aiming for, and that notes should be concise.

For question 3, point out that the first bullet point has been completed. Just as this example consists of just a noun phrase, their own answers for the remaining bullets can do the same.

Suggested answers

Note that it can be a question of judgement which are *main* points and whether or not one point can be split into two separate points (or vice versa). Accept any variations that make sense.

1   •   recording team focus on dialogue – other sounds not picked up well enough

    •   allows sound mixer to adjust levels

    •   allows extra sounds to be added to create mood

    •   allows sounds to be kept if dialogue is replaced with a different language.

2   •   footsteps – for example, different surfaces, shoe types, speed and rhythm

    •   cloth pass – clothes, for example, leather jacket, silk dress

    •   props – for example, putting down a glass, burning fire.

3   Type of surface; type of shoe; speed; rhythm; age; weight

4   •   May not fit context

    •   Risk of duplicating sounds across films

---

12   Vocabulary practice (5–10 minutes)

Answers
a film buffs; **b** named after; **c** tension; **d** imitate; **e** tiptoes; **f** subtle; **g** straightforward; **h** array; **i** infamous

---

B Describing and recommending films

1   Asking for and giving recommendations (5 minutes)

Ask students to try to read with appropriate intonation and expression (avoiding making the dialogue sound too flat). Remind them to practise using stress appropriately (see Unit 2, Section A9.

Before they read, ask if anyone knows the meaning of *sci-fi* (science fiction).

After reading, ask them what they think about the adjectives in the dialogue, before you move on to Section B2.

Answers
What else is worth watching at the moment?

Can you recommend a thriller?

Can you recommend one?

Any ideas?

---

2   Adjectives for talking about films (5–10 minutes)

Using adjectives effectively and precisely is particularly important in reviewing. It is one of the main ways to convey the ideas in the film and opinions about it.

DIFFERENTIATION

Consider reducing the list of vocabulary items for students who require additional **support**, removing the higher-level items. Alternatively, offer a choice of two or three adjectives for each example of 'nice' in the dialogue (numbering the examples). As always, it is useful to have dictionaries to hand to provide a context for each word and so that students can check their choices. This will be useful preparation for Section B3.

3 Collocations (10–15 minutes)

If you share the students' first language, it may be helpful to make cross-cultural comparisons about which words can 'go with' other words. Or, in a multilingual class, you may like to encourage students who share a mother tongue to make these comparisons in their language groups and produce examples for the rest of the class.

DIFFERENTIATION

This is a higher-level exercise, so you may want to reduce the adjective word list to **support** mixed-ability groups or split the class into smaller groups and give each group a section heading to work on.

Challenge the more adventurous to think of further adjectives to add to each category, using a dictionary to help check their suitability. Point out that another good way of adding to their knowledge of collocations is to look for adjectives that go with the nouns in genuine reviews in English. Additionally/alternatively, they could list adjectives to use negatively to describe disappointing aspects of a film or performance (e.g. unconvincing performance, predictable or slow-moving plot).

Suggested answers

a   impressive, magnificent, enjoyable, satisfying, memorable, amusing, hilarious, quirky, dramatic, gripping, breathtaking, mysterious, thought-provoking, engaging, convincing

b   impressive, memorable, amusing, hilarious, quirky, engaging, convincing, appealing, likeable, attractive

c   impressive, magnificent, stunning, spectacular, memorable, hilarious, attractive

d   impressive, magnificent, stunning, spectacular, memorable, dramatic, breathtaking, mysterious, attractive, quirky

e   impressive, magnificent, stunning, spectacular, enjoyable, memorable, amusing, hilarious, dramatic, gripping, convincing

f   impressive, magnificent, stunning, spectacular, enjoyable, memorable, amusing, hilarious, dramatic, gripping, breathtaking, thought-provoking, engaging, convincing

4 Understanding the style of short reviews (15–20 minutes)

This exercise helps students analyse some of the techniques used in very short newspaper reviews, which almost have a language of their own. Clearly, you will want students to develop their own style, but they may like to adopt one or two of these techniques.

DIFFERENTIATION

Reduce the amount of reading for students who require extra **support** by asking them to focus on reviews A–D (and answers 1, 4, 5 and 6).

To **challenge** students, provide a more focused way of analysing the critics' techniques by asking them to find examples in each review of: genre information (thriller, documentary, comedy); dramatic, emotional language; how the writer makes you want to watch the film. Students could compare their answers in pairs.

Answers
1 D; 2 E; 3 G; 4 C; 5 A; 6 B; 7 H; 8 F

After students have completed the exercise, discuss whether they have seen any of these films/performances (all the reviews are based on real films/plays). Do the reviews match their own memory of the film/play? Are they a fan of any similar films in the same genre (e.g. superhero films)?

5   Choosing key words (5 minutes)

This exercise shows the care that is taken by the critic in selecting words that are just right to describe a particular film. Students are given practice in identifying key words.

Answers

1   **a** remote; **b** enjoying; **c** dark secret; **d** will be forced

2   **a** ambitious, doesn't listen, determined; **b** trapped; **c** fight to the death (clarify the meaning here – a fight to the death means a fight that is intended to continue until one of the protagonists dies)

6   Presenting a film or play to the class (25 minutes)

The time required will vary depending on how many students need to deliver their talks.

This exercise consolidates the unit so far by asking students to present a talk on a film or play to their group. If you allow students to plan the talk at home, emphasise that they should only write notes, not a full script.

> **Critical thinking:** Conveying the quality in particular requires students to assess what specially stands out about the film/play and to think critically about what the film/play says to the audience (its message).

Before students present their talks, discuss practicalities (e.g. Is there a time limit? Should they talk sitting or standing? Who are they presenting to?) Clarify the role of those who are listening: they should listen actively, making notes of any positive features they would like to comment on and any questions they would like to ask.

The main focus here is on appropriate content, vocabulary and expression. If students are not used to giving talks like this, you might wish to spend some time discussing presentation techniques (e.g. talking calmly and clearly, making eye contact, glancing at notes but not reading from them)

and listening rules (e.g. paying attention, not interrupting, being encouraging and positive).

Consider allowing students to record or video their talks (e.g. with their phones), and encouraging them to analyse the talks afterwards in their groups. You may wish to select a strong example as a model for positive criticism from the whole class.

DIFFERENTIATION

Support students by making judgements, based on your knowledge of the personalities involved, on who should present to whom. For example, a nervous presenter may need particularly supportive listeners.

7   Pre-listening discussion (5–10 minutes)

> **Critical thinking:** Encourage students to give reasons for their views and to think of examples.

The questions may not be ones that students have given much thought to previously. If they think issues of dubbing and subtitling don't matter, ask them to think of any films or programmes they may have watched that were *badly* dubbed, or any occasions where they may have been put off by subtitles, or spotted mistranslations.

Encourage discussion about whether there is a choice of languages available to them when watching films/programmes, and whether they make a conscious decision to watch in a particular one.

DIFFERENTIATION

To **support** students ahead of Section B8, you could develop the discussion for question 6 by asking for ideas about how dubbing is carried out. This will anticipate some of the information given in the audio recording, thus making the listening task a little easier.

8   Listening for gist (10 minutes)

After this first listening, ask students in what ways the speech related to the discussion they had in Section B7.

Audioscript track 5.2

Listen to a talk about dubbing (the process of changing the speech in a film to a different language).

I'm here today to talk to you about dubbing. Put simply, dubbing films involves stripping away the words spoken by the actors in a film or TV series, and replacing them with dialogue in another language. I'll start by outlining how this is carried out, then I'll compare dubbing with subtitling.

First, then, the film dialogue has to be translated into the target language, making sure the translation sounds as natural as possible and trying to be true to the original meaning. What adds an extra layer of challenge here is the need for lip synching: that means that each new utterance must precisely match the opening or closing of the original actor's lips on screen, as well as aiming for the same number of syllables. We don't want the viewer to see a mouth moving with no sound coming out, or hear words when the lips aren't moving. Unfortunately, this can sometimes mean minor changes to the meaning of the words, but there are a few editing tricks that can help sort out lip synching problems if necessary, such as adding in a few frames with a different camera angle that doesn't reveal the speaker's mouth. Technology is also evolving to a point where it may be easier to alter the lip movements on screen to match the dubbed speech.

In seeking out the right dubbing actor, clearly gender and age must be considered, but crucially also something much more difficult to define, which is whether the audience will believe this voice comes from the face they are looking at. Think of your favourite film or TV character with a much higher- or lower-pitched voice. Could you get used to that? But as well as matching voice and physical appearance as perfectly as possible, with a well-known actor the priority is to use one dubbing voice for all their performances. Viewers will expect that, just as they would be puzzled if a fictional character sounded different in a later film from the same series.

Once they've got the part, the dubbing actor records their lines in sync with the action on the screen. To do this well, they need to get themselves inside the head of the character just as the original actor did, making sure they convey everything about the character's emotions and the on-screen action to the viewer – including for example if they are out of breath from running, or chatting while chewing mouthfuls of lunch!

The main alternative to dubbing is of course subtitling: retaining the original spoken dialogue while displaying a written translation at the bottom of the screen. Many viewers prefer this approach, arguing that you lose some of the original flavour and atmosphere of a film by replacing the language and characters' voices. It's interesting to note, incidentally, that those countries which mainly show English-language films and programmes with subtitles rather than dubbed into their own language also tend to be those where the population has a better level of English, although a direct connection hasn't been proved. It could also be that if you have some knowledge of a language, you're more likely to want to hear it while you skim read the subtitles in your first language.

A further point in favour of subtitling is the cost: you could subtitle ten films for what you'd pay to dub just one.

Reasons to go for dubbing include that it's more relaxing – you don't need to keep moving your eye between the subtitles and the action – and that it makes films more accessible for those with sight or reading problems. In fact, films aimed at children too young to read have always relied on dubbing. In practical terms, subtitles work poorly on a mobile phone screen, too, which is where many people now do most of their viewing. Additionally, young people in particular have a tendency to 'multi-task' rather than focus exclusively on the film, and it's simpler for them to switch between activities when they can still hear the dialogue.

Dubbing is definitely on the rise, whether you like it or not, mainly because of big online streaming services anxious to widen their customer reach. Some of them offer you the option to choose between a dubbed version or a subtitled version of a foreign film: I wonder which *you* will choose.

9   Comprehension check (10 minutes)

The questions require students to listen very carefully to what the speaker says, and to not make assumptions about what the speaker does *not* say. If students have made mistakes, encourage them to listen again (perhaps at home) to work out exactly what was said and where they went wrong, or provide a copy of the audioscript.

Answers

1 A; 2 B; 3 C; 4 A; 5 B; 6 C; 7 C

10 Language study: Viewpoint and evaluative adverbs (10–15 minutes)

This type of adverb is very useful for signalling the speaker/writer's point of view and making connections between phrases or pairs of sentences. Listening out for them can aid understanding in a listening exercise. Some of these adverbs are commonly used in informal speech as well as more formal writing, while others such as *additionally* are much more common in a more formal written context. *Incidentally* is often replaced by *by the way* in everyday speech.

DIFFERENTIATION

Challenge students who need stretching by asking them to explore (in question 3) whether the adverb could be placed in a different position within the sentence. What punctuation would be needed? (The adverbs could be used at the end of the sentences in the exercise, following a comma – e.g. (a) Hardly anybody came, surprisingly.)

Answers

1 A comma is generally used after the adverb.

2 a 3; b 5; c 2; d 4; e 1; f 6

3 Possible answers: **a** surprisingly; **b** personally; **c** incidentally; **d** frankly; **e** presumably; **f** apparently; **g** luckily

4 Uses of the adverb *actually* are varied, but at the head of a phrase or sentence it is often used to suggest a contrast between what is expected and the reality, particularly in speech. For example:

A: That exam was quite easy, wasn't it?

B: Actually, I found it really hard.

C Reading and television

1 Reading habits questionnaire (20 minutes)

As the questionnaire is quite long, you may wish to set it for homework and do the follow-up pairwork discussion in class.

The questionnaire is a way to introduce vocabulary relevant to books and reading, and a lead-in to discussion about reading preferences and habits. If some students say they never read for pleasure, encourage them to use that as a talking point: why? When did they stop? Might they do it again in the future? In what circumstances?

Check understanding of vocabulary and concepts such as the genres in question 2, *tablet*, *book-signing* (a session, typically in a bookshop, where an author signs copies of their book and talks to customers), *blurb*, *peer pressure*. You may wish to discuss what your students understand by *YA* (or get one of them to explain if they are a fan: books aimed at 12–18 year olds, although market research suggests that half of YA-readers are adults). It is not, arguably, a genre, but a category of books with certain characteristics such as teenage main characters, fast-moving suspenseful plots, coming-of-age stories, and similar. The terms *Bookstagrammer* and *BookTuber* are specific to certain very popular photo- and video-sharing services that your students may or may not have access to, but they may be familiar with the concept from other internet services.

2 Listening: Strategies for interrupting (10 minutes)

Students listen to a discussion in which a librarian expresses his fears that TV and films are depriving children and young people of the opportunity to form positive reading habits, thus harming their intellectual and creative development.

DIFFERENTIATION

The audio recording is challenging, so it may be helpful to **support** some students by giving them key quotations either before they listen, or after this first gist listening and before they move on to Section C3.

Reading for pleasure is declining in children.

CONTINUED

Video can't develop the mind in the way reading can.

TV programmes rely on shock tactics to get attention.

Children who watch a lot of violence in films come to accept it as just a normal fact of life.

Parents should set a good example by reading themselves.

They should mark them *agree, partly agree, disagree* or *not sure*, and briefly discuss their views with a partner. This will give an opportunity to check understanding of the language.

Answers

1   Jonathan's key point is that reading develops the mind, whereas TV and videos offer easy entertainment.

2   The interviewer uses the phrases *If I could just butt in here, . . . , Hang on!* and *If I could get a word in here, . . .* Point out that *Hang on!* is informal and quite direct – the interviewer uses it when he starts to lose patience.

Audioscript track 5.3

Listen to a radio interview. Jonathan, a librarian, is concerned that young people are giving up reading because they are too busy watching films and TV programmes online.

Interviewer: What exactly are your concerns, Jonathan?

Jonathan: I think it's very sad to see reading for pleasure decline in children and young people. Reading is a wonderful way to use leisure time. You can escape into an imaginary world of your own. Do you realise the average child watches 20 to 30 hours of TV a week?! Children and young people are not forming the habit of settling down quietly with a book, and getting, you know, the rewards of concentrating on a really absorbing story.

Interviewer: Well, if I could just butt in here—

Jonathan: Children from poor homes watch most TV, maybe because their parents can't afford to pay for other diversions. However, borrowing books from the library costs nothing at all.

Interviewer: But surely a high-quality film can stimulate young people intellectually and creatively?

Jonathan: A video, however well made, can't develop the mind in the way reading can. Reading teaches you to discriminate between good and bad in subtle ways. Most videos are about quick and easy entertainment, just as quickly forgotten.

Interviewer: Oh, now, I think that's a bit unfair! Where's the evidence?

Jonathan: Most videos and TV programmes are pathetic! The characters are shallow, the plots predictable. They rely on shock tactics to get attention – violence, aggression, crime and abuse—

Interviewer: Oh, hang on!

Jonathan: ... just to keep us watching. If crime is a theme in a novel, on the other hand, a child can think it through properly and come to understand the motives behind the actions of the characters. But I think violence on the screen is different. Children aren't using their minds to discriminate about what they see – they're just soaking up violent images!

Interviewer: So you're saying violence is more harmful on screen than when it's written about in a respected novel?

Jonathan: I think children who watch a lot of violence in films and on television come to accept violence and aggression around them as just a normal fact of life.

Interviewer: So you believe films and television actually influence behaviour?

Jonathan:	Why would advertisers spend millions advertising products on TV if they didn't believe it was money well spent?
Interviewer:	So, how would you encourage children to switch off the TV and open a good book?
Jonathan:	Parents should set a good example by reading themselves. Our library has a special young people's section with some wonderful books! Parents can encourage children to join. At the moment, they're taking the easy way out and letting their children become telly addicts! Parents—
Interviewer:	If I could get a word in here—
Jonathan:	... parents should talk to their kids about what they're reading. They. . . they ought to ask their opinions of the plot and the characters. In the end, families would be closer too.
Interviewer:	I don't think you should be too hard on parents! But what you say about screen violence and so on having a more harmful effect is interesting, though I doubt whether you'll be able to prove it! I wonder what our listeners think.

3 Detailed listening (10 minutes)

After the listening, you could ask students what they think the average number of viewing hours is in their own country, and to research it to check.

Answers

1 They lose out on the habit of reading and the rewards of concentrating on an interesting story.

2 Reading uses intellectual powers which help you learn to discriminate between good and bad. Watching a film doesn't develop your mind (it's 'quick and easy entertainment') and you don't remember anything important from films.

3 They come to accept violence as a normal part of life.

4 Parents can encourage their children to borrow suitable books from the library, and they can talk to their children about what they read, asking their opinions of the books.

5 C   interested and concerned.

---

4 Post-listening discussion (5 minutes)

> **Critical thinking:** Encourage students to support their arguments with reasons and examples.

5 Dialogue: Interrupting each other (10 minutes)

Make sure students understand that the em-dash device (—) shows that one speaker is in the middle of talking when someone interrupts.

Obviously, the two speakers will interrupt each other more than is normal in real life, but this gives students valuable practice. The views of the speakers are deliberately rather 'black and white', as this makes their frequent interruptions more natural.

In a follow-up discussion, encourage students to continue practising the interruption strategies by deliberately (but politely) interrupting. Some follow-up questions could be:

- Can violence on screen influence children, even if they come from a good home that teaches them moral values?

- What about the opposite? Do examples of kindness and generosity on TV or in books have a positive influence?

- If children were not watching TV, what else would they be doing? Would it necessarily be something more positive?

- What about the educational value of TV, books and films?

DIFFERENTIATION

Support students with a more basic drill before embarking on the dialogue exercise. Review the phrases for interrupting in Section C2 (or substitute alternatives), then put students in pairs. One student begins a 'conversation' with 'bla-bla-bla' and the other interrupts using one of the phrases and appropriately polite intonation,

CONTINUED

taking over the 'bla-bla-bla' conversation themselves until their partner interrupts them in turn. Continue until they have had a chance to try out several different phrases.

As well as encouraging students to use the phrases for interrupting, you could **challenge** students to practise the body-language signals people use to show that they would like to say something. These may be culturally specific, ranging from slightly opening your mouth and raising your eyebrows to holding up a hand, so consider what is appropriate in your setting.

6 Spelling and pronunciation: The letter c (10 minutes)

Remind students that the rules for pronunciation help with spelling – for example, words like *notice and replace* keep the final -*e* when the suffix -*able* is added, in order to keep the *c* soft.

As students do question 3, encourage them to apply the rules they have just formulated. You could also encourage them to look up any words they are still unsure about in a dictionary, supporting them with understanding the phonetic script as necessary.

Answers
2 a 2; **b** 1; **c** 4; **d** 3

7 Using words in context (10 minutes)

This exercise provides an opportunity to practise contextualising the sounds. Have students swap sentences and read them aloud for further practice. Encourage students to monitor each other's pronunciation.

8 Spelling and pronunciation: The letters ch (10 minutes)

You could follow up this exercise by getting students to write the words in context or by giving them a quiz. In the quiz, you could test their acquisition of the sounds by writing up the phonetic symbols on the board, with an example word under each symbol. Label the symbols 1, 2 and 3. Call out a word and ask students to say whether it belongs to group 1, 2 or 3.

Answers
Group 1: moustache (belongs in Group 3);
Group 2: scheme (belongs in Group 1);
Group 3: chocolate (belongs in Group 2)

9 More practice of c and ch sounds (5 minutes)

The dialogue provides an opportunity to practise the sounds in a reasonably natural context. As always, encourage students to work in pairs (then swap parts) and check each other's pronunciation. Note that the names Alex and Jamie can be for a male or female.

International overview (10 minutes)

This could be done either as a homework exercise (with students using an internet search engine to find the answers) or in class as a quiz. If you choose a quiz, divide students into small groups and award points for correct answers (according to the list below).

Note that the answers to some of the questions are difficult to pin down and, if students do their own research, they may get different results. Statistics will in any case change by year, of course. You could make this a discussion in itself: for which of these questions is there a definite answer that can be proved? What are the problems with some of these answers?

If you wish, you could invite groups to create more quiz questions on the same topic, and choose the best ones to ask the class.

Answers (variable depending on year and source)
1 India; **2** China (the Diamond Sutra, 868 CE);
3 25 000 words per minute; Howard Berg USA;
4 1940s–1950s; **5** Far away, from a long distance;
6 10 years; **7** India (followed by Nigeria, then China);
8 India; from a combination of the words *Bombay* (former name for city of Mumbai) and *Hollywood*, home of USA film industry; **9** The style of animation made in Japan

D Writing a book review

1 Preparing key points for a review (10–15 minutes)

> **Critical thinking:** The activities in this section are based on building the skills for writing a book review. If appropriate, you could offer the alternative of focusing on another film (or TV drama series, etc.) instead. If you have students who don't read at all, some of the questions in this exercise could be answered by bringing in a selection of suitable books and getting them to study the blurb and cover.

At the end of Section D, there is an option to write a complete book review (D10), or else just to focus on the opening paragraph (D8) and build a review from prompts (D9). You may wish to clarify for your students whether or not the notes they are making in this exercise will be used to write a complete review of their own.

Check understanding of vocabulary such as *in a nutshell* (in a very few words), *minimalist, futuristic, dystopian* (referring to an imaginary world where everything is extremely bad, the opposite of *utopian*), *whodunnit* (crime mystery), *flashback*.

2 Reading a review of a classic novel (10 minutes)

This exercise and the next (Section D3) allow students to study features of the kind of book review that would be appropriate for a school magazine, or similar.

This first review is of *Great Expectations* (published in 1861), a classic English novel by Charles Dickens, one of Britain's best-known writers. It is a thought-provoking novel in which character development is a major strength. Ask students if they have heard of it and what they know about it.

Answers

1 *Great Expectations* by Charles Dickens

2 Set in the 19th-century, in England

3 An escaped prisoner and Miss Havisham (described as eccentric and bitter)

4 He becomes more aware of his faults and more compassionate

5 Because he is moved to tears at the end

3 Reading a review of a contemporary YA novel (10–15 minutes)

This second review is of the book *The Knife of Never Letting Go*, the first in the 'young adult' Chaos Walking trilogy by Patrick Ness, first published in 2008. (It has recently been made into a film, named *Chaos Walking* after the trilogy title.)

DIFFERENTIATION

Sections D2 and D3 offer similar activities. **Support** students who find reading activities more challenging by focusing on only one of the two. The questions in Section D4 could apply to just one text.

Answers

1 *The Knife of Never Letting Go* by Patrick Ness

2 Prentisstown; 'a small town with a dark history'

3 It is 'weird' that she is silent because the reviewer has told us that in this world we can hear other people's thoughts

4 *dangerous swamp, pursued by an army of hostile men*

5 A dramatic ending, where what happens next is uncertain (e.g. the hero might live or die)

6 There is unbearable tension

7 *skilfully handled*

8 Because she wants you to read the book first

4 Analysing example reviews (10–15 minutes)

Students analyse why the reviews are effective, and identify useful language for reviews. Explain the meaning of *plot spoilers* (information that might reveal key events in the story, therefore spoiling the surprise for future readers). Students may have seen the words 'Spoiler alert!' on reviews or comments on forums, etc.

Sample answers

1 It makes you feel involved and grabs your attention.

2 a I won't spoil the story by telling you how the plot twists and turns, but I can guarantee surprises!

b . . . dark history which we will only discover later; The cliffhanger at the end will leave you desperate to read the next book.

3 Gilang: how corrupting money is; The novel made me think about how loyalty and integrity are more important than wealth.

Francesca: it made me consider how one person can make a difference in the world by standing up for their values.

4 *Great Expectations*: Students of English language and literature will find it particularly fascinating.

The Knife of Never Letting Go: Whether you are already a fan of YA dystopian fiction or you just love fast-paced, intriguing storylines, I would highly recommend reading the whole trilogy.

5 Gilang: Have you ever liked the hero in a novel so much that you wanted everything to turn out all right for him?; I'd like to recommend it for the school library because I'm sure other students will identify with the main character; I won't spoil the story by telling you . . . ; I think you'll be moved to tears . . .

Francesca: The cliffhanger at the end will leave you desperate . . . ; Don't worry, you'll soon get used to it, and you'll enjoy . . . ; . . . ideally before you see the film adaptations; The novels may be a little bleak and upsetting for sensitive tastes . . .

6 Students' own answers

5 Useful language for reviews (5–10 minutes)

Encourage students to refer back to this list when writing their own reviews.

6 Criticising aspects of a book, film or play (5–10 minutes)

Up to this point in the unit, students have studied examples that are almost entirely positive. This exercise introduces ways of adding in some negative points.

DIFFERENTIATION

Support students by carrying out some further targeted practice of the language. Ask them to think of some books they have recently read or films/programmes they have recently seen that had some features they did not like. They should then practise using each sentence starter in turn to write something negative.

7 Effective openings for book reviews (10–15 minutes)

> **Critical thinking:** Students analyse and evaluate the sample book review paragraphs, ranking them in order of effectiveness.

Point out that these paragraphs were written by real students, and therefore some contain errors of grammar and vocabulary, but correcting errors of this kind is *not* the purpose of the exercise. Instead, in the weaker paragraphs, they should say which of the five tips given in the bullet points have not been followed.

DIFFERENTIATION

Challenge students to rewrite some of the less successful reviews (A, B, D and F) by substituting phrases from Section D5. For example, the phrase *It's hard to put down* could be used instead of *I couldn't leave any single moment in the book without reading it*, at the end of review A.

Suggested answers
C and E are the most successful examples. They are concise and informative. The other reviews are vague, say too little in too many words, and do not make use of appropriate vocabulary.

8 Writing an opening paragraph (15 minutes)

> **Critical thinking:** Remind students of the ingredients of a good opening paragraph for a review: clarity, being concise and engaging interest immediately. If students haven't read a novel recently, let them write about a film or TV show they like.

DIFFERENTIATION

Support students by writing an example with the class as a whole. Decide together on a film, TV show or book that everyone in the class knows, then elicit different ways of beginning a review of it. You can scribe as they make suggestions. A good idea would be to write three openings and then ask students to decide which is the best and why.

It may also help students to prepare their own paragraph orally first. They could work with a partner or small group, telling their partner enthusiastically what is good about their chosen novel (or film) and why their partner should read it / go to see it. Encourage them to focus on what is really good about it in as few words as possible. When moving on to the writing, some students may benefit from a choice of sentence starters to incorporate – for example, *This book/ film will make you . . .* ; *This is the most . . . book/ film I have ever . . .* ; *Set in . . . , this novel tells the . . . story of . . .* ; and so on.

9 Building a review of a thriller from prompts (10–15 minutes)

You might choose to do *either* this exercise *or* Section D10.

The Kidnapping of Suzie Q is a novel aimed at the teenage market, first published in 1994. The exercise provides the content, allowing students to focus on language accuracy.

Example answer

The Kidnapping of Suzie Q by Martin Waddell is the most thought-provoking and atmospheric novel I have read. It is set in modern urban Britain and it tells the story through the eyes of the courageous heroine Suzie. One day she is making an ordinary trip to the supermarket to buy groceries when the supermarket is raided. In the confusion, the criminals kidnap Suzie as she is standing in the checkout queue.

The criminals keep Suzie in captivity. Suzie recounts her ordeal in painful detail. I was impressed by Suzie's courage, determination and refusal to panic or give up. Several incidents in the novel reveal Suzie's ability to cope when she is threatened by them.

The story made me think how ordinary life is changed by one incident. It is also inspiring because it made me realise the inner strength ordinary people can have to cope with disaster.

The novel is skilfully written. Martin Waddell's style is direct and witty, and the characters are strong and convincing. The plot is intriguing and never predictable. If you like tense novels, you'll find this hard to put down.

10 Completing your own book review (25 minutes)

Students bring together all they have learnt in the unit to complete their review of a book (or film), adding to the paragraph they wrote in Section D8 and using their notes from Section D1.

After completing it, students swap reviews and give feedback.

11 Look, say, cover, write, check (10 minutes)

The words in the list include *c* or *ch* spellings, covered in Section **C**. See Unit 1, Section B13 for a reminder of the 'Look, say, cover, write, check' method for learning vocabulary.

GRAMMAR SPOTLIGHT (10 MINUTES)

This section reviews the use of the present perfect tense to talk about experiences, contrasting it with the simple past when a specific instance is described (e.g. at a specified time). There are several occasions in the unit where students are asked 'Have you ever . . . ?' and asked to respond with details, so you may wish to use those opportunities to do a quick review of correct tenses.

CONTINUED

Answers

1   **a**, **b**, **c** present perfect; simple past. In each case, the 'Have you ever . . . ?' question is asking generally about any experiences at any unspecified time up until now, so the present perfect tense is used. The second verb is referring to a specific example at a specific time in the speaker's life, hence the use of the past simple. (Note that in example **c**, the second question assumes that the answer to the first general question was 'yes', and that therefore a specific example is implied.)

2   **a** have watched; **b** has met; spoken (point out that it is not necessary to repeat *has*); **c** Have you heard?

3   In **a**, the mother went and came back; in **b**, she is still there.

Practice

a   have ever had; was

b   rarely had; have been

c   have I told you; haven't done

d   read; stopped; joined; have read; started / have started

e   has performed/played; have not been/travelled/played/performed

WIDER PRACTICE

1   Why not study a short story extract in class and analyse it in terms of plot, theme, characters, language effects and the ideas it conveys?

2   You could watch a popular film in class and analyse it afterwards. Ask students to write reviews and compare them.

3   You could try to arrange a talk to the class by someone involved in TV, radio, the music business, film or creative writing. Failing that, you could show a video interview from the internet, and discuss the ideas it raises.

CONTINUED

4   The class could make a visit to a cinema, theatre, museum, and so on, and upload a review of their impressions onto a reviewing website, or design an advertising poster for it.

5   Students could discuss how to turn a short story or novel into a film. They could discuss what they would include and what they would leave out, as well as the setting/background, special effects, the costumes they would choose and who they would cast in the various roles. They could discuss what kind of films could be adapted for the stage.

6   The ideas below could be adapted for paired conversations, individual talks and class debates. They make excellent practice for a broad range of oral skills. Students can record themselves using their phones, if appropriate, and analyse the recordings, or share recordings for the whole group to discuss.

   •   How is technology shaping our leisure time?

   •   Are we influenced by what we see on screen?

   •   Life is better with a smartphone.

   •   Which apps have changed our entertainment the most?

   •   Nothing can match the excitement of a live performance.

   •   Is it better for our school to spend money on theatre visits or more practical things?

Exam-style questions

Reading and writing

Reading and Writing: multiple matching

This exercise provides practice with multiple-matching comprehension questions. See the notes for the exam-style questions in Units 3 and 4 for suggestions on how to tackle this type of exercise.

Answers

a B; b D; c A; d D; e C; f B; g A; h D; i C

Reading and Writing: informal and formal

You will find advice on general approaches to exam-style writing exercises at the end of the 'Teaching support' section in the Introduction.

If it is not appropriate in your setting to describe a musical event for the review exercise, or your students have not experienced one, you could substitute another kind of entertainment event, such as a poetry recital, play or fireworks display. Encourage students to draw on the range of vocabulary explored within the unit, particularly the range of adjectives.

Example answer

> **Informal writing**
>
> Hi Chris,
>
> I hope you and Aunt Mary and Uncle John are all well. I'm just writing to tell you about a video I made with my friend Tony recently. I had a problem with my phone last year and I asked Tony for assistance. He is so brilliant when it comes to technology. However, on this occasion, he couldn't help so we went online to chat rooms and there was nothing about my problem at all. So I bought a new phone, but Tony took my old one and in the end worked out what the problem was. So we made a film about how to fix it and uploaded it onto YouTube. And guess what! We've had thousands of hits. It's amazing. Now people are asking us for help with other technical problems. I'm so excited and we're going into business together.
>
> Andy
>
> **(145 words)**

Listening

Listening: short extracts and multiple matching

Two exercises are provided: the first involves five short recordings with multiple-choice questions, the second involves matching a list of opinions with six audio extracts.

In the first exercise, students hear a series of short clips from a wide range of situations, and the information

they need comes very quickly. So point out how important it is to read the rubric ahead of each recording because it explains who is speaking and in what context. Students should also be aware that the words in the questions will not directly reflect the words in the recording, so they need to listen for the same idea expressed in different words. For example, for question 1, they are not told specifically who was frightened so they have to work it out from the information provided. If students don't get the answers right, it may be very useful to study the transcript afterwards to work out what they missed or what misled them so they can be better prepared next time.

In the second exercise, students may try to match words they hear on the recording with the same or similar words or phrases in the statements. Explain that this approach is insufficient. They need to listen for genuine understanding and then focus on the specific details that enable them to identify the correct answer. They should read the statements carefully first and then scan the options for the correct answer as they listen. Encourage students to use the second listening to double check their answers. As this is a challenging exercise, you may choose to let them listen more than twice.

Answers

Short extracts

1 A; 2 B; 3 B; 4 C; 5 B; 6 B; 7 C; 8 C; 9 C; 10 B

Multiple matching

1 C; 2 G; 3 F; 4 A; 5 D; 6 E

> **Audioscript track 5.4**
>
> You will hear five short recordings. For each question, choose the correct answer, A, B or C, and put a tick in the appropriate box.
>
> You will hear each recording twice.
>
> **You will hear two friends talking about a film one of them has seen.**
>
> M: Hi Zeynep, I hear you and Sanem went to see that new horror film. Was it as scary as the reviews say?
>
> F: Well, the final scene would have been terrifying, but someone had accidentally told me what happens so it wasn't too much of a shock. But when they're in the thunderstorm

right at the start, that's when I had my hands over my eyes. Then, when the main character's being chased by the monster halfway through, that's when I should have been terrified but Sanem spilt her popcorn, which made me laugh instead.

M: Actually, I'm hoping to see it myself tomorrow.

F: OK, well if you do, look out for the young actor playing one of the sisters, who's got real talent. There's the black-haired one on all the posters, but it's the deaf girl I mean, who I think is related to that fabulous child star who got an award. Oh why can I never remember names?

You will hear two friends talking about visiting an art exhibition.

F: I saw you at the art gallery with your little brother, in the room with the pictures displayed on the ceiling.

M: Ah yes, and did you know they provide rugs for kids so they can lie down and look up at the paintings rather than rushing through as usual? Such a cool idea – and they really try to appeal to all ages.

F: Yeah, they're great at doing things differently, although my grandmother might find it a bit uncomfortable! And if they lowered their prices, I'd really recommend the café.

M: Apparently, their next exhibition will be on urban landscape photography, which I reckon you'll like, although there will be an outdoor sculpture one starting slightly earlier. That's after six weeks of closing for maintenance, though, starting from tomorrow.

You will hear a tour guide talking to a group of students.

F: Welcome to our tour of Greenwood Film Factory. We've had to make some changes to the tour, so we're now including a visit to the room where background noises like footsteps and birdsong are created – that'll be instead of the planned half-hour meeting with the visual effects manager, who's ill, unfortunately. The museum isn't open to the public today, but we have special permission to explore the section about early cinema after lunch. Speaking of lunch, I have to ask you to resist photographing any famous faces you happen to recognise when you're in the canteen, although obviously there's nothing to stop you telling your friends about it afterwards! And do let me know if you need to leave the tour for the toilets and so on at any time – we don't want to lose anyone!

You will hear a teacher talking to the mother of one of her students, Jin.

M: Thanks for coming in today, Mrs Wang. I was seriously concerned about Jin's schoolwork when you last came to see me, and I remember you felt he'd been distracted by spending too much time on computer games. Do you feel that has changed?

F: Well, I've been struggling to make Jin get his homework done before playing those games. But most homework's online, and it's hard to tell whether he's got maths or space monsters on his screen.

M: Yes, I appreciate that, and Jin's exam results last month had improved overall so your efforts may be working, though it's a pity he didn't do so well in science – his strongest subject. I noticed he looked upset about that himself, so at least we know it matters to him. Perhaps the worst is over.

You will hear a woman leaving a voicemail message for her adult daughter.

F: Hello Oksana, I've been up in the attic looking for the two items you wanted for the school play. The mirror wasn't where I expected it to be, although later I moved some old carpets at the back of the garage and there it was. I'm afraid you're going to have to do without the purple blanket, though, unless you don't mind that it got torn on a nail while I was bringing it back down the ladder. I'd love to help with the performance, by the way – my eyesight's rather poor for sewing costumes these days but baking something for the interval might be something I could manage. I'm guessing all the advertising is going to be online, otherwise I'd have definitely volunteered to get involved with that.

Audioscript track 5.5

You will hear six people talking about film-making. For questions 1–6, choose from the list (A–H) which idea each speaker expresses. For each speaker, write the correct letter (A–H) on the answer line. Use each letter only once. There are two extra letters, which you do not need to use.

You will hear the recordings twice.

Now look at the information A–H.

Speaker 1

In my job, I'm responsible for making the film set look as convincing as possible so the audience aren't distracted by items that would be out of place. That's fine if we're using specially made film sets, but if we use real locations we have to make sure any changes we make can be removed at the end of filming and there's no damage. In one film, which was set in a castle in the 19th century, there were modern light switches which needed disguising. It was difficult, but in the end I used white boxes to cover them up. When filming ended, the owners of the castle allowed us to have a wonderful party at the castle, which they also came to.

Speaker 2

I always feel the audience must accept the character and find him or her realistic and true to life. In one film, I had to play the part of an unfit 50-year-old man who disguises himself as a 19-year-old in order to get a place on a university course. My make-up alone took over four hours, but the make-up artist did a fantastic job and I really did look young enough to be a teenager. It gave me confidence that I could be convincing in my role. When my wife saw the film, she was really impressed!

Speaker 3

I work in make-up and I recently had to make someone up to look much older than their real age as, over the course of the film, the character changes from being a teenager to a middle-aged adult. The film schedule had completely underestimated the amount of time this would take. On some days it was a real rush to get the make-up finished on time for the scene, which was very stressful for both me and the actor. This happens more often than I would like and can make my job very difficult.

Speaker 4

As the director, I usually have a clear idea in my mind of what I want in a film but I need to listen to the actors' opinions as well. Recently, I wanted an actor to speak in a particular way to show her character couldn't be trusted, but she persuaded me she should do it in a different way instead and I was happy to change what I thought and go along with that. It happens quite often, actually. People think actors are very moody and difficult to work with, but in my experience most of them try hard to do a good job.

Speaker 5

As an assistant director, I have to give the actors their instructions regarding the film schedule and the timings to be on set. It's essential the actors arrive at the correct time, as the entire schedule is delayed if someone is late. One actor at the moment gets a bit annoyed with me as he doesn't always like being told where to be and at what time. He has to be on the set very early in the morning, which he really dislikes. I've learned to keep calm under this kind of pressure and I work at appearing self-assured even if I don't always feel it.

Speaker 6

Working with a good director can be a great experience and I've learned so much from the directors I've worked with. I usually also have a lot of input into how to portray the character. As I'm already well known as an actor, I have to think about my audience and the ideas they've developed about me over many years. I wouldn't do anything that would damage their view of me and, if there's a difference of opinion with the director, we work to reach an agreement. I've developed good friendships with some of the directors I've worked with and see them outside work.

Speaking

You will find advice on general approaches to speaking exercises at the end of the 'Teaching support' section in the Introduction.

If students are doing this exercise under examination conditions, warm-up questions may help to put them at ease. These are included in the corresponding Coursebook unit.

>6 Travel and the outdoor life

Learning plan

AOs	Key learning intentions	Success criteria
S1, R1, R3	Explore the topics of travel and tourism	• Students can discuss issues relating to tourism and travel using appropriate vocabulary • Students can express opinions about the issues • Students can evaluate the pros and cons of different types of tourism
R1, R2, R3	Scan for detailed information in a brochure and an article about travel	• Students can scan texts and extract relevant information • Students can use information drawn from a text to form their own opinions • Students can identify evaluative language used to persuade the reader
W1, W2, W3, W4	Write a description of an outdoor activity and a place using vivid and engaging language	• Students can identify descriptive language in an article • Students can use descriptive language in their own writing • Students can use adjectives and adverbs as modifiers
L1, L2, L3, L4	Identify detailed information in a conversation and take notes from a lecture	• Students can answer multiple-choice questions while listening • Students can understand tone and attitude in an informal conversation • Students can understand key details and record them • Students can understand the general meaning and purpose of a lecture
S2, S3, S4	Use a range of vocabulary and grammar for talking about blame and responsibility	• Students can use appropriate expressions in informal settings • Students can engage in a conversation and contribute effectively to help move the conversation forward • Students can identify situations when it is appropriate to express blame or responsibility
S1, S3	Plan, prepare and give a short talk about tourism	• Students can list key points to plan their talk before speaking • Students can use real-life examples to support their arguments • Students can communicate ideas clearly, accurately and effectively

Overview

One of the main aims of this unit is to develop students' ability to produce a memorable description. Although students possess basic descriptive skills, they often need help with making their descriptions more vivid, and making them enjoyable to read and of interest to others.

THEME

Constructive use of leisure time is the main theme of the unit. Leisure is a popular topic, and the emphasis is often on the educational aspects of leisure – for example, what do you learn from this exercise? In this unit, active leisure time is considered in a broad context and stresses the value of new experiences. These include activity holidays, leisure activities, camping, foreign travel and tourism.

Students sometimes tend to treat ideas superficially. The course aims to help them develop and demonstrate more intellectual depth. This unit tackles this need by posing questions that help students to think of all aspects of a topic. For example, if students are presented with an attractive idea, such as going on a foreign holiday, they commonly have difficulty in thinking of its less obvious, perhaps less pleasing, points.

Areas for discussion in the unit are:

- How does a webpage advertising a volunteer holiday achieve its effects?
- What are the possible drawbacks of tourism?
- How can you be a responsible tourist?
- Can tourism cause damage to the local environment and community?
- What are the pros and cons of working for the leisure industry as a tour guide?

LANGUAGE WORK

Students extend their range of stylistic techniques by learning more about using comparisons, relative clauses, *-ing* forms and the role of imagery in descriptions. Vocabulary is developed in a variety of ways, with work on adjective suffixes, intensifiers, colloquial expressions and precision in the use of adjectives. It is assumed students will already have some familiarity with the language forms. The exercises reinforce and expand their knowledge.

Punctuation of direct speech is studied. Pronunciation focuses on words with shifting stress.

The 'Grammar spotlight' focuses on the position of adverbs of frequency.

Common misconceptions

Misconception	How to identify	How to overcome
When using **adverbs of frequency**, students often make errors with word order by putting the adverb after the main verb or before the auxiliary. Examples: *He seems always happy.* *I usually can write once a month.*	Write some correct examples on the board, including examples with main verbs and auxiliaries, and ask students to identify the rules for word order with adverbs of frequency. For example: *He always seems happy.* *I can usually write once a month.*	Write example sentences using a variety of adverbs on slips of paper. Cut them into pieces so that students have to re-order them correctly. For some adverbs, there may be several different ways to sequence the words.

Misconception	How to identify	How to overcome
Common errors with the **punctuation of direct speech** include omitting one or more pairs of inverted commas, putting punctuation outside the inverted commas, omitting the comma or using a colon after the quote. Examples: 'Are there any showers in the hotel rooms?_ 'Could you go with me'? He said: Lisa, will you marry me?_	Write some examples on the board without any punctuation. Ask students to copy the sentences using the correct punctuation. Then discuss any differences between their answers. Correct examples: 'Are there any showers in the hotel rooms?' 'Could you go with me?' He said, 'Lisa, will you marry me?'	Play a short segment of dialogue to use as dictation. Then ask students to punctuate it correctly.

Introducing the topic (5–10 minutes)

Working with a partner, students look at the photo and discuss the questions.

Ask students about their ideal holiday. Encourage discussion of why some types of holiday are popular and what most people look for in a holiday destination. In order to elicit prior knowledge, ask students where they went on their last holiday and what was good or bad about it.

Then focus attention on the photo, which draws together the unit themes of travel, tourism, camping and outdoor life. Students might describe the scenery as amazing, stunning, magnificent, breathtaking, impressive or splendid, for example. Reasons why people might go to a place like this may include: to take stunning photos, to feel closer to nature and the wilderness, to feel calm and get away from the stress of busy city life. Brainstorm a list of unusual holiday destinations (e.g. a treehouse holiday in Thailand, an igloo hotel in Iceland, an underwater hotel in the Indian Ocean) and talk about what activities would be good in each place, such as whitewater rafting in Switzerland, kayaking in Canada, butterfly-watching in Cambodia.

You may also want to touch on the environmental and economic impacts of tourism – another theme developed later in the unit.

> **Digital coursebook:** At the start of the lesson, use this video to introduce and review:

- the topic of travel
- a range of vocabulary related to travel
- adverbs of frequency.

Read the title screen and ask learners what they think they might see. Then play the video, pausing to check learners' predictions and discuss what is being shown. The main different interests are in culture, nature and in physical activities.

Play the video a second time, pausing to discuss what is being shown and the questions on the end screen. You can take the opportunity to revise words and phrases associated with the topic of travel. Note that question 4 is differentiated. More confident learners will be able to offer more extensive reasons for their ideas.

You may like to play the video a third time for consolidation.

A Holiday time

1 Holiday quiz (5–10 minutes)

This exercise focuses students' thoughts on what they want from a holiday. To consolidate, it would be interesting to create a class survey chart of the most and least popular holiday activities.

As an extension or warm-up exercise, you could get students to choose the holiday they would like best from a choice of four. Write four very different holiday destinations on four pieces of paper (e.g. a beach holiday in Spain, a skiing holiday in the Alps, a trekking holiday in the Andes, a cruise holiday in the Caribbean) and stick one on the wall in each corner of the room. Then ask students to go and stand next to the holiday they would like best. When they have formed four groups, they should discuss why they chose this holiday and then explain to the rest of the class what its benefits are.

2 Pre-reading discussion (2–3 minutes)

The holiday webpage students are going to read is aimed specifically at young people who want to volunteer abroad to help the environment. The students usually come from many different countries and their common language is English, so it is an opportunity to meet people, make friends and practise English as well. This webpage is for a fictional programme, but there are many such programmes in countries around the world.

Before students read the brochure, encourage them to focus on describing the photos.

3 Brainstorming (10–15 minutes)

> **Critical thinking:** Students may find thinking of bad points about the holiday challenging. You may wish to use prompts, for example:

'Do you think you would be able to do enough to help the environment in just two weeks?'

'Might young students feel homesick and unsure?'

Additional good points

- Learning practical everyday English
- Experienced and qualified staff
- Safe environment to learn new skills
- Making new friends
- Wide choice of activities
- Discovering more about yourself
- Becoming more responsible

Additional bad points:

- Homesickness/feelings of insecurity
- Possibly not enough support for volunteers who don't speak English very well
- Probably very expensive
- May not like the choice of activities on offer
- Little opportunity to experience everyday life and customs in Thailand

4 Reading for gist (2–3 minutes)

> **Critical thinking:** Ask students to skim the webpage and ask these general questions: What kind of programme is being advertised? Who is it aimed at?

Before students read the webpage in more detail, write up an example sentence containing factual and opinion adjectives, such as: *amazing instructors are qualified and experienced.*

Ask students to identify the factual and the opinion adjectives in the example. You could also ask, *'How do you know this is a fact?'*, eliciting the possible response: 'Whether instructors are qualified and experienced can be proved to be true, but whether they are amazing is a matter of perception.'

DIFFERENTIATION

Provide more **support** by writing these words on the board and checking their meaning: *marine life, ecosystem, coastline, destruction, accommodation.* Encourage students to use monolingual dictionaries, if available, or use context clues.

To provide more **challenge**, ask students to write definitions for each of these words.

5 Comprehension: Scanning the text (5–10 minutes)

The questions test scanning skills. Remind students that the answers may be found in various parts of the text. Although the questions might look straightforward, mistakes can be made. Students need to look carefully at the detail, such as the information in the small print which is necessary to answer some questions.

As an extension exercise, students could role play a conversation between a teenager planning this type of holiday and a representative of the volunteer programme. They should work together to create at least five questions and answers, then present their role play to the class.

DIFFERENTIATION

To give extra **support**, ask students to select just five of the questions.

To provide more **challenge**, ask students to add more information to answer questions 1, 2, 4 and 7. You could also ask them to add more questions of their own, such as:

- What kind of information would you expect to provide on the application form? (E.g. age, nationality, language, reasons for applying.)

- What kind of questions would you expect to find on the FAQ page? Write three possible questions. (Examples: *Do volunteers have their own room or do they have to share? How many hours of volunteer work do we do every day? What kind of clothes and shoes should we bring?*)

Answers

1 How to scuba dive, how to observe marine life, how to plant trees

2 Record data, collect plastic, plant trees

3 Yes, but they can't learn to scuba dive

4 To understand instructions, to ask for help, to make friends with volunteers from other countries

5 The accommodation is quite simple

6 You have to stay two weeks

7 Cost, name of place, reviews

8 Example answer: *Could you please tell me how much the programme costs for two weeks?*

6 **Identifying persuasive techniques (2–3 minutes)**

Elicit the ways in which advertisements try to attract our attention – for example, by use of memorable slogans (a short phrase such as Apple's 'Think different'), logos (a symbol such as Nike's tick) and photographs chosen to appeal to particular people. Once students have analysed the webpage in Section A2, you could ask them to design a short advert for an activity holiday to go on a website or in a newspaper. They can use computers to do this, if you have access to them. The class can decide which of the adverts are the most persuasive and why.

Answers

The target groups for the webpage are 15–18 year olds and their parents who will be paying for the trip. The webpage aims to attract these groups by the 'identification technique': potential customers will identify with the pictures of teenagers doing fun things, and parents will be reassured that the programme is safely supervised and well organised.

There is a variety of opinion adjectives – for example, *amazing, beautiful, exciting, fascinating.*

The language, photographs and layout suggest fun, interest, stimulation, supervision and good organisation.

7 **Analysing the message (5–10 minutes)**

> **Critical thinking:** It should be interesting to explore with students how such programmes benefit the environment. Ask them to consider how much can actually be achieved by non-experts in the time period of two weeks. Could these types of programmes do more harm than good? What alternative methods of helping the environment might have a more positive impact?

Ask students to consider the benefits for the volunteers in learning new skills and improving their English. Discuss what kind of English they would learn and use. (e.g. words for marine life, understanding instructions). Ask if they think their English might improve more or less than in a traditional classroom.

Ask students to list benefits for the environment and for the volunteers in two columns. Discuss which aspect of this programme would most likely persuade them to apply.

8 **Language study: Using modifiers before adjectives (2–3 minutes)**

The meaning of *quite* as a modifier depends on the context and, if spoken, on the intonation pattern. In the webpage, *'quite simple'* means *'moderately simple',* implying that it is not luxurious.

It is important to point out that *quite* with the meaning of *completely* is reasonably formal. In informal written and spoken English, people are just as likely to say *The film was really brilliant* as they are *The film was **quite** brilliant.* You may want to draw students' attention to phrases such as *I quite agree, It is/was quite extraordinary* and *quite honestly,* which, though formal in tone, are commonly used, and which students could make good use of in Speaking and Writing activities.

Answers

a moderately; b completely

9 Shifting stress (15–20 minutes)

Monitor students' pronunciation of the example sentences, as it's important that they can show the difference.

You may wish to give further examples:

*A **con**vict is a person who has been sent to prison.*

*They have been con**vict**ed of a crime.*

Some other examples are (verb / noun): *sub**ject** / **sub**ject, re**ject** / **re**ject, de**crease** /**de**crease.*

You may want to challenge students by asking which of the verbs in this exercise change meaning when they become a noun. (The answer is: *object* and *present*). Other verbs that change meaning include: *content, desert, refuse.*

Point out that many two-syllabled words change their function from noun to verb without a shift in stress. Some examples include: *mistake, promise, display.*

DIFFERENTIATION

As shifting stress can be a challenging area, provide more **support** by focusing on a much shorter list of examples when getting students to work out the stress rule. Once students have understood the rule, offer them plenty of practice – for example, get them to make up sentences for their partner using one or more of the stress-shifting words. They should read aloud their partner's sentences with the correct stress, while their partner checks and corrects them. If necessary, demonstrate how stress is marked in dictionary entries (usually with a stress mark immediately before the stressed syllable). Give students a few further stress-shifting words to look up.

Practice

Elicit the fact that, in the examples, the stress falls on the first syllable of the nouns and on the second syllable of the verbs.

Audioscript track 6.1

Listen carefully to each pair of sentences and identify the different stress in the repeated word.

a You'll make good *progress* on the course.

b You can *progress* to a higher level.

c The farmers sell their *produce* in the market.

d The factories *produce* spare parts for cars.

e I *object* to people checking their phones during a meal.

f She brought many strange *objects* back from her travels.

g Black and red make a striking *contrast*.

h If you *contrast* his early work with his later work, you will see how much it has changed.

i The teacher does not *permit* talking in class.

j I can't get a work *permit*.

k I bought Dad a birthday *present* yesterday.

l The artist will *present* his work at the next exhibition.

Answers

a **pro**gress (noun)
b pro**gress** (verb)
c **pro**duce (noun)
d pro**duce** (verb)
e ob**ject** (verb)
f **ob**ject (noun)
g **con**trast (noun)
h con**trast** (verb)
i per**mit** (verb)
j **per**mit (noun)
k **pre**sent (noun)
l pre**sent** (verb)

B Outdoor activities

The following sequence of exercises aims to help students describe leisure activities by highlighting useful language structures and vocabulary. Students are often asked to analyse *why* an activity they like would interest other people too. Here they are offered ideas of things to say and ways of phrasing them.

1 Asking questions (10–15 minutes)

If your students know each other very well, they could be more motivated to do an exercise like this if one of them goes to the front of the class and answers questions. You may also consider turning this into a guessing game by handing one student the name or a picture of an activity and having them answer the questions from the class without naming the activity. The other students try to guess what it is.

Answers

What do you like to do in your free time?

Where do you do it?

What do you feel like when you do it?

What special equipment do you use?

How good are you at it?

How do you feel after doing this activity?

Why do you recommend it?

---

2 Reading: Identifying leisure activities (10–15 minutes)

Task 1 offers practice in identifying key vocabulary. Before they read the descriptions, ask students to identify the main people, places and objects in the photographs. In the first photograph, these are: *skateboarder, skateboard park, skateboard, helmet*.

Once students have done this, ask them to scan the six descriptions to see if they contain any of the key words. Do this with all the photos, pointing out the skill that needs to be developed: the ability to scan images and text to pick out important details.

Task 2 offers practice in comparing and contrasting information in different texts. Discuss which activities would *not* match these descriptions. For example, description A would *not* be a team sport or something you usually do in a group. Ask students to try and match the questions with the pictures before scanning the text again. You may want to set a time limit for students to find the answers.

To **support** students in task 1, you may want to write some key words on the board and ask students to match them with the photos. Choose words that are slightly ambiguous and don't give away the activity – for example, *calm, exciting, challenging*. You can include some false clues as well. Then ask students to scan the texts for the key words. To increase the **challenge**, ask students to predict at least five words they would expect to read in a text about each photo.

CONTINUED

Before beginning the scanning for task 2, encourage students who may need support to narrow down the number of texts to scan for each question by making predictions. They should note down which sports they think each question might apply to: they could compare ideas with a partner (e.g. 'develops strength in the hands and arms' – most likely to be kayaking?). Tell them to start with the ones they are most sure about.

Answers

1 From top to bottom, skateboarding; kayaking; snowboarding; rock climbing; snorkelling; trail running.

2 A rock climbing; key phrases: reach the summit, rope, helmet, get to the top, views

   B snowboarding; key phrases: balance, coordination, easier than skiing, feels like you're flying

   C kayaking; key phrases: pushing off from shore, stroke, leave all my worries behind on land, lake

   D skateboarding: key phrases: park, tricks, flip, twist, helmet

   E trail running: key phrases: trail, road, path, shoes, uphill

   F snorkelling: key phrases: swimming, sea, diving, fish and coral

3 **a** trail running (E); **b** snorkelling (F); **c** skateboarding (D); **d** kayaking (C); **e** rock climbing (A); **f** snowboarding (B)

---

3 Developing your writing style (5–10 minutes)

This exercise will make students more aware of the variety of ways they can describe an activity they enjoy. The contextualised examples (some taken from the texts in exercise 2) remind students of grammatical structures they have met before and show how to use them for particular purposes.

If students have difficulty with structures such as the -*ing* form, it would be a good idea for them to work on some specific grammar exercises. (Suitable grammar practice books are *Recycling Your English* by Clare West or *English Grammar in Use* by Raymond Murphy.)

If they have a reasonable grasp of the structures, a discussion of the examples in the exercise should be sufficient to refresh their memories. Go into as much detail as you feel is appropriate. You could, for example, contrast the use of the infinitive with the *-ing* form:

I plan to start diving lessons next term.

I enjoy training outdoors in the open air.

You could elicit further examples with *like, love, begin/start, intend, continue.*

Students can use 'since' clauses to make a comparison with their state of health, mood, and so on before they began playing a sport or game and their state of health now, for example:

I'm fitter/have stronger arms since I started swimming regularly.

I'm calmer/happier/more flexible since I've been doing yoga.

Remind students of the way comparative structures are formed (adjective + *-er* or *more* + adjective).

Students can also study the use of similes, for example:

If I can't go rock climbing, I feel like a caged bird.

4 Identifying language structures to engage readers (5–10 minutes)

Check that students have underlined the correct parts of the descriptions. Actually, going through the exercise might uncover gaps in their knowledge that you can follow up with some formal grammar exercises, possibly for homework.

5 Describing a favourite activity (15–20 minutes)

This consolidation exercise could be set for homework or as a classroom exercise if you have time. If your students don't do much sport and prefer other outdoor activities such as gardening, walking or photography, encourage them to write about these. The main aim is to achieve a clear, interesting description with enough detail.

6 Reading aloud (10–15 minutes)

Students may well enjoy the chance to read aloud their description, without saying the actual name of the activity and letting others guess what it is.

7 Pre-listening discussion (5–10 minutes)

> **Critical thinking:** Ask students to study the camping picture and explore their responses to a camping trip, building on actual experiences some of them might have had. You could ask:

'What challenges would living in a tent present?'

'What kind of clothes/equipment would you bring?'

'What might a typical day's camping be like?'

Stressful aspects of camping could include coping with living in a small space, cooking outdoors, coping with storms or cold weather.

8 Listening for gist (2–3 minutes)

The listening exercise is based on an informal conversation between two teenagers discussing their feelings about a camping trip. Asking students to listen for gist, which will help them focus on the overall meaning of the extract.

Answers

There are several things they found difficult: putting up the tent, rain getting into their tent, starting a fire, soggy bread for breakfast, cold showers, no wi-fi.

They end their conversation on a more positive note, saying they enjoyed the activities and their intonation indicates that they enjoyed the trip overall.

Audioscript track 6.2

Listen to a conversation between brother and sister, Omar and Natasha, who have just come back from their first camping holiday with a youth club. What did they find difficult about the holiday? Note three things. Do you think they enjoyed the trip despite the difficulties?

Omar: That first night at the campsite was really awful, wasn't it? I mean it was pouring with rain and we were all trying to work out how to get the tents set up, and it was pitch-dark . .

Natasha: I know! It didn't help that none of us had ever been camping before. I think the camp leaders could have helped us out a bit more. We all got soaked!

Omar: Yeah, but it was my fault for not bringing the extra waterproof sheets to go over the top of the tent. I must have left them in the garage at home.

Natasha: Well, don't blame yourself. We managed OK in the end.

Omar: I felt bad about it, though. I thought it was going to rain all weekend!

Natasha: I know! And we had to get up at the crack of dawn to get the campfire started . . . and all the logs were wet.

Omar: And when we opened up our food supplies to make breakfast—

Natasha: . . . the bread was all soggy because I'd forgotten to pack it in an airtight container! I know, I was responsible for that. I should have been more careful.

Omar: Don't blame yourself. Any of us could have done the same. The potatoes were rock hard – I think we roasted them too long in the fire. The worst thing was the showers. They were stone cold. No hot water at all!

Natasha: And no wi-fi either. I was sure they said we could use our phones and laptops. I was so-o-o desperate to check my messages when we got home.

Omar: The camp leader was really good at getting the day trips organised.

Natasha: Yes, he was so incredibly enthusiastic! But some of the other kids were too childish. They made jokes about him behind his back.

Omar: That really wasn't fair. They should have known better. We had a good time on that zip-lining adventure trail, didn't we?

Natasha: Oh yes! And kayaking on the lake was super fun, too. The water was crystal clear.

Omar: Want to go again on the next trip?

Natasha: Count me in!

9 Listening for detail (10–15 minutes)

Answers
1 A; 2 B; 3 B; 4 C; 5 C

10 Post-listening discussion (5–10 minutes)

> **Critical thinking:** The sort of things the teenagers might have enjoyed are exploring the countryside, making new friends, learning new skills, fresh air and physical exercise.

11 Blame and responsibility (8–10 minutes)

Students will probably need to listen to the audio recording again so they can focus on the expressions used.

Answers
Students should tick:

- It was my fault.
- I felt bad about it.
- I was responsible.
- I should have been more careful.
- Don't blame yourself.

(Note that in some cases the speaker used a different tense and/ or pronoun.)

Blaming someone and admitting responsibility are sensitive areas. British people tend to be indirect, so they are unlikely to say to someone's face 'It's your fault' unless they are angry. They do, however, use such language quite freely in talking about someone who is not there.

Suitable expressions for blaming someone to their face are:

'I'm not really very happy about . . .' (formal)

'I really don't know why you insisted on driving/bringing us here. Now look what's happened!' (informal)

Admitting responsibility and telling someone they are not to blame are not sensitive areas, so the expressions listed can be used freely.

12 Comparing cultures (5–10 minutes)

> **Critical thinking:** Draw out language used in students' own culture(s) and any interesting related stories. In some cultures, for example, it is considered polite to apologise and take responsibility, even if it is not your fault. It's a way of making the other person feel better. In other cultures, it is considered wrong to accept blame for something you did not do.

13 Functional language: Writing a dialogue (15–20 minutes)

Remind students to think quite carefully about the blame language they want to use. You may want to suggest that it's unlikely in the picnic situation that anyone would say 'It's your fault'. Perhaps suggest that students disagree over whose fault it is, each one being willing to take the blame – for example, *'It's my fault'*, *'No, it was mine'*.

Before students write their own dialogues, write one with the class as a whole and put it up on the board. This can then be used as a model for students to follow. Encourage students to focus on realistic spoken English. For example, *I am afraid to say that it has come to my attention, Burak, that you have forgotten to pack the cold drinks* is not really how people speak. The following would be more realistic: *Burak! Where are the drinks? You haven't forgotten to pack them? Ohhh, I don't believe it!*

DIFFERENTIATION

Students who require extra **challenge** can be encouraged to expand the dialogue, perhaps explaining why the drinks were forgotten, apologising and going on to discuss what they are going to do to remedy the situation. Students

CONTINED

could also think of their own scenario and present the dialogue to the class as a short sketch, using props and gestures to support their performance.

Students who need **support** with the exercise could be given a more basic structure: Speaker A says what has happened; Speaker B apologises and admits responsibility; Speaker A tells B they are not to blame; Speaker B offers to get some more drinks. You could also write a simple dialogue on the board and ask students to change words that are underlined.

14 Colloquial expressions: Adjective collocations (10–15 minutes)

In informal English, these noun + adjective and adjective + adjective expressions are common.

You may like to ask students if they know any other of the numerous meanings of *pitch*. For example, it can be used as a verb in *to pitch a tent* and to mean 'a field' as in *cricket/football pitch*. This could be a good opportunity for some dictionary work.

As this is a challenging exercise, you could narrow the vocabulary options and give students who find it difficult a pair of words to choose the correct collocation from, for example:

This jacket is ruined and it was brand / bone new!

Answers
a brand; **b** freezing; **c** wide; **d** fast; **e** boiling; **f** bone; **g** wide

15 more colloquial expressions (5–10 minutes)

English is very rich in all kinds of colloquial expressions. Understanding their use and being able to use them will make a huge difference to students' fluency.

Answers
a a bite to eat; **b** a drop of rain; **c** hear a pin drop; **d** a hair out of place; **e** at the last minute; **f** from time to time

Before students try to create their own sentences, remind them that they need to use the whole phrase. You could round off the exercise by asking them to share any similar colloquial expressions from their own language(s).

16 Word building: Adjective suffixes (10–15 minutes)

You may like to discuss adjectives that can be formed by adding one of the three suffixes to a few of the words listed with the whole class. You could list them in three columns (-*proof*, -*ish*, -*ic*). Then let students, in pairs or small groups, discuss and form other adjectives. Encourage them to use a good dictionary to help with this exercise.

You could also ask students what other adjective suffixes they are aware of, for example:

-ical:	*grammatical, theatrical, alphabetical*
-ous:	*poisonous, dangerous, courageous*
-ious:	*ambitious, suspicious, infectious*
-ful:	*helpful, delightful, meaningful, peaceful*
-y, -ly:	*windy, spicy, friendly*
-able:	*memorable, fashionable, advisable*
-ible:	*edible, legible, intelligible*

DIFFERENTIATION

To give more **support**, give definitions of suitable adjectives and ask students to write them down, listing them in the correct categories. For example, *something that is more or less red* (= *reddish*).

For more **challenge**, ask students to add two more words to each list – for example, *fireproof, rainproof, Arabic, traumatic, childish, oldish*.

Answers

-proof: bulletproof, foolproof, heatproof, soundproof

-ish: foolish, pinkish, stylish, twentyish, warmish

-ic: ironic, nomadic, panoramic, scenic

---

17 Punctuating direct speech (15–20 minutes)

Many students can use inverted commas – also called quotation marks – around the actual words used by a speaker, but they don't use other elements needed for direct speech, such as commas or capital letters. This exercise aims to encourage students to work logically, so allow them sufficient time to analyse the examples, prompting where necessary.

Remind students that if you start a new paragraph when the speaker is in the middle of a speech, you don't need to close inverted commas at the end of the paragraph. They do need to be opened, however, at the beginning of the next paragraph.

Answers

'What was the best part of your holiday in America?' Juliana asked when she saw Paolo again.

'Going along Highway One from Los Angeles to San Francisco,' said Paolo, without hesitation. 'I wouldn't have missed it for the world.'

'What's so special about Highway One?' Juliana asked, 'Isn't it just another dead straight American highway?'

'Well,' replied Paolo. 'The road runs between [. . .] full of redwood trees. Yes,' he paused for a moment, 'it's truly magnificent.'

'What was the weather like?' Juliana asked. 'Every time I checked the international weather forecast, there was one word: hot.'

'In fact,' Paolo laughed, 'we had stormy weather, but when the sun broke through it created fantastic rainbows. We visited a cove where you can hunt for jade. Anything you find is yours and I'd almost given up looking when I found this.' He reached into his pocket and pulled out a tiny green fragment. 'Here,' he said, 'it's for you.'

C Tourism: The pros and cons

1 Brainstorming (15–20 minutes)

〉 **Critical thinking:** The course is about developing and displaying depth of thought. Awareness of topical issues and an ability to discuss them thoughtfully are good skills to acquire. This exercise is very challenging, and it's a good idea for students to do it in small groups before coming into a larger group to pool their ideas.

Suggested answers

1   **Pleasures**

- Having new experiences, observing customs, sampling local cuisine, visiting local places of interest perhaps very different from home.

- Having more time to explore things / learn a skill / meet people.

- Practising the local language.

- Going home with more understanding of a different part of the world.

Drawbacks

- You may be adversely affected by strange food, a different climate, different culture.

- Lack of knowledge of the area/language may cause frustrations/misunderstandings, and you may even be exploited by unscrupulous people.

- You may be homesick.

- You may find the country you are visiting disappointing and very different from your expectations.

- You may get sunburnt / bitten by insects / lost in a strange place or lose your valuables.

2   **Advantages**

- Tourism creates employment of various kinds in service industries, construction, manufacturing.

- Tourism earns foreign currency.

- Tourism can create more international harmony.

- The wealth generated by tourism can be invested in the economy to improve the infrastructure: roads, hospitals, schools, and so on.

- Some facilities built with tourists in mind may benefit the local population – for example, wildlife parks, swimming pools.

Disadvantages

- The natural beauty of a locality may be destroyed by increased number of visitors.

- Tourists cause damage by using up resources, damaging sites and leaving rubbish.

- The local economy of farming and fishing may be destroyed by the construction of hotels and resorts.

- The cost of food, accommodation and transport may increase for local people.

- Wildlife may be negatively affected.

3   How can tourists behave responsibly when they go abroad?

- Save precious natural resources and energy – for example, they shouldn't waste water and should switch off lights.

- Avoid buying items made from endangered species – for example, ivory, turtle shells, coral.

- Ask (using gestures if necessary) before taking photos/videos of people.

- Respect the local etiquette – dress modestly and avoid behaviour in public which may offend.

- Learn about the host country's history and current affairs.

- Use companies that invest their profits in the local economy and community.

You may like to ask a student to write up the ideas from the whole class on a board or flip chart, if there is time.

2   **Introducing eco-tourism (15–20 minutes)**

Before listening to the audioscript, ask students for their definition of tourism and how they think eco-tourism might be different from normal tourism.

Answers
2 **a** sightseeing tours; **b** hotels; **c** 2.9 trillion; **d** 1.5 billion; **e** 1.8 billion; **f** natural disaster; **g** Machu Picchu; **h** negative impact; **i** respect; **j** Costa Rica

Audioscript track 6.3

Listen to the introduction to a lecture about tourism.

Today we're going to talk about tourism and the effects of mass tourism on a global and on a local scale.

First of all, what is tourism? Tourism can be defined as the activity of people travelling to other places and countries away from their home, usually for short periods of time, for the purpose of leisure, curiosity, fun and relaxation. Types of tourism include beach holidays, sightseeing tours, outdoor activity holidays and individual trips such as backpacking or camping.

Tourists on whatever kind of holiday usually make use of various kinds of commercial services, such as transportation, hotels, tour companies and tourist attractions. Tourism is a multi-million-dollar industry around the world. For many countries, it is the main source of income for their economy, creating jobs and attracting investment. In 2019, for example, global travel and tourism contributed 2.9 trillion dollars to the global economy. In the same year, there were 1.5 billion international tourist arrivals, and it's projected that by 2030, this number will have reached 1.8 billion.

Of course, large numbers of tourists travelling from one part of the globe to another is not without significant negative consequences as well. Many critics point to the excessive pollution created by air travel, especially long haul flights. Furthermore, many local economies that depend solely on tourism suffer greatly when there is a natural disaster or – as happened during the pandemic of 2020–21 – people were suddenly unable to travel. The sheer numbers of people visiting sites of natural beauty and of historic importance, such as Machu Picchu in Peru or Pompeii in Italy, have also caused lasting damage to the actual sites that are being visited.

This brings me to the main topic of today's talk – and that is eco-tourism. What is eco-tourism? Eco-tourism has been defined by the International Eco-Tourism Society as 'responsible travel to natural areas that conserves the environment, sustains the well-being of the local people, and involves interpretation and education'. In other words, it aims to minimise the negative impact on local cultures and the environment, and emphasises the importance of mutual respect between tourists and local residents. Let's look at one example of an eco-tourism project in Costa Rica.

Let's start by looking at the regional economic data . . .

3 Post-listening discussion (10–15 minutes)

1 Encourage students to relate the information in the lecture to their own personal experience. Talk about the photo and ask if they have ever stayed in this type of resort and what their experience was like. Discuss the different ways a resort like this could damage the environment. Ask for suggestions on how this type of resort could do more to help the environment.

2 Students could read out their advertisements and take a vote on the hotel or holiday that sounds most attractive.

4 Pre-reading discussion (5–10 minutes)

The reading comprehension exercise that follows is based on a magazine article encouraging holidaymakers to visit two lovely Italian islands, Sicily and Sardinia.

> **Critical thinking:** Before they begin reading, it would be interesting to hear students' perceptions of these islands, and also to find out how they think foreigners view their own country(ies). You could link their answers to the results of the earlier discussion about tourism as a worldwide issue.

If students have travelled abroad, you could ask what their expectations of the country were before they went and how the visit changed what they thought.

5 Vocabulary in context (5–10 minutes)

Answers
a 8; b 5; c 1; d 6; e 10; f 4; g 11; h 2; i 9; j 3; k 7

Incandescently is an unusually long word. You could ask students to work out how many different words they can make from it by rearranging the letters.

6 Identifying descriptive language (5–10 minutes)

Underlining the descriptive language will reinforce awareness of description, one of the unit's main aims.

It would be a good idea to do the underlining exercise with the class as a whole. Firstly, elicit the fact that descriptive language describes people or places in such a way as to help the reader visualise them. For example, *He was tall and thin* doesn't offer us much. By contrast, *Tall and sickly-thin, with bald head hidden under an old fedora, and eyes like the lifeless black holes of forgotten space* creates a mood and helps us picture the character.

Once students are clear as to the purpose of descriptive language, read out the article about the Italian islands, pausing as necessary, and guiding students towards its use of descriptive language.

7 Comprehension check (8–10 minutes)

The comprehension questions require both short answers and the selection of the correct option about each island from either/or questions. Students also have to decide on the author's attitude to the islands by selecting the correct option from the choices given.

DIFFERENTIATION

Tell students who may need **support** to read only about Sicily (to line 57). They can answer questions 1–3 and, for question 5, change the questions to 'Which of the following are true of Sicily?' Alternatively, the reading task could be done as a jigsaw reading with one of each pair reading about Sicily and the other about Sardinia.

For more **challenge**, ask students to explain the following words/phrases from the article: *cuisine, exotic gardens, rolling plains, slow pace, sleepy hilltop town, prehistoric ancestors, vulture, flamingo.*

Answers

1   A poor economy; physical separation from the mainland

2   Markets like souks and couscous cafés in the capital

3   There are some of the most beautifully decorated buildings in that part of the world

4   any two of: fishing, cycling, walking, riding

5   a   Sardinia (eagles, black vultures and flamingos)

    b   Sardinia (mountain wildness, eagles and black vultures soar over mountains)

    c   Sicily (agriturismo)

    d   Sicily (amphitheatre, temples)

    e   Sicily (Mount Etna)

    f   Sardinia (prehistoric buildings)

    g   Sardinia (childminding services available at Forte Village)

6   **C** The author gives a balanced view; there is no evidence of recommending one island more than another.

8 Post-reading discussion (10–15 minutes)

The mind map is a springboard for students to think about the pros and cons of different types of holiday accommodation. Students can work in pairs to explain and justify their choices. To wrap up the exercise, gather ideas from the class and draw an extended mind map on the board. This task is preparation for one of the exam-style speaking tasks.

DIFFERENTIATION

To offer more **support**, brainstorm some possible reasons on the board before they start.

To make it more **challenging**, ask students to find at least three reasons for their final choice.

9 Language study: Adverbs as modifiers (5–10 minutes)

It is quite common to use adverbs to modify adjectives in English. It's difficult to give rules about their use, but you could tell students that adverbs like *appallingly, horrifyingly,* and similar, collocate with negative words. Adverbs like *staggeringly, amazingly, incredibly* are used when there is a suggestion of surprise – for example, *The balcony had a staggeringly beautiful view of the bay.*

DIFFERENTIATION

If students need **support** with the vocabulary, consider reducing the number of examples. Try focusing on a reduced number of more widely used examples, such as *surprisingly* for things which are not as you expect; *badly* or *seriously* to emphasise something very negative. Provide some practice examples (or get students to come up with their own): *I thought the shop would be cheap but it was surprisingly expensive; The water looked cold but it was surprisingly warm,* and so on.

Suggested answers

a   alarmingly/surprisingly/seriously; **b** fully;
c   strikingly/strangely/seriously/surprisingly;
d   badly; **e** seriously; **f** utterly; **g** alarmingly/

dazzlingly/surprisingly; **h** surprisingly; **i** fully/
painstakingly/badly; **j** fully/surprisingly/faintly;
k alarmingly/seriously; **l** strangely/surprisingly

10 Imagery in descriptions (5–10 minutes)

The following sequence of exercises focuses on
bringing together what students have learnt so far
about describing, building on the earlier work on
describing a leisure activity.

Encourage students to draw on all their language
resources in responding to the question on imagery.
For example, a good response to *'a lovely, broad
landscape with rolling plains and corn-coloured hills'*
would be: 'When I hear this, I think of an open,
peaceful landscape, with an unhurried way of life.'

By contrast, the description of the starker
landscape of Sardinia in *'Eagles and black vultures
soar over the mountains, pink flamingos flash their
wings by the coast'* might elicit the response: 'It
suggests a wild atmosphere, lots of contrasts, very
colourful, lots of fascinating things to see.'

11 Adjectives: Quality not quantity (5–10 minutes)

Students continue to investigate the power of
language by observing how many descriptive
adjectives are used before a noun. It's usually
only one or two, and students can reflect on the
effect that well-chosen adjectives have on creating
atmosphere.

Encourage students to choose an example of
descriptive language and explore it.

12 Comparing two styles (10–15 minutes)

> **Critical thinking:** Comparing and contrasting
the two styles will bring descriptive techniques
into sharper focus. Text A reflects the way many
students write in simple, short sentences, with
a limited vocabulary, resulting in a repetitive
style. Students need to move on from this.
Text B integrates the techniques students have
been learning so far, using intensifiers, a broad
vocabulary and more complex sentences.

13 Developing your writing style

Practice (10–15 minutes)

Students could work in pairs to draft and redraft
the description. Encourage them to make use of the
ideas introduced in this exercise.

To give more **support**, elicit the key ideas of the
paragraph: the marketplace, the people, the
town, its buildings and restaurants, and so on.
Assign one key area to each group of students.
Encourage them to experiment with combining
the sentences in different ways so that they are
more concise. Compare ideas as a class before
asking students to rewrite the whole paragraph.

Example answer

> The town developed around an ancient
> rectangular marketplace. It has many medieval
> buildings and a wide diversity of restaurants
> offering delicious food from several different
> cultures. The local people have a traditional
> way of life and dress, and are very hospitable,
> honest and welcoming.

14 Writing your own description (15–20 minutes)

This would be a good homework exercise.
Encourage students to make as many drafts as they
feel are necessary.

Provide a basic partial frame for students
who need more **support** to make a start. For
example, *We stayed in a . . . hotel/house/town,
which . . . It was beautifully/conveniently located
in/near . . . One of the best things about our
holiday was . . . which . . ., and so on.*

International overview (5–10 minutes)

1   The top four international tourist destinations at
the time of writing were France, Spain, the USA,
China (in that order). It should be interesting
to hear students' reactions to this fact and their
opinions about the reasons.

Questions 2–4 should also produce some interesting
ideas and discussion.

15 Giving a short talk (20–30 minutes)

You may like to record a few of the best talks for analysis later.

16 Words from names (5–10 minutes)

Some verbs such as *pasteurise* (milk) or nouns such as *sandwich* are, of course, named after the individuals who invented them. In this exercise, students match the invention to the name of the person or place.

Names, their meanings, origins and associations are a source of great interest. Sometimes students have an adopted English name or are aware that the name of their country or city has a different name in English. Some people moving to settle in an English-speaking country anglicise their family names.

The discussion could also stimulate exploration of how family and place names originated. Many English family names were derived from place names (*Worthington, York*), nicknames (*Armstrong*), family relationships (*Johnson*) and trade names (*Carpenter, Baker, Fletcher, Smith, Miller*).

Ask students to contribute what they know about the origins of names in their culture(s).

The impact of modern life on names could also be investigated. For example, you could ask students to reflect on trademark names such as Google, Amazon, Twitter, Instagram, YouTube and Bluetooth, which have become a part of everyday language.

Answers
1 a Sandwich; b Marathon; c Fahrenheit; d Denim;
e Morse; f Volta; g Rugby; h Diesel

17 More homophones (5–10 minutes)

This exercise gives further practice with homophones taken from the reading texts. Some are less obvious than others – for example, *boar/bore*. This will give students more insight into the range of homophones in English.

Answers
blue/blew; boar/bore; deer/dear; flower/flour; herd/heard; meet/meat/mete; real/reel; route/root
scene/seen; sea/see; soar/sore/saw; wear/where/ware

D Personal challenges

1 Reading an example email (5–10 minutes)

This email provides a reliable example of the sort of writing students should be aiming for. Start by describing the photo and asking what students know about Tasmania.

2 Comprehension check (5–10 minutes)

Answers
1   Tasmania
2   She was nervous. Her feelings weren't justified; she didn't feel lonely because the group leaders were so thoughtful.
3   Canoeing. The instructor made her laugh and forget her fears; she made quick progress and was happy with what she learnt in a week.
4   She thinks Lucia would like the place, the people and all the different things that can be done on an activity holiday.
5   She loved it and wants to do it again.

3 Analysing the email (5–10 minutes)

Answers
1   **Paragraph 1:** reason for writing

   Paragraph 2: description of place and weather

   Paragraph 3: description of canoeing lessons

   Paragraph 4: why Lucia would enjoy it too
2   Students should try to comment on the use of adjectives and intensifiers such as *so* and *really*.
3   Students sometimes find it difficult to say why something they like would also interest others. This paragraph gives another example of how to do this, with useful expressions for closing an email.

4 Vocabulary check: The weather (5–10 minutes)

Before students do the exercise, check their understanding of the following vocabulary:

Blizzard: A severe snowstorm

Shower: A brief, usually light fall of rain

Dew: Very small drops of water that form on the ground overnight

Dusk: The time between day and night

Overcast: The sky is covered in cloud

Gale: A very strong wind

Drizzle: Very light rain that falls in small drops

Thaw: A period of warm weather that causes ice and snow to melt

Drought: A long period without rain which causes a shortage of water

---

DIFFERENTIATION

To provide more **support**, write the definitions on the board and ask students to identify the matching words.

For extra **challenge**, ask students to write their definitions for these words. Students who finish early can be asked to brainstorm five more weather words and write definitions for them. For example: *downpour, breeze, heatwave, sleet, hail, slush.*

Answers

a false; b false; c true; d true; e false; f true; g true; h true; i true; j false

---

5 Spelling revision (2–3 minutes)

This exercise gives students the chance to revise some of the spelling rules they learnt in earlier units (see Unit 2, Section D8 and Unit 3, Section D8 in the Coursebook).

6 Writing about the weather (5–10 minutes)

Example answer

We're having a good time here but the weather isn't great. Every day starts *misty* or even *foggy*. This clears up by midday and we get a little *hazy* sunshine. We had a *rainy* day yesterday and the ground was too *muddy* for walking. It's generally *chilly* and I'm glad we brought warm clothes. Our boat trip was cancelled because it was *stormy*. We're hoping for calmer weather tomorrow.

7 Discussion (5–10 minutes)

> **Critical thinking:** You could begin by reading out the information about voluntary work abroad in the Coursebook. Students then work in pairs to discuss the questions. If students struggle to think of how volunteers abroad can overcome the problems they face, suggest the following ideas: volunteers can take part in an induction scheme in which they learn about the host country; volunteers can do some training in a particular area before they go aboard; volunteers can talk to other people who have had experience of living and working abroad.

8 Building a blog from notes (15–20 minutes)

Elicit the fact that a blog is a website that takes the form of a diary or commentary on particular subjects or events. You may like to tell students that the word *blog* is a combination of *web* and *log*, with *web* being an abbreviation of *world wide web*, and *log* being a kind of record of events during the voyage of a ship or plane. Point out or elicit that people who write blogs are called *bloggers* and that bloggers write *posts*. The blog could be checked by getting students to complete it on the board.

Example answer

At first, I was very busy but now I have time to update my blog. I'm enjoying myself here. The weather is warm and sunny, except for last night when there was a big storm which turned (the) paths into rivers.

The family I'm staying with are very kind. The house is three-bedroomed and is quite comfortable. I am very close to my 'sisters', who tell me off if I do anything wrong! Each morning I wake up to the sound of exotic birds darting among the trees.

Yesterday, I took a bus through breathtaking countryside to the local city. I went to a bustling market. Everywhere people were selling things but I'm not sure who was buying!

I'm helping to look after young children in a nursery school. The children are delightful and are very polite. The work is demanding but rewarding.

I miss everyone at home but I feel I am growing up / have grown up quickly and I'm more confident now.

I will / am going to upload photos tomorrow and would love to read your comments.

You may like to circulate a copy of the completed magazine article or project it on the whiteboard. Ask some comprehension questions about the article – for example, What is the overall purpose of the article? What does she like / dislike about her job? What kind of place is Rhodes? Why do tourists like to go there? On the whole, would you be interested in this kind of job? Why or why not? What other kinds of benefits or drawbacks might there be?

9 Look, say, cover, write, check (5–10 minutes)

Regular short tests give students a sense of progress. In this exercise, they learn problematic spellings. Ask students if they have any other tips for remembering difficult spellings. See Unit 1, Section B13 for a reminder of the 'Look, say, cover, write, check' method for learning vocabulary.

10 Discussion (15–20 minutes)

You may like to check that students understand what a tour guide actually does before going into the exercise in the Coursebook. They need to understand that tour guides are normally employed by a travel company to look after tourists who have booked holidays with the company. Their duties may include interpreting and explaining things tourists need to know about the places they are staying in – for example, the opening times of banks and shops, how to get a doctor, and so on. They will help sort out problems that tourists encounter, such as getting ill, losing valuables, problems with accommodation. The job sometimes includes taking the group to places of interest and places of entertainment in the evening. Depending on the type of trip, a tour guide may accompany the group to other cities or destinations on the itinerary, or even across continents. Tour guides usually wear some sort of uniform so they are easily recognisable.

Point out that, unlike a tour guide, a resort rep (representative) is usually based in one specific holiday resort.

11 Reordering a magazine article (5–10 minutes)

Answer
The correct order is: l, j, e, m, c, d, n, f, a, h, k, b, g, i

DIFFERENTIATION

For students who need **support**, give them the topic of the three paragraphs and tell them to begin by dividing the sentences by paragraph: 1 Describing Rhodes, 2 Describing the job, 3 Final conclusions and recommendations. For an extra **challenge**, ask students to add one more sentence to each paragraph.

GRAMMAR SPOTLIGHT (10–15 MINUTES)

Students will be familiar with adverbs of frequency, but they often misplace them in sentences, so they will appreciate some clarification about where the adverb should go. You may want to start by writing the adverbs on the board in random order and asking students to rank them in order of frequency.

Answers
1 usually, always, often, seldom, sometimes, hardly, rarely, never
2 a I always ride my bike to school.
   b Maria often goes swimming with her friends. (*already correct*)
   c He usually prefers the buffet-style breakfast.
   d Visitors to the Taj Mahal are seldom disappointed.
   e We sometimes play tennis after college / We play tennis after college sometimes.
   f Lewis is hardly ever on time – it's so annoying!
   g The children rarely go to the cinema.
   h She has never been on holiday abroad.

DIFFERENTIATION

Provide **support** with further controlled practice – for example, based on their daily routine (e.g. eat breakfast – *I always eat breakfast*; get the bus to school – *I usually get the bus to school*, etc.). For extra **challenge**, ask students to make sentences using other adverbs of frequency – for example, *occasionally, frequently, regularly, normally*.

Occasionally, sometimes, often, frequently and *usually* can also go at the beginning or end of a sentence. *Rarely* can be used at the beginning of a sentence with inverted verb / subject. For example, *Rarely have I seen such an amazing sunset* as opposed to *I have rarely seen such an amazing sunset*. Rarely can also go at the end of a sentence, often with 'very'. For example, *We go to the cinema very rarely*.

WIDER PRACTICE

1   If tourism is a big issue in the area in which you are teaching, you could ask local tourist officials to talk to students about employment prospects, ways of managing tourism that respect the environment and heritage, and future tourism projects.

2   The travel theme lends itself well to the study of maps. Map reading is a very useful life skill, as well as understanding the points of the compass, so it is well worth practising.

3   If you have access to the internet, you may be able to find interesting websites and videos that reflect the unit themes. Travel review websites and blogs are popular, and there is a growing emphasis on activity / adventure / special interest holidays, eco-tourism, and so on. Students could watch these and do the following: listen for factual detail; compare places to stay; decide which of the places presented they'd like to visit and why; review the programmes, offering suggestions for ways in which they could be improved.

4   Students might like to do a cross-curricular project in which they investigate a topic that draws on geography, history, literature or technology, and so on and present it to the class. The following topics might give you some ideas:

   –   An investigation into popular pastimes – their origins and reasons for their popularity

   –   Any topic around the seven natural wonders of the world

   –   An investigation into the history, design and decoration of buildings the students are curious about

   –   An investigation into an ancient civilisation, describing its impact on the world.

5   If you know of someone who has visited an unusual or exciting place, they could either come into the class to describe it and answer questions, or you could record him or her talking about it and replay the talk for discussion. Sometimes a parent or relative of a student is delighted to be invited to share their experiences with the class.

6   As a change from brainstorming ideas for a topic, why not try brainwriting? Each student writes an idea about the topic on a slip of paper. No names are used. The slips of paper are collected and each anonymous idea is discussed in turn in the group.

Exam-style questions

Reading and writing

Reading and Writing: note-taking

This exercise provides practice with answering comprehension questions that require note-taking.

You might wish to recommend these simple steps for successful note-taking:

1   Read the question carefully and underline the key words as you read.

2   Look carefully at the heading and any pictures to pick up clues about the content before you begin to read the text.

3   Read the text fairly quickly, with as much concentration as possible. Then reread more slowly any parts you found confusing. Don't worry if you don't understand bits of the text – you may need to read through the complete text before you understand it all properly. Reread the text again if necessary.

4   Underline key parts of the text that are relevant to the question as soon as you notice them.

5   Write short notes by copying short, relevant words and phrases from the text, or by using words of your own. You do not need to write complete sentences. Be selective, and remember that you are making notes not writing paragraphs. Your notes should be brief, relevant and easy to understand.

Answers

1   Knowledge of engineering, architecture and astronomy; built beautiful cities with roads and palaces; Quechua language that was widely spoken but was not written down

2   It is very high in the mountains; it is built on a steep mountain slope; they had no metal tools; they had no wheels

Reading and Writing: informal and formal

You will find advice on general approaches to exam-style writing exercises at the end of the 'Teaching support' section in the Introduction.

Example answer

Formal writing

Bullen's is perfectly located in the centre of the country, between a lake and a river, with woods to the west and mountains to the east. The accommodation is simple, but perfectly adequate, and the staff are helpful and friendly.

Although the activities are limited in number, those that are available are really exciting and I was happy to repeat some of them, for example, kayaking on the lake because the instructors were so good. By the end of the week I had really improved my skills. Ziplining across the river was also a magic experience. For the evenings, there was a games room with table tennis and board games - but no TV.

I can recommend Bullen's to everyone, especially people who enjoy outdoor activities. Moreover, there are lots of animals and birds nearby, making it a paradise for nature lovers. While not cheap, the prices are quite reasonable, bearing in mind what is on offer.

Try it for yourself!

(160 words)

Listening

Listening: sentence completion

Students complete gapped multiple-choice questions based on a talk.

Ask students to look first at the photo and say what clues it gives them about what they are going to hear. Then ask them to read the questions very carefully before listening to the recording, underlining key words or phrases that will help them identify the answers. Point out that answering this question relies on understanding paraphrase, so students should be prepared to listen out for words and phrases that mean the same as some of the options.

Students should listen twice to the recording. In a class situation, they can listen as often as you think is necessary. It is helpful to check the answers by pausing the recording in the appropriate places. If they find part of the recording tricky and can't answer a particular question on a first listening, they should make sure they move on to the next question, otherwise they may miss the answer to that one too. For this kind of multiple-choice exercise, a useful strategy may be to eliminate the incorrect answers before deciding on the correct answer.

Point out that question 7 is an inference question where the meaning is implied but not stated explicitly.

Answers
1C; 2C; 3A; 4A; 5C; 6C; 7A; 8B

Audioscript track 6.4

You will hear a museum tour guide giving a talk about Viking history and culture.

For each question, choose the correct answer, A, B, or C, and put a tick in the appropriate box.

You will hear the talk twice.

Now look at questions 1–8.

I am delighted to show you our museum's marvellous collection of Viking artefacts. The Vikings were fierce warriors but also clever traders and adventurous travellers.

The Vikings were superb sailors and left Norway, Sweden and Denmark and went to areas now called Western Europe, the Middle East, Canada, Greenland and Russia. They used the sun, stars and winds to navigate across stormy, dangerous seas. Their wooden longships were narrow and light, which made them versatile. They could be landed on beaches and rowed upriver when they were inland. In modern times, some of the actual boats the Vikings sailed in have been excavated intact from the bottom of riverbeds. It seems the thick, mud-like clay acted as a preservative, which stopped the wood of their boats from rotting away.

On our left, we can see a magnificent reconstruction of a Viking longship. The intricately carved longship you see here is a warrior ship and has 40 oars for rowing when required. The sail is painted red because the Vikings thought that would frighten the enemy. The rack that runs alongside the side of the ship was made for holding wooden shields.

Vikings were skilled craftsmen and, on the wall here, behind the longship, you can see examples of their weapons: iron spears, swords, battle axes, crossbows and arrows. Archery was learned at an early age, as archery skills were essential for hunting as well as for fighting. The wooden shields and crossbows you see are replicas, as unfortunately wood rots quickly and very few of the real shields and crossbows have been found.

On my tablet, I can show you a famous engraving of a Viking. You'll see he is wearing a heavy bearskin cloak and a helmet made from a bear's head. If you look closely, you can see the frightening expression on his face and his threatening body language. To develop the correct mental state for warfare, warriors dressed in helmets and cloaks made from bearskins and then worked themselves into a fierce rage. In English, we get the word *berserk*, which means being so angry that we are out of control, from an old Norse word for bearskin.

Making weapons look beautiful was also very important. Notice how the hilt of the sword is beautifully decorated with a pattern of inlaid silver. A warrior's most treasured possession was his sword, and he gave the sword a particular name and had it engraved on the hilt. When the warrior died, his axe and sword were buried with him.

Speaking

You will find advice on general approaches to speaking exercises at the end of the 'Teaching support' section in the Introduction.

If students are doing this exercise under examination conditions, warm-up questions may help to put them at ease. These are included in the corresponding Coursebook unit.

>7 Student life

Learning plan

AOs	Key learning intentions	Success criteria
R3, L3, S1, S3	Explore the topic of study and student life	• Students can discuss issues related to student life • Students can express opinions about life at college or university • Students can talk about exam anxiety, stress and ways to relax
R1, R2, R3	Identify ideas, opinions and attitudes in a magazine article about exam stress	• Students can scan texts and identify relevant information • Students can use information drawn from a text to form their own opinions • Students can evaluate different responses to a problem
W1, W2, W3, W4	Give advice in an email, using appropriate register and style	• Students can use appropriate register and style in an informal email • Students can respond and give advice in an encouraging and supportive manner • Students can organise their ideas into a coherent written text
L1, L2, L3, L4	Identify factual details and understand what is implied in a talk about student counselling	• Students can predict what they will hear and check their predictions • Students can identify and select specific information • Students can understand the general meaning and purpose of a lecture
S1, S2, S3	Use a range of vocabulary and grammar for talking about problems and giving advice	• Students can identify language for asking for and giving advice • Students can use a variety of expressions to give advice • Students can use a range of vocabulary for talking about problems, anxiety and stress

Overview

The main aim of this unit is to develop the skills that students need for writing advice in an email. Giving advice, particularly in written English, presents difficulties even for native speakers. This is partly because the tone and register are tricky to get right – subtle variations of tone can have a powerful impact on the effect of what is said, and there are important cultural differences between languages in terms of what is socially acceptable.

This unit also focuses on the techniques that help sustain an idea and develop it into a complete paragraph. This is one of the key areas where students need support if their

hard work is going to translate into success.

The unit includes an analysis of tone and register in spoken English as part of a broader analysis of interactive techniques in conversation. This will help students become more familiar with the discourse strategies needed in the Speaking test and improve classroom talk in general. In addition, there are opportunities for students to practise taking notes while listening to a talk about college counselling and understanding what they read in a magazine article on exam tension.

THEME

The unit is thematically linked through a number of topics of particular interest to young students. These include:

- leaving home to study – independence versus security
- coping with exam tensions and developing study skills
- making friends in a new environment

- responses to bullying.

The language study and themes have been selected to combine popular topics with skills practice.

There are many exercises in the unit, and you could choose to really focus on those areas where development is needed.

LANGUAGE WORK

The language work includes detailed work on useful phrases for asking for and giving advice, modals and idiomatic expressions. Language study sections focus on the use of *should* in the past as well as in the passive form. Idioms are natural in informal contexts; students enjoy learning them, and they can greatly enhance the effectiveness

of tone and register. Spelling and pronunciation exercises focus on silent letters. Vocabulary is developed with more work on word building, and punctuation is also revised.

The 'Grammar spotlight' looks at text messages and how 'text speak' differs from more formal, grammatical written English.

Common misconceptions

Misconception	How to identify	How to overcome
Using the infinitive after *should* instead of **should + have + past participle** when talking about past events. Example: *The show should start at 19.30 but it started 45 minutes later.*	Take some (anonymous) examples from students' written work (correct and incorrect) and write them on the board. Ask students to identify the incorrect examples. Point out the surrounding context and ask whether it is about the past, the present or the future. Correct example: *The show should have started at 19.30 but it started 45 minutes later.*	Give some examples of past and present situations and ask students to give advice on what should have happened for each one.
Using the past form of *have* with **should** in the passive. Example: *The restaurant should had been opened last week.*	Write a mixture of examples using the passive, some with *should* and some without. Ask why the verb *have* is in the past in some sentences and not in others. Correct example: *The restaurant should have been opened last week.*	Create a situation that will help students remember these two structures. Example: *The students arrived 30 minutes late for the test. Why? They hadn't been told about the new starting time. They should have checked on the test website the day before.*

Introducing the unit topic (5–10 minutes)

Working with a partner, students look at the photo and discuss the questions.

Ask students to look at the photo carefully. What does it show about the atmosphere of this college? Are the students relaxed or stressed? Happy or worried? Serious or carefree? Confident or shy? What can we tell from their clothing, hairstyles, facial expressions and the things they are carrying convey? What are the students talking about? What kind of study habits and routines are probably encouraged at this college? You may want to brainstorm ideas for what the students in the photo are talking about and suggest mini-dialogues between them.

Encourage students to think about how their lives will be different at college or university. They might think about study habits and routines, teacher expectations and the new skills they may need to learn, but they might also discuss aspects of everyday life that may be new or different. They should realise that everyone will have different challenges, depending on their personality and previous experiences.

> **Digital coursebook:** At the start of the lesson, use this video to introduce and review:

- a range of vocabulary related to the topic of higher education

- *should* + past participle.

Read the question on the title screen and ask learners what they think they might see. Then play the video all the way through and check learners' predictions.

Play the video a second time, pausing to discuss what is being shown and the questions on the end screen. You can take the opportunity to revise words and phrases associated with the topic of higher education. Note that questions 2 and 3 on the end-screen are differentiated two-part questions. The first part should be relatively easily accessed from the video. The second part requires reasoning and personal opinion. More confident learners will be able to offer more extensive reasons for their ideas. Take note of whether learners use *should* + *have* + past participle in their answers to question 1.

You may like to play the video a third time for consolidation.

A Challenges of student life

1 Completing a checklist (15–20 minutes)

The topic opens with a discussion about looking after yourself at college or university. Use the photos to elicit different aspects of life at college or university that might be exciting or stressful. If you feel this is culturally or socially outside students' experience, you may prefer to start by getting them to think about transitional times in their lives, such as moving to a new town or starting a new school. You could ask them to think about what was good or difficult about a particular situation, and what they feel they learnt from it. Elicit concepts relating to self-sufficiency, developing a larger range of social and practical skills, making new friends, relating to different kinds of people, understanding new rules, finding one's way around a strange area, and so on.

If you have students who have already experienced being away from home to study, then it would be ideal to capitalise on their experience and let their views be your starting point.

Let students complete the checklist by themselves.

DIFFERENTIATION

To give more **support** with the checklist, suggest that students choose five topics they know most about.

For more **challenge**, ask students to add five more topics to the list.

2 Pre-listening task (10–15 minutes)

Once students have given their answers to questions 1–4, it would be a good idea to demonstrate how to interact with someone badly and how to do it well. You could choose a student to play the role of someone about to go to university. You play the role of their friend wanting to know how they feel about leaving home. Do two role plays. In the first, look bored, do not make eye contact, do not smile and do not use any of the communication strategies listed. In the second, do the reverse: look and sound interested, ask open questions, offer encouragement, paraphrase, ask for more information, and offer advice. Then ask the class to describe the differences in your attitude in the two role plays and to say why your interactive skills were better in the second.

The aim of this sequence of exercises is to increase students' understanding of a lively conversation. It will help them cope better with the Speaking test and improve their classroom talk. In the audio recording, Luke and Malika take an equal part in the conversation, whereas in the test students are given the best possible opportunity to demonstrate their oral skills. In oral pairwork in class, students sometimes tend to take turns giving their opinion, listening to each other but not really interacting. The work on interactive skills will help them move on from this to greater fluency.

3 Reading and listening at the same time (5–10 minutes)

Once students have listened to and read the dialogue, check that they have underlined the phrases that show that the speakers have good interactive skills. Language note: Note that the word 'college' can be used to refer to either university or to another type of tertiary education, such as technical college (UK) or community college (US). It can sometimes also refer to a part of a university, such as the colleges of Oxford, Cambridge or London University.

Ask students why it is important to show enthusiasm, kindness and affection while listening to a friend who is talking about a problem. Elicit the idea that, when we give advice to someone, it should not sound as if we are giving them a command. We should try to put ourselves into the position of the friend and imagine what it would be like to experience their difficulties.

Suggested answers

Asking open questions: What are you anxious about?

Giving encouragement/reassurance: You always seem such an independent person.

Paraphrasing: You mean you've already found a part-time job?

Asking for more information/clarification: What do you mean exactly? Can you give me an example?

Empathising / asking for empathy: Do you know what I mean? I know exactly how you feel. It's the same for me.

Making suggestions/offering advice: Maybe you could . . . ? Have you thought about . . . ?

If you share a common language with your students, it's a good idea to compare and contrast ways of offering advice in the two languages. It may also be worth comparing the similarities and differences of tone and register between the two languages.

Giving advice orally

Elicit from students the unique elements of face-to-face contact: body language, the opportunity to smile / to look sorry / to tailor what we say to the person's reactions, the scope for the listener to ask questions.

You can set up the following mini role plays as extension activities if you think it's appropriate. Ask students what they would say in these circumstances:

- Your friend is keen to leave school and take a job but you feel they would be wiser to stay on and get some qualifications. What do you say?

- A young man hoping to be promoted at his firm is rejected after an interview because he lacked knowledge about how the company wanted to develop in the future. He asks his manager for advice about how to do better next time. You are the manager. What do you say?

- Your sister wants to take a year off before college to travel. You think she might not want to study when she comes back. What do you say?

Audioscript track 7.1

Luke:	How do you feel about starting university this autumn?
Malika:	Oh, you know, I'm excited, but a bit anxious, too.
Luke:	Really? What are you anxious about?
Malika:	Well, I've never had to organise my timetable before and manage my study time. My teacher or my parents always remind me to study. I'm just not sure if I'll be able to stay motivated. Do you know what I mean?
Luke:	But you always seem such an independent person! I think you're underestimating yourself. I'm sure you'll get the hang of it once you start. Is there anything else worrying you?

Malika: Well, I'm worried about making friends. I don't think I'm very good at meeting people and—

Luke: Oh, don't worry about that! I'm sure there will be plenty of opportunities to socialise and meet new people. Anyway, everyone'll be in the same boat!

Malika: That's true. How about you? Do you feel anxious about starting university?

Luke: Yes, I'm a bit anxious about finances. My parents are paying the tuition fees for me, but I'll also have a part-time job to help pay for my food and accommodation.

Malika: You mean you've already found a part-time job? I'm impressed!

Luke: Yes, it's in student services so I'll be on campus all the time.

Malika: That sounds excellent! Maybe you could start with just a few hours and increase them later when you have a better idea about your studies?

Luke: That's a very good idea. I'll try that! I'm also a bit worried that I won't be able to keep up with coursework.

Malika: What do you mean exactly? Can you give me an example?

Luke: I mean, what if I'm not clever enough to write all the essays and pass the exams? My parents have really high expectations of me!

Malika: I know exactly how you feel. It's the same for me. My parents want me to be a professor one day! Have you thought about talking to some of the students in the previous year and asking them for some tips?

Luke: No, but my mum's friend has a daughter who started there last year. Maybe I'll ask her for some advice.

4 Conversation study (5–10 minutes)

This exercise encourages students to notice how we use specific phrases to make a conversation sound friendly. Put students into pairs or small groups to highlight the parts of the conversation which illustrate each of points a–d.

Answers

a Malika's use of questions (*What do you mean exactly? Can you give me an example?*) shows that she is trying to understand what Luke is saying to her.

b Malika's suggestion *Maybe you could . . . ?* is friendly. She doesn't tell her friend to do it, but simply suggests that this might be a good idea.

c Luke says, '*But you always seem such an independent person! I think you're underestimating yourself.*' This suggests that he has a high opinion of Malika and wants to boost her self-esteem.

d Malika's use of empathetic language (*I know exactly how you feel. It's the same for me.*) shows that she understands Luke's feelings.

5 Developing your own conversation (15–20 minutes)

Tell students they are going to practise having a conversation about doing something challenging such as going away to college. Read out the five bullet points and make sure that students understand them. You can do this by asking students to give an example of how to explain an idea clearly, be a good listener, offer appropriate advice, and so on.

Give students a couple of minutes to look back at their answers for Section A1. Once you have put students in pairs, give them time to decide what they are going to talk about. If students respond well to this task, you could ask them to role play further conversations on similar topics.

DIFFERENTIATION

To provide more **support**, tell students to focus on just two or three of the points from Section A1. The first time they do the role play they should focus on keeping the conversation going rather than trying to correctly use phrases from Section A2; they can look back at these afterwards and have a second go. Some students may prefer to write their dialogue before they record it.

For more **challenge**, set a target of using at least five expressions from Section A2.

6 Recording your conversation (10–15 minutes)

Students can make recordings using their phones. Alternatively, if your school has audio recording equipment, use that. Put students into small groups to listen to their recordings. Encourage them to give one another constructive feedback: What did they do well? What could they improve? You may want to encourage them to use a checklist to evaluate their performance. Remember to encourage positive and supportive feedback.

7 Comparing languages (5–8 minutes)

› **Critical thinking:** This exercise would be best set for homework. Encourage students to make a short recording of two conversations, one in English and one in their own language. The conversations should be on exactly the same theme. Students can then analyse the recordings, looking at the differences and similarities between their language and English. Point out that they need to consider tone as well as the interactive techniques used.

8 Reading and discussing an email about problems (10–15 minutes)

› **Critical thinking:** Before they begin reading, ask students to find out if the writer of the email has difficulties at university that they anticipate for themselves. This will help them focus on the email and provides continuity with the earlier work in the unit. The pairwork after the email provides more opportunities to exploit and reinforce advice language.

9 Reading an email offering advice (5–10 minutes)

This email serves as a good example of how a friendly tone can be achieved while giving advice. Point out that students could look back at it as a good example of an advice email.

It's important after the pairwork to get feedback on this reply to Sheryl's email to make sure there have been no misunderstandings. Check comprehension of the following idiomatic expressions. In Sheryl's email: quite at home (= very much at home), get my act together (= get organised). In Bianca's email: keep on top of things (= keep things under control), pace yourself (= to do something at a steady pace so that you don't get too tired or run out of time).

Answers

Students should underline these phrases:

One thing you might find helpful is . . .

Try to . . .

all you really have to do is . . .

why not . . . ?

don't forget to . . .

It's not a good idea to . . .

You won't forget to . . . , will you?

10 Analysing the advice email (15–20 minutes)

This is a key exercise, so you may prefer to monitor the discussion through a whole-class approach. Use this opportunity to ask students why the tone of the reply is particularly appropriate. How does Bianca express empathy and reassurance? Encourage students to think about the differences between giving advice in an email and face to face. Discuss how language in an email has to compensate for the fact that you can't smile or show sympathy through non-verbal communication. The pair of emails exchange views between peers, and students should note the relaxed tone and register.

11 Advice phrases (5–10 minutes)

› **Critical thinking:** Many students can make basic use of modals such as *should* and *must*. They should, however, be aiming for more sophisticated advice language. This exercise provides further practice in discriminating between registers and shades of tone and meaning.

Draw out that stronger expressions include direct commands (*You should / need to / had better*). Intensifiers such as *absolutely* in '*You absolutely must*' also make the advice much stronger. You could ask students to suggest alternatives to *absolutely*, such as *certainly, definitely, really*. Ask them to suggest ways of softening some of the stronger expressions – for example, *I think . . . I wonder if . . . Have you tried . . . ? Might it be a good idea if you . . . ?*

More low-key advice sounds more like a suggestion or a question (*Why don't you? / How about?*) and often uses softeners such as *perhaps, maybe, could* or *might*. Discuss ways in which intonation and tone of voice could make some of these expressions sound stronger or more bossy.

Check that all students can use the correct verb form after the different phrases. Go through the list with them, eliciting examples of advice you might give to someone starting life at university and allowing other students to comment on and correct the grammatical forms as necessary – for example, *Why not join a sports club . . . ?* (not *to join*), *You may like to try working in the college bar . . . ?* (not *to work*).

DIFFERENTIATION

For more **challenge**, ask students to suggest some more indirect ways of giving advice – for example, by referring to one's own or another's experience as in *Something I've tried is . . . ; My sister found it very useful to . . .*

12 Expressing problems and asking for advice (10–15 minutes)

The way we express problems is linked to who we are and the culture we come from.

You may like to highlight the indirectness of the informal statement *I'm not sure what to do.* This invites the listener to advise/suggest without asking directly for help. Advice/suggestions would then be offered in a seemingly casual way – for example, *I suppose you could always . . .*

If students are having difficulty thinking of problems, possible prompts are:

- A mother is waiting for her young child to return from school. They are three hours late.

- An expensive pair of shoes you bought ten days ago have completely fallen to pieces. On the receipt, it says that faulty goods have to be returned within seven days.

- You're talking to your friend about redecorating your bedroom. You're undecided between redoing the room in white or another colour.

- You're on holiday in a foreign country. You know no one and do not speak the language. You find that your bag with your passport and money has been stolen. What do you say when you telephone home?

You may want to discuss different contexts where problems can occur. Discuss problems at school or at work that might be difficult for someone to talk about.

13 Listening to students' problems (10 minutes)

1   Before students tackle the question, ask them to read the statements in the second column and discuss the kinds of problems they may relate to. Make sure they understand that they will hear six different voices on the audio recording and have to match the statements to the speakers.

2   Ask students to use expressions for giving advice from Section A11. When playing the recording for the second time, you may want to pause after each segment to check the answers.

DIFFERENTIATION

To give more **support** for question 1, ask questions about each segment. *How does speaker 1 feel about his new school? Why does speaker 2 like football? Why did speaker 3 choose science? What does speaker 4 dislike about French lessons? What does speaker 5 have to ask another student about? What kind of tasks is speaker 6 good at?*

For more **challenge**, discuss which problems are most easily solved. Ask students to rank the problems in order of difficulty or categorise them in different ways – for example, whether they are problems the speakers can solve by themselves or need outside help with.

Answers
1 C; **2** D; **3** A; **4** F; **5** G; **6** E; (B is not used)

Audioscript track 7.2

Listen to six students talking about their problems.

Speaker 1:   We moved to this town when my parents changed jobs a year ago, so I've been at this school for about six months now. The teachers are quite nice and I'm enjoying the course work. My favourite subject is art, and I can use the art studio after school whenever I want. But I find it really difficult to talk to the other students. They've all known each other for three years and they're just not interested in me. I feel like I'm being excluded.

Speaker 2: I've been in the football team for two years and I love it! There's usually a match with a team from another school every other week. And we've been doing quite well in the league this year. We train at least twice a week and it's really good for keeping fit, and also for my general mental health. The thing is, I've got big exams coming up this year and my parents say that I've got to give up football so I can study more. I understand why, but I really want to stay with the team!

Speaker 3: In Year 2, we had to choose whether to study physics and chemistry or music and art. I chose science because maths was my best subject and I got top marks in all my exams. I thought that in the future, I might become a medical researcher developing new medicines or vaccines to help people. But now I'm at the end of Year 2 and I've realised I'm not enjoying these subjects at all! In fact, I can't ever imagine having a career in this field. I'd really rather study literature or art.

Speaker 4: My favourite subject is French. I love everything about France! The art, the literature and films. I think I'm quite good at communicating in French conversation lessons too. The problem is that our French teacher makes us do presentations and it just makes me really nervous. I hate standing in front of the whole class – I'm afraid they're going to laugh at me! And I never do well in them.

Speaker 5: I've just started doing a laboratory science class on my chemistry course. I love doing the experiments, setting them up and trying things out. It's fascinating! The teacher is really nice too, but she speaks really fast and I don't always catch what she's saying. Sometimes I end up doing the wrong thing and have to check with another

student. Then the teacher gets annoyed because it looks like I'm chatting and not paying attention.

Speaker 6: I think I'm quite good at getting my homework done on time. I like doing worksheets and essays and tasks that have a clear outcome. But when it comes to tasks that are less clearly defined, I get really stuck. The teacher asked us to think of an idea for a science project and I just can't seem to come up with anything good enough. I mean, the field is so broad, it could be anything, and I just don't know where to start.

14 Tone and register in students' emails (15–20 minutes)

> **Critical thinking:** In this exercise, students study extracts from emails giving advice. The extracts reveal typical weaknesses at this level, when students struggle to convey ideas and attitudes with limited language resources.

DIFFERENTIATION

The exercise is ideal for mixed-ability work in small groups. **Challenge** students who have a quicker 'feel' for tone and register by asking them to **support** classmates who may be more caught up with the basic meaning of the language.

Answer
Extract e is the most suitably written paragraph.

15 Rewriting a paragraph (10–15 minutes)

Encourage students to rewrite one of the paragraphs they thought was inappropriate, with help if necessary. Brainstorm ideas with the class for a list of points they should pay attention to: appropriate tone, register, vocabulary, expressing empathy, reassurance, and so on. Refer back to the email in Section A9.

B The pressure of exams

1 Pre-reading task (15–20 minutes)

Before students do the exercise, it would be useful to focus the whole class on the pressures that exams cause by asking students how they feel about preparing for and taking exams. You could write their comments on the board. How do their views compare with the opinions given in the Coursebook?

Discuss possible solutions to each problem. You may want to assign one problem to each small group and ask them to come up with a number of possible solutions. Alternatively, write each problem on a separate piece of paper. Pass the papers from group to group so that each group can write a different piece of advice on the page. Students can then discuss the various solutions and vote for the best one.

You could turn this into a critical thinking exercise by asking students to list the positives and negatives of taking exams. For example:

- For exams: they measure progress, give students a goal to aim for, can be motivating, provide evidence of your level for colleges or employers.

- Against exams: they are stressful, only test how well you do under exam conditions, don't give an overall picture of your abilities, don't test all skills – for example, team work, creativity.

Then divide the class into two teams to debate the issue or, for homework, ask students to write an essay on the advantages and disadvantages of exams.

2 Reading for gist (5–10 minutes)

The magazine article is about four students with very different attitudes to exam study and revision. Their views and those of their parents are evaluated by a counsellor who offers solutions to the issues.

3 Comprehension check (10–15 minutes)

The comprehension questions require students to contrast and compare the different students in order to identify what differentiates them from each other.

DIFFERENTIATION

To **support** students in finding the answers, guide them with suitable questions. For example, *What kind of symptoms of stress does Radek have? Is he good at talking about his anxiety? Why does Fauzia feel overwhelmed? Why does she feel stressed by her parents? Why does Kenzo run out of time in exams? Why do Kenzo and his dad disagree? Why does Ayesha's mum nag her? Why does she chat with friends on her phone?*

For extra **challenge**, ask students to find similarities between any two of the students in the article and say if they feel this is typical for teenagers of their age.

Answers
a Fauzia; **b** Ayesha; **c** Kenzo; **d** Radek; **e** Fauzia; **f** Ayesha; **g** Kenzo; **h** Radek; **i** Fauzia; **j** Ayesha

---

4 Post-reading discussion (15–20 minutes)

> **Critical thinking:** Elicit students' thoughts on the experiences of the students in the article using the questions provided. The discussion is a valuable opportunity to draw out some cultural comparisons about styles of exams, approaches to exams and exam results, study in general, free time and family attitudes.

Particular issues to explore could be:

- Exams are undoubtedly stressful, but does stress have any positive effects? (It can make you work harder / some students thrive in a competitive atmosphere / you appreciate relaxing time more fully.)

- Is coursework a good idea, or can you end up feeling overloaded?

- How can you build confidence for exams?

- How can the family help the student who is in the middle of exams?

- What do you think is the best time of day for revision? (Experts suggest our brains are at their peak at around 10 a.m.)

To **support** students with question 8, elicit ideas about what makes a good or a bad place to study. Then ask them to make notes about where they like or don't like to study. Finally, ask them to work in groups of three to have the discussion, with one person role playing the moderator.

For extra **challenge**, ask students to summarise the results of their discussion to present to the class.

5 Vocabulary: Colloquial words and phrases (5–10 minutes)

Making suitable use of colloquialisms helps students achieve a good, informal tone. This exercise recycles words and phrases they met in the text.

Answers

1   **a** open up; **b** exam nerves; **c** stick to; **d** nagging; **e** stressed out; **f** sailed through

2   Encourage students to compare ideas and opinions about the value of stress and the need to avoid it.

6 Word building (5–10 minutes)

Students could use dictionaries for this word-building exercise. Encourage them to create sentences to show meanings, as this will test their understanding of how to use the words in context.

Answers

Building nouns from verbs

Achievement; appointment; arrangement; astonishment; disagreement; entertainment; improvement; management

Other examples include: disappointment, postponement, enlargement, enjoyment, enhancement, encouragement

Building adjectives from nouns

Magical; cultural; musical; functional; classical; mathematical; personal; natural

Other examples include: national, political, logical, emotional, recreational

You could extend this exercise by considering the suffix *-ful*. The examples *stressful* and *helpful* are found in the text. Other examples to elicit are: *colourful, useful, harmful, thoughtful, beautiful*. You could also ask students which of these words have an opposite with the suffix.*-less* (all the above except *stressful* and *beautiful*).

7 Language study: Giving advice (5–10 minutes)

Students have come across the sort of language the counsellor uses earlier in the unit. The aim of this exercise is to help students use their existing knowledge to further explore contrasts and similarities between advice expressions. It also encourages them to look for meaningful patterns in the grammar and helps them work out guidelines for using modals correctly.

The questions draw attention to the special features of modal auxiliaries. The main ideas to elicit are as follows:

Answers

1   *Need(s) to* and *should* sound more indirect than *must*. Students might add that the counsellor uses a passive construction in A and C, which sounds less prescriptive than an active one.

2   *Need* is followed by *to* + infinitive. *Must* and *should* are never followed by *to*.

3   **A** Should Radek be encouraged . . . ?
     B Does Fauzia's father need to . . . ?
     C Does Ayesha need to . . . ?

4   **B** Don't encourage Fauzia ...; **C** Using her phone doesn't need to be seen as . . . ; **D** Ayesha doesn't need to . . .

5   *Ought to* can replace *should* and *need(s) to. Has to* can replace *must.*

8 Should/shouldn't have (10–15 minutes)

Should/shouldn't have + past participle express blame and criticism of someone's actions. They are very direct, so students need to be careful of the way they use the structures when addressing other people, especially as they can imply blame. If used about one's own action, this structure can imply regret for having made a mistake or done something wrong.

Practice

Answers

a   Joseph shouldn't have taken a part-time job when he had exams coming up.

b   Indira shouldn't have gone to the concert when she had an exam the next day.

c   He should have checked his bank balance before he spent a lot of money.

d   I shouldn't have shouted at my brother when he was trying to be helpful.

e   I shouldn't have borrowed my sister's jacket without asking her first.

f   You should have bought some extra bread when you knew we needed to make sandwiches.

9 Using a more informal tone (5–10 minutes)

> **DIFFERENTIATION**
>
> To give extra **support**, provide or elicit the word that begins each answer (**a** I; **b** You; **c** You; **d** I; **e** Abdul; **f** I; **g** He). You can also simplify the instruction by telling students to use *should, should have, must* or *need* (i.e. removing the extra complication of *ought* and *had better*). Also check understanding of *vital*, which will influence students' choice of modal. Some students tend to overuse *must*; recap by asking them the difference between when we use *must* and *should* (*must* is stronger and can sound too direct).
>
> To give more **challenge**, ask students to write about anything they regret having done. They should write a paragraph or describe the situation to their partner.

Answers

a   I don't need to cook as Bruno is taking us out for a meal.

b   You should do / ought to do / need to do your homework at a regular time each evening.

c   You shouldn't have made / oughtn't to have made a promise you can't keep.

d   I shouldn't have left / oughtn't to have left all my revision to the last minute.

e   Abdul must get / had better get some rest or he will fail his exams.

f   I should have listened / ought to have listened to her advice.

g   He shouldn't have played / oughtn't to have played computer games instead of revising for the exam.

You could finish this exercise on register by asking students to consider the underlying strength of emotion in this kind of statement: I'm a bit annoyed, I must say. It is a typical English understatement and native speakers hearing it would guess that the speaker was angry about something. This is shown particularly by the phrase *I must say.* Contexts in which you might make this comment could be:

•   Your friend returns a book they borrowed from you and you find that several pages are torn.

•   You pay quite a lot of money for a second-hand bicycle that the previous owner assures you is in very good condition. After a few days, you detect a lot of faults.

10 Spelling and pronunciation: Silent letters (2–4 minutes)

Silent letters are often the cause of spelling errors; students can't hear them so they forget to use them. Before beginning the exercise, you could write a word (e.g. *castle*) on the board and ask if all the letters in it are pronounced. When you have established that the *t* is silent, you could ask for examples of similar words. These could be categorised according to particular letters – for example:

silent l: *chalk, palm, would*

silent c: *muscles, scene*

silent p: *pneumonia, psychology*

silent w: *sword, wreath, who*

silent k: *knot, kneel, knight*

silent g: *design, reign, gnat*

silent gh: *straight, bought, caught*

silent t: *thistle, fasten, soften*

silent h: *exhaustion, vehicle, heir*

Monitor students' pronunciation as they practise saying the words aloud.

11 Identifying silent letters (5–10 minutes)

Allow time for students to agree on the silent letters and practise saying each word.

DIFFERENTIATION

To give **support**, allow students to use dictionaries to check their pronunciation.

For more **challenge**, elicit other examples of words with the same silent letters.

Answers
1 a g; b w; c h; d w; e gh; f c; g l; h l; i u; j g; k gh; l h

12 Adding silent letters (5–10 minutes)

DIFFERENTIATION

Students who finish early can be **challenged** to close their books and write down as many words as they can remember from Sections A11 and A12. Ask students who need more **support** to work in pairs and test each other on the spelling of random words from sentences a–o.

Answers
a brightest, knows, talk; b wouldn't, listen; c circuit; d Whereabouts; e half, whole; f write, answers; g lights; h wrist, knee; i white; j Honesty; k scent; l whistle, wrong; m wrote, pseudonym; n reigned; o psychic

13 Detecting patterns (5–8 minutes)

The aim of this exercise is to help students use what they already know about silent letters to come to conclusions about meaningful patterns. This will help them with pronunciation when they come across unfamiliar words, and with spelling.

Students might need some help to detect the patterns, so you could start with an example. You could write *psychic* on the board and ask them to think of other words which start with *ps* (e.g. *psychiatrist, psychology*). Make sure students

understand that when the letters *ps* come at the beginning of a word, the *p* is silent.

Other patterns students might notice are:

- *pn* at the beginning of words has a silent *p* – for example, *pneumonia, pneumatic*

- *gn* usually has a silent *g* – for example, *design, assign, gnaw*

- *kn* usually has a silent *k* – for example, *knee, know, knowledge, knot*

- *wh* has an almost completely silent *h* in the question words (*what, which, why, when, where*) and in the numerous other words beginning with *wh* – *for example, white, wheel, whisper*

- *st* usually has a silent *t* when followed by *l* or *e* – for example, *whistle, fasten*

14 Idiomatic expressions (5–10 minutes)

Answers
a *hustle and bustle*: noise and activity
b *light as a feather*: very light
c *risked life and limb*: took dangerous chances

15 Look, say, cover, write, check (5–10 minutes)

Using a visual strategy will help students recall the actual 'look' of words that use silent letters. Ask students which words they found most difficult to remember and try to come up with mnemonics to remember them. See Unit 1, Section B13 for a reminder of the 'Look, say, cover, write, check' method for learning vocabulary.

C Studying effectively

1 Punctuation reminders (15–20 minutes)

These punctuation reminders will provide useful revision. The topic is homework, which ties in with the study skills theme. Homework is not universal, so make sure students understand what it is, if necessary. Elicit their approach to tackling homework – you could make a list of tips on the board. Questions can include:

- Should the TV be on and social network sites be on screen during homework time?

- How long should you spend on homework?

- What should you do if you can't understand your homework?
- Should you work at a desk or table?
- What time should you start your homework?
- Is it right to get help from parents or friends to complete homework?

Example answers

> 1   I need a few quiet moments to myself when I get in from school. I have a drink and relax for a while. Then I get out my homework. I work at a desk in the corner of the living room. It's peaceful but not silent. I like French and Maths homework the best.
>
> 2   I've got a few reference books which I keep on a shelf above my desk. I borrow my brother's paints for artwork and I use my sister's laptop for essays. I've used my dad's tools for some technology projects too. They don't mind me borrowing their things as long as I look after them.
>
> 3   Our school has a homework link on the school website. This means that you can use the homework page to check the homework you've been set. It also prevents students getting too many subjects for homework at once. About two years ago, I had English, history, German, physics, biology, maths and technology homework on the same night. It was a nightmare. The homework page prevents these problems. However, it also means teachers refuse to accept silly excuses for not handing in homework.

---

2   Rewriting an email (10–15 minutes)

In this exercise, as well as deciding on paragraphing, students are asked to analyse tone and register. Firstly, they need to establish the sense of the email. Then they should work out the writer's intention (to console and advise), and discuss why he does not succeed in achieving a suitable tone.

To help focus on improving the tone, ask students to picture the situation and to imagine how Gustavo,

who has failed an exam most of his friends have passed, is feeling. Ask them questions along the lines of: *Will he want to be criticised? To be given lots of advice? To be reminded he has failed? Have you ever been in a similar position? Can you remember what it felt like?* Elicit the need for a sympathetic but controlled response that focuses on what Gustavo can do, rather than on his failings. This involves leaving out anything that could be interpreted as disapproval or criticism. Encourage students to decide what's worth saving and what they should discard, and let them discuss suitable alternative phrases – for example, *I'm keeping my fingers crossed for you.*

DIFFERENTIATION

After setting the context and discussing how Gustavo must be feeling (see suggestions above for whole-class discussion), put students into pairs to **support** each other. Ask one student in each pair to scan the letter and underline two criticisms Victor makes of Gustavo, and the other to underline three good pieces of advice that Victor gives Gustavo. They should then compare notes before moving on to drafting their own version. Tell students to write their email in three paragraphs, eliciting what should go in each:
1 – sorry to hear Gustavo can't come, **2** – advice to Gustavo (using the ideas from Victor's email); **3** – something encouraging.

Example answer

This is just one possible answer, which students may like to compare with their own.

> Hi Gustavo,
>
> I was really sorry to hear that you're unable to join us on the trip because you have to resit your exam. You must be feeling really fed up and I do sympathise with you.
>
> It might be a good idea to contact Oscar, as I know he's resitting too. How about revising together? I'm sure he'd be glad of your support and companionship.
>
> An approach I found helpful, which you may like to try, is to get hold of the syllabus and underline the relevant sections. I know you've

probably done this (if so, ignore me), but I found checking past papers to identify typical questions helped a lot. There's a lot of time pressure in the exam, so it's definitely worth practising the answers in the specified time.

Let me know as soon as you get your results. I'll be keeping my fingers crossed for you. We'll miss you a lot on holiday, and it won't be the same without you.

Your friend,

Victor

3 Reading aloud (5–10 minutes)

Students can try out on a small audience the effect of the tone and register they have achieved.

4 More idiomatic expressions (10–15 minutes)

Before students start the exercise, it's worth making sure they understand the literal meaning of the component words of the idioms. You could also encourage students to relate the idioms to similar ones in their own language(s).

Answers
1 A; 2 B; 3 D; 4 B; 5 B; 6 A

5 Increasing your stock of idioms (5–10 minutes)

Using idioms effectively is obviously more difficult than just understanding them. You will need to emphasise that idioms have a precise meaning and are only applicable in specific situations. You might like to ask students to keep records of those idioms they like and to use them as much as possible until they are really sure they know the appropriate contexts for them.

6 Sentence correction (5–10 minutes)

These sentences, taken from students' actual writing, are quite challenging to rewrite. Students may like to treat them as problem-solving exercises, working on them together to identify the intended meaning and then rephrase them.

DIFFERENTIATION

To **support** students, do this exercise as a whole-class activity. Read out the sentences in turn, encouraging students to identify the errors and suggest replacement words or phrases. In item **a**, for instance, *be wisdom* is incorrect – you can *be wise* but you can't *be wisdom*. Elicit ways of rewriting the phrase – for example, *If you were wise / It would be wise / If I were you*. Then the verb *follow* comes in the middle of the sentence and links to *advice* at the end. *Follow someone's advice* is a correct phrase. Students should then identify that *teacher advice* is incorrect – it is missing a possessive apostrophe. Finally, encourage students to try different ways of rewriting the whole sentence – for example, *If you were wise you would follow your teacher's advice. / It would be wise to follow your teacher's advice. / If I were you, I would follow your teacher's advice.*

Alternatively, give students different sentences, each containing one or more grammar/vocabulary mistakes based on language studied recently.

For more **challenge**, ask students to analyse the types of errors in the given sentences, whether of vocabulary, register, tone or grammar.

Suggested answers
a   You would be wise to follow. / If I were you I'd follow your teacher's advice.
b   Try to develop a positive attitude to / frame of mind for your work.
c   Remember that a good friend can be a tremendous help.
d   You should never tell anyone your password, or they can access your personal information.
e   Many people would agree with the points in your email.

International overview (10 minutes)

Check basic understanding of what the pie chart shows to make sure that students have assimilated the facts. For example, you could ask them how many students chose Germany for their studies.

This activity also provides useful practice for saying large numbers, which can be challenging.

Styles of teaching and learning vary a lot across the world. Find out how students like to learn things and ask whether going abroad to study, where there might be a different teaching style, would be difficult. Ask if they would prefer to study at a university where there is a lot of freedom and emphasis on group work and problem solving, or in more structured classes or lectures where everyone is taught in the same way at the same pace.

Answers

1   10

2   China

3   Japan

D Advising and helping

1   Pre-listening tasks (5–10 minutes)

Elicit or teach the meaning of *counselling* (the professional help given to people with personal or psychological problems), and that someone who counsels is called a *counsellor.* Ask why people turn to counsellors for help. Elicit ideas such as: problems with stress at college or at work, family or relationship problems, problems with lack of confidence, depression and anxiety.

Students can then do tasks 1 and 2 in groups or pairs and give feedback to the whole class. Possible disadvantages of counsellors include the difficulty of checking their credentials, the difficulty of knowing whether any advice is indeed sound, the risk of becoming dependent on counselling, the expense if you have to pay.

2   Listening for gist (5–8 minutes)

After you have played the audio recording once, ask students if any of the questions they wrote have been answered.

DIFFERENTIATION

To provide more **support**, ask students to listen for the four main areas of support that are offered.

For more **challenge**, ask students to listen for one detail about each of the four areas.

Audioscript track 7.3

Listen to a university counsellor talking to a group of new students about the counselling services available at the university.

Thank you for coming to this informational talk today about university counselling services. I'm sure you're all very excited to be starting your first term here and getting to know each other and all that the university has to offer. The student counselling service is just one of the many resources available to you to help you make the most of your time here with us. First, I'll tell you where to find us and give a general description of what we do. Then I'll describe the specific types of services we offer. And finally, I'll explain how you can access more information.

First of all, where and who are we? The student counselling centre is located on the third floor of the university administration building. We have a team of trained counsellors who can offer advice on a wide range of issues. We also have a resource centre which is open to all students, where you can find up-to-date information about everything from academic support to careers advice. We run workshops and talks throughout the academic year and we welcome walk-in visits as well as being able to schedule one-to-one appointments.

So, what kind of counselling services do we offer? There are four main areas. First, we offer free academic support through specialist workshops. Do you sometimes need help understanding your tutor's feedback on your essay? And I don't just mean the handwriting! *[laughter from student audience]* We're not going to write your essays for you *[laughter from student audience]* but we can help you ask the right questions so you'll be able to develop your independent study skills. Here you can get advice on how to improve your essays, how to prepare for exams, and much more. In addition, it's also possible to schedule one-to-one meetings with a student volunteer adviser and to get advice on a particular essay, project or dissertation question. We encourage you to look first at the workshops on offer, to see if any of those would help solve your problem, before making an individual appointment.

The second area involves advice on choosing a future career and how to take steps towards achieving your goal. How do you choose the career that's right for you? How can you get started? That's where we come in! As well as talks by past alumni, covering a wide range of professions from legal and medical professionals to business entrepreneurs, we also provide help with writing applications, preparing your CV, applying for grants and scholarships, and applying for internships so you can get the experience you need to help you make a decision.

The third area includes help with your personal mental health and well-being. Our counsellors offer advice on a range of topics, for example, managing your budget, maintaining motivation and dealing with exam nerves. It's normal to feel overwhelmed from time to time, so don't feel shy about talking to a counsellor about issues of stress or anxiety. Often it's really hard to struggle on with problems on your own. Just having the opportunity to talk to someone can help you put things into perspective. Please be assured that any information you give us is entirely confidential and will not be given to any other person without your written consent.

Finally, we also offer support for students with disabilities. We can arrange specialist support for accessing resources or doing exams. We can also offer help to students with learning difficulties, such as dyslexia or attention deficit disorder or any other long-term learning difficulty. Our aim is to help all students to access resources equally and make the most out of their time at university.

To conclude, let me tell you where to find more information. Of course, you're all welcome to drop into our counselling centre at any time. We're open every weekday from 9 a.m. to 3.30 p.m. We think of our centre as a cheerful friendly place and you're welcome to drop in for a chat. You can also phone or email us. And I would encourage you to take a look at our website, which is updated on a weekly basis with news about our workshops, talks and other informational resources.

Thank you! Now do you have any questions?

3 Detailed listening (5–10 minutes)

Let students listen to the audio recording again to complete the notes. Only one or two words are required to fill each gap. Check the answers by pausing the recording in the right places.

The occasional spelling or grammar mistake will not matter as long as the answers are clear.

Answers
a third; b workshops; c appointments; d career advice; e well-being; f permission; g access resources; h 3.30pm; i a chat; j week

---

Inference

Students may feel some social stigma about asking for counselling or may feel they are to blame and have to handle the problem alone. Draw attention to this sentence in the audio, which implies that students may feel stigma: 'It's normal to feel overwhelmed from time to time, so don't feel shy about talking to a counsellor about issues of stress or anxiety. Often it's really hard to struggle on with problems on your own.'

To explore this idea further, ask students to role play a conversation between a student who thinks counselling is a good idea and another student who is hesitant or doubtful. They should try to persuade their friend to go to the counselling centre.

4 Rewriting an email giving advice (15–20 minutes)

Before students begin to rewrite the email with a more tactful tone and register, encourage them to consider Roberto's problem and what could be done about it.

Example answer
This is a possible version of the email, for students to compare with their own attempts.

> Hi Roberto,
>
> I was sorry to hear that you are having a tough time getting on with your little brother. I know small children can be very annoying, and it's not an easy problem to resolve.
>
> My younger brother Tom used to drive me up the wall. Like your brother, he was always interfering with my things and even

damaging them. I used to get bad-tempered and impatient with him, and we often had a strained atmosphere at home. Eventually, I decided to discuss the problem with my parents and, to my surprise, they saw my point of view. Tom now agrees not to touch my things, and I put anything really precious somewhere he can't reach.

Nowadays, we get on quite well. I play football with him and give him a hand with his homework. He has become more of a friend than an enemy. Do you think this approach could work for you? You could always give it a try.

Looking forward to hearing from you.

All the best,

Daniel

---

drive someone up the wall: make someone very angry and annoyed

5 Building a letter from a list of points (20–30 minutes)

The main challenge in this exercise is for students to select a few relevant tips from the list and expand on them with more detail. Discuss some of the dangers of using the internet for homework, such as the temptation to get distracted and sidetracked by irrelevant websites, or the problem of filtering internet material effectively. After students have brainstormed some ideas of their own about how to resolve the problem, you could take one point from the list and show how it could be expanded with interesting details or examples.

Example answer

It's a good idea not to leave it too late in the evening to start your homework. For example, I usually prefer to have a short rest and a snack when I get in from school, and then get down to my homework. I concentrate better earlier on, and I have the rest of the evening free to relax or see friends. If you start your homework late, you may find you have to stay up late to finish it, which makes you feel tired the next day.

For more **support**, ask students to rank the tips in order of usefulness. Then assign three tips each to small group. Each group can write one paragraph, giving their tips to Polly.

For more **challenge**, ask students to include at least three of their own ideas to their advice to Polly.

6 Pre-writing discussion (5–10 minutes)

> **Critical thinking:** Bullying is an issue that needs to be handled sensitively. You could start by asking for a definition or some examples of bullying, either in person or online. Ask students whether bullying is a problem only for younger children, or whether it can happen in other contexts – for example, among teenagers or older people. You can also discuss what causes it.

Possible definition of bullying: unwanted and repeated aggressive behaviour which often involves rumours, lies, insults and other ways to make the victim feel humiliated.

Bullying in person: it is usually direct and targets one person; there are often witnesses; it can involve physical threats, shouting or violence; it usually occurs in a specific location (e.g. school or playground), and you can get away from it by going to a safe place.

Online bullying: it can be done anonymously; it can spread quickly on social media (by people passing on messages); it's hard to avoid if you are on your phone or social media all day long; it can happen anywhere; bullies can see victims' reactions.

Effects of bullying: Victims of bullying often feel isolated and helpless. They can show symptoms of depression and changes in mood, behaviour, sleep pattern and appetite. They may start to do poorly in schoolwork or miss days at school.

It's important to discuss the problem of bullying in the classroom, so everyone knows what to do when it happens. Remind students not to pass on messages that are cruel and hurtful, and never to post any messages or images of themselves online that are personal or private.

(If possible, find out if there are any helpline or support services in your area that you can direct students to should they need help.)

Possible ways to respond to bullying:

- Report online bullying to teachers, parents and to the website where it appears.
- Contact a teacher, counsellor or helpline for support.
- Share your experience with friends you trust.
- Unplug from social media for a while.
- Take part in activities for Anti-Bullying Week, or organise them yourselves.

Finally, I think we all have to get together to stop bullying in our schools. Why not start or join an organisation that helps to stop bullying? You could invite a speaker to your school, create posters or leaflets about bullying and organise events that raise awareness of bullying. Above all, don't feel you are alone!

7 Email completion (15–20 minutes)

Point out that the introduction contains thanks for Leroy's email, an expression of sympathy and a note of hopeful encouragement. This approach could be continued throughout the email.

This exercise offers more much-needed practice in developing ideas into interesting paragraphs. You may wish to suggest students turn back to the email offering advice in Section A9 for guidance.

DIFFERENTIATION

To give more **support**, break down the advice into different categories. For example, things Leroy could do himself, ways to get help from others and ways to fight bullying in general. Look back at the email in Section A9 and pick out phrases that may be useful.

For more **challenge**, encourage students to use some idiomatic expressions from earlier in the Coursebook – for example, Sections A14 and C4 in this unit, Unit 2, Section A3 and Unit 1, A9.

Example answer

. . . It's important to tell other people about what is happening. Don't be afraid to speak out! If someone bullies you, it's not because you have done anything wrong. You should talk to your parents or teacher and explain the problem. I know it may be difficult to talk to them about it, but please give it a try.

Another thing that might be helpful is to contact a national helpline. They have really good advisers who can help you understand what to do next. Sometimes it's easier to talk to a stranger than to someone who knows you well.

GRAMMAR SPOTLIGHT (5–10 MINUTES)

With Coursebooks closed, you may like to open the discussion on 'text speak' by asking which features of their mobile phones students use most frequently. They could discuss the advantages of texting (it's convenient, usually cheap, etc.) and also its disadvantages, such as whether people feel disappointed to receive a text on a special occasion instead of getting a greetings card in the post.

Before asking students to answer the questions in the Coursebook, elicit a text message or use one from the exercise and write it on the board. Students can then identify how it is different from a proper sentence: missing pronouns, articles, prepositions, special abbreviations, and so on.

Answers

a   Hi Libby! I hope your weekend in Dublin went well.

b   I'm sorry, but I can't come tonight. I'll phone you when I get home.

c   I'm on my way, but I'm going to be 20 minutes as there is a lot of traffic. Please wait for me.

d   Dear Mr Poulos, I would like to accept the position you have offered me. Many thanks.

e   I'll text you before I come round to make sure you are in.

WIDER PRACTICE

1   You could set up role plays and ask students to imagine they are addressing very different groups of people. Encourage them to adjust their tone and register to suit their audience.

Scenarios could include:

- encouraging an elderly person to use a mobile phone or tablet

- comforting a parent whose son/daughter is about to leave home to study overseas

- explaining to a small child what to expect on the first day at school.

2   Students who are less confident at speaking could be given, or pre-prepare, prompt cards listing key phrases to remind them what to say. They could also focus on simpler situations, such as apologising for accidentally breaking something when visiting someone they don't know well.

3   Students could further explore the pros and cons of using the internet as a tool for study. They could discuss how they evaluate the usefulness of a website, share website addresses they have found helpful, and say how they resist being distracted by links to irrelevant sites, and so on.

4   If students are interested enough in the theme, you may like to invite an ex-pupil who speaks English well, and now attends a university, to visit the class and give them his/her opinions of university life. Similarly, university officials (student union officers, careers advisers, lecturers, welfare officers) could be invited to answer students' queries.

5   You may like to collect further examples of letters/emails which contrast tone and register. A formal register, using longer words of Latin origin, passive forms and no contractions could be contrasted with the style of informal registers.

6   To explore the topic of managing exam stress and anxiety, ask students to do some research on websites that give advice about managing stress. They could then create a poster giving ten top tips, adding cartoons or illustrations if they want.

Exam-style questions

Reading and writing

Reading and Writing: open response

This exercise provides practice with answering open comprehension questions.

The text recycles themes and language that students have already encountered in the unit.

Remind students to take their time and pay attention to the detail in order to find the correct answers. Point out that they do not need to write their answers in full sentences and that a brief answer is sufficient in this exercise. It is also fine to use words from the text (they don't need to paraphrase) but, as always, they need to take care with spelling. Point out that the questions follow the order of the text, except for the last question, which covers the whole text.

Answers

1   1856

2   They allowed female students

3   Eastern suburbs

4   Leadership skills

5   By tapping your student card on the reader by the door

6   Any three of: grants; scholarships; counselling (service); mentors

Reading and Writing: informal and formal

You will find advice on general approaches to exam-style writing exercises at the end of the 'Teaching support' section in the Introduction.

For the review exercise, you might like to give students these sentence starters:

- We learnt a lot about . . .
- The best thing about the trip was . . .
- I was a bit disappointed that . . .
- Everyone enjoyed looking at . . .

Example answer

Informal writing

Hi Eleni,

I was sorry to hear you are feeling nervous about your exams. I know it's a horrible feeling!

A revision plan is always a great idea, if you haven't already got one. I know you would stick to it, and seeing your progress would give you confidence. You will soon have loads done! And why not make playlists for your revision sessions? Choose the best music for getting into the right mood to concentrate and it can help you remember things too.

Relaxing, eating well and early bedtimes are vital before exams, so do look after yourself. Do you still run? It's great exercise for stress. If you take enjoyable breaks, you will go back to studying feeling refreshed.

In the exam, don't forget to read the questions carefully and underline the key words. Even if a question doesn't make sense at first, ideas will start to come, and you will get great results.

Loads of luck,

Adriana

(160 words)

Listening

Listening: dialogue

Students select the picture that matches what they have heard in each short recording. Note that there are three recordings in this exercise. The number of recordings that may be used in an examination may differ. Please see the details of the assessment section of the syllabus for more information. Each recording is in a different context.

Remind students to read the questions carefully. Encourage them to study the pictures before they listen, noting the differences between them and considering what words they might hear in the recording that distinguish one picture from another. It might be helpful for students to think of a key word for each picture, such as the name of the type of place or activity shown.

Point out that all four options for each question may be mentioned in the recording, but only one of them is the correct answer.

After they have listened, it may be useful to show students the transcript so they can work out why they made any mistakes.

Answers
1C; 2B; 3A

Audioscript track 7.4

You will hear three short recordings. For each question, choose the correct answer, A, B or C, and put a tick in the appropriate box.

You will hear each recording twice.

Question 1: Where is the boy going to study?

F: Are you going to work on your presentation now? Where are you going?

M: I was thinking of going to the library, but it's closed this afternoon, so I thought I'd work on it at home.

F: Why don't you go to the student lounge? They have nice comfy seats there.

M: Oh, it's always so busy with people coming and going all the time, and they talk on their phones a lot.

F: I know what you mean. How about going for a coffee first? I need to ask your advice about something.

Question 2: What did the boy do on Saturday?

F: Did you have a good weekend?

M: Yes, it was good! I was going to play football with my friends in the park, but the forecast said rain so I went to the gym instead. I'd planned to meet a friend to go and see a film in the afternoon, but she phoned to say she wasn't feeling well so I went home. I managed to get out for some cycling on Sunday, though.

Question 3: What is the girl going to do first?

M: Hi Magda! How're you enjoying your first week at uni?

F: Oh it's fun! But I can't stop to chat! I have to rush off to student services to get my student card. And after that, I have to pick up some milk and bread at the shop.

M: Oh, I got my card yesterday. You have to pay five dollars to get your photo taken.

F: Oh really? I'd better go and get some cash at the ATM before I do anything else then.

M: Let's meet up for a sandwich at the student café later on?

F: Sure! About 12 o'clock okay?

Listening: interview

Students answer multiple-choice questions based on an interview.

Make sure students read through the questions before they listen to the recording. They should use the second listening to check their answers.

Answers
1 B; **2** A; **3** A; **4** C; **5** B; **6** B; **7** C; **8** A

Audioscript track 7.5

You will hear an interview with a student counsellor. For each question, choose the correct answer, A, B or C, and put a tick in the appropriate box.

You will hear the interview twice.

Now look at questions 1–8.

Interviewer: What are some typical problems students bring to you?

Counsellor: A very common one is, um, not having enough finance to get through college, um, getting into debt. And they come needing advice.

Interviewer: How can you help?

Counsellor: We break down their spending and see if there are any economies – moving to a cheaper flat near the college saves rent and travel costs, erm, for instance. We also talk about funds they can tap into like, for instance, outside agencies that can give small grants . . . and I help them write letters. The college itself has a hardship fund they can apply to.

Interviewer: Is that reasonably successful?

Counsellor: Yes, it helps, but as a counsellor, I'm also concerned that financial problems bring about other problems. So I look at whether needing financial assistance is putting an extra strain on their personal relationships.

Interviewer: Are there other times when problems seem to peak?

Counsellor: Before exams. Er, maybe they're finding exams stressful, they're worried they can't retain information . . . it . . . it just goes, and they get mental blocks leading to being stressed in the exam period.

Interviewer: What do you offer?

Counsellor: I do things like study techniques – summarising their notes very briefly into key words. I emphasise that, you know, quality is better than quantity – do a bit at a time, but really try to take it in. Relaxation and exercise are important, too, in helping them to cope. I try and see if there are underlying problems. I mean – why should exams be a problem now if they've done all right before? Is something in their personal lives worrying them and, you know, we get them to talk about those things as well.

Interviewer: I see you normally are prepared to go quite deeply into things?

Counsellor: It depends. For example, if young people are still living with their parents and, um, they don't feel they're listened to, that their needs are not catered for, then we need to tackle that. I get the . . . the rest of the family to come and see me, too. And I help students to say how they feel to their parents. One problem, for instance, might be overcrowding, having to share a bedroom, that sort of thing, and I suggest ways that a student can get more space and privacy at home.

Interviewer: So you look at each case in an individual light?

Counsellor: As a counsellor, I think it's very important to make them feel comfortable, not be judgemental. Everything is confidential – I don't discuss a student's problems with anyone else without their permission. Unless . . . well, there is one main exception . . . something illegal is involved. Good quality counselling can't happen without trust.

Interviewer: So you would never openly criticise what a student is doing?

Counsellor: I try to get away from being critical. Often students have suffered too much from that. The most straightforward cases are where people want clear advice, for example, on choosing the best course for them, but counselling is not quite like that. In my view, it's primarily about supporting people who are confused or unhappy to explore their own issues. What they're going through now may be linked back to bad childhood experiences, for instance. It's . . . it's no good me just telling them what to do – it's essential they see things for themselves.

Interviewer: In general, how do you cope with what must be a fairly draining kind of job?

Counsellor: We see so many people! We always have appointments unless it's an emergency. This allocates a set amount of time to each student. And, erm, it helps if you remember you're not responsible for their problems. Only they can, ultimately, make changes in their lives. I couldn't afford to be any other way. I'd be swamped!

Speaking

You will find advice on general approaches to speaking exercises at the end of the 'Teaching support' section in the Introduction.

If students are doing this exercise under examination conditions, warm-up questions may help to put them at ease. These are included in the corresponding Coursebook unit.

〉8 The search for adventure

Learning plan

AOs	Key learning intentions	Success criteria
R3, L3, S1	Explore the topic of adventure, exploration and the sea	• Students can describe a coastal scene • Students can discuss what makes the sea fascinating • Students can talk about why people undertake risky adventures
R1, R3, R4	Understand the sequence of events in a story and a newspaper article about adventures at sea	• Students can identify and make notes about advantages and disadvantages in a text • Students can compare and contrast facts and opinions • Students can understand what is implied but not directly stated
W1, W2, W3, W4	Write a narrative with effective use of tenses and engaging opening and closing paragraphs	• Students can use a variety of past tenses to tell a narrative • Students can describe a sequence of events • Students recognise how a good opening and ending can make a narrative more interesting • Students can use appropriate language to engage the reader and make their writing vivid and descriptive
L1, L2, L3	Identify and understand key points in an interview and a lecture	• Students can ask questions and predict ideas before listening • Students can identify the main idea and details • Students can make notes while listening • Students can relate information in a lecture to their own experience
S1, S3, S4	Use appropriate stress and intonation for expressing surprise, consoling and sympathising	• Students can recognise and produce correct stress and intonation to show surprise in questions • Students can select the correct expressions to console or commiserate according to the situation

Overview

This unit focuses on narrative technique. When writing a story, students are expected to use their imagination to build a narrative around something that could conceivably happen in their real lives. They will encounter a wide variety of stimuli – for example, recounting an incident on a journey, losing something, a burglary, a storm, an accident, a fire – and they are usually given a scenario with a brief outline of what happened.

The theme of exploration has been chosen for this unit as the thrill of adventure appeals to students. Many of the exercises are sea-related because dramas at sea provide key ingredients for a good story: heroism, adventure, rescue missions, and so on.

Areas for discussion, which are relevant to other aspects of the course, are:

- Why are people so fascinated by the sea?

- What do we mean when we talk about heroism?
- How can negative experiences that cause hardship and struggle be turned into something positive so that we ultimately come to benefit from them?
- Is the desire for adventure also a wish for greater self-knowledge and personal development?
- What lessons can be learnt from dangerous, frightening or disappointing events?

LANGUAGE WORK

Structuring a narrative means ordering the events coherently and making the links between events clear. While most students will have met the narrative tenses they need to use before, putting them all together still presents a challenge. The unit deals with this through exercises analysing how and why narratives work, and through follow-up activities.

Students who show they have a wide vocabulary and can manipulate structures to dramatic effect are likely to be more successful. The unit helps students build up these skills by vocabulary expansion exercises, using emotional and dramatic language, and writing more complex sentences. Reported speech, which students will probably already have met, is revised using a variety of reporting verbs. Relative clauses, including both defining and non-defining types of clauses, are presented and practised.

The 'Grammar spotlight' focuses on the interrupted past continuous.

Common misconceptions

Misconception	How to identify	How to overcome
Students sometimes use an extra object pronoun at the end of a **relative clause** when the relative pronoun is the object of the clause. Example: *We spend a lot of money on things (that) we don't really need them.*	Ask questions to help students identify whether the pronoun refers to the subject or the object of the previous part of the sentence. Explain that in the case of object pronouns, the relative pronoun already refers back to the previous noun and we don't need to repeat it with another pronoun. Correct example: *We spend a lot of money on things (that) we don't really need.*	Write pairs of sentences on the board that can be joined using a relative pronoun. Ask which pronouns can be deleted. Example: *I bought a new jacket. I wore it to my interview. → I bought a new jacket which I wore to my interview.* (The pronoun *it* is not needed.)
Students may use the simple past instead of the **past continuous** for an ongoing action that is interrupted by another action or event. Example: *They swam in the ocean when they saw a big shark.*	Read out some examples and ask students to notice the duration of each event or activity. Ask which action continues for some time and which happens suddenly. Draw a timeline on the board, showing how one activity is interrupted by another. Correct example: *They were swimming in the ocean when they saw a big shark.*	Write some pairs of sentences on the board and ask students to compare them. Examples: *She was reading a book when she saw a mouse.* *She jumped out of her chair when she saw the mouse.*

Introducing the unit topic (5–10 minutes)

Working with a partner, students look at the photo and discuss the questions.

The questions should encourage students to think about why the sea is such a source of mystery and fascination. They might be curious about what the diver is doing. Taking photos, gathering samples, exploring, looking for buried treasure, searching for a rare species of coral or fish? Some students might be able to share what it's like to wear a wetsuit and use goggle and fins, to swim under the sea or even to use an oxygen tank. Encourage them to discuss why a place like this is fascinating – for example, for the marine life, the unusual rock formations, the brilliant colours, the unexpected discoveries. They might wonder what it is like to be under the sea – weightless in a silent world untouched by humans and observing marine life close-up.

You may also want to explore what students know about the world's oceans and whether they have experience of sailing, diving or swimming in the sea or the ocean. Encourage them to exchange stories about visiting or living in places on the coast. Is life in a coastal area different from life inland? What occupations are associated with living on the coast (fishing, lobster or oyster farming, seaweed collecting, pearl diving, scuba diving instructor, marine biologist)? Would students prefer to live near the sea or far away from it?

⟩ **Digital coursebook:** At the start of the lesson, use this video to introduce and review:

- the topic of adventure
- a range of vocabulary related to exploration and the sea
- defining relative clauses.

Read the question on the title screen and ask learners what they think they might see. Then play the video all the way through and check learners' predictions.

Play the video a second time, pausing to discuss what is being shown and the questions on the end screen. You can take the opportunity to revise words and phrases associated with the topic of adventure, exploration and the sea. Questions 1, 2 and 4 invite learners to use their imagination and think about how Mr Doba felt. These questions allow for differentiation, as more confident learners will be able to offer more extensive descriptions and reasons. Take note of whether learners use defining relative clauses in their answers to question 1.

You may like to play the video a third time for consolidation.

A The call of the sea

1 Visualisation (5–10 minutes)

Explain that visualisation is creating a mental image of something even though you cannot see it. It is a helpful technique for stimulating imagination and generating new ideas as well as helping to remember details of past experiences. Allow plenty of time for the visualisation so students can freely associate with any aspect of the sea that comes into their mind. Writing down what they visualised might best be done in their own language. They may write words or phrases that can later be turned into sentences. Ask them to share ideas with a partner.

Write these categories on the board and ask students for words that go in each: Sights, Sounds, Feelings.

DIFFERENTIATION

To give extra **support** with visualisation, you could start with some guided questions, pausing after each question to allow time for students to visualise. For example:

Close your eyes. You're walking along a beach. Feel the ground beneath your feet. What does it feel like? Breathe in deeply. What can you smell? Is it windy? Listen to the sounds around you. What can you hear? Look around you. What can you see? Are there trees or flowers? What colour is the sky? Are there clouds? What kind? Now open your eyes and write as much as you can remember.

Students can then be asked to write phrases or sentences to describe the scene (five to ten phrases according to their ability).

---

2 Discussion (5–10 minutes)

> **Critical thinking:** Students compare statements encompassing the romantic and adventurous aspects of the sea with their own views. Many of the ideas are followed up in greater detail later in the unit, so it's useful to hear students' views. Encourage them to be as speculative as possible.

To follow up, ask which of these statements might likely be expressed by each of the following people: a sailor, a deep sea diver, an explorer, an artist, a writer.

3 Sea vocabulary (5–10 minutes)

> **Critical thinking:** The vocabulary work prepares for many of the lexical items later in the unit. It's a good idea to remind students to make a note in their vocabulary records of unfamiliar words.

DIFFERENTIATION

Ask students who need more **support** to work in pairs and give each student three categories to deal with. When they have had time to check the meaning of all the items in their list, students should look at their partner's categories and ask their partner to explain the meaning of any words they don't know. Follow this up with a quick quiz: give definitions for some of the words and ask pairs to come up with the words.

To add more **challenge**, ask students to add three more words to each group. Alternatively, write the following words in random order on the board and ask students which group they belong to: *pier, seafoam, squid, dinghy, lifeguard, parasailing.*

Answers
1   **a** hive; **b** spanner; **c** squirrel; **d** tram; **e** solicitor; **f** abseiling
2   **A** jetty; **B** shells/sand; **C** turtle; **D** trawler

4 Writing a descriptive paragraph /
5 Reading aloud (20–30 minutes)

In these two exercises, students consolidate this stage of learning by writing a descriptive paragraph. You may want to use the photo to model one or two opening sentences. They then read the paragraphs aloud to their groups for

comments. As always, encourage positive feedback and constructive criticism.

DIFFERENTIATION

To provide extra **support**, write questions on the board. Students can use the answers to write their paragraph.

Where did you go? How did you get there? How did you feel on the way there? How did you feel when you arrived? What did you see and hear? How did you feel at the end of the day?

For extra **challenge**, brainstorm verbs to use with each of the following nouns:

Waves (lapping, rippling, beating, crashing, rolling, splashing)

Seagulls (screeching, floating, swooping, perching)

Water (shining, glistening, glittering, shimmering)

Wind (roaring, howling, whistling, whispering)

Suggest the following structure as models for students to incorporate in their work: I could see/ hear/feel + noun + verb with -ing . . . (e.g. *I could hear waves lapping on the beach, I could feel the sand squelching under my feet*).

6 Pre-reading discussion (4–5 minutes)

Encourage students to exchange views about what role the sea has played in the history of their country. For example, Japan is an island country surrounded by the sea and for centuries was isolated from the rest of the world, so its culture developed quite separately. The sea was also an important source of food, so Japanese dishes typically include many kinds of fish and shellfish.

Ask students if they know any famous stories or novels about the sea. Some famous novels about the sea written in English include: *Moby Dick* by Herman Melville, *The Old Man and the Sea* by Ernest Hemingway, *Treasure Island* by Robert Louis Stevenson. You may want to ask students to research summaries of these stories for homework or find abridged versions to read from the library.

You may also want to discuss myths or legends about the sea – for example, mermaids, sea monsters and shipwrecks.

7 Reading and sequencing (5–6 minutes)

Before they begin reading, you could ask students to predict the content by looking at the photos. Ask: *When were they taken? How do you know? How are today's ships and equipment different?* Discuss the meaning of the word *endurance* and probable reasons for why this name was chosen for the ship. (Endurance is the ability to do something difficult or painful for a long time.)

Students could also discuss what makes a good story – for example, strong characterisation, powerful scenes, dramatic incidents, an intriguing or fast-moving plot, a surprising ending.

If appropriate, encourage them to use insights they have gained in other parts of the curriculum (e.g. from the study of literature).

DIFFERENTIATION

For extra **support**, pre-teach the meaning of these words that appear in the story, or ask students to look them up.

salvage, magnet, endurance, tantalising, gale, drift, remote, gruelling

This may be a good opportunity to remind students that the meaning of a word depends a great deal on the context; the meaning may not always be exactly the same as the one found in the dictionary.

To provide more **challenge**, ask students to guess the meanings of the words listed above from the context and suggest synonyms before checking their dictionaries.

Answers
a 5; b 2; c 6; d 1; e 10; f 3; g 4; h 8; i 9; j 7

8 Comprehension check (5–6 minutes)

Answers
1 To cross Antarctica from coast to coast via the South Pole

2 The ship was trapped in ice before they could reach land

3 128 days

4 Ice, bad weather, freezing conditions

9 Making inferences (5–10 minutes)

❭ **Critical thinking:** Remind students that inferences are not directly stated in the text. These are logical deductions based on evidence in the text.

DIFFERENTIATION

To help students who need more **support**, suggest some multiple-choice options for each question. For example, for question 1, *Do you think they joined because they wanted to be famous, were bored or wanted a challenge?*

Challenge more confident students to come up with several (up to five) answers for each question.

Answers
1 To achieve something no one had done before, to test the limits of their strength and endurance.

2 Ability to set up camp, make a fire, keep warm, walk long distances, fish and hunt and find food, keep themselves mentally and physically healthy.

3 loneliness, despair, hopelessness, desperation, homesickness

4 They didn't have GPS or satellite communication devices. They didn't have modern materials such as plastic and fibreglass for their equipment.

5 Students' own answers

6 Students' own answers

10 Drawing a timeline (5–10 minutes)

> **Critical thinking:**

Students may wish to explore different ways of presenting the timeline, for example, as a vertical or a horizontal line, with information boxes above or below the line (or alternating) or within the timeline itself.

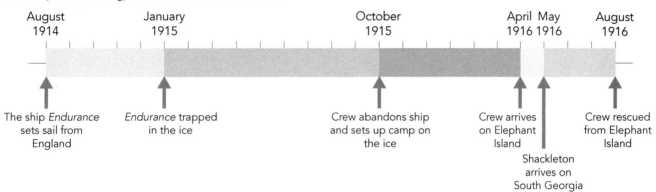

11 Language study: Narrative tenses (10–12 minutes)

The idea of this exercise is to help students use the grammatical knowledge they already have and apply it to a study of tenses in the story. Note that the past perfect continuous is also used in the last paragraph ('had been waiting') and you may also wish to extend students' knowledge.

The difficulty for many students at this level is not in understanding the theory of tenses or the underlying rules, but in applying their knowledge in different situations. Seeing how tenses are used in authentic texts is a dependable way to reinforce and extend understanding, which students can then build on in their own writing.

You could pair a student who needs support with grammar with another who is more able if you think the pairing is appropriate and will benefit them both.

After students have worked out their own ideas for formation and usage, you could open up the discussion to the whole class. You could ask an able student to record notes on the board.

The past simple

The past simple of regular verbs is formed by adding *-ed* or *-d* – for example, *reached, remained, drifted, intended.* Exceptions include: *was, set, became, began.* The past simple is common in storytelling as it shows one completed action or event following another and it moves the story forward. Paragraphs 6 and 7 of the story contain good examples.

The past continuous

The past continuous is formed with *was/were* and the *-ing* form of the verb – for example, *The ship was gradually sinking.* It is used for actions in progress in the past, often interrupted by another action – for example, *He was escaping the anger of his countrymen and I gave him refuge.* In storytelling it is often used for background information and descriptions setting the scene. You could extend the discussion by eliciting a further example, such as:

It seemed like any other ordinary day at the market. Stallholders were selling fruit and vegetables, shoppers were buying food for the weekend, dogs were barking and children were playing near the fountain. I was walking towards the café to meet a friend when I noticed a strange object lying on the ground . . .

The past perfect

The past perfect is formed with *had* + the past participle – for example, *It wasn't what they had imagined.* It is used to show that something had already happened at the point in time we are talking about, before another action – for example, *Roald Amundsen had already reached the South Pole.* Once the earlier point in time is established, we don't need to keep using the past perfect – it's more natural to use the past simple.

The past perfect continuous

The past perfect continuous is formed with *had* + *been* + the present participle – for example, *They had been waiting*. It is used to show that an action was continuing up to a past point in time: *We had been walking for hours before the sun finally appeared*.

You may wish to draw a timeline on the board to help students understand the past perfect tenses.

12 Beginnings and endings (3–5 minutes)

The beginning takes us right into a dramatic scene from the middle of the story. Then the story backtracks to fill in the details of what happened before and after. The last paragraph describes how the men were finally saved and the remarkable fact that everyone survived.

In the opening paragraph, the past continuous sets the scene for the events taking place. The past perfect describes events that took place before this opening scene in order to engage the reader in wondering why the explorers went on this expedition. In the final paragraph, the past simple is used to describe the final events of the story. The past perfect (and the past perfect continuous) are used to emphasise the period of time leading up to this final scene.

As a challenge, you may want to ask students to write an alternative last sentence for the ending of the story.

13 Discussion: Heroism (5–10 minutes)

1 > **Critical thinking:** A hero or heroine is a person who is admired for having done something very brave or having achieved something great .

Possible answers in relation to Shackleton could be:

- He was determined to save his men.
- He didn't give up despite many obstacles.
- He did his utmost to the limits of his physical strength.
- He did not let his men down.

---

2 For this part of the discussion, you could ask *Is it only people faced with extraordinary problems who can be called heroic?* Can ordinary people who show exceptional qualities be called heroic too – for example, people with disabilities who manage to succeed against the odds, or elderly people who lose a partner and face old age alone?'

3 Encourage students to give examples of their own heroes and heroines. Ask them to identify the qualities/attributes that make them heroic. You could ask *In what way would you like to be like your hero or heroine? How could you achieve that ideal?*

4 The discussion could then be extended along these lines: *Imagine that you tried hard to win a race. You trained and practised a lot, but in the end, you came third or fourth. Would you give up or would you try again? How would that experience help you?*

14 Continuing a story creatively (10–15 minutes)

Let students identify with a member of Shackleton's team and think through the possibilities. Would their friends and family understand the kinds of difficulties and hardships they had been through? How would they describe it to people so they will understand? It may be helpful to refer back to questions 1–3 in Section A9 where they made inferences about the men.

Before students begin writing, ask them what form their continuation of the story will take. Elicit that it should be written in the first person and that it could be written as a diary entry. Then consider its tone. The men are on their way back home and will have a great deal of time to think about their experience. The writing should therefore have a reflective tone.

DIFFERENTIATION

To **support** students who find this challenging, you could put some ways of beginning this piece of writing on the board – for example, *It is hard to believe that I am on my way home: there were times I thought I would never see England again. When I fall asleep, I imagine that I am still camped out on an ice floe with the wind howling in my ears.*

To provide extra **challenge**, ask students to add three more questions to the list and include the answers in their writing.

15 Writing from notes (5–10 minutes)

Example answer

> We had been waiting for over two months. Some of us had given up hope of ever being rescued.
>
> Every day, we scanned the horizon, hoping for sign of a ship. We were making a fire to cook some meat, when we saw a ship. After 128 days, at last help arrived!

16 Comparing cultures (5–10 minutes)

> **Critical thinking:** You may prefer to ask students to research a favourite story, perhaps from their childhood, for homework and then present it to the group.

17 Showing surprise: Stress and intonation (10–15 minutes)

In *wh-* questions the sentence normally has a falling intonation, with the main stress towards the end: *When did you arrive?*

However, when we want to show surprise, the voice rises and the question word is stressed instead: *When did you arrive?*

Let students listen carefully to the examples and have a chance to hear the contrasts. When the question is first asked, the stress and intonation are normal. When the second question is asked, the speaker shows surprise and wants clarification.

Pause the audio recording after each question and let students practise the intonation patterns. Finally, they can make up questions and answers of their own.

Audioscript track 8.1

Listen to the stress and the intonation patterns in these *wh-* questions and answers. When does the intonation rise? When does it fall?

a   What was the goal of the expedition?

   To cross Antarctica.

   What was the goal?

b   How many men were on the ship?

   There were 27 men.

   How many men were there?

c   What destroyed the ship?

   It was crushed by ice.

   What destroyed it?

d   What did the men eat?

   They ate seal meat and penguins.

   What did they eat?

e   How long did the men wait to be rescued?

   One hundred and twenty eight days.

   How long did they wait?

B Adrift on the Pacific

1 Pre-listening tasks (10–15 minutes)

Students are going to listen to an interview with a sailor talking about a book that inspired him. The book is a true story about a couple, Maurice and Maralyn Bailey, who in 1973 sold everything they owned to buy a yacht and sail it to New Zealand. Unfortunately, the boat was hit by a whale off the coast of Panama and it sank. They survived for several months on a life raft before they were rescued. Maurice always maintained that it was Maralyn, her positive attitude and her love that had kept him alive. Afterwards, they returned to England and wrote a book about their experience entitled *117 Days Adrift*, using the notes that Maralyn had made in her diary every day during their ordeal. It became a bestseller. Maralyn died in 2002 at the age of 61, Maurice in 2019 at the age of 85.

Narrative questions

Remind students that a complete narrative should answer the questions *Who, What, Where, Why, How* and *When*. To help them focus on the content of the story, students make up interview questions beginning with the above words before they listen. For example:

- What happened?
- Why did the boat sink?
- Where did the boat sink?
- How did they survive?
- What did they eat?
- Who rescued them?
- When did they get home?

DIFFERENTIATION

To provide **support**, revise the basic formation of past simple questions with students, eliciting the rules and giving some examples to practice (e.g. They bought a boat – *Why did they buy a boat?* / She saw something in the water – *What did she see in the water?*) Remind students of the difference between questions where the question pronoun refers to the *subject* rather than the object. Ask them to discuss and explain the difference between *Who rescued you?* And *Who did you rescue?* (i.e. there is no *did* when the question pronoun is the subject).

For extra **challenge**, ask students to write two questions for each question word listed.

Vocabulary check: answers
a 6; b 2; c 5; d 3; e 1; f 7; g 4

 8.2

2   Detailed listening (5–10 minutes)

Let students listen to the audio recording and find answers to their own questions.

Audioscript track 8.2

Listen to a podcast interview in which the guest describes the story of a couple, Maurice and Maralyn who were attempting to sail across the world when their boat sank. They survived on a life raft for four months before they were rescued and then wrote a book about what happened.

Presenter: Today, I'm delighted to present our monthly podcast 'Stories that inspired me'. This month we've invited Yann Pasulek, world-class sailor, to the podcast to talk about a book that has inspired him. Yann, welcome!

Guest: Thanks for inviting me!

Presenter: Can you tell us which book you've chosen and then a little about why it inspired you?

Guest: The book I've chosen is one that I read when I was a teenager – it made a huge impression on me. It's called *117 Days Adrift* and it was written by Maurice

and Maralyn Bailey. It describes what happened to them when they set out to emigrate from England to New Zealand by boat. They decided to sell their house and everything they owned in order to buy a yacht and make this journey. But while they were sailing from Panama towards the Galapagos Islands, suddenly something crashed into their yacht.

Presenter: Another ship?

Guest: No, a whale! They could see the injured whale struggling in the water alongside their boat. At first, they were more concerned about the whale, but then they realised that it had damaged their boat, which was sinking.

Presenter: Oh no! What did they do then?

Guest: They immediately launched the life raft and filled it with supplies of food and water, and abandoned ship. They weren't too worried at first because they had some supplies and they thought there was a fair bit of shipping traffic in the area. They decided to row towards the Galapagos Islands, but this turned out to be a big mistake because they used up most of their energy and water supplies, and also they didn't get very far.

Presenter: What did they do next?

Guest: It got worse. They headed for the Equatorial Counter Current, hoping it would take them to the Central American coast. But then, to their horror, a hostile current dragged them to the middle of the ocean.

Presenter: That must have been very frightening. Did they see any other ships at all?

Guest: From time to time, they caught sight of vessels in the area. Each time they tried to catch their attention by firing flares, waving and even setting fire to clothing in turtle shells, but to their despair, the boats sailed on, oblivious to them. They sighted seven vessels altogether. By that time, their life raft was deteriorating and had started to leak. They were constantly bailing out water.

Presenter: Unbelievable! How did they manage to get food?

Guest: Their supplies had run out, so they ate birds, fish, sea turtles and even sharks, which they caught with their bare hands or by improvising fishing lines. It was really upsetting for them because they loved animals and hated killing them. They became emaciated and malnourished. Amazingly, dozens of sea animals followed them as if to keep them company. Dolphins, turtles, sharks, a variety of birds and fish, even a whale, swam alongside them and didn't seem to be afraid of them at all. They felt very close to the sea.

Presenter: How did they get rescued in the end?

Guest: They'd been at sea for almost four months and they hadn't seen any ships for well over a month when suddenly Maralyn said she could hear a boat. Maurice thought she was imagining things, but it really was a ship – a South Korean fishing vessel. One of the fishermen had spotted them and the ship came to their rescue. The crew took them to Honolulu where they received medical attention. They were so weak, they couldn't walk. They said they had survived by just focusing on each day, one day at a time. Afterwards, Maurice said it was his wife's positivity that had kept them alive. It took them several months to recover and, after this experience, they both decided to become vegetarians.

Presenter: That's an incredible story! And can you tell us why it means so much to you?

Guest: I think it's an amazing account of fortitude and courage. I mean, they were tested to their limits and managed to survive, despite not having any hope in sight. I think that's what inspired me and is one of the reasons I took up sailing and am now planning my third solo voyage across the Pacific.

Presenter: Thank you so much for sharing a book that inspired you and good luck with your voyage!

3 Checking your answers (3–5 minutes)

Students can discuss the answers to their own questions. Elicit some examples from students of questions that were or were not answered in the interview.

4 Listening and note-taking (5–10 minutes)

Students should listen to the audio recording again and complete the notes. Remind them that, when taking notes, they should write key words and don't need to write complete sentences. However, the notes should be legible and make sense so that they can be read and understood easily at a later date.

Suggested answers

a   They were emigrating to New Zealand

b   Near Panama in Pacific Ocean; they were hit by a whale

c   worried about whale; didn't panic; got onto life raft

d   used up energy and water

e   turtles, birds, sharks, fish

f   raft started to leak; had to bail out water constantly

g   almost 4 months (117 days)

h   flares, waving, set fire to clothing .

i   several months

j   taking one day at a time; positivity/ positive attitude

5 Discussion: Motivation and adventure (5–10 minutes)

1 ⟩ **Critical thinking:** Each year, many people take part in risky expeditions to climb mountains, sail or row across the ocean, and so on. Use the photo to elicit ideas about the attractions and hardships of such an expedition. You could discuss the extreme mental resolution required and the types of risks taken out of choice rather than necessity. Possible questions to prompt discussion:

- Are they in search of a dream?

- Do they want fame and success?

- Are they encouraged by their group to do more and more risky things?

- Are they afraid of failure and letting people down?

- Are spiritual goals important – do they want to discover their own inner potential and limitations when put to extreme tests?

- Are they bored and dissatisfied with ordinary life?

You could ask which of these ideas, if any, students would apply to Maurice and Maralyn or to Ernest Shackleton and his team.

2   The discussion is now extended to consider the wider implications of adventurous projects.

You could finish the discussion by asking whether it's possible to develop as a person and build inner strength in ordinary circumstances, or whether it's necessary to go to extremes to do it.

DIFFERENTIATION

To give more **support** for question 1, you could suggest some real-life expeditions and ask students what motivated the expedition members in each case. For example, the first people to reach the summit of Mount Everest were Edmund Hillary and Tensing Norgay; the first person to fly across the Pacific Ocean was Amelia Earhart; the first teenager to sail single-handed around the world was Laura Dekker.

For more **challenge**, ask teams to come up with one real-life expedition and suggest what motivated people to take part.

6   Ordering events (5–10 minutes)

1   It's a good idea to revise the use of time expressions by putting a few examples on the board and checking that students understand their function, such as:

I'll ring you as soon as the email arrives.

(Ask: Is he going to ring a long time after, or just after the email arrives?)

He waited until the rain stopped before going out.

(Ask: Did he go out when it was raining?)

2   You could suggest students check the order of events by listening to the audio recording again and using their notes for reference.

Answers

1   1 k, 2 a, 3 j, 4 d, 5 b, 6 c, 7 e, 8 f, 9 i, 10 g, 11 h

2   The statements could be linked as follows:

> First, they left England for New Zealand. When the yacht was damaged by a whale, they escaped onto a life raft before the boat sank. First, they rowed towards the Galapagos Islands. Next / After that / Then they attempted to get to the Central American coast but a hostile current dragged them back out to sea. They tried to attract the attention of passing ships, but they sailed by, unaware of the couple's situation. Eventually, they were rescued by South Korean fishermen and were taken to Honolulu to receive medical care.

7   Expressing emotions (5–10 minutes)

Remind students that emotional expressions such as *to our horror, to my dismay* make a narrative more dramatic and personal. The phrases listed are used to describe emotional reactions to dramatic situations – for example, *My friends and I were sitting on a bench outside the zoo when, to our great astonishment, we saw a Sumatran tiger walking towards us.* Point out that these phrases are quite formal. In informal language, when describing more ordinary surprises than tigers appearing in front of us, we don't usually use these phrases or say things such as *To my horror, the supermarket had run out of chocolate biscuits.*

You could extend this exercise to discuss modifiers (e.g. *great, intense, serious, enormous*) and the ways these collocate. For example, we say *to our great relief/astonishment* and *to our intense relief,* but not *to our intense astonishment.* Unfortunately, there are no rules. Familiarity can be improved by wider reading and practice.

DIFFERENTIATION

To provide more **support**, ask students to first identify the emotion in each situation. For example, for question 1a: *How would you feel if you suddenly saw some lightning above you?* (worried). Then students can match the emotions with the correct expressions.

For more **challenge**, ask students to create sentences for the expressions that were not used (annoyance, disappointment).

Suggested answers

1   a   when, to my alarm/concern

    b   yesterday, to our great relief/joy

    c   when, to his alarm/horror

    d   and, to my delight/amazement/
        astonishment

    e   saw, to his alarm/concern/horror

    f   when, to our amazement/astonishment

2   Sentences **a**, **c**, **d**, **e** and **f** illustrate using the interrupted past continuous to show that an action stopped at a specific point when something else happened. This grammar point will be practised again at the end of the unit.

    a   past continuous, past simple

    b   all past simple

    c   past continuous, past simple, past
        continuous

    d   past continuous, past simple, past perfect

    e   past continuous, past simple

    f   past continuous, past simple

8   Dictionary work: Prefixes (5–10 minutes)

    This exercise is quite high level, so you could treat it as a good opportunity for dictionary practice.

    You could round off the exercise by discussing examples of other prefixes and their meanings, such as *miscalculate, outgrow, overcompensate, intercity, derail, reconsider.*

DIFFERENTIATION

To **support** students in remembering the meaning of the prefix *mal-*, ask them to find three more examples of words with the prefix meaning badly or wrongly (e.g. malnourished, malady, malware) and to write example sentences.

For extra **challenge**, ask students to find three words with the prefix *bene-*, which has the opposite meaning to *mal*, and means good or well (e.g. benevolent, beneficial, benign, benefit, benefactor).

Answers

1   **a** malnutrition; **b** malignant; **c** malfunctioning;
    d malpractice; **e** malevolent; **f** malicious

2   **a** counterbalance; **b** counterproductive;
    c counterattack; **d** counteract; **e** counterpart;
    f counterarguments

9   Revision of reported speech
    (5–10 minutes)

    Incorporating some reported speech adds variety and immediacy to a story. Many students will already be familiar with the rules. You could revise them by discussing the example from the dialogue and encouraging students to formulate the rules – for example, tenses shift one tense back, many modals do not change, pronouns change to reflect who is being spoken about, infinitives do not change.

    Remind students that *that* is often omitted in reported speech, especially after *say* and *tell – for example, She said (that) she wanted to be alone.*

    The rules governing reported speech are often broken in informal spoken or written English. A way of avoiding reported speech is to simply quote someone. In modern informal English, *be like* is often used to do this instead of *said. Be like* can be used in either its present or past form – for example, *And I'm like, 'why did you do that?' and he was like 'I've no idea!'* However, students do need to master the rules with regard to reported speech so that they can become competent users of more formal styles of written and spoken English.

10 Reporting verbs (10–15 minutes)

After completing the exercise, you could extend the work by eliciting other examples of reporting verbs such as *accuse, deny, apologise, think, offer, advise, reply, encourage, agree, recommend, complain*. Give a direct speech example for each verb in random order and ask students to identify the verb. For example, *'This hotel is badly heated.'* (= complain). Then ask students to write one sentence for each verb using reported speech. Students may choose to write examples with all the verbs or choose the ones they feel most confident about.

Note that some verbs use a preposition followed by a gerund (*accuse, apologise*) and some verbs are followed by an infinitive (*advise, encourage*). Some verbs also need to be followed by an object. Examples: *She accused me of wasting her time. He apologised for being late. They advised us to wait until morning. We encouraged them to go on the trip.*

Suggested answers

a   She declared/explained she was attempting to break the world record for sailing non-stop around the world.

b   She revealed that she was being sponsored by several businesses.

c   She admitted/confessed that her worst fear was personal failure.

d   She acknowledged she was doing it because she was hoping to beat the present world record of 161 days.

e   She said she was taking food and drink to last her up to 200 days.

f   She revealed/explained that the food included 500 dried meals, 150 apples, . . .

g   She confessed that when she was thousands of miles from shore, and if she was injured, then she would be scared.

h   She mentioned that she had been taught to stitch her own flesh wounds in an emergency.

i   She said that if there was a crisis, she thought the answer was not instant action but to think about it.

j   She declared/revealed/added that she knew she could handle the boat and she would find out whether she had the strength to beat the world record.

11 Writing a report of an interview (10–15 minutes)

International overview (5 minutes)

The quiz highlights many interesting facts about the world's oceans. One aspect of the topic for students to look up on the internet or in printed material could be how we use the oceans as a resource. Possibilities include investigation into the mineral wealth of the ocean, the food it provides or wave power. Alternatively, students could explore the world of fishing, either by researching a traditional fishing community or finding out more about a commercial fishing company. Other aspects of the oceans to focus on include the development and use of coral reefs, pollution of the oceans from sewage, dumping of chemicals and pesticides, oil spillages, and so on. Students could present their information to the class or they could interview each other, taking the part of journalist and representative.

Answers
1 B; **2** True; **3** C; **4** B; **5** A; **6** B

Provide a basic writing frame for students who need more **support** – for example:

Silvia Camilletti is a . . . yachtswoman, who . . .

This morning I spoke to her at/on . . . where . . .

I began by asking her about . . .

I was particularly interested to know . . .
She told me . . .

To provide more **challenge**, ask students to include all the statements (a–j) in Section B10, paraphrasing whenever appropriate.

Example answer

> Silvia Camilletti, 24, is planning to sail around the world single-handedly. She is hoping to beat the present world record of 161 days.
>
> I interviewed Silvia on her yacht, as she made last-minute preparations for her adventure. As we spoke, Silvia was organising boxes of food supplies in her kitchen. 'I am taking food to last me 200 days,' declared Silvia. The food includes 500 dried meals, 150 apples and 144 bars of chocolate.
>
> I was intrigued to know why Silvia wanted to undertake such a dangerous voyage by herself. She assured me that she was not doing the trip to prove herself. 'I have always been involved in challenging projects,' she insisted. Undoubtedly, however, she may face serious problems. Silvia confessed, 'When I'm thousands of miles from shore, and if I'm injured, then I'll be scared.' Silvia also revealed she has been 'taught to stitch her own flesh in an emergency'.
>
> Whatever the risks she faces, Silvia is a brave young woman who is determined to test herself to the limits.
>
> 'I know I can handle the boat, and I'll find out whether I have the strength to beat the world record,' she said.

C A remarkable rescue

1 Pre-reading tasks (5 minutes)

1   This gives students practice in structuring a narrative. Use the photo to elicit students' experiences of helping an animal, such as a sick pet or an injured wild bird. Encourage them to share their experiences with the class.

2   Students try to predict what will happen in the article. Ask them to describe the photo and say what kind of dangers whales may face in the ocean.

3   This task asks students to explore the language of the article and its audience. The text comes from a popular newspaper aimed at a general audience and is an example of a typical human interest story. You may want to discuss different types of newspapers and how some are more formal, are more text-heavy and have fewer photos than others.

2 Reading for gist (5–10 minutes)

Some students may meet plenty of unfamiliar vocabulary in this text, but most of the meanings can be deduced from the context, so discourage them from using dictionaries here. Demonstrate how to use context clues to guess meaning – for example, *tangled = caught or trapped*. It is possible to guess this meaning by looking at the previous sentence, which says that the whale was *'cut free from the nets.'* If it wasn't free, it must have been caught or trapped. You could also brainstorm a list of vocabulary that students might expect to find in this article.

To extend the exercise, you could ask students to identify any sentences where the past perfect tense could be used – for example:

*'The amazing hour-long performance was caught on camera moments after the creature **had been** cut free from fishing nets.'*

*'We were all proud and thrilled that we **had saved** this fantastic young life.'*

Suggested answers
Past simple: saved, came, thought, decided, swam

Past continuous: was floating

Discuss any cases where an alternative past tense might be used.

3 Multiple-choice questions (5–10 minutes)

Answers
1 B; 2 C; 3 B; 4 A; 5 A; 6 C

4 Vocabulary check (5–8 minutes)

Answers
a breathtaking; b came across; c helpless;
d stricken; e fatigued; f panicked; g dramatic;
h show

5 Narrative structure (3–5 minutes)

⟩ **Critical thinking:** Although students are not expected to display great sophistication in shaping a narrative, this exercise will increase students' awareness of possible starting points in a story. It will also help them become more aware of the shifts in viewpoint and time, which are typical of longer and more detailed newspaper reports.

All the points given in the Coursebook are possible reasons for telling the story in that particular style.

6 Writing a summary from notes (5–10 minutes)

Note: Summary writing is beyond the requirements of the Cambridge IGCSE English as a Second Language syllabus, but is a useful study skill that will help students to identify the key points of a text and remember them.

Example answer

A humpback whale was trapped by fishing nets off the coast of California. A whale-watching boat found the whale and the crew decided to help. One of them decided to dive down and used a knife to cut the nets off. Afterwards, the whale put on a show of diving and jumping to say thank you to its rescuers.

7 Vocabulary: Adjectives (3–5 minutes)

Suggested answer
Physical condition: 1 stricken, 2 injured, 3 hurt, 4 fatigued, 5 frightened

Experience: 1 breathtaking, 2 dramatic, 3 impressive, 4 amazing, 5 interesting

8 Pre-listening exercise

⟩ **Critical thinking:** Draw a mindmap on the board and elicit as many effects that humans have on ocean life as possible. For example: oil tankers crash and leak oil into the oceans, ships throw rubbish and waste into the water, chemicals from farming (fertilisers and pesticides) flow into rivers, which end up in the ocean.

9 Listening: A lecture about the Earth's oceans (10–15 minutes)

Ask students to read the questions before they hear the audio recording. Play the recording while students select their answers. Let students compare answers in pairs before listening again.

After checking the answers, go back to the mindmap and ask the class which points were not mentioned or to add other points that were mentioned in the lecture.

DIFFERENTIATION

For more **support**, play the recording again and ask students to add any additional points they hear.

For more **challenge**, ask students to create two or more multiple-choice questions to test each other.

Answers
1 C; 2 C; 3 C; 4 B; 5 B

Audioscript track 8.3

Listen to the introduction to a lecture on the impact of human activity on the oceans.

Good morning, everyone! Today's lecture is about the impact of human activity on the oceans. Let's start by getting an overview of some of the main issues.

As we all know, water covers about 71 percent of the Earth's surface. Although we often think of the Earth as having five separate oceans, it may be more helpful to think of them as all being joined together into one global ocean. This is even more relevant when we start thinking about the global effects of human activity on the planet.

Needless to say, the main factor affecting every ecosystem on our planet is climate change. Changes in temperature cause sea levels to rise, and also affect our weather systems and severe weather events. They affect the migration and feeding patterns of all wildlife, on land as well as in the sea.

Climate warming is partly caused by greenhouse gases such as carbon dioxide. As the amount of carbon dioxide increases, the ocean starts to absorb some of the excess gas. The gas reacts with seawater and increases the acidity of the water. This affects the growth of animals and plants in the ocean, weakening, for example, the ability of coral and shellfish to form shells.

But climate change is not the only way in which oceans are affected. Marine habitats are continuously being harmed by underwater drilling and mining. Habitats are also destroyed by pollution, whether from oil or chemical spills, or from the dumping of waste such as plastic.

Finally, oceans are obviously a vast resource for food, but fishing can be destructive. Excessive overfishing can depopulate whole sections of the ocean, and the use of nets and trawlers can also damage and kill fish that aren't eaten for food. Any kind of shipping activity can easily damage and harm sea mammals such as whales and dolphins, which can be struck by ships or caught up in fishing nets.

So now let's go into further detail on some of these wider issues and look at ways in which we may go about lessening the impact of humans on the ocean . . .

10 Language study: Revision of defining relative clauses (10–12 minutes)

The aim of this and the following exercise is to revise the difference between defining and non-defining clauses and to help those students who are still writing mainly in simple sentences to vary their style of writing. Sentences that demonstrate variety in length and complexity as well as accuracy show greater skill. Using defining and non-defining clauses accurately is one way to achieve this.

Ask students who need **support** to first identify what kind of pronoun matches each sentence. Then suggest some key words to help students complete the sentences (e.g. *happy, lottery, saved, bought, grandfather, helped*).

For extra **challenge**, ask students to come up with two different ways to complete each sentence.

Suggested answers
a They prefer stories that have happy endings.
b The man who won the lottery has donated a lot of money to charity.
c The student who saved the boy's life received an award for bravery.
d The shoes that I bought last month have already fallen apart.
e The factory where my grandfather worked is now a tourist hotel.
f The doctor who helped us comes from Guatemala.

11 Language study: Revision of non-defining relative clauses (5–12 minutes)

Students could treat this exercise as a problem-solving one and work together to come up with the extra information for each sentence.

Suggested answers
1 a Rahmia Altat, who retired last year, now does voluntary work.
  b We heard about the heroic acts of the rescue workers, which impressed us all.
  c Nurse Mara, who attended the meeting specially, demonstrated the lifesaving techniques.
  d Drowning, which can be a risk for children playing in water, can usually be prevented.
  e Smoke alarms, which are quite cheap, should be fitted in every home.

f My cousin Gina, whose parents died when she was a baby, is being brought up by her grandparents.

2 **a** Mrs Nazir, who had never entered a competition before, won a trip to the Caribbean.

   b The new hospital, which opened last month, is the biggest in the country.

   c Our sailing teacher took us to an island, where we had a picnic lunch.

3 Students' own answers.

12 Consoling and sympathising (5 minutes)

Some students can find it hard to get the balance of sympathy right, and this quiz provides more practice in choosing appropriate responses to sensitive situations. The expression 'Oh dear!' is a useful sympathetic response in many situations and is heavily used by British people.

Suggested answers

1 A or E

2 A or C

3 A (B and E would be possible, but express blame rather than sympathy)

4 A, B or C

5 **a** I'm sorry, you must be really disappointed.

   b Are you? Why? It looks all right to me.

   c Oh no! How terrible!

13 Spelling and pronunciation: The suffix -tion or -ion (3–5 minutes)

This exercise will boost students' awareness of the sound and spelling pattern of this suffix, usually pronounced /ʃn/.

After marking the stress, students should then practise the pronunciation of each word. Ask students to notice that the stressed syllable in these words is always the penultimate syllable.

The matching exercise (question 3) will ensure that the meaning of each word has been understood properly.

To round off, you could elicit more examples of words ending in -ion – for example, *inspiration, comprehension, expression, attention*.

Answers

1 **a** exhibition; **b** fashion; **c** occupation; **d** demonstration; **e** passion; **f** invention; **g** qualification; **h** definition; **i** recognition; **j** ignition; **k** promotion

3 **a** qualification; **b** occupation; **c** invention; **d** passion; **e** exhibition; **f** definition; **g** promotion; **h** ignition; **i** recognition; **j** fashion

---

Audioscript track 8.4

Listen carefully to the following words on the audio recording and mark the main stress in each word. Then practise saying them.

a	exhibition	**b**	fashion
c	occupation	**d**	demonstration
e	passion	**f**	invention
g	qualification	**h**	definition
i	recognition	**j**	ignition
k	promotion		

---

14 Language study: Adverbs (5–10 minutes)

Students often make spelling mistakes when forming adverbs. They tend to overgeneralise about the -*ly* ending and don't make the adjustments necessary to take account of adjective spellings. The rules aren't complex, however, and mastering them needn't take long.

After the brief refresher on adverb functions, students can go straight into the basic spelling rules for adding suffixes. Or you could adopt a problem-solving approach by giving them some examples and asking them to look for meaningful regularities in the spelling changes.

Examples:

comfortable	*We sat comfortably.*
incredible	*We were incredibly lucky.*
guilty	*'I haven't taken anything,' said the thief guiltily.*
merry	*She laughed merrily.*
rhythmic	*They danced rhythmically.*
terrific	*It was terrifically expensive.*

Practice

You may want to stage the exercise so that students first read the text for meaning and say which of these careers would interest them most. Then ask them to identify which words in italics need to be changed. It may be helpful to refer back to the rules for adverbs and ask which rule applies to each example. Students can then write the correct adverbs, then check the spelling.

Discuss the reasons why a career in marine science might be attractive and what the disadvantages might be. Advantages might be that you get to visit different countries, do a lot of diving, learn about marine animals and plants. Disadvantages might be that you have to study a lot, you might need an MA or PhD, and you might need to do a lot of training before you can get a well-paid position.

DIFFERENTIATION

To provide extra **support**, ask students questions about the text that require an answer using an adverb – for example, *What do marine biologists do with the samples they collect?* (They analyse them carefully.)

For extra **challenge**, ask students to think of an alternative adverb for each example. They could also think of three extra adverbs that could be added to the text.

Answers
Surprisingly; finally; carefully; eventually; technically; quickly; normally; safely; independently; clearly; verbally; safely; responsibly; patiently; accurately

---

15 Look, say, cover, write, check (5 minutes)

The spelling list will help students recognise spelling sounds and patterns by developing visual awareness. See Unit 1, Section B13 for a reminder of the 'Look, say, cover, write, check' method for learning vocabulary.

D Reacting to the unexpected

1 Pre-reading task: Making notes (5–10 minutes)

This next series of exercises pulls together the skills students have been building up and gets them writing narratives. They start by making notes on something that has happened to them. Encourage them to keep their notes and use them to write a complete account for homework.

2 Reading an example narrative (5–10 minutes)

The example narrative shows the style and format students should aim for.

Answers
Simple past tense: seemed, sat, noticed, realised, plunged, grabbed, swam, was, was, felt, laid, appeared, gave, revived, was, was, arrived, were, rang, had

Past continuous: was thinking, was telling, was sitting, (was) talking

Past perfect: had decided, had gathered

Present perfect: have arranged

Non-defining relative clauses: who was a boy of about five; who appeared to be unconscious; which revived him immediately; which I think is a very good idea

---

3 Comprehension check (10–15 minutes)

Answers
1 She was watching the children on the beach paddling and throwing pebbles.
2 No
3 Mouth-to-mouth resuscitation
4 She is only dimly aware of the crowd gathering around her.
5 They are going to arrange for him to have swimming lessons.

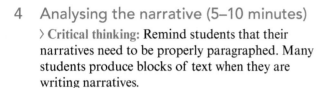

4 Analysing the narrative (5–10 minutes)

> **Critical thinking:** Remind students that their narratives need to be properly paragraphed. Many students produce blocks of text when they are writing narratives.

DIFFERENTIATION

For more **support**, ask students to write questions about the events in the story.

For extra **challenge**, ask students what kind of information is missing from the story. (Where were the boy's parents, for example?)

Answers

1 '*It seemed like another ordinary day.*' This opening tells you immediately that something extremely unusual is about to happen.

2 The main tense is simple past to describe a sequence of actions of events. Past perfect is used to give some background to the scene, and past continuous to emphasise that a continuing activity was interrupted.

3 To my consternation/dismay; Without a second thought; To my tremendous/considerable relief.

4 The article ends with some helpful advice based on her experience. Alternative ways to end the story could be: that she met the boy again a year later and he was a swimming champion; that the parents sent her a thank you gift; that she was invited to talk about her experience on a TV programme.

5 a Naila, her family, a young boy and his parents

   b She saved a boy from drowning in the sea.

   c On the beach.

---

5 Dramatic expressions (5–10 minutes)

Dramatic expressions can increase the pace and excitement of a narrative. Encourage students to use them. Other dramatic expressions to elicit include *was thunderstruck*, *quick as a flash*, *in the nick of time*, and show how they could be used.

Students could read their own sentences out loud.

Answers

1 **a** 5; **b** 2, 3 or 4; **c** 2, 3 or 4; **d** 1, 2, 3 or 4; **e** 5 or 6; **f** 1 or 3

2 Students' own answers.

---

6 Pre-writing discussion (5 minutes)

Make sure students understand what a windsurfer does and what the sport is all about, especially if they have little experience of watersports.

7 Ways of developing an outline (15–20 minutes)

The outline of a story about a windsurfer carried out to sea by strong winds gives students a basic plot to work from so they can concentrate on structuring the story well and providing interesting background details. Put students into small groups to develop the story from the outline. Make sure that there is a mix of abilities in each group. Encourage students to discuss the best way of opening the story, how to make it more interesting by adding details and what dramatic expressions might bring it alive for the reader.

This exercise does not involve the search for a correct answer, which means that students could be stretched and encouraged to give and justify their opinions – for example, *I think we should open the story with 'I had no idea what was going to happen' as it makes the reader really wonder what took place. What do you think?*

DIFFERENTIATION

The task may be more manageable for students who need extra **support** if you break the story into two halves. When they have finished, you could have two groups read their versions consecutively so that they hear the complete story read aloud. You could also provide students with a short tick list of features you want them to include – for example, two time expressions, one non-defining relative clause, one dramatic expression, and so on.

For extra **challenge**, ask students to come up with two or three different ways of starting or ending the story.

---

8 Building a story from a dialogue (15–20 minutes)

Students write a narrative based on a conversation about an incident on a school trip to the seaside. The teacher lost her purse and one of the children helped her look for it. Students may not immediately see how they can produce a composition from a conversation, so it's useful to clarify how they can transfer the information revealed in the dialogue into a story told from Ethan's point of view.

Discuss with them how to shape the narrative and how to change the pronouns, and so on before they start. Using some direct and reported speech would add interest and variety to their stories. You may want to refer back to the example narrative in Section D2 for some useful techniques for starting the narrative and setting the scene.

9 Post-discussion task: Correcting and writing a report (20–30 minutes)

> **Critical thinking:** Before they proofread the report, make sure students understand what they have to do. Elicit the pros and cons of giving funds for the explorers' expedition either before the class read the report, or afterwards as reading comprehension. The following are useful points to discuss.

Reasons for supporting the expedition:

- students are interested in the project and want to find out what happens
- good example to students of explorers' courage, bravery and determination
- local people involved, so it's good to support them
- hopefully, explorers are well-prepared
- they may have learnt/learned survival skills and done training
- expedition might find things out which benefit our knowledge – for example, climate change factors.

Reasons for not supporting the expedition:

- waste of money giving to inexperienced teenagers who just want to have fun
- dangerous – things might go wrong and end in disaster
- lack of experience and preparation

- wouldn't be able to give money to help a different cause with a tried and tested reputation – for example, fire service.

Students should enjoy improving the report, as it is quite a straightforward exercise and they will produce a perfect report at the end with good audience awareness – for example, '*I have spoken to other students in my year to find out of their views / At school, we are all looking forward to reading the Antarctica Expedition blog*'.

You could draw attention to the formal tone and register – '*The positive points of supporting the expedition are that, firstly . . .*' / '*To sum up, I believe that . . .*'. You could ask students to comment on the fact that the report sounds polite.

Finally, it is also worth pointing out that small extra words get into our writing unnoticed, so it is important to proofread carefully. Students may have views on why we make mistakes when writing and therefore how that may be avoided.

Answers

1   The extra words which should not be there are highlighted in bold and crossed through below.

2   The 'missing' sentence has been inserted and is underlined below.

This report will consider ~~at~~ the pros and cons of supporting the young explorers going to Antarctica. I have spoken to other students in my year to find out ~~of~~ their views and these are given in the report.

The positive points of supporting ~~to~~ the expedition are that, firstly, the people taking part are from our town, so we would be helping local people. <u>In fact, a ~~some~~ member of the expedition previously attended our school.</u> In addition, many of us admire the explorers because they are prepared to take risks and are testing ~~in~~ themselves to the limits. Their courage is a shining example and ~~for~~ encourages us to think about the importance of having challenging projects ourselves.

On the other hand, a few students have said it would be better to give the money to the Town Emergency Services rather than a group of teenagers who ~~they~~ want to have fun. Also, the trip might ~~it~~ end in disaster. While it is true that exploring the coast of Antarctica is dangerous, in my view, the people going on ~~if~~

the expedition are taking the project seriously and are well-prepared. They have spent a long time learning ~~how~~ survival skills. They are also going to do some research ~~there~~ in Antarctica, which will increase scientists' knowledge of climate change.

To sum up, I believe that we should support ~~our~~ the expedition. The explorers ~~who~~ deserve our help. The project is a worthwhile and inspiring ~~one~~ challenge. At school, we are all looking forward to reading ~~on~~ the Antarctica Expedition blog.

GRAMMAR SPOTLIGHT (10–15 MINUTES)

The 'Grammar spotlight' gives further practice with the interrupted past continuous. Students will hopefully have developed an appreciation of the way this structure can make a real difference to their writing. It should certainly help consolidate the work they have done earlier in the unit.

To extend the task, ask students to choose one or more sentences in question 2 and suggest how the story might continue.

Answers

1 was walking; *walking home interrupted when a passer-by collapsed*

was doing; *doing homework interrupted when water started pouring*

was chatting; *chatting interrupted when a guest insisted*

2 a Tomaz was sitting on his life raft feeling hungry and scared when, to his relief, a rescue ship appeared on the horizon.

b The shipwrecked couple were having a conversation about what to do next, when they saw/noticed a rowing boat coming towards them.

CONTINUED

c Alan was alone on the desert island trying/hoping/struggling to make a fire without matches when, to his amazement, he saw/noticed/spotted some children walking/running/skipping along the beach.

d Maha was walking home one evening when to her surprise several bright white circular objects suddenly appeared in the sky.

e The class were listening quietly to Mr Hamsun's science lecture and making notes when the teacher suddenly put his hand in his pocket and threw a fistful of fabulous diamonds onto the desk.

f Anton was hiking with his children in the woods when, to his amazement, he spotted a mysterious, veiled woman dressed in golden robes.

DIFFERENTIATION

Some students may be puzzled by the extra words sometimes used between the auxiliary verb and the main verb (e.g. *Alan was alone on the desert island trying . . .*). To give **support**, demonstrate that this makes no difference to the structure of the past continuous form, putting brackets around the 'extra' words (*alone on the desert island*). Also point out that there may be more than one past continuous verb before the verb that 'interrupts' (*the class were listening quietly and making notes when the teacher put . . .*).

WIDER PRACTICE

1 The sea is a fascinating topic and students may enjoy researching many of its other aspects – for example, the creatures that live in it. If appropriate, cross-curricular links may be made with other subjects that students are studying – for example, geography, science.

2 Students could extend the theme of adventure and exploration further by investigating space travel or life in space. They may like to research the lives of famous astronauts, look into space missions, find out about everyday life on a spacecraft or investigate space tourism. Presenting their mini-projects to the class in the form of short talks would be enjoyable for everyone.

3 Students could extend their storytelling skills by choosing a current news topic that absorbs them, tracing its development over several days. This could then be presented to the class.

4 Students could explore poetry or extracts from literature, from their own cultures or English literature, which focus on bravery, heroism, adventure and exploration.

5 Students who are interested in conservation and the environment may want to do more research about how the world's oceans are being affected by climate change and pollution, and what is being done to prevent that.

Exam-style questions

Reading and writing

Reading and Writing: multiple matching

This exercise provides practice with answering multiple-matching comprehension questions.

Encourage students to read the rubric and scan the nine statements so they get a general idea of what the text might be about. Then they should read the texts for general meaning. When they have finished reading, they should tackle the first statement. In this particular exercise, students are asked to decide which person received public recognition for achievement. They should scan the text again to identify possible candidates, eliminating people who do not match the statement. They should then compare the likely candidates more carefully, as only one answer will be right.

Students can then tackle the next statement and repeat the process, and so on. Students' knowledge of vocabulary and topic will be crucial in helping them distinguish between ideas that are similar but not the same. When students have finished the first round of reading and matching, they should return to any problematic matches and refine their choice by checking the detail of the question against the detail of the text.

Answers
1 D; 2 B; 3 A; 4 B; 5 D; 6 A; 7 C; 8 B; 9 C

Reading and Writing: informal and formal

You will find advice on general approaches to exam-style writing exercises at the end of the 'Teaching support' section in the Introduction.

When writing the email, remind students of some of the vocabulary used in this unit to describe the sea. If necessary, refer back to some of the photos and ask students to imagine themselves in the scene.

Example answer

Formal writing

When we went inside the caves, we were amazed at the strange atmosphere. It was a sunny day outside, but inside, the caves were dark and silent. Some of us found that scary, but I didn't mind because we had torches and the guide had a big flashlight.

We followed the guide, who led us down some very steep entrance steps, reminding us to hold tightly onto the safety rope. She explained that the caves are ancient but had only been discovered recently. Occasionally there was not enough space to stand up, so we had to crawl slowly like turtles.

After our visit, we got ice creams and sat outside in the sunshine. Some classmates admitted they felt scared at first but gradually started to enjoy the feeling of exploring underground. Overall, it was wonderful to discover a place very few people had seen before. It was cold, though, so I would advise next year's group to take warm jackets.

(160 words)

Listening

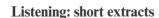

Listening: short extracts

Students answer multiple-choice questions on five short recordings.

In the first exercise, students hear a series of short clips from a wide range of situations, and the information they need comes very quickly. So point out how important it is to read the rubric ahead of each recording because it explains who is speaking and in what context. Students should also be aware that the words in the questions will not directly reflect the words in the recording, so they need to listen for the same idea expressed in different words. If students don't get the answers right, it may be very useful to study the transcript afterwards to work out what they missed or what misled them, so they can be better prepared next time.

Answers
1 B; 2 A; 3 C; 4 C; 5 C; 6 B; 7 A; 8 B; 9 B; 10 A

Audioscript track 8.5

You will hear five short recordings. For each question, choose the correct answer, A, B or C and put a tick in the appropriate box. You will hear each recording twice.

You will hear a camp leader giving some information about an adventure trail camp.

Camp leader: Hi everyone and welcome to our adventure trail weekend! We hope you've brought a lot of energy and enthusiasm – as well as your tents and sleeping bags, of course. Any sports equipment you'll need – such as helmets and goggles – is available here for you to borrow. And all food and drink will be provided for everyone as well. We've got an amazing choice of activities for you, including water sports, wilderness trails and a trip to explore some underground caves!

Before learning more about all the activities you can do here, we'll go over some simple rules for staying safe during the weekend. After that, you'll be able to meet the team leaders and you can ask any questions you like before signing up for your choices.

You will hear two classmates talking about a presentation they are preparing for school.

Girl: Have you finished preparing your presentation yet?

Boy: Not yet. I can't decide whether to do Arctic Explorers or Space Travel. I think Space Travel might mean reading more technical stuff and I'm not too good at that. Hopefully, Arctic Explorers won't be as difficult, even though it isn't as exciting. What did you choose?

Girl: I almost chose Space Travel, but in the end I decided to do something about the Vikings. I haven't started writing yet but I found some amazing websites with videos and everything.

Boy: Are you going to take notes from the websites and then write your own description?

Girl: Actually, I'm going to look for some interesting photos first and then write a short description to go with each one.

Boy: Hey, that sounds like a good idea! I think I'll do that, too.

You will hear part of a radio interview with an open water swimmer.

Interviewer: Tell us why you decided to start open water swimming.

Swimmer: I've always loved swimming and used to swim in the pool every day, but I thought I'd like to try something a bit more challenging and joined a club for open water swimming about two years ago. And I've never looked back!

Interviewer:	What's your next swim going to be? Will it be difficult?
Swimmer:	I'm going to do an open water swim off the coast of Sweden. Of course, the water will be very cold. That's not a problem if you have a good wetsuit. The strong tides off the coast there could push me off course, but it's not the longest swim I've ever done. I'm looking forward to it!

You will hear a boy leaving a voicemail message for a friend about a sailing club.

Hi Tania! Have you heard about the open day at the sailing club this weekend? It's open to the public and free all day from 10 a.m. to 3 p.m. You can learn about the kinds of boats they have, and I think they give you a sailing lesson too! I've never been to the club before but I'm sure it's a lot of fun! Do you want to go? I expect there will be a lot of people there, so why don't we go half an hour before opening time so we can get a place at the front of the queue? Let's meet at the main entrance to the park, next to the playground. Oh, wait a minute, that's the wrong side of the park! Let's meet at the benches near the water fountain instead. We can go to the riverside café for an ice-cream afterwards!

You will hear a boy talking to a friend about a trip he made to the coast.

Girl:	How was your trip to the coast last weekend?
Boy:	It was good! Except it was too cold to go for a swim!
Girl:	Oh no! You were going to search for fossils, weren't you?
Boy:	Yes, we had a lot of fun looking for fossils, but I didn't find any. Only some shells and pieces of stone. I brought some of them home with me.
Girl:	That's too bad. Did your friends have better luck?
Boy:	No, but one boy was searching among the rocks and wandered off into some caves. We had to wait in the bus while the teacher walked back to look for him.
Girl:	Poor thing! Was he alright?
Boy:	Yes, he was just a bit afraid that he'd get left behind. But he was fine.

Speaking

You will find advice on general approaches to speaking exercises at the end of the 'Teaching support' section in the Introduction.

If students are doing this exercise under examination conditions, warm-up questions may help to put them at ease. These are included in the corresponding Coursebook unit.

>9 Animals and our world

Learning plan

AOs	Key learning intentions	Success criteria
S1, S2, S3	Explore the topic of animals in zoos, on farms, in the wild and in medical research	• Students can identify and respond to others' opinions • Students can use a variety of expressions for expressing opinions • Students can use appropriate vocabulary to express ideas on topics related to animals
R1, R2, R3, R4	Skim for general ideas and identify bias in an article about animal research	• Students can predict ideas in an article • Students can identify bias in an argument • Students can identify the main idea of each paragraph
W1, W2, W3, W4	Write a blog post using examples and explanations to develop your argument	• Students can plan the structure and organisation of a blog post • Students can choose appropriate tone and register to engage their reader • Students can express a nuanced view of an argument • Students can add emphasis appropriately
L1, L2, L3, L4	Identify key details and understand what is implied in an interview	• Students can predict ideas they might hear in an interview • Students can identify details and say if they are correct or incorrect • Students can identify inferred or implied meanings
S1, S2, S3, S4	Use appropriate register and intonation for expressing disappointment and disagreement	• Students can use a variety of expressions for describing disappointment • Students can use stress and intonation to emphasise their feelings • Students can respond and elaborate on others' opinions

Overview

The main aim of this unit is to further develop students' ability to express reasoned opinions and arguments in emails, letters, articles and reports. There is also further practice in note-taking. Unit 4, Sections C and D focused on presenting both sides of arguments. This unit looks at a wider variety of arguments using the topic of animals. There is also a multiple-matching question based on a text about birdwatching and a report-writing question about whether to help fund a tiger sanctuary or a bird reserve.

Sometimes students are asked to present views and opinions explaining how or why a thing could happen. For example, in a discussion on endangered species, rather than being asked to take a stand for or against a proposal to help endangered species, students could be asked to express their opinions in a more measured way – for example, *Why do endangered species need our help and how can we ensure their protection?*

THEME

Students consider a number of questions on the theme of animals, including:

- How can zoos be more animal-friendly?
- How can medical understanding and health standards be improved without resorting to experiments on animals?
- How can we ensure working animals are treated fairly?

- What can we do to help protect endangered species?

The items include a magazine article about animal experiments, an interview with a zookeeper and a leaflet about 'adopting' zoo animals. There is also a multiple-matching question based on a text about wild birds.

LANGUAGE WORK

The language work further develops the skills needed to present a convincing argument. These include opinion language, rhetorical questions and ways of adding emphasis, including the use of *what* clauses, which can be especially problematic when used with a preposition. There is a range of vocabulary expansion exercises related to animals. Spelling and pronunciation work focuses on plurals, and students practise disagreeing informally and expressing disappointment.

The 'Grammar spotlight' focuses on the past perfect passive.

Common misconceptions

Misconception	How to identify	How to overcome
Students often make mistakes with word order when using **what clauses with a preposition.** Examples: *About my phone what I like is its design. What about it I like is the colour and functionality.*	Contrast examples of *what* clauses with and without prepositions and ask students to identify the differences. Correct examples: *What I like about my new phone is its design.* *What I like about it is the colour and functionality.*	Write the words of a sentence using a *what* clause with a preposition in scrambled order on the board and ask students to sequence them correctly.
Students may sometimes use the past simple passive when **the past perfect passive** would be more suitable. Examples: *I noticed that my new bike was stolen.* *He told us that he was kidnapped.*	Take some incorrect examples from students' written work and write them on the board. Ask students to identify when each of the past events occurred and whether one of them occurred before the other. Correct examples: *I noticed that my new bike had been stolen.* *He told us that he had been kidnapped.*	Explain that this tense is most often used to contrast with an event using the past simple tense. Provide examples of sentences in the active form and ask students to rewrite them in the passive.

Introducing the unit topic (5–10 minutes)

Working with a partner, students look at the photo and discuss the questions.

The questions should draw out what students think about wild animals and how they are impacted by human activity. They might describe the animal in the photo as *strong, powerful, proud, independent, savage,* for example. What do they know about this particular species, its habitat, diet and special characteristics?

Move the discussion on to the difference between the concepts of being in danger and being endangered. Wild animals face a number of dangers in their natural habitat, from predators to lack of food, but being endangered means that a species is in danger of extinction because the population has reached a critically low number. This could be caused by the destruction of their habitat to satisfy human needs or because of climate change or increased pollution. Can students name any endangered animals (e.g. mountain gorillas, tigers, orangutans, Asian elephants)? How do they feel about the animals' future? What do they know about what threatens these animals and what is being done to protect them?

Some students may know about biodiversity from other subjects such as geography – how a range of different species living together create an ecosystem that helps and sustains all creatures within it. When species become extinct, often because their habitat is destroyed by human action, the biodiversity of Earth, which is essential to life on this planet, is in danger.

Studying wild animals can give us a lot of information about how they live together in particular ecosystems, maintaining a balance that allows all animals and plants to thrive. It can help us learn how to maintain biodiversity and live in harmony with other creatures on our planet.

> **Digital coursebook:** At the start of the lesson, use this video to introduce and review:

- the topic of animals and their relationship to humans
- a range of vocabulary related to animals
- the past perfect passive.

Read the question on the title screen and ask learners what they think they might see. Then play the video all the way through and check learners' predictions.

Play the video a second time, pausing to discuss what is being shown and the questions on the end screen. You can take the opportunity to revise words and phrases associated with the topic of animals and their relationship to humans. Note that the end-screen contains two differentiated two-part questions. The first part should be relatively easily accessed from the video. The second part requires reasoning and personal opinion. More confident learners will be able to offer more extensive reasons for their ideas.

Take note of whether learners use the past perfect passive in their answers to question 1.

You may like to play the video a third time for consolidation.

A A fresh look at zoos

1 Animal vocabulary (5–10 minutes)

> **Critical thinking:** The unit starts with some key vocabulary. It's a good idea for students to work in pairs for Sections A1 and A2.

To extend the exercise, ask students to each choose a wild animal. Then play a game of '20 questions'. Their partner can ask up to 20 Yes/No questions to find out the chosen animal – for example, *Does it live in the forest? Does it eat meat?* If the partner can guess before 20 questions are up, they get a point. This can also be done as a group/team quiz activity.

DIFFERENTIATION

To reinforce the categories in question 2 and recycle other wildlife vocabulary, ask students to add two more animals to each group.

For an extra **challenge**, you may also want to elicit other animal classifications such as amphibians and insects, and ask for examples of each.

Answers
1   **A** snake; **B** parrot; **C** kangaroo; **D** wolf; **E** crocodile; **F** gorilla
2   **mammals:** bear, rhino, gorilla, cheetah, lion, elephant, leopard, camel, dolphin, monkey, wolf, kangaroo
     reptiles: crocodile, lizard, snake
     fish: shark, salmon
     birds: vulture, penguin, eagle, parrot

2 Definitions (5 minutes)

You could also elicit the meaning of other animal-related words: *herbivorous, omnivorous, carnivorous, cold-blooded, warm-blooded, invertebrates, marsupials*, and so on.

Answers
1 B; 2 A; 3 C; 4 A; 5 B

3 Pre-reading discussion (5–10 minutes)

> **Critical thinking:** Allow the discussion about zoos to be as open as possible so that students have a real chance to think through the issues for themselves. You may want to brainstorm possible reasons for having zoos – for example, to educate, entertain and conserve.

DIFFERENTIATION

It may **support** students to pre-teach (or provide a glossary for) the following vocabulary from the text, or to bring up some of them in the pre-reading discussion and write them on the board: *perspective, enclosure, living quarters, diet, exploit, endangered species, predator*.

For extra **challenge**, ask students to predict three points they would expect to find in the article.

4 Reading an article for the school website (10–15 minutes)

Encourage students to underline the opinion language as they read.

5 Comprehension check (5–8 minutes)

Answers
1 Because their teacher wanted them to see a modern zoo
2 Very positive – he thought the animals seemed happy
3 The origins and habits of the animals
4 They protect animals from predators, provide a caring environment and educate people about wildlife.
5 Bad points about zoos to elicit could be:
  - Wild animals find conditions cramped; they lack space and privacy, and they are herded together when some animals are naturally solitary.
  - Animals are frustrated because they can't get enough exercise or have the opportunity to respond to hunting instincts.
  - Animals become lazy as they have no need to search for food.
  - Animals suffer by having to live in unnatural climatic conditions.
  - Zoos are unnecessary – we can see animals in their natural habitat by watching wildlife programmes on television.

6 Analysing the article (8–10 minutes)

> **Critical thinking: Answers**
1 The opening paragraph is effective because it explains the background to the zoo visit. It shows audience awareness because it provides typical school details.
2 Paragraph 2 questions attitudes to zoos with phrases such as '*I was pleasantly surprised by what I found*', '*people had said that zoos are full of smelly cages . . . Metro Park Zoo, however . . .*' and '*In my opinion . . .*'.
3 The phrase expressing disagreement is '*nothing could be further from the truth*'.
4 '*I wasn't sure about the rights and wrongs of zoos*' tells us he has thought about both sides of the argument. '*On balance, I feel that*' sums up his view of zoos and pulls the contrasting ideas together.
5 The final paragraph ties together the whole structure effectively. It shows audience awareness by including a reference to his classmates.

7 Typical opinion language (5–10 minutes)

> **Critical thinking: Answers**
1 I just wasn't sure; As I see it, nothing could be further from the truth; On balance I feel that; to my mind; I think
2 In my view; Let's put it this way; I believe; If you ask me; As far as I'm concerned; As far as I can see

Disagreeing with other people's views

Answers

3   Some people accuse them of . . . but nothing could be further from the truth.

Many people say that . . . However, . . .

8   Making your mind up (2–3 minutes)

> **Critical thinking: Answers**
On balance, I feel that . . .

9   Writing a paragraph (10–15 minutes)

Students could write their paragraphs either individually or in a group with others who want to write about the same topic.

DIFFERENTIATION

To **support** students in developing their opinions, ask them to write down their ideas first in the form of a mind map. They should use the mind map to list ideas for and against their chosen topic. Provide some examples to help them get started. Encourage students to come up with at least three ideas for and against before making up their mind.

Challenge more confident students to come up with at least five ideas.

---

10   Reading aloud (5–10 minutes)

When they have finished writing, ask students who chose the same topic to sit together and compare their paragraphs. Reading aloud provides a good opportunity to compare and contrast language structures and content. If you prefer, this could also be done as a whole-class activity.

11   Expressions of contrasting meaning (5–10 minutes)

Before students start the exercise, it's worth pointing out that there is more than one possible answer each time. For example, *a bare, cramped room* could be contrasted with *a well-furnished, gracefully proportioned room*.

The main aim of the exercise is for students to explore different possibilities and then choose the one that seems best to convey a contrasting

meaning. At the end of the exercise, they can share their answers and you can discuss different shades of meaning.

Suggested answers

1   a   a lively/interesting/informative lesson

b   a well-polished/shiny/smart pair of shoes

c   a healthy/fit child

d   a tasty/delicious meal

e   a graceful/elegant dance

f   a tidy/neat/well-maintained garden

g   attractive, easy-to-read/clear handwriting

h   a gleaming bicycle in perfect condition

i   a peaceful/calm, friendly/tolerant person

j   a soft, comfortable bed

12   Pre-listening task (3–5 minutes)

Brainstorm ideas about a typical day in the life of a zookeeper. Make a list of possible daily tasks on the board. Discuss what students might like and dislike about this job.

13   Vocabulary check (2–3 minutes)

Answers
animal welfare: health and well-being of the animals

conservation: saving and protecting species from extinction

enclosures: cages or closed-off areas where animals are kept

enrichment: making animals' lives more interesting

virtual tour: tour by video or live webcam

14   Listening for gist

DIFFERENTIATION

For additional **support**, you may want to pause the audio recording after each question and ask students to predict what the speaker is going to say in response.

For extra **challenge**, pause at the end of each answer and ask students to take notes of two key points from each section.

Audioscript track 9.1

Listen to an interview with zookeeper Jo. Does she mention the topics you predicted?

Jo: Hi everyone! My name is Jo Nazeen and I'm here today to answer all your questions about zookeeping!

Jo: OK, Terry what's your question?

Terry: Why did you decide to become a zookeeper?

Jo: Good question! I've loved animals ever since I was a small kid. We always had pets at home and at school I just loved all the lessons about wild animals. Then when I was about 12, I went on a summer 'zookeeper experience' at our local zoo. That's where you spend a day with a real zookeeper and help out with the daily tasks. Sort of a good way to find out about what a zookeeper's job is like. And I just loved it so much! I went on to take courses in biology and animal behaviour and zookeeping technology . . . and now here I am!

Yes, Sylvie?

Sylvie: Hi! Can you describe what your typical day is like?

Jo: OK, so of course we have to make sure the animals have enough food and exercise. But the main thing is to check that animals aren't sick. We weigh most animals once a week – weight is a really good way to tell if an animal is unwell – and take their temperatures. And it's important to keep careful records, especially if I'm handing over to another zookeeper – they have to know what I've done. After that, it's mainly cleaning out their enclosures – not everyone's favourite part of the job *[laughs]*!

Yes, Ali?

Ali: Hi! Do you think that animals sometimes get bored in the zoo?

Jo: Right! So we do something called enrichment activities – which is basically keeping the animals active and making sure they *aren't* bored. One way we do that is by giving them challenges to solve; for example, instead of just giving them food, we put the food inside a toy or a tube so that they have to work a bit harder to find and get the food – a bit like what they would do naturally in the wild.

OK, Jay? What's your question?

Jay: What's the best part of your job?

Jo: The best part is just spending time with the animals. When an animal gets to trust you, that's so cool! But I also love talking to people about the animals, like we're doing now! Recently, one of my jobs has been setting up virtual tours of the zoo. Visitors to our website can view a live webcam of some of our animals and they can speak to a specialist zookeeper who can tell you more and answer your questions. We're also planning to do virtual tours of the whole zoo, where you can follow the zookeeper on a webcam. We want everyone to learn more about what we're doing for animals and animal conservation!

OK, so I think that's all for today. Thanks for your questions and join us again for regular updates on the Virtual Zoo! Goodbye!

15 Multiple-choice questions (5–10 minutes)

DIFFERENTIATION

Allow students who need extra **support** to read the audioscript and underline the relevant parts for each question.

For extra **challenge**, ask students to write two more multiple-choice questions.

Answers

1 C; 2 B; 3 B; 4 C; 5 A; 6 A

16 Post-listening discussion (5–10 minutes)

> **Critical thinking:** Encourage discussion of how technology may change the way we think about zoos and animal conservation. Could extinct animals be brought back to life, as in the film *Jurassic Park*, for example?

17 Expressing disappointment and disagreement, and making your opinions clear (5–10 minutes)

Encourage students to express their views on the appropriateness of using large animals in the circus.

Silvia's voice goes down as she expresses disappointment. You could present a model of a disappointed tone – for example, *'I was looking forward to seeing (name someone familiar from TV) at the theatre in real life, but she didn't give a very good performance.'* You could ask students to relate their own experiences of disappointment arising from unfulfilled expectations, such as a boring film, meal or party.

Adjectives and comparative structures are important in this exercise so you may like to revise the *not as . . . as . . .* form (which can be tricky), with the relevant adjectives (*spectacular, fascinating*, etc.) for description.

You may like to ask pairs of students to take the parts of Malik and Silvia and read the dialogue aloud. Students usually like doing this, and you can ask the rest of the class to decide how disappointed 'Silvia' manages to sound.

Audioscript track 9.2

Listen to a dialogue about Silvia's visit to the circus. She is expressing disappointment. Does her voice go up or down?

Malik: What did you think of the circus?

Silvia: Well, to be honest, I was just a bit disappointed.

Malik: Why was that?

Silvia: The trapeze artists weren't very exciting and I didn't like seeing large animals performing tricks.

Malik: Surely the jugglers were good fun to watch?

Silvia: As a matter of fact, they weren't as skilful as I thought they'd be.

Silvia: As a matter of fact, they weren't as skilful as I thought they'd be.

Malik: But wasn't seeing a real live fire-eater amazing?

Silvia: To be frank, I've seen better things on television.

Malik: Sounds like a waste of money, then.

Silvia: It was! In fact, we left before the end.

Expressing disappointment

You could ask students to tick any expressions they recognise from the dialogue. Focus on intonation and pitch, replaying sections from the dialogue as needed so that students can listen and repeat. Discuss different ways of saying these expressions to change their meaning.

18 Practice dialogues (10–15 minutes)

Students progress from the prompted dialogue in question 1 to making up their own conversations in question 2. You may want to ask them to present their dialogues to the class.

DIFFERENTIATION

Students who need more **support** can read their dialogues aloud, but encourage them to look down only when they read the lines and look up at their partner when they speak.

To give more **challenge**, students can use notes or try to improvise without using a script.

B Animal experimentation

1 Pre-reading discussion (10–15 minutes)

> **Critical thinking:** The following sequence of exercises focuses on the rights and wrongs of animal experimentation. The magazine article in Section B5 puts forward a highly positive view of the issues, but students then explore why this may or may not give a complete picture of all that animal experimentation involves. It's a difficult text, so students do a variety of tasks to prepare them for it, intellectually and linguistically.

After students have commented on the photo of the laboratory rat, you could ask how they feel about using animals for dissection in science lessons (if their studies involve this). You could ask if they have been immunised, and say that the vaccination against polio, for example, was discovered through animal experimentation.

Make sure students have understood the concept of ethics before they go on to discuss the ethical questions in question 1 in pairs or small groups. Ethical questions will be central to later discussions on the treatment of animals, but they are very culturally based. What is 'ethical' in one culture isn't necessarily seen as right in another. You could check this by asking about wider issues that students may have a view on. It might be most helpful to choose examples that relate directly to students' culture(s).

Finally, students are asked what they think about animal experiments, after having had a chance to review the various ethical issues. They are offered some further useful vocabulary for giving opinions.

2 Predicting content (1–2 minutes)

DIFFERENTIATION

For extra **challenge**, ask students to predict three opinions they expect the writer to include in the article.

For more **support**, read out some opinions and ask if students think the writer will agree or disagree with them – for example, *Animal testing is cruel. Animals don't suffer a lot. It's better to test animals than humans.*

Answers

As the writer is a medical research scientist, the arguments are likely to be balanced.

3 Vocabulary check (2–3 minutes)

Answers

An *emotive* issue is one that arouses strong feelings. (Contrast *emotional* which means feeling strong emotions.)

A *controversial* issue is one about which people disagree strongly.

4 Reading for gist (8–10 minutes)

> **Critical thinking:** This question helps students to understand the overall purpose of each paragraph. Make sure that students understand that each paragraph *contradicts* one of the statements (myths) in the list.

Answers

Paragraph 2: B; **Paragraph 3:** E; **Paragraph 4:** C; **Paragraph 5:** A; **Paragraph 6:** D

5 Vocabulary practice (5–6 minutes)

Answers

a 3; **b** 6; **c** 4; **d** 2; **e** 5; **f** 5

6 Post-reading discussion (5–6 minutes)

> **Critical thinking:** In order to support students with this discussion, you could elicit some ideas for and against the idea that experiments on animals are humane and necessary.

Arguments for include the following: Scientists do not set out to hurt animals and, because they do everything they can to minimise suffering, the experiments they perform can be described as humane.

Arguments against include the following: If human beings are more intelligent than other animals, then humans ought to use that intelligence more wisely – nothing gives people the right to willingly hurt other living creatures.

7 Note-taking (8–10 minutes)

This exercise is useful practice for note-taking and making lists of points. Before students begin making notes, it would be useful to draw attention to three key words in the exercise: *reasons*, *achievements* and *steps*.

Answers

a To find cures and treatment for human illnesses.

b Advances in medical understanding; advances in the practical applications of medicine.

c To reduce the number of animals in each experiment; replace animals with alternatives where possible; refine experiments so they cause the least possible harm to animals.

8 How the writer achieves an objective tone (8–10 minutes)

1 > **Critical thinking:** The aim of this exercise is to study devices the writer uses to achieve a dispassionate style. You could ask *'Does the writer seem aggressive and angry about medical experiments being the right thing to do?'* Questions along these lines will help students become more analytical about the techniques the writer is using.

This, and the subsequent exercises, would be challenging even for native speakers, so a number of prompts are given to help students think along the right lines.

2 Students should find the checklist helpful in exploring the devices the writer uses. This statement is incorrect: 'She uses emotive language.'

3 The writer uses an objective neutral style of language, using mainly passive structures and avoiding the use of the first person. She acknowledges arguments against animal testing, but frames them as subordinate to her main arguments: 'While concern for the inhumane treatment of living creatures is undeniably valid . . . '. She emphasises that her argument is fact-based, in contrast to the myth: 'In fact, there are many similarities between humans and animals which . . . '.

9 Finding the right angle (2–3 minutes)

This is a good opportunity to contrast the notion of a 'for and against' approach to an argument with the 'how' approach, which requires reasoning and explanation from different standpoints. To give another example, you could ask *'Are you more likely to be asked for your opinions for or against reducing road accidents, or for your opinions as to how they might be reduced?'*

This section refers to the angle of an argument, while Section B10 mentions bias in an argument. Students need to be clear as to the meaning of these related concepts:

- An *angle* refers to the approach that a writer takes to a topic – for example, looking at the subject of experimenting on animals from the perspective of how those experiments have led to improvements in medicine.

- *Bias* refers to the way that someone's viewpoint is affected by their prejudices. We can show bias for or against something. For example, we might expect a scientist who experiments on animals to show bias in favour of colleagues who do the same, but bias against animal-rights campaigners who want to put a stop to such experiments.

10 Understanding bias in an argument (8–10 minutes)

1 > **Critical thinking:** The aim of this exercise is to show how the impression of objectivity can be reduced when we consider how much the writer has left out of the argument. Students try to find points against medical experiments on animals. The term 'points against' is a slight oversimplification: what students are doing, in fact, is considering a wider variety of aspects of the issue in order to establish a more complete picture.

2 Each point is quite condensed, so it's worth taking each one in turn and making sure students understand what is being said.

You could finish the work on understanding bias by asking students to sum up how fair they feel the writer is to the topic, now that they have had a chance to consider more aspects of the issue.

11 Writing an article for the school blog (20–30 minutes)

Students are asked to use their understanding of medical experiments on animals and the language used for opinion and persuasion to write an article to post on the school blog. The question is intellectually quite challenging and has a different slant from the 'for and against' compositions they have written before.

Make sure students understand that they are writing a measured argument. They can show this by using contrast expressions such as *while, although, even though* – for example, *While animal experiments have led to important medical advances, there are other ways in which health care can progress.*

Key points to include could be: the limitations of medical experiments (animals react to drugs and experiments in different ways from humans); the alternatives to research on animals (e.g. more tests on human volunteers, which can be more reliable; the use of medical technology such as lasers and ultrasound techniques); preventive measures to reduce human illness (e.g. better health education, the provision of clean water supplies).

Allow students enough time to ask any questions and to write the composition, as they are likely to find it a demanding task. Remind them of the need to use a firm closing paragraph and that the main idea to convey is that there are alternatives.

DIFFERENTIATION

To **support** students, simplify the task by offering a ready-made list of three points 'for' and three points 'against' animal testing; for example:

For: Animal testing can help make medical treatment safer for humans; it can help us find cures for diseases; laws make sure that the animals are well treated.

Against: We could test new medical treatments on humans or using technology instead; animals are not a reliable way of testing treatments designed for humans; some laboratories treat animals better than others.

For more **challenge**, ask students to do some research and include some facts and statistics about animal research – for example, how many animals are used in research every year and whether this number is increasing or decreasing, and why. They could also find out about more recent medical research and whether animals were used for testing or not.

12 Prepositions after verbs (5–6 minutes)

It is always useful for students to practise using prepositions as accurate use takes a long time to master. Other examples to elicit include:

I can only *guess* <u>*at*</u> his whereabouts.

Animals *differ* <u>*in*</u> many ways <u>*from*</u> people.

I want to *complain* <u>*to*</u> the manager <u>*about*</u> their attitude.

Answers

1 a experiment on

   b bother about, dying from/of

   c surprised at

   d object to

   e contribute to

   f quarrel with

   g depend on

   h died of

   i provide him with

   j respond well to

2 Some other verbs that can be followed by the same prepositions are:

   • about: worry/gossip/think/speculate/ argue *about*

   • at: look/wonder/hint/smile/throw *at*

   • from: hear/depart/benefit *from*

   • of: accuse/remind/dream *of*

   • on: concentrate/bet/rely/ congratulate/agree *on*

   • to: listen/dedicate/appeal *to*

   • with: collaborate/sympathise/help/ agree *with*

13 Spelling and pronunciation: Regular plurals (5–10 minutes)

However familiar students are with plurals, they still present problems and are at the root of many spelling mistakes and pronunciation difficulties.

Ask students to read the list of nouns silently and to double-check the meanings of more tricky words – for example, *wasps, spiders.*

Students then listen to the words listed and identify the pronunciation of each ending. The words are spoken twice.

Answers

/s/: cats, insects, wasps, goats

/z/: hens, donkeys, spiders, birds, cows, monkeys, bees

/ɪz/: cages, faces, horses, houses, roses

Audioscript track 9.3

Listen carefully to each word and identify if the –s at the end is pronounced /s/ (as in cats) or /z/ (as in hens) or /ɪz/ (as in faces).

a	cats	g	spiders	m	houses
b	hens	h	faces	n	monkeys
c	insects	i	horses	o	bees
d	cages	j	goats	p	roses
e	wasps	k	birds		
f	donkeys	l	cows		

14 Spelling and pronunciation: Irregular plurals (5–10 minutes)

Ask students to practise the pronunciation of the irregular plurals. Other examples to elicit could be:

1 *-es:* branches, watches, wishes

2 *-ves:* ourselves, wives, thieves, shelves, halves, lives, loaves (common exception: *roofs*)

3 vowel change: *foot – feet*

4 *-es:* heroes

5 *-ies:* babies, families

6 always plural: headphones, glasses (spectacles), clothes, species

7 always singular: aircraft

15 Vocabulary practice (5 minutes)

Answers

a sheep, lambs

b bears, wolves, wildcats

c deer, geese, foxes

d mice

e crocodiles, rhinos, teeth

f fish

g caterpillars, butterflies

16 Look, say, cover, write, check (5–6 minutes)

The word list recycles vocabulary students have met and helps them learn problematic words. See Unit 1, Section B13 for a reminder of the 'Look, say, cover, write, check' method for learning vocabulary.

C Animals in sport and entertainment

The following sequence of exercises explores the role of animals in sport and entertainment. You could begin by asking students if they are involved with animals in any sport they do – for example, horse riding. Ask them to describe what they enjoy about the activity and whether the animal enjoys it too.

1 Discussion (5–10 minutes)

Horse racing is popular in many countries. You could ask whether training animals to perform under pressure and in public is unkind in any way, or whether it depends on how the animals are treated.

Field sports, or bloodsports, are much more controversial ,and there are many groups actively campaigning either in their defence or against them. Encourage students to express their views on such sports and see if they modify their opinions after considering the letter in Section C3.

2 People's opinions (5–10 minutes)

Asking students to tick the views they agree with will help them focus on what they are reading. The sentence structures contain examples of emphatic forms, which they will be studying in more detail in later exercises.

3 Letter completion: My views on animal charities (10–15 minutes)

You may like to complete the first (or more) of the sentences as a group to help students think about how to do this cloze exercise.

To finish, you may like to discuss the angry tone of the letter, which is in contrast to the cool and more measured tone of the article on animal experiments. The opening paragraph gets straight to the point, but does not use any polite or softening expressions and therefore sounds very forceful and direct. A softer approach would be: *I am writing to express my concern about . . .* or *It has recently come to my attention that . . .* The end of the letter leaves the reader in no doubt that the writer is disgusted by the plan. A softer approach would be: *. . . to ensure that charitable funds are donated to more useful projects in future.*

To increase the **challenge**, ask students to try to predict the missing words and expressions before looking at the questions. They could also suggest alternative words or phrases for each gap.

Answers
1   **a** I think this is a very; **b** foolish; **c** argued; **d** but; **e** insist; **f** yet; **g** unfair; **h** As I see it; **i** and; **j** nothing could be further from the truth; **k** Nevertheless

4   Vocabulary check: Words for feelings (5–10 minutes)

For more **support**, you could recommend that students use dictionaries for this exercise, as the level is fairly demanding.

For more **challenge**, ask students to make up their own sentences using these words.

Answers
a horrified; **b** uneasy; **c** immoral; **d** apologetic; **e** absurd; **f** saddened

5   Language study: Adding emphasis (15–20 minutes)

There are many different ways to express emphasis in writing. The structures in this exercise have been selected as some of the most straightforward to learn, so hopefully, students will be confident in using them later.

You may like to ask students to read the sentences aloud to show the emphasis through stress and intonation. You could discuss the fact that, in speech, we are less reliant on changes in structure to show emphasis, as we can use other features such as stress, intonation and tone of voice to convey meaning. Point out that overuse of these forms can make writing or speech sound artificial and affected.

Answers
What I find most impressive about bullfighting is . . . ; What makes me cross is . . . ; What I love about horse racing is . . .

Practice

Answers
1   a   What she admires are attempts to reduce animal suffering.

    b   What we need are better fences to stop animals wandering onto the road.

    c   What the safari park wardens worry about is animals escaping.

    d   The place where you can see owls, eagles and hawks is a falconry centre.

    e   What we didn't understand was that animals have adapted to live in certain habitats.

    f   What I didn't realise is how animals depend on each other.

    g   The people who are responsible for the reduction in rhino numbers are hunters.

    h   The place where the golden eagle prefers to nest is in treeless, mountainous country.

    i   What ought to concern us are endangered species in our own country.

    j   What I want is the right to object to things I think are wrong.

2   a   Having a purpose in life has made her so happy.

    b   We all shouted, 'Do tell us more about your adventures.'

    c   Do take lots of photos when you visit the wildlife park.

    d   I never realised that baby rhinos were so affectionate.

    e   Raising funds for charity is so worthwhile.

    f   Your granny does enjoy her garden, doesn't she?

    g   You do look tired today. / You look so tired today.

    h   Thirsty animals are so miserable.

    i   Gordon felt so sorry for the animals he saw at the circus. / Gordon did feel sorry for the animals he saw at the circus.

j I do worry about you, you know.

k Do turn off the tap properly when you have finished washing.

l Do come in, Sophie. I'm so pleased to see you.

6 Comparing languages (2–3 minutes)

You may want to compare and contrast written and spoken language. For example, how are stress and intonation used to convey emphasis? Discuss ways of adding emphasis to text and email messages using emojis or other text features such as asterisks, capital letters, bold and highlighting in different colours.

7 Writing sentences (5–10 minutes)

Example sentences

> *Do* help yourself to anything you would like to eat.
>
> Helping at the animal rescue centre was *so* worthwhile.
>
> *Do* speak up; I am a little deaf.
>
> Seeing a lion in real life was *so* exciting.

D Animals at work

The following sequence of exercises considers the role of working animals, including police dogs and dogs for the blind. The topic then focuses on animals that are kept by people to generate income. The discussion points centre on the responsibilities people have towards their animals and what can be done about cruelty to working animals. Students also consider whether intensive farming is ethical.

1 Thinking about working animals (5–10 minutes)

Ask students to look at the pictures of animals and elicit ideas about what animals are used for in their country(ies).

Other responsibilities owners have towards animals could include: giving them water, sheltering them, keeping them in a reasonably clean and comfortable condition, making sure they get enough rest and exercise, getting a vet for them if they are ill.

2 Discussing ethical issues (5–10 minutes)

> **Critical thinking:** Students may have strong opinions about whether animals are overworked or treated harshly by their owners. Encourage them to be specific about any problems they may have observed, as this helps them think through their ideas more analytically.

You could extend the discussion to consider the use of animals to help people in difficulty (rescue dogs, dogs for the blind, etc.) or to detect criminals (police dogs, guard dogs, anti-poaching dogs, etc.). Such dogs often have a high level of intelligence and training. Exploring more about how they can help humans fight crime or save lives might be a useful follow-up.

3 Building an email from prompts (20–25 minutes)

Example answer

> Dear Sir,
>
> I am writing in response to recent articles saying that people who keep animals for profit are 'cruel and heartless'. My family makes a living from keeping sheep. In my view, our life is harder than the animals'!
>
> In lambing time, for example, there is no day off and no rest. My father gets up as soon as it is light and hurries out to the first task of the day without even bothering to have a drink. He works for several hours without a break. He checks the lambs that were born in the night or attends ewes that are having difficulty giving birth. He brings poorly lambs indoors to be bottle-fed.
>
> He tries to get round the flock four or five times a day, often in snow or cruel winds. If there is a specific problem, he has to go out several times a night with a flashlight. Although expensive, the vet is always called when needed.
>
> It is true that every ewe or lamb that dies is a financial loss to us, so it is in our own interest to care for the sheep.

The sheep are eventually sold at the market. How could/can we live any other way? But we are certainly not the 'ruthless exploiters' of your article. In fact, nothing could be further from the truth.

Yours faithfully,
Orla O'Connor

4 Assessing the argument (2–3 minutes)

Encourage students to re-read the email when it is correct to get a sense of textual flow, as this is difficult to do when they are building it up from the prompts. You could ask a student who has a good command of intonation to read it aloud to the group, or you may prefer to do this yourself.

Ask students to identify the main arguments that Orla uses. (The farmers work hard. They take good care of the animals. They bring in expert care if needed.) What other arguments could she have used? (The sheep have plenty of space and good food. They are given medicine when they are ill. They are warm in winter. They are treated humanely.)

5 The closing paragraph (2–3 minutes)

As always, ask students to pay particular attention to the end of the email, which finishes with an opinion. Explain that this is appropriate for this type of text, and compare it with how you might end a 'for and against' essay.

6 Vocabulary check: Young animals (5–6 minutes)

Answers
a cub; b duckling; c chick/chicken; d calf;
e kitten; f pup/puppy; g kid; h foal; i calf; j calf;
k cygnet; l cub

7 Comparing languages (5 minutes)

You could also discuss what characteristics are associated with different animals in different cultures with the class. For example, in Britain, an owl is often said to be wise, a fox is crafty, and so on.

8 Vocabulary check: Collective nouns (5 minutes)

Point out that *flock* is also the collective noun for birds and that *herd* is generally used for hooved animals (reindeer, bison, horses, donkeys, etc.).

Other collective nouns for animals include: a gaggle of geese, a colony of bats / ants.

You may like to extend this exercise by considering the names of the sounds animals and birds make (e.g. *buzz, bark, moo, roar, squawk, twitter,* which are onomatopoeic in English) or by eliciting the names of animal homes *(kennel, pen, stable, cage, nest, lair,* etc.). (Activities on onomatopoeic words are extension material and not required by the syllabus.)

Answers
a cows, elephants, deer
b sheep, goats
c fish
d dogs, wolves
e bees, locusts, ants

9 Discussion: Intensive farming (10–12 minutes)

> **Critical thinking:** Intensive farming of animals may or may not be familiar to students, so the discussion will need to be adapted to their experience. Depending on their background, students may have positive views of intensive farming: because it uses more technology, the results are more dependable, it can produce greater quantities of food and it is labour-saving.

It would also be useful to check students' understanding of the 'food chain' concept. They may be familiar with this from their science or geography lessons.

Reasons people may object to intensive farming (called factory farming by those who criticise it) usually centre on the conditions in which the animals are kept – for example, hens may be kept in dark, windowless sheds, with very little space to move around, and their feeding is controlled automatically. People claim that animals kept in these conditions usually produce tasteless meat, eggs, and so on. There is concern that livestock which is fed regular doses of hormones and antibiotics could pass these on to consumers in the food chain. It is also possible for diseases to spread more quickly in these intensive farming environments, and then huge numbers of animals or birds may have to be slaughtered.

Some farmers are attempting to farm organically and sustainably, raising a smaller number of animals so that they can have space to graze and forage without the stress they experience in confined environments. Some farmers are also integrating livestock and crops instead of keeping them separate. These farms can often be more efficient and profitable, using natural fertiliser and producing less waste, but it takes time to replenish the soil, and meat or dairy products produced in this way tend to be more expensive.

Organic and sustainable methods could be made more attractive to farmers by providing financial support or subsidies to produce food on a smaller scale using more humane methods and adopt organic sustainable methods. It may also be helpful to educate the public about their buying choices. If everyone chose to buy free-range eggs, for example, the price is more likely to go down. Food companies could be obliged to give fuller information to consumers on food labels. You may want to discuss the definitions and various possible interpretations of words used on food labels such as: *organic, cage-free, free-range, grass-fed, non-GMO*, and so on.

10 Punctuation (15–20 minutes)

It would be useful to revise students' grasp of the main points of punctuation before going into the exercise.

DIFFERENTIATION

To provide more **support**, go over the paragraph breaks with the class and assign one paragraph to each group. Then have them exchange their work and correct each others' answers.

For more **challenge**, ask students to add one sentence to each of the main paragraphs.

Example answer

Dear Sir,

Fair methods of food production

Like many of your readers, I want to buy healthy food which is produced in a way which is fair to farm workers and animals. Furthermore, I don't believe food production should damage the environment.

Many farmers in our area say that it is cheaper to rear animals under intensive conditions than it is to give them a decent life. However, if farmers were given subsidies, they would be able to afford more space and comfort for animals. Farmers get subsidies for intensive methods, so why not pay them for a kinder approach?

Similarly, many of the farms around here use hormones and antibiotics, which can get into the food chain. Farmers say it is less expensive to add growth hormones to animal food than it is to use more natural or 'organic' methods, which require a bigger labour force and so would be more expensive. What is more expensive in the end – subsidies to the farmers for organic farming or a damaged environment?

In my view, we have a right to know what is in our food. Tins, packets and fresh food should be labelled by food companies as 'free-range' or 'factory farmed', or if antibiotics were used, so that we know exactly what we are eating.

I realise my ideas might lead to higher food prices, but I have no doubt at all it would be worth it.

Yours faithfully,

Shahar Rishani

11 Checking the text flow (5–10 minutes)

Encourage students to read the letter again when they have corrected it to get a sense of textual flow. While the opening expresses a clear, strong opinion, the closing might be considered a little weak as most people would probably be against higher food prices. Ask students to summarise the main idea in each paragraph. (The letter opens with a clear expression of the writer's opinion and reason for writing. The second and third paragraphs consider opposing arguments and present arguments against them. The final paragraph suggests a clear course of action from the consumer's point of view. The final sentence concedes that prices may be higher as a result while insisting that the overall purpose is worthwhile.)

12 Discussion (10–15 minutes)

> **Critical thinking:** Encourage students to evaluate Shahar's arguments and say whether they agree or disagree, and why. Students can work in pairs, each taking one side of the argument.

Against: Higher prices mean that people won't be able to afford healthy food in their diet. People will buy cheaper, less nutritious food instead. Also, it may mean that smaller quantities of meat and dairy are produced and only wealthy people will have access to it, thereby increasing food inequality. Organic farming is more labour-intensive and farm work is usually low paid and seasonal, so workers may be paid less.

For: Sustainable farming methods can benefit the environment in the long run, reducing chemicals not only in our food but also in the water and soil. Organic farming methods can reduce pollution and waste of natural resources. Animals will not suffer from lack of space and mistreatment and will be happier. Workers can enjoy working in a safe and kind environment. We will feel better knowing that our food is produced in an ethical and human way.

You may want to extend the discussion to include reasons for becoming a vegetarian and how this might impact environmental damage and climate change.

13 Rhetorical questions (5–10 minutes)

It can be artificial to think of rhetorical questions out of context. However, when they have assimilated the pattern, students should be able to incorporate this device into their writing styles.

Rhetoric is the art of speaking persuasively by using certain techniques to make listeners find it hard to disagree with what is being said. One feature of this form of communication, commonly used by public figures such as politicians, is the rhetorical question, which is not a question at all, but a statement put into the form of a question. The point of the rhetorical question is to make a statement more dramatic. For example, *How can we ever forget our beautiful queen?* might be said

by a heart-broken king hoping to make more of an impact on the audience than *We can't forget our beautiful queen.* Rhetorical questions are very useful in compositions because they are such an effective way of making a point.

DIFFERENTIATION

You may want to **support** students with analysing and forming rhetorical questions by working through the questions orally with them.

For more **challenge** in question 2, ask students to suggest a couple of different questions for each one.

Suggested answers

1   a   People ought to show more sympathy to farmers.

     b   No one could enjoy eating a battery hen.

     c   It is better to pay a little bit more for food produced ethically than to make animals suffer terribly in factory farm conditions just so we can get cheaper prices in the supermarket.

     d   Everyone would be happier knowing our food was ethically produced.

     e   We don't really need all this food from thousands of miles away.

     f   No one should worry about animals when little children are starving.

     g   Pets are not always safe and happy with their owners.

     h   You cannot put a price on a child's life.

2   a   Is a vegetarian meal always healthy?

     b   Who can say the farmers are wrong?

     c   Which is more important/better: to save an animal or (to) save someone's life?

     d   Who knows the extent of the problem?

     e   Wouldn't we all be happier knowing that our food was free of chemicals?

     f   Isn't it about time we remembered endangered species at home?

     g   Shouldn't we consider farm workers before worrying about animals?

3   Asking students to find examples in the email and letter they have corrected will reinforce learning. They should underline the following:

How could/can we live any other way? Why not pay them for a kinder approach? and *What is more expensive in the end . . . environment?*

E Helping animals in danger

1 Discussion: Could you help animals? (8–10 minutes)

> **Critical thinking:** Students may need some further clarification about how human activities have a harmful effect on animals. You may like to elicit the way new roads and housing developments restrict wild animals' range of movement and reduce the scope they have for roaming and finding food. Rather than perceiving a need to live alongside wild animals, people who settle in these areas may see the animals as a nuisance, perhaps causing traffic accidents or foraging for food near rubbish bins. Agricultural development often leads to pesticide use, and this – and the resulting run-off into streams and rivers – is harmful to wildlife.

The idea that we should develop ways to coexist peacefully with wild animals is explored in Section E5 in a report for the headteacher about a scheme to alert local people to the presence of elephants in their area and in the exam-style listening question at the end of the unit.

International overview (2–3 minutes)

Answer
Asiatic lions, snow leopards and tigers are the most endangered species on the chart.

2 Reading for gist (10–15 minutes)

Discuss the photos and ask how they might relate to the topic and title of the text.

DIFFERENTIATION

To give more **support**, pre-teach the meaning of these words: *breeding ground, cost-effective, plaque, acre, orphaned, poacher.*

For extra **challenge,** encourage students to try to work out the meaning of unfamiliar words from the context and to suggest substitute words that could be used instead of the unfamiliar word.

3 Comprehension check (5–10 minutes)

Answers

1   Most animals at the zoo are available for adoption.

2   It uses the money for breeding programmes to save animals from extinction.

3   An adoption certificate, regular copies of 'Zoo Update', and four free entry tickets.

4   To save an area of rainforest in Central America as a sanctuary for wildlife.

5   They are in Thailand, and they provide natural sanctuaries for rescued Indo-Chinese tigers.

4 Writing a report from notes (20–30 minutes)

The report is a substantial piece of work that involves many skills, so it is helpful to allow enough time for it and to encourage students to write more than one draft.

You may like to allow students to discuss the example answer below and compare it with their own writing. It shows how material in the Student's Book, particularly the previous few exercises, can be used as a resource and combined with original writing.

DIFFERENTIATION

To give more **support**, simplify the task. Students could just make the case for adopting a zoo animal, ignoring the 'Points against' section in the notes. Revise and elicit the language students could use to present their first argument and then to add further points: *Firstly . . . , In addition, Furthermore, . . . Most important of all . . .* , and so on. Demonstrate how to expand sections of the notes, eliciting students' ideas – for example, *invitations* to special events (e.g. see newborn animals) might be expanded to: *The school would receive invitations to special events at the zoo, which could include seeing newborn animals. This would be very educational for the younger children.*

Report to the headteacher on the adoption of a zoo animal

Our local zoo, the Queen's Zoo, has an animal adoption scheme, with many animals to choose from, and if we use the funds in this way, there are many benefits. Firstly, adopting a zoo animal means we would get a plaque at the zoo with the school's name on it, which would make us all very proud. We could also get discounts on entrance tickets and in the gift shop. Furthermore, we would be invited to special events, such as seeing newborn animals. Perhaps most important of all, however, is the fact that the funds would help support breeding programmes, which encourage animals from endangered species to breed in captivity. When they are ready, the animals are returned to the wild.

On the other hand, if we adopt a zoo animal, we cannot support other conservation projects, which are also worthwhile. Rainforests contain a wealth of wildlife but habitats are under threat. Rainforest conservation projects, such as Rainforest Action Costa Rica, provide a safe haven for a vast number of wonderful birds and animals by protecting their habitat. In addition, there are some very special projects which help animals that are hunted for their body parts. Tiger numbers have fallen below 4000 due to hunting. The Tiger Trust does very valuable work rescuing endangered tigers in Thailand, for example.

I have discussed the adoption scheme with the members of the Wildlife Club, and we believe the school should use the funds to adopt a zoo animal. The club would prefer to adopt a tiger or a tamarin monkey, if possible. We agreed there is nothing like seeing a living, breathing rare wild animal in real life and observing its behaviour. It will be more meaningful for younger students than just listening to the reasons why animals need to be protected. It would also help older students with their science projects, especially those thinking of a science career or who want to work with animals. Finally, the adoption scheme is not just about having fun at the zoo, it helps the zoo's breeding programme, which plays a very important role in preventing endangered species from extinction.

5 Improving paragraphing and punctuation in a report (10–15 minutes)

You may also like to ask students to underline key phrases that show awareness that the report was written for the headteacher and explain why these phrases are important. For example:

- *encouraged the little children to practise the right way of feeding a baby elephant who has lost its mother. As a result, they understood as much as the older ones* (shows awareness that the headteacher would like evidence that the event benefited students of all ages and abilities).

- *. . . we felt extremely lucky that we had been given the chance to meet a true wildlife pioneer and we all learnt so much* (shows appreciation of the school's efforts to arrange the meeting).

- *I would certainly recommend it for next year's group, if the opportunity is still available* (makes a polite recommendation, implying need for permission).

Corrected report

Mr Bavsar's talk about his work in southern India was so inspirational. Mr Bavsar explained why he started his special project, the Elephant Information Service. One night a child woke up to see a small elephant calf standing by his bed. Somehow, the elephant had got into the house and gone into the bedroom without disturbing the boy's parents. The elephant made a strange noise and then turned around and left the way he had come, without causing trouble.

As Chief Wildlife Officer, Mr Bavsar was asked to investigate the incident. When he visited the family, they said they were not distressed but they were shocked. They said that if they had known wild elephants were so near, they would have been better prepared for potentially dangerous situations. This made Mr Bavsar realise that animals and humans could coexist peacefully, as long as they took sensible precautions to avoid conflict. Mr Bavsar set up the Elephant Information Service and now there are early warning systems in the area. The service alerts families when animals are nearby by sending texts, flashing warning lights and making phone calls.

The whole class loved Mr Bhavsar's talk. He was so knowledgeable and showed us his personal photograph collection of the rare and beautiful animals he has cared for, including elephants. Elephants sadly, are often orphaned when their parents are killed by hunters and have to be cared for in an elephant sanctuary before being returned to the wild. Mr Bhavsar even brought in a large toy elephant, a blanket and feeding bottle, and encouraged the little children to practise the right way of feeding a baby elephant who has lost its mother. As a result, they understood as much as the older ones about the needs of infant elephants.

Overall, we felt extremely lucky that we had been given the chance to meet a true wildlife pioneer and we all learnt so much. I would certainly recommend it for next year's group, if the opportunity is still available.

CONTINUED

Answers

1   Small ponds had been dug out . . .

2   a   If the Siberian tiger cub had not been found in time, it would have died in the snow outside its den.

   b   The tiger cub's tail had been badly damaged by severe frost.

   c   His leg had been badly bitten too.

   d   The wildlife officials who found the cub said they had been shocked by the cub's condition. 'We believe the poor little thing had been attacked by a predator and the severe temperatures made everything worse.'

   e   After a year, the tiger cub had made a full recovery and was returned to the wild.

GRAMMAR SPOTLIGHT (10 MINUTES)

The past perfect passive

If students need help in grasping the idea of the past perfect as a time in an earlier past, or need more practice with the passive form, it might be useful to draw a timeline on the board to contrast the past perfect with the simple past. The past participle of irregular verbs is often an obstacle in the correct formation of the structure, so it may be helpful to give students a few irregular verbs to learn each week. This can be more manageable for them than learning long lists of verbs.

DIFFERENTIATION

Students who need more **support** on the basic structure of the past perfect passive may benefit from some controlled oral practice. For example, set up the following scenario. *Our local zoo raised so much money from their adoption scheme that they spent some of it on improving the zoo. When we went to visit last week . . . The animal enclosures had been painted. Lots of new trees . . . Some broken windows . . . New play equipment for the monkeys . . . The elephants' very small enclosure . . . A completely new visitor centre . . . , and so on.*

WIDER PRACTICE

1 You may like to discuss further the concept of peaceful coexistence with wildlife, given the fact that in many parts of the world wild animals are a danger to people, cause accidents and threaten jobs. The report in Section E5 and the exam-style listening question at the end of the unit, which suggest ways to overcome the problems wild animals cause without hurting the animals, could be a useful aid for the discussion.

2 Having studied animal rights in detail, it would be interesting for students to discuss workers' rights – for example, the right to be paid a fair wage. You can discuss ethical trade associations that guarantee food was produced in an ethical way with respect for workers' rights, such as Fairtrade International.

3 The topic of animals lends itself well to cross-curricular work. You could arrange for teachers of biology and geography to talk to the class about ecology, the food chain, and so on.

4 There is a lot of factual information available about animals themselves: animal families, origins, habits, breeding patterns, endangered species. Students could find out about an animal they are interested in and give a talk to the group.

5 Watching or listening to a controversial discussion about farming, zoos or animal management could provide a basis for debate, as could inviting a speaker on the topic to the class.

6 Supporting an animal or wildlife charity might be worth considering. Students would receive a lot of information, and it would give them a valuable sense of making a difference to some issues of global concern.

7 Students could be asked to research hobbies and leisure-time pursuits that involve animals and give a short talk to the class.

8 Students could research a specific sports event using animals and write a report on how well the animals are treated and whether they think the sport is ethical or not.

Exam-style questions

Reading and writing

Reading and Writing: multiple choice

This exercise provides practice with multiple-choice comprehension questions.

Point out to students that some of the questions require them to use inference skills: using clues in the text to work out what the writer means without saying it directly. They also need to read the text quite carefully. For example, an option might *seem* to represent the writer's view, but does the writer actually say as much? If students are unsure which option to choose, advise them to focus on identifying which options are clearly incorrect. It may be particularly useful with this exercise to go through the questions afterwards as a class and highlight/underline the words that provide the answers.

Answers
1 C; 2 B; 3 A; 4 B; 5 C; 6 A

Reading and Writing: informal and formal

You will find advice on general approaches to exam-style writing exercises at the end of the 'Teaching support' section in the Introduction.

For the email exercise, remind students of language they could use for inviting someone and ways to sound enthusiastic. For example: *Let's . . . ; Why don't we . . . ? How about . . . ; It'll be so much fun! We'll have such a great time!*

Example answer

Informal writing

Dear Chris

I don't know if you read about it, but an incredible new aquarium has just opened in my town. It's a really cool building mostly made of glass sited right by the sea. I've seen video clips of the exhibits and they are amazing - massive tanks with a huge variety of fish. What's more, they give you headphones, and you can learn all about all the fish, where they can be found, what they eat, their breeding habits, if they are endangered and even if they are good to eat!

If you're interested, would you like to come with me next Saturday morning? You're welcome to stay over at my house on Friday so we can get there early and avoid the crowds. Afterwards, we could go for a swim in the sea, and have a seafood lunch! Let me know what you think,

Bobbie

(160 words)

Listening

Listening: multiple matching

Students match a list of opinions with six audio extracts.

This is a challenging exercise, so you may like to let students listen more than twice. Remind them that they should listen for accurate understanding of ideas. If they simply match words on the recording with words in the statements, they might choose an incorrect answer, so it is useful to draw attention to the way paraphrasing is used.

You may like to pause the recording when checking the answers in order to focus on a particular expression of an individual word. Encourage students to discuss why this particular word or phrase is important in choosing the correct answer. You may also like to explore the fact that there is no evidence on the recording for statements C and H.

Answers

Speaker 1: D	Speaker 2: G	Speaker 3: A
Speaker 4: E	Speaker 5: F	Speaker 6: B

(Statements C and H are not needed.)

Audioscript track 9.4

You will hear six people talking about wildlife.

For questions 1–6, choose from the list (A–H) which idea each speaker expresses. For each speaker, write the correct letter (A–H) on the answer line. Use each letter only once. There are two extra letters, which you do not need to use.

You will hear the recordings twice.

Now look at the information A–H.

Speaker 1: We went camping in an area where grizzly bears and other dangerous wild animals live. We never actually encountered any dangerous wildlife but we still took bear spray with us when we went out, just in case we met any. We were also warned not to keep food in the tent, as this attracts animals too. We were told to put food in the campsite's storage lockers to keep it away from wildlife.

I think camping in an area where wild animals live is safe as long as you follow the campsite rules and avoid taking silly risks that could endanger the lives of other campers as well as your own.

Speaker 2: Wildlife was here long before people settled in this region. Things we have done to the environment, including agricultural development, housing projects and road building, have destroyed much of the habitat of many wild animals. I heard recently of plans to cut down a large section of forest in order to extend an industrial area near here, which would be terrible for the wildlife living in the forest. If we were more appreciative of our wildlife heritage, we'd all benefit. I certainly support the idea of underpasses for safer road crossings for wildlife.

Speaker 3: Grizzly bears and other wildlife living near us are a problem as they frequently cross the main road and come into the town. Parents get worried about their children being attacked and sometimes animals get hurt, just because people panic and don't think clearly. I'm hoping to go on a course to learn more about wildlife, so I can teach my community how to respond to the wild animals living locally without causing any harm to them.

Speaker 4: I think we should all do more to care for wild animals and protect them, as they are part of our heritage. However, let's not forget that wild animals can still be a real problem for the human population. My uncle is a sheep farmer and he has money worries because his sheep keep being killed by dangerous wild animals. Lambing time is when his sheep are most vulnerable, and he has to take special care as he can't afford to keep losing sheep. He once had a lucky escape from a wolf when he went out late one night to try to protect his flock.

Speaker 5: I attended a town council meeting last night where we discussed the idea of building underpasses so wildlife can cross roads safely. Lots of people were in favour of the idea, but, although it sounds very good in theory, in practice I doubt that animals would use the crossings. They might ignore them. I think other ideas, such as more lighting after dark and lowering the night-time speed limit, are better and would be a lot cheaper too. There's another meeting next week, and I'll definitely attend so I can put forward my views.

Speaker 6: We have packs of wolves and other dangerous wildlife living not far from where our sheep graze. They used to be a real danger and our sheep were always being attacked, especially at lambing time. Then we got some financial help from the government to train guard dogs and install spotlights and special alarm systems. These measures have really helped keep the predators away and we hardly lose any sheep now. I would recommend these measures to any farmer who's troubled by wolves or other predators, as they've really worked well on our farm and given us so much more peace of mind.

Speaking

You will find advice on general approaches to speaking exercises at the end of the 'Teaching support' section in the Introduction.

If students are doing this exercise under examination conditions, warm-up questions may help to put them at ease. These are included in the corresponding Coursebook unit.

> 10 The world of work

Learning plan

AOs	Key learning intentions	Success criteria
R3, L3, S1, S3	Explore the topic of work and employment	• Students can describe qualities needed for a job • Students can compare being a freelancer with being an employee • Students can use work-related idioms and expressions
R1, R2, R3, R4	Identify connections between ideas, opinions and attitudes in an article about work	• Students can identify and make notes about advantages and disadvantages in a text • Students can compare and contrast facts and opinions • Students can understand what is implied but not directly stated
W1, W2, W3, W4	Write a formal letter and an article using appropriate style and register	• Students can plan the structure and organisation of an article, a job ad and an email • Students can choose appropriate tone and register • Students can edit a text and identify mistakes
L1, L2, L3, L4	Understand key points and bias in a lecture about marketing strategies	• Students can predict ideas they might hear in a lecture • Students can identify details • Students can identify bias, and inferred or implied meanings
S1, S2, S3, S4	Take part in a role-play discussion for developing a new product using a range of interactive skills	• Students can use appropriate language to express opinions, agree and disagree • Students can negotiate and come to an agreement in a discussion • Students can use appropriate grammar, vocabulary and pronunciation to express their ideas in a business meeting

Overview

This unit consolidates the skills needed if students are to show evidence of language ability in reading, listening or speaking skills and the ability to sustain quality in their writing, whether that is in writing reports, articles, emails or letters.

THEME

The theme of the unit is work. This is approached through developing more understanding of the skills and qualities needed for work, common problems faced in the workplace, and the way in which school prepares you for work. Students sometimes lack confidence because they think they will need exceptional academic qualifications to have a chance in today's competitive job market. In fact, recent research shows that employers particularly look for good communication skills. Improving communication skills has been the focus of this course and is an attainable target for all students.

The issues raised are:

- How do surveys and the portrayal of teenagers in the media influence public opinion and adversely affect their chances of training or employment?
- How does stereotyping operate at work, and why might it be harmful?
- How does school promote maturity and responsibility for work?
- How can employment levels be increased (using examples and knowledge based on students' own countries)?

The texts include an article about people who decided to work freelance and a magazine article about the employment of people with disabilities. Listening exercises are a lecture about internet marketing strategies and an exercise with short conversations based on work scenarios.

LANGUAGE WORK

The unit consolidates the functions and skills approach of the earlier units. New language work focuses on expressing figures and approximations, and criticising statistical information. Pronunciation focuses on linking sounds.

The 'Grammar spotlight' looks at superlatives of long and short adjectives and at adverbs of degree, including correct word order when using the adverb *enough* with an adjective.

Common misconceptions

Misconception	How to identify	How to overcome
Students may use *most* + the -est ending or *most* with a short adjective when trying to express a **superlative**. Examples: *It is the most biggest one in the country.* *It was the most clear water I've seen.*	Write some example adjectives on the board. Ask students to categorise them according to whether they use *most* or *-est*. Then ask for example sentences using each one. Correct examples: *It is the biggest one in the country.* *It was the clearest water I've seen.*	Write a selection of short and long adjectives on the board. Then write a list of jobs. Ask students to use these adjectives to say which job is, for example, the most difficult, the most/least interesting, etc. Examples: *I think that firefighting is the most dangerous job because your life is in danger.* *I think that being an office assistant is the unhealthiest because you are sitting at a desk all the time.*

Misconception	How to identify	How to overcome
Students often use incorrect word order when using **enough with an adjective**. Example: *Our product range isn't enough large.*	Write sentences using *enough* + adjective and *enough* + noun, leaving out the word *enough*. Ask students to add the word to each sentence and notice its position after the adjective and before the noun. Correct example: *Our product range isn't large enough.* *We don't have <u>enough products</u>.*	Write a list of products on the board (e.g. phone, coat, shoes, bag, bed) and ask students to make complaints about each product. They can then choose one product and create a customer service dialogue using *is . . . enough, isn't . . . enough*, etc. for as many complaints as they can.

Introducing the unit topic (5–10 minutes)

Working with a partner, students look at the photo and discuss the questions.

The questions should encourage students to think about the world of work and, in particular, about how to choose the right sort of job and career path for themselves. They could start by finding words to describe the person and setting in the photo. What do they think this person's daily job routine is like? What tasks and responsibilities might they have? Might it be a rewarding job, and in what ways?

You could move the discussion on to what motivates a person to do their job. To help others, to help the environment, to make money, to buy a home and have a family? Students could explore different ways of evaluating a job, according to what you can get or achieve, how far you can use and develop your talents, or how much you can contribute to society. Do they think all jobs should be paid equally, or is it fair that some people are paid more than others? Are some jobs more valuable than other jobs? Which are the most valuable jobs in society in their country?

You may also want to help students explore more unusual jobs or workplace settings which they may not have considered. They could discuss what their dream job might be and what steps they might need to take to achieve it.

> **Digital coursebook:** At the start of the lesson, use this video to introduce and review:

- the topic of the world of work
- a range of vocabulary related to work
- superlative adjectives.

Read the question on the title screen and ask learners what they think they might see. Then play the video all the way through and check learners' predictions.

Play the video a second time, pausing to discuss what is being shown and the questions on the end screen. You can take the opportunity to revise words and phrases associated with the topic of work.

Note that the end-screen contains differentiated two-part questions. The first part should be relatively easily accessed from the video. The second part requires reasoning and personal opinion. More confident learners will be able to offer more extensive reasons for their ideas.

You may like to play the video a third time for consolidation.

A The rewards of work

1 Discussion (4–5 minutes)

The introductory discussion focuses on why people work. The reasons are wide and varied. Encourage students to come up with ideas such as:

- to earn money/raise their standard of living
- to use skills and qualifications
- to have fun
- to travel
- to enjoy company benefits: car, health insurance, tax-free loans, and so on
- for security
- to get out of the house
- for standing in the community
- to give routine and structure to the day
- to make a difference to society

- to have a break from domestic chores and commitments
- to express different aspects of their personality
- to get a sense of achievement
- to enjoy using specialised equipment only available at work
- to enjoy wearing a uniform/special clothes.

You could also ask *'What is the effect on people when they lose their job?'* This could elicit interesting ideas which can be developed later in the unit, where there is a focus on unemployment.

2 Skills and qualities for work (5–10 minutes)

1 Use the photos to elicit vocabulary for the skills and qualities needed for the jobs.

2 The matching exercise encourages students to focus on what skills and qualities are really essential for an occupation.

DIFFERENTIATION

To provide more **support**, ask students to add an additional skill or quality for each job, adding three to five words, according to their ability. Make sure students focus on skills that are really essential for each job.

For extra **challenge**, students may add five more jobs and the skills that are essential for each of them.

Answers
2 a 3; b 9/10; c 5; d 9; e 8; f 7/9; g 4; h 6; i 2/6; j 1

To extend this task, ask students to suggest other jobs that require each of these skills or qualities.

3 Pre-listening task (2–3 minutes)

Introduce the topic of choosing a job by brainstorming what aspects of a job are most important. These could include: working hours, flexible working (working from home), opportunities for training, workplace environment, atmosphere, colleagues, and so on.

4 Listening: Why I like my job (5–10 minutes)

1 Students are going to listen to six people talking about why they like their job. Ask them

to read the questions first. You may want to pause the audio after each speaker to allow time for students to make their choice.

2 Help students to identify clues to what the jobs are – for example, speaker 1 mentions visuals and logos.

Answers
1 1 E; 2 D; 3 C; 4 B; 5 G; 6 F (A is not required)
2 1 Graphic designer
2 Factory manager
3 Shop assistant in a toy shop
4 Restaurant chef
5 Electric appliance repair person
6 Medical lab researcher

Audioscript track 10.1

Listen to six people talking about their jobs.

Speaker 1: I started this job about a year ago. Before that, I was working from home and mostly on my own. Now I'm working full-time for a marketing company in their main office, and I'm much happier because I can work face to face with other people. We have brainstorming sessions where we all try to come up with creative ideas for visuals and logos. Advertising is a really competitive market these days and it's easier to come up with an original concept if you're collaborating with other people.

Speaker 2: I've been doing this job for about five years, and it's probably the best job I've ever had. I've learnt about every aspect of the production cycle, and now it's up to me to keep everything flowing smoothly so that production is on time and up to standard. There are so many things that can go wrong. A supply shipment can be delayed, for example, or a machine can break down and cannot be fixed right away. You have to be ready for anything! In the end, you just have to stay calm and do your best.

Speaker 3: Sometimes customers come in and say, 'I want a present for my 7-year-old nephew.' That's a really broad category! My job is to ask them about their nephew's hobbies and interests, what sports they like and so on, and finally narrow ideas down to two or three choices that seem to work. It might be a computer game, a piece of sports equipment or a book. Then I leave them alone for a bit to make their decision. There's nothing worse than feeling you've been pushed into buying something you don't want.

Speaker 4: I probably work longer hours every day than most people. Work starts at about 11 in the morning when we start preparing food for the evening. Then we take a break in the afternoon, and after that, it's straight through until midnight. But what I really love about it is having the ability to get everything ready on time while maintaining the very best quality. At the end of the day, if the customers are happy, then I'm happy too!

Speaker 5: We open up at 9 a.m. every morning and are open all day until 6 p.m. We have a good customer base – lots of regulars who have been coming to us for years. I like taking things apart and putting them back together. Always have! What I like best about the job – apart from chatting with the customers, of course! – is being able to mend things that are broken. We live in such a throwaway culture. It feels good to make things last just that little bit longer. Know what I mean?

Speaker 6: I like working here because all my colleagues are very serious about their work and everyone concentrates really hard on what they're doing. Of course, there's a fair amount of routine work which isn't that exciting – collecting samples, analysing data, writing up charts. But every once in a

while, you make a real discovery and it's that wonderful feeling of Wow! I've really made a difference! I'm not sure if it really *has* helped make medical history, but every small step is a step along the way really, isn't it?

5 Predicting (5 minutes)

Students are going to read about two people who have decided to work as freelancers (independent self-employed workers) instead of working full-time for an employer. Some reasons might include: they can work from home, have flexible working hours, be their own boss. At this stage, accept all suggestions and leave discussion until after reading.

Speculate with the students about how the workers in the photos might feel about their workplace and what they might miss about working in a company office.

Discuss the title of the article. What does *tied down* mean in this context? (trapped, lack of freedom)

6 Reading for gist (5–10 minutes)

DIFFERENTIATION

To provide extra **support**, write some comprehension questions on the board – for example:

- What did Melody do in the past?
- Why did she leave her job?
- What kind of work does Melody do now?
- How does she feel about being a freelancer?
- What did Kelvin do immediately after school?
- Why did he decide to study more?
- What problems has he faced as a freelancer?
- What does he love about being a freelancer?

To provide more **challenge**, ask students to work in pairs. Each student will read half the text, about either Melody or Kelvin. Then they will summarise the main points to their partner. They can try to find similarities and differences between the two people. Afterwards, they can read the second part of the text to check their answers.

7 Comprehension check (5–10 minutes)

This task requires students to compare and contrast the two stories to see which sentences match or don't match each person.

Answers
1 B; 2 C; 3 A; 4 C; 5 A; 6 B

8 Note-taking and discussion (5–10 minutes)

⟩ **Critical thinking: Answers**

1 a Choosing work she loves; loving the work she does, having a carefree lifestyle; irregular income

   b Having a heavy workload; being stuck in a cubicle; being trapped in an office hierarchy; stable income with contributions and benefits

2 Benefits of freelance work: can work as much or as little as you want; can choose what kind of work you do; can choose where you work (e.g. at home or in a coffee shop).

Disadvantages of freelance work: have to look for work, make contacts, negotiate fees and rates; fees may not be paid regularly so you need to manage your budget carefully; may feel isolated working alone and not having the opportunity to discuss work with colleagues; no paid holidays or pension when you retire; may not have as many rights to legal protections.

Benefits of being an employee: can work with colleagues, which is more social; have regular hours (not always on call); clearer division between family and work life; paid holidays and sick pay; other perks such as private health insurance and gym membership.

Drawbacks of being an employee: may have to work with or for people you don't like; don't always have control over what kind of work you do; can't take time off whenever you want; sometimes have to work in noisy or unsafe environments.

9 Vocabulary check (5 minutes)

Students can work in pairs to produce a lexical set for business and work-related vocabulary. Monitor the exercise and encourage them to use dictionaries.

Answers
1 a retired; b full-time; c colleagues; d contacts; e juggling; f cubicle; g hierarchy; h credentials; i portfolio; j income

2 industry, company, organisation, earn, manager, workload, qualified, nine-to-five job, run a business, benefits, freelancer

10 Idioms (10 minutes)

Answers

a When she was young, she would never have imagined that she would be a freelancer later on.

b It made her aware that her situation wasn't good, and she needed to do something about it.

c He is working for a fixed period of time that is not intended to be permanent.

d He had to take out small amounts of money from his savings.

11 Look, say, cover, write, check (4–5 minutes)

Double letters and ie / ei can sometimes be a problem. Ask students to identify the difficult words and think of ways to remember the correct spelling. See Unit 1, Section B13 for a reminder of the 'Look, say, cover, write, check' method for learning vocabulary.

12 Is freelance work for everyone? (10–12 minutes)

⟩ **Critical thinking:** The aim of this exercise is to develop students' understanding of how different types of working may suit different people depending on their personality and lifestyle. Use the photo to discuss the challenges of this type of work and how difficult it may be to earn a living wage.

Possible answers

1 Being able to: work independently; keep to a timetable; monitor your own work; be on time; not get distracted, not procrastinate.

2 Jobs that involve working from home, and also other jobs such as taxi-drivers, messengers and food delivery workers.

13 Understanding visual data (8–10 minutes)

> **Critical thinking:** Understanding visual data is a useful academic and work skill. Being able to describe a graphic and what it represents will help students to navigate different types of visual data including bar charts, line graphs, word clouds, flowcharts, pie charts, Venn diagrams, and so on.

Answers

The graphic shows the percentage of income generated by freelance workers in different countries around the world. It shows that the opinions of the people in the article may be relevant to many economies globally.

Discuss possible cultural differences in attitudes to freelance workers; for example, in some countries they may be considered less professional, less trustworthy or less dependable. Also, in some countries, it may be difficult or too expensive to get health insurance if you are freelance.

14 Pre-role-play discussion (8–10 minutes)

Suggested answers

1 To find out about new trends in the market; to get fresh new ideas; to expand their customer base.

2 Encourage students to think of flavours that will use local ingredients and appeal to people in their country. They may want to start by listing interesting ingredients, then pick the top six flavours or flavour combinations and think of creative names for them.

15 Product development meeting and role play (25–30 minutes)

Encourage students to read and understand the context for the multiple-matching exercise carefully. Some questions involve inference so students should take care that they have grasped the implications of information given in the text. Remind students to: read the rubric, scan the questions, read the texts for general meaning, and finally tackle each question methodically, re-reading the text(s) to help them decide, especially where answers to task 1 seem 'close'. If students feel the question applies to more than one person, they should study the evidence in the text with extra care. For example, question 3 asks, 'Which person wants to produce an ice cream aimed at the narrowest age range of customers?' Students might think this applies to both the marketing manager and the advertising executive, as both mention a wide range of customers. On closer reading, however, the marketing manager uses the key words 'older teenagers and adults' which is a wider age range than the advertising executive, who refers to 'adults'. As always, it is a good idea to ask students to provide evidence from the text to support their choices, in order to discourage the temptation to answer through guesswork.

The role play enables students to act out the occupational roles suggested by the texts. They work in groups of four to discuss the feasibility of researching and developing a new ice-cream flavour. The role play includes a discussion of the ingredients, the name, the target audience and advertising strategies.

The aim is to enable students to activate as much passive knowledge as possible. However, it would be useful to revise the functions of interrupting, offering advice/suggestions/opinions and expressing disagreement, so students are well-prepared (see the contents chart at the front of the Coursebook for the relevant units). Tell them that the emphasis will be on fluency, spontaneity and activating passive knowledge.

Allow groups some time to quietly read and absorb the information about their roles, and check any problems with comprehension. Alternatively, you could draw together all those with the same role. Make sure students understand what is expected of them, and clarify any misunderstandings before they begin. If appropriate, you or students themselves could record or video the role play and play it back, pausing in key places, so that students have the chance to identify the good points of the interaction and where it could be further improved.

At the end of the role play, compare the results and which names and flavours were chosen. Then take a vote on the best one.

To provide more **support**, write some useful phrases on the board. For example:

Suggestions: *I think we should . . . Don't you think it would be better to . . . Maybe we ought to consider . . .*

Agreement / Disagreement: *That's an excellent idea. I totally agree. I'm not sure about that. Do you really think that's a good idea?*

Opinions: *As far as I'm concerned . . . As I see it . . . My personal opinion is . . .*

Answers
1 a Food tester; **b** Advertising executive;
c Marketing manager; **d** Marketing manager;
e Public relations manager; **f** Food tester;

B Facts and figures

1 Approximations (5–10 minutes)

Answers
1   The stress in *percent* falls on *cent*.

2   **a** 8; **b** 3; **c** 2; **d** 1; **e** 6; **f** 4; **g** 5; **h** 7

3   Elicit from students the idea that approximations are used to make bare statistics more understandable by comparing them to amounts that the general public find easy to imagine.

The disadvantage might be that approximations can be used to slant information so that it creates a positive or negative impression. It is not, strictly speaking, a disadvantage, but simply something that students should be aware of.

2 Questioning statistics (10–15 minutes)

> Critical thinking: The aim of this exercise is to develop students' ability to question statistics that look authoritative.

1   Discuss what image of working mothers is presented in this statement. Is it positive or negative? Is being absent from school presented as a positive or a negative factor? What other explanations might there be for fewer absences?

(You may want to discuss the definition of *working mother* as a term that implies that not all mothers work.) The statement does not distinguish between single parent families and families where both parents work. Does the statement imply that mothers are solely responsible for their children's care? Does it imply that mothers who work outside the home are less concerned about their children? How could this be rewritten to present a positive image of working mothers?

2   The answers to the questions might reveal that the survey was carried out by a market research company on behalf of a political pressure group that is opposed to working mothers and wants to influence public opinion against them. The size of the sample might reveal that it was too small to be meaningful. The questions could be too vague; *absence* is a general term, and absences might be due not to illness but to things like dental appointments, which might be arranged differently by working mothers (after school hours) and non-working mothers (during school hours). Moreover, the two groups of children may not be similar in terms of age, social background, and so on, making comparison less useful.

The questions are important because you need to be sure the information was gathered objectively and that the results have not been distorted in the interests of a particular pressure group.

3   The same kind of questions should be asked for task 3. In the second survey (b), it would be very important to know if the intake of the schools surveyed is similar, to ensure that 'like is being compared with like' (a phrase that means that two things which are similar in some way are being compared).

3 Criticising statistics (5–10 minutes)

> Critical thinking: Before students read the reactions in the speech bubbles, you could ask *'How do you think local teenagers felt when they saw this written about them? Pleased? Angry? What do you think they said?'* Elicit some reactions expressing indignation and a refusal to believe the results. Drill appropriate responses, including those in the Student's Book. Check that students sound annoyed and disbelieving before asking them to practise in pairs with the information in Section B2.

4 Young lives: Good or bad?

> **Critical thinking:** Students work in pairs to analyse the statements about teenagers.

1 You could encourage students to think about the situation in their own country by asking:

- Are teenagers in your country less materialistic than those in the survey?

- Are they more community-minded than the teenagers in the survey?

- Where do teenagers you know get their spending money from?

2 Before students tackle this task, you may wish to discuss what an employer might be looking for in a worker (maturity, reliability, experience, responsibility, and so on) and how a youth leader might try to persuade employers that training schemes for young people are a good investment.

Answers

1 **Positive:** b, c, f, g, j; **negative:** a, d, e, h, i

2 a Statistics a and j seem to show that some teenagers are committed to work.

b Statistic b may show that training schemes are needed because students find it hard to get work experience.

International overview (8–10 minutes)

You may want to clarify the meaning of each type of education and the usual age range for each one.

Encourage students to criticise these statistics using the language and techniques they have practised in Section B.

Answers

1 Upper secondary

2 About three billion people

3 The overall trend shows an increase in the number of people completing higher levels of education (upper secondary and tertiary). This may be because the world population is increasing and also because more people from lower secondary and primary levels are getting access to higher levels of education or because the job market is getting more competitive.

5 Rewriting in a more formal style (20–25 minutes)

The aim of this exercise is to consolidate work done in earlier units about appropriateness of style, tone and register. The letter, which is too informal for its purpose, could be analysed in small groups. It is packed with inappropriate expressions (*Hi you guys, got me mad, Talk about . . . , totally worried,* etc.), so all the students should be able to find some.

After they have analysed the letter in pairs, ask students *When would you write a letter in this style?* (to a friend, or perhaps to a college newsletter if the normal tone of the newsletter is very student-centred and informal).

You could ask a student to come to the board and write up examples of inappropriate language under the headings in the bullet list.

Before students attempt to rewrite the letter, suggest some phrases they could use – for example:

With regard/reference to the comment about . . .

I disagree with/object to the comment that . . .

DIFFERENTIATION

Check understanding of the terms in the bullet list, eliciting examples. Provide some sentence starters if students need **support** with the rewriting (e.g. *I feel annoyed that . . . , I disagree that . . . , I really can't agree that . . . ,With regard to . . .* , etc.).

Example answer
A copy of the letter below could be circulated to students for comparison with their own attempts.

Dear Editor

I am a student at a local high school. I have just read your report 'Young Lives Shock!' and I feel most annoyed about the way it describes teenagers. We are not 'unconcerned about employment'. My friends and I are very worried about the chances of getting a job in a town with high unemployment like this one.

I also disagree with your report's suggestion that 'teenagers value their spare-time jobs more than their studies'. Like the teenagers in the survey, I too have a part-time job to earn extra spending money. My parents are unable to afford to buy me the trainers or kind of phone I would like. I work in a café twice a week after school. It does make it hard to concentrate at school the next day, but I do extra homework to catch up.

With regard to the comment 'the youth of today show a strong preference for the company of their peer group over that which their parents can offer', I think it is more natural to want to spend time with friends of your own age than to stay at home with your parents. However, I would like to point out that teenagers do respect their parents.

I would be most interested in hearing the responses of other readers to this survey.

Yours faithfully,

Ollie Debeer

C Internet marketing

1 Pre-listening discussion (4–5 minutes)

The pre-listening exercise focuses on the topic of shopping from a consumer's point of view. Students can work in pairs or as a class to brainstorm ideas.

Suggested answers
Read reviews on the internet; look up product comparison websites; look up reviewer blogs, videos, top ten best lists, and so on.

2 Predicting content (4–5 minutes)

Remind students that predicting the content of a lecture or talk will help them to understand and remember new information. Predicting will also help them to activate vocabulary relevant to the topic and prepare them to connect new information with already known information.

Suggested answers
Advertisements, banner ads, pop-up ads, spam or junk mail, browser-sponsored links, and so on.

3 Vocabulary check (5–6 minutes)

Answers
endorsement: recommendation

engagement: involving your audience and creating interactions with them

credibility: trustworthiness, reliability

followers: people who follow you on social media

niche market: a small segment of a larger market that has unique needs and preferences

target audience: the particular group of people at which a product is aimed

4 Listening for gist (8–10 minutes)

After listening once for gist, elicit the four main categories and write them on the board (company website, emails, videos, social media influencers). Then ask if students can remember any good or bad points about each one.

Encourage students to focus on key words in the lecture in order to get the gist. Remind them that they don't need to understand every word a speaker says to enjoy listening and to understand the general ideas. They should also try to listen out for signpost words that indicate a new segment (*Firstly, secondly, thirdly, Finally*). The speaker also uses intonation and stress to show that a new point is being made.

DIFFERENTIATION

To provide more **support**, tell students that there are four main segments in the lecture. They should try to write the key word for each segment.

For more **challenge**, ask students to write the key words and one good or bad aspect of each one from the point of view of a marketer.

5 Detailed listening (10–12 minutes)

Ask students to read the questions and answer choices carefully and try to answer them if they can before listening again.

After checking the answers, ask some general questions to elicit students' responses to the lecture, for example:

- *Which method of internet marketing would most likely persuade you to buy something?*

- *What products do you think are best suited to each kind of marketing?*

- *Would you believe the recommendation of an influencer? What would make you trust their advice?*

DIFFERENTIATION

If students need more **support**, pause the audio recording at the end of each segment so they have time to choose their answers.

Answers
1 A/C; **2** C; **3** A; **4** B; **5** A; **6** C

Audioscript track 10.2

Listen to the beginning of a lecture about internet marketing. Which of your ideas are mentioned?

Good morning! And welcome to today's podcast about marketing. This is the first of two lectures about internet marketing strategies. And in today's session, we're going to consider different strategies for using the internet in marketing and how to make optimal use of social media.

Right! Let's get started! So when you think of internet marketing, what do you think of first? Advertisements? Pop-up ads? They're certainly important marketing tools. But there are many other ways that companies can use the internet to market their products.

First and foremost is, of course, the company or product website. This is the place where consumers may go first to find out about new products and ultimately make their purchases. It's vital,

therefore, that the website is easy to navigate and is inviting and attractive to the target audience. Research has shown that consumers who have a negative experience on a company website are very unlikely to return and will immediately go to a rival company.

A second, highly effective tool is email marketing. This is the process of sending out emails to prospective customers. I'm sure you've all had the experience of finding dozens of advertising emails in your spam folder *[laughs]*, so obviously the key factor here is making sure your emails are targeted at the right people and knowing how to optimise your emails so that people want to open them and read them – and not just click the delete button.

A third way to advertise is to create videos and podcasts about your products. It's worthwhile trying to think outside the box with these. For example, rather than just a straightforward presentation video demonstrating the features of your product, it can be more effective to create an instruction video, such as 'How to make the perfect omelette . . . ', which would be a good way to demonstrate your new cookware range.

Finally, a growing trend in marketing campaigns is the use of social media. According to some <u>recent research</u> , 3.484 billion people actively use social media – that's 45 percent of the world's population.

Recently there has been a tendency to reject traditional forms of marketing as less credible and less trustworthy. Social media users are more likely to believe recommendations from someone whose opinion they trust. And this is where the role of the social media influencer comes in.

Of course, there are mega influencers out there with millions of followers, celebrities like Rihanna and Taylor Swift. They have a huge online following, and major brands – especially fashion and beauty brands – often pay them to endorse their products, although it isn't usually cheap! In contrast to these celebrity influencers, there are hundreds of bloggers who have built up an audience for their videos or blogs that are focused on a specific kind of niche lifestyle or interest – for example, a travel blog for backpackers, or a cooking blog for people who live alone. These bloggers interact and engage with their followers in a very personal way and have built up trust in their audience. So when they endorse a product, their followers are more likely to go and buy them. This can be very useful to the internet marketer.

So how do you go about choosing the right sort of influencer for your products? There are a number of different factors to consider, but mainly you'll want to look carefully at their target audience. Are these the people who will buy your product? Then ask what they are passionate about (influencers are always passionate about something!) and what kinds of interactions they have with their readers. It's not only about numbers. Engagement is a much more useful way to evaluate how successful they are. Do they have a lot of comments – and what kind of comments are they? Do they engage in real conversations or do they just post smiley emojis? These criteria will help you decide if an influencer really has the right sort of audience for your brand.

6 Post-listening discussion (15–20 minutes)

> **Critical thinking:** The aim of the discussion is to explore stereotyping. The lecturer's comment that all influencers 'are always passionate about something' is a stereotype because it suggests that all influencers are the same (in this respect). The stereotype could be positive (influencers are all enthusiastic and energetic people who know a lot about their specific topic area) or negative (they are heavily biased towards a certain point of view and do not give an objective opinion).

You could now write the occupation *librarian* on the board and ask students *'How would you describe a typical librarian? Are all librarians serious? Do they all wear glasses? Are they all fond of reading?'* Discuss ideas about appearance, lifestyle, clothes, spare-time interests, and so on. Discuss whether the stereotypes are positive or negative, or both. Students could then discuss the occupations in the bullet list in pairs.

To help students focus on whether stereotypes are a good or bad thing, you could ask *'Are school or college leavers put off some occupations by stereotyping? How far have you found stereotypes to be true to life? Who do you know who doesn't fit the stereotype for their occupation?'*

7 Common work-related expressions (5–10 minutes)

Answers

1 *'Thinking outside the box'* means thinking creatively in unexpected ways in order to come up with new ideas.

2 **a** talks about work; **b** an ambitious person; **c** money given when he retired; **d** not working; **e** person who does menial jobs at work; **f** have control over how and when I work; **g** a high-achieving person; **h** manual workers, office workers

8 Pronunciation: Linking sounds (5–10 minutes)

Tell students that if a word ends with a consonant sound, it will link with the next word if that word begins with a vowel sound. Read the first advert so that they can hear how some words are pronounced distinctly and others 'run into' the next word. Before they practise reading the advert aloud, remind them that, as always, pronunciation is part of meaning – for the meaning to be conveyed clearly, the pronunciation must be satisfactory too.

Answers

1 Brighten up; Get a (job); If you need extra (cash); Lots of vacancies in; (It's) fun, it's

2 Career opportunities; Learn in; got energy and enthusiasm; Contact Elma

9 Writing a job advert (10–15 minutes)

2 The linking sounds are underlined in the example answer below.

To extend the exercise, you could ask students to role play a student phoning to find out about the job. Write some key phrases on the board to get them started:

Hello, I'm calling about the job ad I saw on your website. Could I get some more information?

Yes, of course. What would you like to know?

Sample answers

> **GENERAL ASSISTANT FOR LABORATORY**
>
> Saturday help needed to <u>wash up</u>, <u>sweep up</u> and generally tidy the laboratory.
>
> $8.00 per hour plus <u>travel expenses</u>.
>
> <u>Contact Amy</u> Jones 013452 78642 <u>a.jones@labresearch.com</u>

Monitor the pairs as they read to each other, and correct any faulty pronunciation.

D Recruitment with a difference

1 Pre-reading task (3–5minutes)

The article is about a fast-food restaurant which employs deaf staff. The text is based on an interview with the restaurant manager, who relates how his feelings of anxiety changed to enthusiasm when he realised how smoothly the system worked and all the benefits it offered to the disabled employees.

1 Possible advantages of fast-food restaurants are:

- good when you are in a hurry
- clean, hygienic surroundings
- informal – you can go alone or with a group of friends
- relatively inexpensive
- consistent quality of food
- familiar menu wherever you are.

2 Encourage students to write open questions – for example:

- Why did you decide to employ deaf staff?
- How do the staff communicate with customers?
- What roles do the staff have in the restaurant?
- What training do they have?
- How do hearing people communicate with them?

- What difficulties have you had?
- How do customers react?
- How successful has it been?

2 Vocabulary check (3–4 minutes)

hearing impairment: reduction in ability to hear

recruiting: finding new employees

agile: quick in movement

criteria: standards for judging/deciding something

mentor: more experienced person who inspires and advises

3 Reading for gist (5–10 minutes)

Students should enjoy finding answers to the questions they wrote.

4 Comprehension check (10–15 minutes)

DIFFERENTIATION

To **support** students with this exercise, tell them in which paragraph the answers can be found: **1** para 4; **2** para 5; **3** paras 8–9; **4** para 11.

To provide more **challenge**, ask students to come up with two more questions about information in the text. Also ask them to explain the meaning of the following phrases: *crash course, eye-opening, groundbreaking, easier said than done, embarking on an adventure.*

Answers

1 The management were aware of the large numbers of deaf people in society and felt they had a duty to help them.

2 They used the same criteria as when they select hearing applicants.

3 In previous jobs, the employees felt isolated, but here they feel normal, which is very positive for them.

4 They become more energetic and better tempered.

5 Any two of: learnt basic sign language; changed his attitudes towards disabled people; gained a sense of personal fulfilment because he has made a difference to people's lives.

5 Post-reading discussion (10–15 minutes)

1 › **Critical thinking:** Discuss employment opportunities for people with disabilities generally, then students' reactions to the idea of employing people with disabilities in situations other than restaurants. You could ask, for example, *'How would a blind teacher deliver their lessons? What special aids might they need?'*

2 When students discuss the contrasting rewards and stresses of people-orientated jobs and product-orientated jobs, they will be generalising to some extent. It may be quite a difficult abstract concept for those who have not had employment experience. Prompt them if necessary, to elicit ideas along these lines:

- In a people-orientated job, you have to learn to cope with many different kinds of personalities and expectations. People may have more needs than you can satisfy, and so the work might feel outside your control at times. You can gain rewards through a feeling of being valued and respected by the people on whose behalf you work.

- In a product-orientated job, you have the satisfaction of producing something that you can, in a sense, stand back and admire at the end of the day. On the other hand, the work can be more monotonous as it does not have the unpredictable element that a people-orientated job brings.

3 Encourage students to give their views on mentoring. You could develop the idea to include mentors in the family or social sphere, such as aunts and uncles who support younger relatives who need someone to confide in and who may feel isolated in their immediate family.

6 Vocabulary practice (5–10 minutes)

Students can work in pairs for this exercise.

Answers

1 hyperactive; energetic; lazy; indolent

2 loving; affectionate; supportive; friendly; indifferent; cold; critical

3 placid

7 Language study: Similes (10–15 minutes)

You could ask students to read their sentences aloud.

You may like to point out that in informal English, *like* is sometimes used instead of *as if/though.* Example: *Her face turned red like a tomato.*

Like metaphors, similes are an example of figurative language. However, there is an important difference: with similes we make a direct comparison between things, actions and feelings, using words such as *like, as* and *as if.* You could introduce similes by putting a few common examples on the board – for example, *sing like an angel; sleep like a log; as busy as a bee; as strong as an ox; as cold as ice.* You could *challenge* students by asking them to come up with a few similes of their own to describe the qualities of family and friends, the classroom, and so on. They can do this alone before they share similes with a partner. You could then bring the whole class together and ask students to share a few of the similes they came up with.

DIFFERENTIATION

To provide more **support**, ask students to identify which sentences can be completed by a noun or a gerund, and which require a clause. (*Like* can be followed by a noun, gerund or clause; *as* (in this case) needs a noun or a gerund; *as if* needs a clause.)

To provide more **challenge**, ask for at least two different ways to complete each sentence.

Suggested answers
a an oven; **b** ice; **c** it was covered in volcanic ash; **d** she had won the lottery; **e** being in prison; **f** life wasn't worth living

8 Spelling: *-able* or *-ible*? (5–10 minutes)

Before students start the spelling exercise, you could write up *preventable* and *responsible,* and highlight the endings. Then you could elicit other words with these endings. Unfortunately, there are no clear and simple rules for the spelling patterns, so remind students of the importance of learning the endings by heart. The word *responsible* is commonly misspelt by students.

You can remind students that usually if the word ends in *-e*, this is dropped when adding -able or -ible, but sometimes it is kept – for example, in the word likeable.

Answers

1 **a** available; **b** invisible; **c** curable; **d** responsible; **e** incredible; **f** sensible; **g** reliable; **h** advisable; **i** inaccessible; **j** irritable

2 **a** washable; **b** inedible; **c** digestible; **d** desirable; **e** approachable; **f** excitable; **g** bearable; **h** incomprehensible

9 Phrasal verbs (5 minutes)

Answers

2 **a** gets by; **b** carry out; **c** turn down; **d** leave anyone out; **e** drawn up

10 'Eye' idioms (5 minutes)

Answers

1 An *eye-opening experience* is one which makes you realise things for the first time.

2 **a** 8; **b** 7; **c** 6; **d** 1; **e** 3; **f** 5; **g** 2; **h** 4

E Preparing for work

1 How well does school prepare you for work? (12–15 minutes)

1 Discuss the jobs shown in the photos. Draw out what kinds of skills would be needed in these jobs and whether any of these skills could have been taught or learnt while at school.

Students may not have a specific idea of their future career, but you could invite them to think of the positive ways school is preparing them, in general, to be successful in employment. Their ideas could range across the subjects of the curriculum – for example, good communication skills and being numerate and computer-literate are essential for work in many areas; an understanding of science helps you use technical equipment safely, and so on. Moreover, personal qualities that are needed at work such as team leadership, being a good team player, creativity and imagination are developed at school by many subjects including sport, art and extra-curricular activities.

Some schools arrange work experience, so you could discuss what students gain from this – for example, learning about how the organisation works, teamwork, relating to employees of different ages and backgrounds, mastering some basic tasks, getting a 'feel' for a job to help them decide whether this field of work would suit them, and so on.

2 Holding a position of responsibility at school also develops personal qualities. Encourage students to identify strengths they have gained – for example, confidence, good organisational skills, empathy, self-discipline.

For extra **challenge**, ask students to write a paragraph they could include in a CV, saying what qualities make them a suitable candidate for a job.

2 Pre-reading task (2–3 minutes)

The pre-reading task leads into a reading and writing exercise.

Before students begin the task, it's useful to clarify the concept of head boy or girl, as not everyone will be familiar with this position, especially if your school does not have them. Explain that it's a position filled by a student in the final year of school who has shown outstanding qualities of leadership. A head boy or girl may be elected by students or chosen by teachers. The chosen student does such things as negotiate with teachers over matters of discipline and student grievances, and is trusted by teachers to act as an 'ambassador' to other students, explaining the teachers' point of view on unpopular rules, and so on.

You could also discuss the disadvantages of the head student system. It is sometimes thought to encourage resentment among students and has been stopped in some schools for this reason.

If the school does not have the prefect system, you could discuss the pros and cons of alternative systems such as a student council. Elicit the idea that the council is composed of elected students who meet to discuss ideas or problems. Councils usually elect representatives who talk to the teachers about the student council's ideas. They discuss matters such as changes to school uniform, school dinners, new student clubs or new facilities.

3 Reading, analysing and writing (15–20 minutes)

Luke's article is suitable in terms of its style. It begins well, uses a range of structures, shows awareness of its audience, and is well organised into paragraphs that follow a logical progression of ideas.

Students should work together to identify how Luke has used complex sentence constructions, collocations describing qualities and skills, and so on before they decide how his article could end. Point out that a good conclusion would offer a short summary of what has already been said, and might, in its final sentence, include one new point.

Example answer

Matthew is the best candidate and would be an ideal head boy. He has good all-round skills, and he has proved his ability to work for the school and get on with all kinds of people. I would definitely trust him to represent our point of view to the teachers.

4 Comparing two styles (15–20 minutes)

Students should not have too much difficulty in recognising the weaknesses of Leila's style. You could ask *'Which article carries more authority/ would influence you more? Why?'*

A suitable answer would be something like:

'The short, simple sentences, plain tone, abrupt register and lack of organisation make Leila's article much less authoritative than Luke's article.'

5 Developing your writing style (10–15 minutes)

Rewriting Leila's article is quite challenging, and you may like to invite students to work on various possible drafts in groups until they have produced a draft everyone is satisfied with. Remind them that Luke's article should give them some ideas for structure, vocabulary, and so on.

Students who need more **support** with writing may benefit from choosing a few sentences from Leila's report and connecting them with clauses or linkers. Demonstrate with one or two examples, eliciting ideas from students, then let them continue on their own or in pairs – for example, *She set up a social club. She worked after school every day. She worked on Saturdays as well. = She set up a social club, where she worked after school every day including Saturdays.*

Students who need more **challenge** can think of some extra sentences to add to the article.

Example answer

> **HEAD GIRL ELECTIONS**
>
> My personal choice for head girl is Mira Patel. She has worked extremely hard for all of us and her behaviour is a shining example to the rest of the students.
>
> Do you remember how many of us were being bullied and were afraid to come to school? She tackled this problem very effectively and the bullying is no longer an issue. It was also Mira's idea to start a 'Welcome Day' for new students, which has really helped new students integrate quickly and happily.
>
> The fact that we have a brilliant social club is due to Mira's hard work too. She worked round the clock to set one up. We now have a wonderful place to meet our friends and unwind after school.
>
> In addition, she negotiates confidently with teachers. Her discussions with the headteacher led to the girls being given permission to wear trousers in winter, which is much more comfortable for us and something we had wanted for a long time.
>
> Her work visiting patients at our local hospital who do not normally receive visitors has developed her understanding of people's needs. This is a great asset in a big, mixed comprehensive like ours.
>
> Mira is not as egotistical as many of the other prefects, and I know I speak for many of us when I say 'Vote for Mira'. She is trustworthy, hardworking and, what is more, so very likeable!

6 Brainstorming (10–12 minutes)

> **Critical thinking:** Unemployment may not be a big problem for your students in their particular situations. Nevertheless, they should be developing an ability to discuss issues of global concern. This exercise is a good opportunity for them to think about the problem of unemployment in their own country. As always, encourage them to give local examples so that they develop the ability to adapt a composition question to a local situation. If you have an international class, share ideas about the various economies students come from.

Asking students to read a newspaper article or watch a TV programme about unemployment a day or two before you intend to cover the topic will focus on some of the issues and give them food for thought. Alternatively, they could interview their parents or other adults they have contact with about the causes of unemployment and possible remedies.

Encourage students to write down all their ideas during the brainstorming, no matter how unusual they seem!

7 Reading an email to a newspaper (8–10 minutes)

The email follows on from the discussion about unemployment. It raises some ideas that could be followed up after the reading – for example, *Should unemployed people receive welfare payments to provide the necessities of life? What is life like for unemployed people in your country? Why might some people genuinely prefer unemployment to having a job?*

Answers

Young people need effective careers guidance; a mentoring scheme would be helpful; a partnership of local firms and schools could be set up to teach computer skills; we are aware of the personal effects of unemployment.

8 Analysing the email (10–15 minutes)

Answers

a I read your report, which suggested . . . (paragraph 1); schools should start a 'mentoring scheme', which would match pupils . . . (paragraph 2); to develop training schemes that would enable us to . . . (paragraph 3).

b school leavers need much more detailed careers guidance (paragraph 2)

c an eye-opener (paragraph 2)

d like a high wall you have to climb (paragraph 5)

e Moreover (paragraph 2); Furthermore, . . . whereas (paragraph 3); I would also like to add that . . . (paragraph 4) f   I do not usually write to newspapers but . . .

g   Young people need all the help they can get, not criticism.

h   The overall impression is formal, which is appropriate for a formal email/letter to a newspaper.

9   Writing an email of reply (25–30 minutes)

Remind students that the reply should be formal but not excessively so. Some students are fond of language such as *'I am honoured that you have read my letter'*, which is too formal. The right tone should be that of two equals sharing views.

10   Correcting a report for the headteacher (15–20 minutes)

Students should enjoy a pre-task discussion of the text, which states that personal skills and qualities are just as important as good exam results.

It will be intriguing to find out what students think of this idea. Hopefully, it will give some encouragement to less academic students by emphasising the sometimes overlooked truth that being effective at work is not solely dependent on academic ability, as many other qualities are just – if not more – essential.

DIFFERENTIATION

To provide more **support**, give each half of the class just half of the report to correct. When they have finished, they can check each other's work.

For extra **challenge**, ask students to suggest an additional final line to the letter.

Answers

The extra words which should not be there are highlighted in bold and crossed through.

Mr Chen's talk was the most interesting careers ~~the~~ event we have attended. He began by explaining how he had built up ~~with~~ his factory, 'Chen's Engineering,' from a small company to a large business. He explained that, when he was growing up, he helped ~~them~~ in the family engineering business. Mr Chen most enjoyed ~~it~~ repairing motorcycle engines.

At a young age, he realised he liked working with machines, and got a lot of satisfaction from making a damaged engine ~~to~~ work well again. Most of all though, he learnt ~~him~~ about giving good customer service. He saw that his parents ~~they~~ were always patient and pleasant to customers, no matter what the effort. His father ~~he~~ would say, 'A man without a smiling face should not open a shop.' Mr Chen says he has never forgotten ~~of~~ those words, as they have been essential to the success of his business.

Mr Chen then told us what he looks for ~~in~~ when he recruits new employees. He said that job applicants think high exam grades are everything, but they are ~~in~~ wrong. He chooses people, including school leavers, because they are polite, enthusiastic and willing ~~them~~ to learn. He expects ~~it~~ employees to speak in a professional way to customers, and not to say, for instance, 'Hi you guys, wanna have a coffee?' He said everyone can ~~you~~ learn to be respectful, talk confidently on the phone, take notes and ask for help when necessary.

We appreciated ~~and~~ Mr Chen's careers talk very much, especially the emphasis on communication skills at work. As a result of the talk, some of us now want to get wider ~~our~~ experience. We are thinking of doing voluntary work or getting ~~us~~ a part-time job in the holidays.

Peter Lee, Head Boy

---

11   Choosing appropriate vocabulary (20–25 minutes)

You may like to reinforce the message about not misinterpreting questions. Question interpretation is a tricky area because the questions nearly always have some cultural content. Problems can arise because students' interpretation is too literal, or because they are put off by the artificiality of the exercise and can't think into the situation quickly enough.

Sometimes misinterpretation can be deliberate: students try to stretch the definition of the task to exploit previously prepared material. Remind them that what they write must be relevant to the question set and that going off the point is not a good idea.

Also remind students that this exercise is about making sure that vocabulary is relevant to a specific topic; they are not being asked to answer the specific example questions.

DIFFERENTIATION

To provide more **support** for students, do a few examples on the board. Begin with basic topics (e.g. family, school, free time) and then move on to more specific topics (e.g. school sports day, a job interview). Finally, you could move on to abstract concepts (e.g. love, loss and happiness).

To add extra **challenge**, encourage students to think of vocabulary that is relevant to each of the subjects. Make sure that they understand that this can be any part of speech, i.e. noun, verb, adjective.

Answers

1   sales figures; share prices

2   disappointed; irritated; isolated; saddened

12 Timed writing (15–20 minutes writing; 10–15 minutes reading aloud)

Timed writing is important because students find concentrating their thoughts and producing coherent compositions in a short space of time very challenging. Let them have more classroom practice on other questions if necessary.

Allow students to read their compositions aloud either to their group or in pairs. Emphasise the value of honest but constructive criticism. Insist that each 'listener' finds two positive things to say about the compositions before suggesting criticisms and positive ways the writing could be improved.

DIFFERENTIATION

To **support** students before giving their feedback, brainstorm a list of criteria that they could listen and look for in each others' work – for example, a wide range of vocabulary, interesting details, logical organisation, a good beginning and a strong ending.

For extra **challenge**, ask students to write a brief reflection on their composition, what they learnt and what they would improve for next time.

13 Listening: Four work scenarios (15–20 minutes)

Answers

1   **a** Friday morning; **b** seeing the specialist

2   **a** none; **b** patience and stamina

3   **a** very good experience; **b** next week

4   **a** good news; **b** pilot

Audioscript track 10.3

Listen to four short recordings. Answer each question in the Coursebook using no more than three words for each detail. You will hear each recording twice.

1   **a** Maria is ringing up to change the time and date of a job interview. What alternative is she offered?

     b What is Maria doing on Tuesday?

     'You said the interview was Tuesday at 4 p.m., and that's when you're seeing the specialist? Yes, well, if you think you can get here on Friday morning, we can fit you in then.'

2   **a** According to the careers talk, what special qualifications are needed to enter training schemes for the police force?

     b What two personal qualities are needed?

     'Well, many of you will be surprised that, apart from a good standard of general education, no special qualifications are needed for our basic entry scheme. More important, in fact, are patience and stamina, as the hours are often long and the work is demanding.'

3   **a** What did the headteacher think about your friend's idea of helping at the children's clinic?

     b When does your friend want to visit the clinic?

     'I told the headteacher I wanted to help at the children's clinic. She agreed it would be very good experience for me and she encourages us all to do something for the community. But she felt I should visit the place first – so I've decided to ring the clinic and ask if I can visit next week.'

4 a Has the speaker received good news or bad news?

   b What job does he want to train to do?

   'I'm really sorry – I won't be able to make it. Do give my love to everyone. I've just received a letter saying I've been accepted onto a trainee pilot course. You know I've always wanted to fly, so I'm off to Rome to meet the other trainees.'

GRAMMAR SPOTLIGHT (20–25 MINUTES)

Superlatives of long and short adjectives

You may like to write two sentences on the board first to contrast the use of superlatives for short and long adjectives, and elicit other superlatives – for example:

We have had the warmest/coldest/hottest/driest summer for years.

He was the most ambitious/competitive/supportive/annoying man she had ever met.

You could also point out that superlatives are often used with the present perfect and past perfect tenses, as in the examples above.

CONTINUED

Adverbs of degree

Students will have some familiarity with adverbs of degree and, as always, the 'Grammar spotlight' enables them to explore their intuitive knowledge. If you have more advanced students, you may like to elicit the idea that the adverbs a little and a bit are used with adjectives that have a negative meaning. We can be a little disappointed or a bit tired but not a little happy or a bit interesting.

Answers

1 The best candidate; the youngest senior prefect; the most fantastic negotiating skills

2 Marketing manager: very important, quite critical

   Food tester: a bit cautious, too unusual

   Advertising executive: rather forceful, extremely expensive

WIDER PRACTICE

1 You could ask students to bring in examples of articles from the internet or from print media which, in their view, distort statistical information. They could argue their case in their groups.

2 Students might like to devise a questionnaire to use with local firms to find out more about their employment policies – for example, working conditions and pay, health and safety, equal opportunity issues, recruitment, training schemes. Alternatively, a human resources officer or senior member of a firm could be invited to talk about their approach to employment. You could arrange for this to take place at the same time as a careers lesson, if possible.

3 Students can research employment opportunities online and present a short talk to the class on an area of work that interests them.

4 Students can research the best way to prepare their curriculum vitae (CV, or resumé), including all their hobbies and interests, skills and abilities. Then they can work in pairs or groups to help each other improve their work.

Exam-style questions

Reading and writing

Reading and Writing: multiple choice

This exercise provides practice with multiple-choice comprehension questions.

Point out to students that some of the questions require them to use inference skills: using clues in the text to work out what the writer means without saying it directly. They also need to read the text quite carefully. For example, an option might *seem* to represent the writer's view, but does the writer actually say as much? It may be particularly useful with this exercise to go through the questions afterwards as a class and highlight/underline the words that provide the answers.

Answers
1 A; 2 C; 3 B; 4 C; 5 A; 6 B

Reading and Writing: informal and formal

You will find advice on general approaches to exam-style writing exercises at the end of the 'Teaching support' section in the Introduction.

To help with writing the email, advise students to look at the picture, to suggest extra details for their email. In this case, they might include details about the fun of learning new skills and working together with other people.

Example answer

> **Formal writing**
>
> Our trip to the careers event was exciting. Mrs Azar took us into a room where local business people were sitting at tables. She said they wouldn't mind if we didn't know what we wanted to do in the future and would be happy to answer any questions, including about the companies they represented.
>
> This made us all feel confident. I would like a job in design, and a food manufacturer told me that their designers design appealing packaging for their products. She showed me some amazing examples on their website. She also said no one starts their

> first job with a lot of experience, so I shouldn't worry. When they choose new employees, they select applicants who are polite, enthusiastic and willing to learn.
>
> It was a rewarding and eye-opening day. Some of us would have liked to find out more about training courses, so if the visit is repeated next year, it would be useful to have someone who could tell students about those.
>
> **(166 words)**

Listening

Listening: interview

Students answer multiple-choice questions based on an interview.

Make sure students read through the questions before they listen to the recording. They should use the second listening to check their answers.

Answers
1 B; 2 C; 3 A; 4 A; 5 B; 6 C; 7 B; 8 A

> **Audioscript track 10.4**
>
> You will hear an interview with a writer called Peter Robinson.
>
> For each question, choose the correct answer, A, B or C, and put a tick in the appropriate box.
>
> You will hear the interview twice.
>
> Now look at questions 1–8.
>
> | | |
> |---|---|
> | Presenter: | Hello – and welcome to our weekly podcast where we invite people in different professions to come and talk about their work. Today we're delighted to welcome Peter Robinson, bestselling author of mystery novels set in Ancient Greece. Hello Peter! |
> | Peter: | Hi, and thank you for inviting me. |
> | Presenter: | Can you tell us a little about how you got started in your career as a writer? |

Peter:	I think I wrote my first story at the age of eleven. It wasn't very long – about fifty pages, I suppose – and it was complete rubbish! I didn't really start writing seriously until my twenties when I'd finished university and was still trying to decide what kind of job I wanted to do. I studied history, and I thought it would be fun to write a mystery based in Ancient Greece, so I tried it out as an experiment. The first novel wasn't good, but the second novel seemed good enough to send to different publishers.
Presenter:	I see, and how easy was it to get published?
Peter:	Not easy at all! Most publishers won't look at a book unless it's from a literary agent. And it's very hard to get an agent to take you on. But I had a stroke of luck with one of the publishers who was really interested in Ancient Greece, and he actually read my book.
Presenter:	Did he publish it?
Peter:	No! But he gave me some good feedback and it helped me to improve the book. And then it got picked up by another publisher.
Presenter:	Fantastic! And how do you come up with the ideas for your mysteries?
Peter:	I often start with a mental image of a scene and then I build a story around it. I get to know the characters and each of their stories, and then fill in details until I'm almost living with them in their world. It's important to make the plot and the characters as convincing and realistic as possible. That's the difficult part.
Presenter:	Do you ever have difficulty writing – I mean do you sometimes get stuck?
Peter:	Oh, all the time! I think that's part of the job really. If that happens, I tend to take a break and go for a run or a swim or something just to take my mind off it. Then I come back,

	and somehow something's clicked in my subconscious and I can move forward again.
Presenter:	What's your daily routine like?
Peter:	Well, I get up early as I like to write in the morning when my mind is most focused. I aim for six to seven hours of writing a day. I don't count the pages. It's just important to be making progress. I have a quick lunch break, then finish work at about 2pm. I think you have to be quite self-motivated as a writer. No one's going to tell you when to go to work or what to do . . .
Presenter:	Do you ever have to help with publicising your books?
Peter:	Oh yes, I do that quite a bit. I go to book festivals four or five times a year, and I also do talks and interviews on the radio and on TV. Personally, I like the book festivals best because I can meet up with my audience – people who actually read my books. They sometimes ask me the most detailed questions about my books, details that I've often forgotten about myself. That can be a bit embarrassing – but it's all good fun!
Presenter:	Do you think novels are important for us?
Peter:	I think they're tremendously important. Reading a novel is like entering another world – it stimulates your imagination and helps you make sense of your own story. That's the important thing. I think we're all writers in a way, telling our own stories.

Speaking

You will find advice on general approaches to speaking exercises at the end of the 'Teaching support' section in the Introduction.

If students are doing this exercise under examination conditions, warm-up questions may help to put them at ease. These are included in the corresponding Coursebook unit.

> Answers to Workbook questions

Unit 1

A Our outlook on life

1   Quick language check

a	for	f	dealing
b	set	g	purpose
c	resolution	h	motivated
d	determined	i	she was
e	eating	j	maintaining

2   Vocabulary for planning your life

a	aspirations	g	rewards
b	process	h	admitted
c	obstacles	i	flexibility
d	pursued	j	honest
e	focused	k	realistic
f	volunteered		

3   Reading for gist

Circle the correct words from the pair: up, in, possible, taught, excuse, imaginative, passionately, made, yet, inspired, forgave, prevent

Multiple choice: 1 B; 2 C

4   Style features

a   How much do you know about Albert Einstein?

b   Einstein showed **us** that a small amount of matter could be changed . . .

c   I was fascinated to learn that he didn't speak until he was three years old!

d   If you've heard about him but don't know much about his life and work, then read on!

5   Figurative language

Replace the figurative language:

a	very proud	d	disappeared
b	very sad	e	reminders
c	based on	f	very noisy

Match the expressions to their meanings:

g   change ambitions, plans or targets

h   criticise yourself yourself, usually unfairly

i   be able to accept a range of possibilities

j   have a single goal you really want to achieve

k   achieve far more than those in a similar position

l   achieve a goal you have set yourself

Write sentences using figurative expressions:
Students' own responses.

B Facing challenges

1   Comparing information in charts

a   ✓

b   ✓

c   ✓

2   Pre-listening task

a	burst into laughter	e	have a laugh
b	sense of humour	f	stony-faced
c	crack a smile	g	laugh along with
d	roar with laughter	h	get into trouble

3   Listening

A	3	D	x
B	1	E	2
C	x		

C Personal qualities

1 Describing character

a   absent-minded

b   good-natured

c   untidy

d   ambitious

e   placid

f   optimistic

g   artistic

h   private

Not used: sensitive

2 Vocabulary check

Makes sense (✓): d, e, g

Does not make sense (✗): a, b, c, f, h

3 Negative prefixes

Making opposites:

un – unenthusiastic, unconscious, unsympathetic

il – illegal, illiterate

im – impatient, impossible

in – insecure, incorrect, insignificant

ir – irresponsible, irregular

dis – disappear, disobey

mis – misunderstand, misbehave

Students then write their own sentences.

4 Commenting on positive and negative qualities

a   by far

b   incredibly/extremely/so

c   incredibly/extremely/so

d   absolutely

e   rather/a little bit/slightly

f   rather/a little bit/slightly/incredibly/extremely

g   can be

h   rather/a little bit/slightly

i   always the best/great

j   great

k   incredibly/extremely/so

5 Sentence correction

a   for

b   of

c   out

d   that

e   top

f   them

6 Developing your writing style

Example answer:

The first thing you notice about my grandmother is her brown eyes, which twinkle when she smiles. She is small and fair-skinned, and her hair is snow white. Despite a painful arthritic knee, she still enjoys life and is very artistic. She paints beautiful pictures of nature scenes. Around her neck she wears a gold locket, which my grandfather gave her when they first married. I know she treasures it. Ever since I can remember, my birthday has been made more special by the thoughtful presents she buys me.

7 Homophones

Correct words:

a   warn

b   fought, War

c   ate

d   flaw

e   whether

f   grown

g   break

h   great

Students then write their own sentences.

D People we look up to

1 Sentence correction: multi-word verbs

a   Olivier really takes <u>after</u> his father – they look very similar.

b   Chioma's very sociable and gets <u>on</u> well with more or less everyone she meets.

c   Alessandro's really upset because he's fallen <u>out</u> with his best friend.

d   Pernille treats everyone as though they're equal – she doesn't look down <u>on</u> anyone.

e   Ding is someone who will never let you <u>down</u> – he's very reliable.

f   I look <u>up</u> to both of my grandparents as they're both wonderful, kind people.

g   Asha and Olga had a massive argument, but made up <u>with</u> each other a day later.

h   Jimmy is very cheeky, but he gets <u>away</u> with it because he's so charming as well.

2   **Pre-listening task**

a   the culture or country that someone comes from

b   a person who lives in a particular place

c   to encourage someone to do something

d   to get better after an illness or accident

e   the government or organisations that have power

f   not enough of something

g   to decide what the meaning of something is

h   a difficulty or problem experienced in life

3   **Listening**

1	B	3	C	5	B
2	A	4	C		

4   **Draft and redraft a structured email**

Example answer:

Dear Editor,

Literacy is very important for people's happiness and (for) the development of the/our country. Research studies show/have shown that people who are unable to read or write are more likely to be dissatisfied with their lives. They lack confidence and find it difficult to get jobs/a job. In addition, they can't/don't help their children with their schoolwork or play an active part in their community. They find it difficult to do ordinary things like reading (the) newspapers or filling in forms. Many cannot use the internet or social media. Some of (them) feel ashamed. They cover up their problems and pretend (that) they can read.

I think it is very important that people who can't read or write get help. In our area, there is a literacy scheme which helps / to help adults (to) improve their skills in reading and writing. Schemes like this (can/will) help the government to achieve its/their goal of 100 percent literacy in/for our country.

Yours faithfully,

Vicki Sansa

5   **Language study: Using apostrophes**

Omission of letters:

a   haven't

b   you'd, You're

c   She's, who's

d   Don't, you'd, it's

e   Let's, It's, I've

f   doesn't, they've

g   Aren't

h   coffee's

Possession:

i   Billy's, teacher's

j   sisters', Eddie's

k   students', college's

l   people's

m   women's, men's

n   Alicia's, neighbours'

Omission and possession:

o   Elena's, weeks'

p   I'll, sister's

q   That's, boys'

r   It's, doctor's

s   girl's, couldn't

t   can't, customers'

Grammar spotlight: Present simple and continuous

a   enjoys/is enjoying; hates

b   suppose; 's playing/is playing/plays

c   avoid; are arguing

d   'm/am reading; contains

e   don't/do not understand; 's/is saying

Unit 2

A What is a healthy lifestyle?

1 Vocabulary

1	B	3	A	5	B
2	A	4	C	6	C

2 Understanding pie charts

a swimming

b table tennis

c basketball

d basketball

e keep fit

f judo

3 Suffixes and spelling

a achievement

b motivation

c memorable

d diversity

e noticeable

f careless

g advisable

h courageous

B Note-taking and sports

1 Note-taking practice

social-media campaign

videos to schools promoting mental benefits

structured training courses

supervised training for safety

only friendly competition is allowed

qualified instructors

instructors trained in first aid

redecorated club house

hot showers, hairdryers, lockers, mirrors

2 Linking ideas

a	2	c	6	e	4
b	3	d	5	f	1

3 Sentence correction

a When the referee blew the whistle at the end of the game, neither team <u>had scored</u> a single goal.

b <u>Have</u> you ever won a big competition?

c My bicycle had a puncture today although I <u>replaced</u> the tyre last week.

d Did Hala <u>tell you</u> you why she wasn't chosen for the team?

e The child was in tears because he had <u>fallen</u> off his bike.

f Where <u>did you buy</u> your tennis racket?

g Dentists <u>take</u> care of people's teeth.

h Last week <u>I twisted</u> my ankle playing hockey.

4 Language study: Measurements as adjectives

The correct answers are:

a He lives in a seven-million-dollar house.

b The 500-million-pound contract was to provide six new aircraft.

c The 3000-kilometre cycling race takes place over three weeks.

d I'm exhausted because I worked a 15-hour shift last night.

e Although it was only a three-star hotel, it was actually quite luxurious.

C Fitness and technology

1 Pre-reading task

a intention

b simulation

c gather dust

d astonishing

e high-resolution

f real-time

g monitor

h enhanced

i hooked

j toned

2 Reading for gist and detail

Multiple choice:

1 C

2 A

True or false:

a	T	e	T	i	T
b	F	f	F	j	DS
c	T	g	DS		
d	DS	h	T		

3 Pre-listening task

a set up   e running

b approaching   f simulated

c sort out   g demonstration

d struggle   h unnatural

4 Listening for detail and attitude

Speaker 1: E   Speaker 3: D

Speaker 2: A   Speaker 4: B

They are all talking about the Tour de France Elite Cycling Machine from Activity C2.

D Different approaches to well-being

1 Vocabulary check

a beating   f encouragement

b inconceivable   g slump

c immersed   h consultation

d key   i danger

e fresh   j take

2 Pre-reading task

Thinking about superfoods:

Example answers:

a Because they are much better for you than most other foods.

b More energy; lots of vitamins and minerals; protect from certain illnesses.

c Maybe some fruits and vegetables, and perhaps some types of meat or fish.

Matching words and definitions:

a a fashion that is only popular for a short time

b something positive that is hard to believe or explain

c designed to make people believe something that is not true

d to cause worry or fear

e a member of the public who buys goods or services

f an unnecessary show of excitement or concern

g to argue or disagree about something

h certainly

3 Reading

a 2   b 3   c 1   d 3

4 Style and features

a 2   b 1   c 3   d 1   e 1

5 Note-taking about superfoods

Example notes:

Positive aspects: proven health benefits; can encourage healthy eating; introduces consumers to new foods

Negative aspects: only as beneficial as other fruits, vegetables, etc.; may make consumers avoid other essential foods; food companies/shops likely to charge more for them

Students then write their own short article.

6 Sentence correction: Zero, first and second conditionals

a If the weather <u>is</u> hot, ice cream melts very quickly.

b If I won a million dollars, I <u>would</u> buy a really nice house.

c If it rains a lot, the cricket match <u>will</u> be cancelled.

d <u>If</u> I met someone famous, I wouldn't know what to say.

e Plants die if they <u>do</u> not get enough water.

f If the racket doesn't cost too much, <u>I'll/I will</u> buy it.

g If I lived close to a lake or the sea, I would <u>go</u> swimming every day.

h Sergio's parents are <u>going</u> to be so pleased if Sergio wins the tournament.

Unit 3

A Our neighbourhood

1 Forming open questions

Example answers:

a How long have you lived in your neighbourhood?

b What changes have there been?

c How do you feel about growing up there?

d What are your friends like? / Tell me about your friends.

e What clubs do you belong to? / Tell me about any clubs you belong to.

f Where can you spend free time near you? / What places are there to spend free time near you?

Students then write their own answers to the questions.

2 Pre-reading task

a do up

b affordable

c worn-out

d transform

e renovated

f adequate

g scandalous

h investment

3 Reading letters

Multiple matching:

a 3   d 3   g 1

b 2   e 1   h 2

c 1   f 2

Features of letters:

a A

b All three should be ticked.

c 1: On the plus side, plenty has been spent on rented accommodation . . . I think the council should try to attract a greater number of businesses into the area, though.

2: There's only one green space in the neighbourhood, which is really popular . . .

I know it's impossible to create more parks out of nowhere, but the council should prioritise doing up the one we've got.

3: I must say that I've never been short of things to do here . . . However, I wish the council would provide more bins and employ more people to pick up all the rubbish that people throw away.

4 Colloquial language

1 A   3 B   5 B

2 C   4 B   6 B

5 Language study: Using the gerund

1 seeing   3 Doing   5 having

2 staying   4 missing   6 waiting

B Living in different locations

1 Choose the best word

1 B   5 C   9 D

2 C   6 B   10 A

3 A   7 B

4 B   8 A

2 Pre-listening task

a protection of people and buildings against dangers

b in every part of something or during the whole period of time

c work needed to keep buildings, machines, etc. in good condition

d comfortable and pleasant because it is small and warm

e a small insect that lives in colonies, often underground

f a person who designs buildings

g someone who enters another person's property without permission

h a rounded roof on a building

i the quality of being hard and strong

j someone or something that gives you ideas for doing something

3 Listening comprehension

1 A

2 C

3 B

4 A

5 B

6 C

C Describing places and belongings

1 Order of adjectives

a tall young Russian

b medium-sized, green leather sports

c beautiful old round Italian

d large modern rectangular wooden dining

e strange long green plastic

2 Developing your writing style

Example answer:

I'm lucky enough to have my own bedroom, and to me, it is a very special place with a tranquil atmosphere. The room overlooks the garden and, if I lean out far enough, I can touch the walnut tree which grows just under the window. In autumn, I can even pick walnuts from the tree. When I get in from school, I love curling up on my soft, comfortable bed to read, relax or just daydream. There are lots of cushions on the bed and a beautiful Indian silk bedspread. I find its soft colours particularly relaxing.

3 Word formation

b converted

c own

d traditional

e reductions

f relaxing

g light

h charm

i inspiring

D Welcoming an exchange visitor

1 Improving the tone of an email

Example answer:

Dear Ahmed,

I'm really looking forward to your visit to our home. My family consists of my mother and father and my younger brother, Joseph. He's only 10, so he can be mischievous at times, but don't worry – he's really friendly too.

I've arranged for you to come to school with me and I think you'll enjoy it. Most of the other students are easy to get on with. I'll explain everything you need to know about the school timetable, like when to bring your gym kit, for example. Our form teacher is Mrs Tait. She's usually pretty kind, and, like most of the other teachers, only a tiny bit strict.

I've got lots of exciting activities planned for after school, like swimming, badminton and trips to the cinema.

We've got high-speed internet at home, so you can keep in touch with your family as often as you like.

I can't wait to meet you.

Best wishes,

Oliver

2 Writing an email

Things that are important when writing an email:

appropriate beginning and ending

appropriate tone

all content points covered

spelling and grammar checked and corrected

appropriate paragraphing

writing positively

appropriate level of formality/register

Sample response:

Dear Isabel

I hope both you and your family are well.

I apologise for not getting in touch with you sooner about this, but I'm afraid we're going to have to postpone your stay with us next month. I'm really sorry to disappoint you! I was really looking forward to your coming over.

Unfortunately, we've had some family problems. Dad has had a pain in his back for quite a long time, and the doctor has just told us he's going to need an operation, and this is scheduled for the exact same time as your visit! He'll have to stay in hospital for a while, and when he comes out, he'll need complete rest. Mum and I will have to go to the hospital every day, and it wouldn't be much fun for you to be left at home alone. Also, the trips we had hoped to do would have to be cancelled, as neither Dad nor Mum will be able to drive us anywhere.

What about trying to rearrange your trip? Mum and Dad think it will be fine if you come in July instead of next month. The weather will be better then, so there'll be even more things we can do and places we can go together. We're sure to have a really great time. Anyway, talk to your parents about it and let me know.

All the best,

Bianca

3 **Understanding information in a table**

a   Coulden   e   Williams

b   Morel   f   Lilkova

c   Carter   g   Bloome

d   Khan

4 **Passive forms**

a   Their new house was much bigger than the old one and <u>was</u> built in 1924.

b   Many more bus routes are <u>planned</u> / <u>being planned</u>, both into and out of the city centre.

c   A book describing the history of the town has been <u>written</u> by Daniel Rickman.

d   A bridge <u>was</u> first constructed across the river as long ago as 1482.

e   The first houses in the new estate will be <u>finished</u> in around six months' time.

f   The product is <u>being</u> advertised online and on television at the moment.

Unit 4

A Global warming and industry

1 **Choose the best word**

a   on   e   greater

b   garments   f   fossil fuels

c   carbon footprint g   materials

d   designed   h   consumers

2 **Reading: Scanning practice**

a   asthma

b   the roads are too dangerous

c   half a dozen/6

d   don't make unnecessary journeys by car

e   electric car or hybrid

3 **Vocabulary check**

a   upmarket   d   debris

b   byproducts   e   brainchild

c   mould   f   substitute

4 **Using connectives to guide the reader**

Example answers:

Because, since, as:

a   The roads are getting more crowded because/since/as the number of cars manufactured is increasing.

b   My parents won't allow me to have a motorcycle because/since/as (they think) it is too dangerous.

c   (The) Swimming lessons were / have been cancelled because/since/as the pool was/ is leaking.

d   Train travel became more popular because/since safety checks were introduced.

As a result of, therefore, that's why:

a   Therefore they would land / were going to land in Manchester.

b   Consequently, many people feel inadequate.

c   As a result, house prices have risen / are rising.

d   . . . so she bought a new one.

In addition, furthermore, what's more, as well:

a   are a relatively dangerous form of transport as well.

b   Furthermore, large amounts of water are required for it to grow well.

c   What's more, most people use bikes to get to work.

d   In addition, there were long queues to get on the rides, and some of the rides were not working.

e   Furthermore, a factory would encourage more people to move into the village and as a result, (the) local shops would get more customers.

5   **Understanding graphs**

a $50 000

b   March

c $70 000

d   May

e   Up

B Transport

1   **Pre-listening task**

a   a physical substance

b   able to damage something or someone

c   a disadvantage or problem

d   to estimate using information already known

e   in a gradual but increasing way

f   to show something in public for the first time

2   **Listening task: Hydrogen, the fuel of the future?**

a   75

b   costly

c   2.5 / 2½

d   trucks/lorries

e   2035

f   200

3   **Euphemisms**

a   truth

b   away

c   days

d   Citizen('s)

e   between

f   careful

C Looking for solutions

1   **Paragraphing and punctuation**

At the end of the spring term, our class held a fundraising barbecue. We decided, after some disagreement, to donate the funds to the local hospital. Some students argued that the school needed the money to help replace our classroom laptops. However, in my opinion, we made the right decision to donate the money to a good cause.

Although organising the event was hard work and time-consuming, I think most of us enjoyed selling the tickets and cooking the food. In addition, the nurses told us our donation helped to buy oxygen cylinders for emergency use, which made us feel very proud. The majority of us agreed saving lives is more important than state-of-the-art computers. Nevertheless, a few students disagreed and I understand their point of view.

In conclusion, I think that, although most of our fundraising efforts should continue to benefit local charities, we should have one event each year just for our school. If the headteacher gives permission, perhaps we could use the money we raise to have our classroom computers replaced.

Please let me know if you require any further information about our fundraising activities and plans.

Jordan Inara

Student Representative to the School Management Committee

2   **Presenting the pros and cons**

Listing: Secondly

Contrast: but, however, However,

Reasoning: because, Therefore,

Emphasis: in particular, as surely

Addition: Another point to consider, Moreover

Consequence: As a result, Consequently

Opinion: In my view, I think

Summing up: In conclusion

3   Further connectives

B; F; G

4   Text completion

a	because/as	f	but
b	will/would	g	where
c	with	h	when
d	been	i	which/that
e	which	j	Finally

D The community's views

1   Relating to your target audience

Internet users = C

Residents = F

Teenage magazine readers = E

People looking for a job = A

Parents = D

A penfriend = B

2   Writing a balanced report

Example answer:

This year, the annual class visit was to the alternative energy centre.

At the centre, students were given some very interesting talks about alternative energy sources and also watched a fascinating film on wind power. Unfortunately, several students were unable to see the screen adequately, which made the experience less enjoyable than it could have been.

Students were issued with many useful handouts throughout the day. However, some students did not bring folders with them, so they had difficulty looking after their papers, resulting in some of the handouts being lost.

At the end of the day, the group visited the gift shop and saw an intriguing range of recycled goods. Most of those present bought some gifts to take home for themselves or for others, but many of the items on sale in the gift store were rather too expensive for people our age to afford.

The atmosphere on the bus home was extremely positive. Most students felt they had learnt a good deal and that this would help them in their studies, especially science. Everyone in the group was more aware of the importance of renewable energy sources and what everyone can do to save energy and care for the planet.

It was felt that another visit to this cutting-edge centre would be highly beneficial, as there is still so much to learn.

3   Making predictions

Correct the mistakes:

a   Local authorities have said that it <u>is</u> likely the town will be flooded soon.

b   Energy use is almost <u>certain</u> to rise in the next few years.

c   There's little doubt that world population<u> will continue</u> to rise for many years.

d   A scheme to help people repair their own bikes may <u>be</u> set up if there's sufficient funding.

e   Traffic congestion in the city is expected <u>to</u> improve after road-use charges are introduced.

Order the sentences:

1 c; **2** b; **3** e; **4** a; **5** d

4   Listening: Making predictions

1	C	3	B	5	C
2	A	4	C		

Unit 5

A Cinema and other forms of entertainment

1   Film vocabulary

a	costumes	e	scene
b	reviews	f	genres
c	cast	g	box office
d	characters		

2   More film vocabulary

a   special effects   e   suspense

b   Oscars   f   message

c   settings   g   performance

d   role   h   star

3   Language study: *So . . . that* and *such . . . that*

Example answers:

a   a powerful performance

b   an exciting story

c   an amazing actor

d   convincing/appealing/attractive

e   poignant

f   long

g   beautiful/magnificent

h   sad

B Describing and recommending films

1   Odd word out

a   conscious

b   sufficient

c   substantial

2   Collocations

(Words in brackets are possible, but less likely, collocations.)

stylish: thriller (animation, horror film, documentary, comedy, crime film)

atmospheric: horror film, crime film, thriller (animation, documentary)

witty: animation (horror film, documentary, comedy)

terrifying: horror film, thriller (animation, documentary, crime film)

thought-provoking: documentary (animation, crime film, thriller)

skilful: animation, horror film, documentary, crime film, thriller

3   Describing films

a   5   c   1   e   4   g   6

b   7   d   2   f   8   h   3

4   Describing plots

Verb tense mistakes:

a   Anja <u>decides</u> to change / and <u>meets</u> Max

b   Bond <u>investigates</u> a CIA agent / <u>becomes</u> a weapon

c   to <u>begin</u> a new career / but can he <u>do</u> it

d   then nearly <u>ruins</u> it / who <u>detects</u>

e   Life <u>changes</u> / Zoe <u>falls</u> in love

f   <u>knocks</u> on the door / why <u>does</u> she have

g   <u>catches</u> fire

In which review(s):

a   a, c, e   d   c, d, g

b   f   e   a, b, d, g

c   b   f   e

5   Pre-listening task

a   take shape

b   making a name for herself

c   lapped up

d   milestone

e   in earnest

f   two-dimensional

g   endearing

h   breakthrough

6   Listening for gist and detail

1   A   3   B   5   A   7   C

2   C   4   C   6   B   8   A

7   Word formation: Adjectives and evaluative adverbs

(Words in brackets are possible, but less likely.)

a   expectations

b   personally (frankly)

c   entertaining

d   pleasant (pleasing)

e   likeable

f   mysteriously

g   incidentally

h   powerful (gripping)

i   gripping

j   Unfortunately

k   frankly

l   thankfully

8 Comprehension

1   B

2   C

3   A

C Reading and television

1 Choose the best word

1	A	4	A
2	B	5	C
3	D		

2 Text completion

a   for

b   is

c   to/with

d   of

e   as

f   Furthermore/Also/Additionally

g   if/when

h   with/using

i   one/a

j   to

k   up

l   When/If

m   take/carry

n   than

3 Sentence correction

a	waste <u>of</u> time	e	<u>a</u> discussion
b	better <u>than</u> mine	f	was <u>not</u> able
c	growing <u>up</u>	g	brought <u>up</u> by
d	right <u>to</u> decide	h	as modern <u>as</u>

4 Understanding pie charts

a	✗	d	✓
b	✓	e	✓
c	✓	f	✗

Other possible sentences:

(Books of) poetry and plays were twice as popular as foreign-language books.

Novels accounted for nearly half of all books borrowed.

The most popular kind/type/category of books borrowed was novels.

Short stories were slightly more popular than poetry and plays.

D Writing a book review

1 Developing your writing style

a	1	c	7	e	4	g	5
b	8	d	3	f	6	h	2

2 Language round-up

The following sentences make sense: b, h, i

3 Writing a book review

Example answer:

Have you ever read a book that you wish wouldn't end? Have you got to know the hero so well that you feel like you've known them all your life? Well, that's what happened to me when I read *Step by Step*, the autobiography of explorer and TV film maker, Simon Reeve.

Step by Step is, of course, not a novel, so the 'hero' is real, and has become a well-known presenter of travel programmes. I must admit, I was expecting a typical autobiography, with very few intimate details about the writer's actual life, just a series of stories which create a good impression of them. *Step by Step* is different, however. Simon tells us in full detail the complete story of his difficult teenage years and challenging relationship with his father. As I was reading it, I was actually thinking, 'so it's not just me that feels down sometimes!'

Simon also goes into detail about how he started his working life in the post room at a newspaper, then ended up writing a book about news stories he researched in his own time. He also explains the fortunate series of events that led to him starting to make TV documentaries about various places around the world.

His style of writing is excellent. It is very easy to read, and he almost makes you feel as though you're a close friend who he's telling stories to!

I would recommend this book, not just to anyone who likes Simon Reeve's TV programmes, but also those who love finding out that celebrities are just normal people who have ups and downs in their lives just like you and me.

4 **Using the present perfect to talk about experiences**

a ~~has~~ started, he **has** developed

b she **has** ever **read**, I ~~have~~ finished

c Laura ~~doesn't go~~ hasn't **been**, she ~~has gone~~ went / **did go** a lot

d television **has** changed, there ~~has been~~ **was** much less variety

e I ~~saw~~ **have seen** this film, since it ~~has~~ first ~~come~~ **came** out

Unit 6

A Holiday time

1 **Vocabulary check**

a fully equipped campsite

b travel websites

c culture and customs

d holiday resort

e nightlife

f scenery

Unused: tourism; activities

2 **Pre-reading task**

1	B	3	C	5	A
2	A	4	C	6	B

3 **Five-minute reading task: Scanning**

a	2	c	1	e	1	g	3
b	3	d	3	f	2	h	1

4 **Paragraphing and punctuation**

Recently our class looked at a website advertising an activity holiday. We identified the persuasive techniques advertisers use to convince potential customers to choose this kind of holiday.

Firstly, we looked at the photographs showing young people doing interesting activities. The activities looked very appealing and succeeded in the advertiser's aim of making us want to find out more about the holidays. The target group for this kind of holiday is teenagers, and we noticed how, in order to increase a sense of identification, young people of similar ages and backgrounds to ourselves were chosen for the pictures.

We also studied the information given on the website. This was also persuasive, as comments such as 'every minute of the day is filled with fun' were used to look like real facts, rather than just the advertiser's opinions.

I think by choosing scenic locations, happy-looking people and exciting activities, the holiday company achieved their aim of making the holiday seem attractive. In addition, they cleverly disguised any negative aspects of the holidays.

If you are thinking of booking on a holiday website, remember the advertiser wants you to buy the holiday and will only show its good points. So think of its potential drawbacks for yourself before making your mind up.

5 **Language study: Using modifiers before adjectives**

a fairly

b extremely

c quite

d slightly

B Outdoor activities

1 Text completion

a	flexibility	g	risky
b	strain	h	warnings
c	costume	i	sea
d	trunks	j	shallow
e	supervised	k	life-saving
f	sensitive	l	emergency

Extra word: exercise

2 Developing your writing style

being; since; exploring; where; completely; identifying; capture; from looking; a; like; who; physically; which

3 Pre-listening task

Students' own response.

4 Listening for gist

a Anna seemed to enjoy it a lot. There were some things she didn't like, but she says that overall it was a wonderful experience.

b The long working hours; cleaning the dining areas); going on stage / entertaining the teenagers.

5 Listening for detail

a	eight	d	acting
b	windsurfing	e	east
c	dining areas		

6 Blame and responsibility

a blame; fault

b responsibility; down

c guilty; should

d responsible; things

7 Colloquial expressions: 'Body' idioms

a	*bite my tongue*	d	give me a hand
b	behind my back	e	off my chest
c	blew my mind	f	a straight face

8 Word building: Adjective suffixes

a	memorable	d	changeable
b	poisonous	e	courageous
c	dramatic, basic	f	spacious

C Tourism: The pros and cons

1 Text completion

arranges; According to; with; observe; study; to; do; disturb; argue; where; on; even

2 Building an email from prompts

Hi Wayan,

Just a quick email to tell you about our wonderful holiday visiting the beautiful islands of Sicily and Sardinia. They are places I had never been to but had always wanted to visit.

Sicily has a grand but stormy past. We saw traces of Arabic and Greek influence in the buildings and ruined temples (which/that) we visited. We spent two nights in the capital, Palermo, which was full of life. We also hired bicycles and cycled through/ to sleepy villages. We were impressed by the gentle pace of life and the warmth of the people.

The highlight of our trip was a picnic in a magical mountain setting. We sat near a stream. Far below (us) we could see the Mediterranean gleaming in the sunshine. The only sound was the rustling of the wind in the trees.

It was a holiday I'll never forget!

Write soon!

Love,

Esther

3 Understanding maps

a Palermo, Messina and Catania

b Naples

c Sardinia

d Mount Etna, 3323 m

e false

4 Language study: Adverbs as modifiers

a incredibly painful

b   exceptionally interesting

c   frantically busy

d   dazzlingly bright

e   hardly recognisable

f   bitterly cold

g   completely exhausted

h   mentally tiring

5   **Developing your writing style**

Example answer:

Tranquil Paradise Island has everything: stunningly white, palm-fringed beaches; a dramatic, rocky coastline; sparkling sea full of fish. The air has the scent of exotic flowers, and often the only sound is the song of the birds. In the evenings, the setting sun turns the sky a deep pink and the starlit nights that follow are especially beautiful. Forget pollution, traffic and tower blocks. This diamond-shaped island is truly special, and you'll want to return. I promise you.

D Personal challenges

1   **Reading an example email**

Gap-filling an email:

a   hard to believe

b   marvellous to visit

c   awful to live in

d   expensive to heat

e   idealistic of me to think

f   easy to maintain

g   pleasing to look at

Not used: difficult to know

Students then write four sentences of their own.

Order of sentences and functions: 1 C; 2 E; 3 A; 4 D; 5 B

2   **Compound nouns with *snow* and *sun***

sunshine, sunburn, snowstorm, sunlight, sunhat, snowball, sunroof, sunscreen, snowflake,

sunstroke, snowplough, sunbathe, snowdrift, snowboard, suntan

3   **Spelling revision**

a   thundery   c   icy

b   smoky   d   windy; rainy

4   **Building a text from notes**

b   We went fishing in a nearby lake, but we didn't catch anything.

c   We were caught / got caught in a thunderstorm and, as we had no coats with us, we were/got soaked to the skin.

d   We went to a country market where I bought a brand new DVD dirt cheap.

e   We went on / did a terrific walk through a pine-scented forest and had a picnic near a waterfall.

f   We met a man in the forest who lent us his binoculars to look at a deer.

g   We spent a whole hour watching a breathtaking sunset until the sky went completely dark.

5   **Adverbs of frequency**

Most frequent: always

usually, often (in either order)

sometimes

seldom, rarely, hardly ever (in any order)

Least frequent: never

a   I hardly ever / rarely / seldom go to the cinema – maybe just once or twice a year.

b   Kendra doesn't always go to Italy on holiday – she goes to other countries from time to time.

c   Sometimes Marek sometimes likes going on day trips sometimes when he's on holiday sometimes, but most of the time, he stays at the beach. (correct in any of these positions)

d   Maria usually/often eats out when she's on holiday, but occasionally she cooks something at her rented apartment.

e   Hector is never late when he has to catch a plane – he arrives early every time!

Unit 7

A Challenges of student life

1 Challenges of student life

a	6	c	7	e	4	g	2
b	1	d	8	f	5	h	3

2 Conversation study

1 C   2 D   3 C

3 Tone and register in students' emails

1   This paragraph is rather rude in tone, with very direct language used to turn down the invitation and lots of praise given to an alternative event. The writer appears to criticise the recipient by suggesting they need to check the social calendar more carefully.

2   The writer uses a very positive tone throughout the email and explains fully why they can't attend the recipient's party. They make no criticisms of the recipient or their arrangements for the party.

3   The writer starts out positively but then starts to criticise what they expect the recipient's party to be like. The final two sentences suggest that the recipient's party is much less important than Barry's party so could easily be cancelled.

Paragraph 2 is the best.

B The pressure of exams

1 Pre-reading task

a   happening all the time

b   a detailed plan for achieving success

c   highly planned, organised and structured

d   in a successful way that achieves what you want

e   extremely important or necessary

f   doing something again to practise it

g   completely or very much

h   refers to something that is very close to something else

2 Reading comprehension

a	1	d	1	g	3
b	2	e	2		
c	3	f	not used		

3 Vocabulary: Colloquial words and phrases

e   *at a loose end* is not associated with unhappiness from having too much to do.

a	5	c	2	e	4	g	8
b	9	d	1	f	3	h	7

6 is not used

4 Language study: Giving advice

Choose the best expression:

a   needs to be seen

b   should be encouraged

c   needs to learn

d   encourage

Complete the texts:

1   B

2   D

5 Using a more informal tone

Rewrite the sentences:

a   You shouldn't have forgotten Mum's birthday . . .

b   You needn't buy any milk when you go out . . .

c   You had better take warm clothes with you . . .

d   I should have gone to bed earlier last night . . .

e   You oughtn't leave your revision to the last minute . . .

f   You needn't have booked a taxi . . .

Choose the best informal expressions:

a	loads	d	stick to
b	push me	e	make up
c	nag you	f	do my best

6 **Homophones with silent letters**

a	**(h)**eir	f	w**(h)**ich
b	**(h)**our	g	w**(h)**ether
c	rei**(g)**n	h	weig**(h)**
d	weig**(h)**t	i	s**(c)**ent
e	**(k)**nig**(h)**t	j	**(w)**rote

Students write their own sentences.

C Studying effectively

1 **Punctuation reminders: Capital letters**

Mr Jones, Joseph, University of Colorado, Baltic Sea, Wednesday, Chinese, September, India, River Nile, Asia, Harvey Street, BBC, Himalayas, Professor Grivas

2 **Punctuation reminders: Punctuating a text**

Having just marked her last revision test, I am concerned that Jennifer's poor English is holding her back. Fortunately, she is seeing Mr Barnes, the Language Support teacher, every Tuesday afternoon for help with grammar, spelling, vocabulary and handwriting. She needs to make a special effort to improve in these areas.

3 **Idiomatic expressions**

Make sense: a, d

Don't make sense: b, c, e

4 **Increasing your stock of idioms**

a Try to do better / improve your work

b Not being as good at something as before

c Accept punishment or negative consequences

D Advising and helping

1 **Pre-listening task**

True: b, c, d, f, g   False: a, e, h, i, j

2 **Listening for gist**

a Very happy – the flat is still quite clean and he hasn't had his study disrupted yet.

b Very. Selena gives relevant responses to all of Jack's comments, so is clearly listening carefully, and even gives some indirect advice about being diplomatic with his flatmates.

c There is a suggestion that Jack thinks the flat will become untidy when he says, 'so far, at least.' Jack also thinks there will probably be problems with students needing to study while others are making too much noise.

3 **Detailed listening**

a	NG	d	F	g	T	j	T
b	T	e	NG	h	T		
c	F	f	F	i	NG		

4 **Email completion**

a	knocking	h	wonderful
b	embarrassed	i	choose
c	advice	j	discuss
d	training	k	organise
e	occupation	l	effect
f	appointments	m	confidential
g	earning	n	positive

5 **Grammar spotlight**

a The show should <u>have</u> start<u>ed</u> at 19.30, but it actually started 45 minutes late.

b A better time could <u>have</u> been chosen for the concert.

c <u>Some improvements might be made</u> next year.

d The order <u>should</u> have been delivered on 23 October, but it never arrived.

e I'm glad I took that map because, without it, I <u>would have been</u> lost!

Unit 8

A The call of the sea

1 **Sea vocabulary**

Definitions:

a	pebbles	e	current
b	seaweed	f	liner
c	driftwood	g	shore
d	surf	h	port

Extra words: dunes; rock

Choose the correct words:

a docks; cargo

b horizon

c tide

d snorkelling

e smugglers

f dinghy

2 **More sea vocabulary**

a whales

b skipper

c oceans

d voyage; pirates; cargo

e coastguard

f lighthouse

g dolphins

h shells

i vessel

j dinghies; yachts

3 **Reading and sequencing**

a	6	d	10	g	3	j	9
b	5	e	8	h	1		
c	2	f	4	i	7		

Correct order: g, c, b, h, d, j, f, i, a, e

4 **Language study: Narrative tenses**

a they <u>had not eaten</u> a proper meal

b he <u>was/had been</u> devastated

c the ferry we <u>were</u> going to catch

d This sentence is correct.

e before it <u>sank</u>.

f and <u>asked if I had</u> lost anything.

g when I <u>fell</u> over

5 **Text completion**

been, staying, cancelled, woke, delightful, quietly, glorious, violent, crashing, drowned, cruelly, recovering, screeched, splashed, reminding, collection, inspect, passing, astonishment, decided

B Adrift on the Pacific

1 **Forming questions**

a Did you ever give up hope?

b How big is the Pacific Ocean?

c Are you in good health now? / Are you now in good health?

d How much longer do you think you could have survived?

e What preparations did you make for the journey?

f How big is a sperm whale?

g What are your plans for the future?

h What did you think about while you were on the raft?

i What do sharks taste like?

j Are you still keen on sailing?

2 **Ordering events**

The correct order is: g, i, e, b, h, a, f, d, c

3 **Reporting verbs**

a boasted

b admitted

c congratulated

d offered/agreed

e apologised

f estimated

g agreed/offered

h explained

i complained

4 **Writing a report of an interview: Pre-listening task**

Match words and meanings:

a a long, thin strip of land surrounded by water

b relating to the sea and things that live in it

c relating to a large city

d a place where nature is protected

e the people who do the work on a boat

Describe the route:

Example answer:

They started off initially in San Diego, and flew down to La Paz in the south of Baja California. From there, they took a boat to Manzanillo on the Pacific coast of Mexico, via Mazatlán. From Manzanillo, they continued by bus down to Acapulco, and then flew inland to Mexico City. From Mexico City, they took a bus across to Veracruz, from where they went by boat through the

Gulf of Mexico to New Orleans. Finally, they took a plane back to San Diego.

5 **Writing a report of an interview: Listening task**

Possible notes:

La Paz: bottom of peninsula (Baja California), helping at turtle rescue centre

Mazatlán: 1½ weeks there, big tourist city with beaches, went to beaches and whale-watching, saw humpback whale and dolphins

Manzanillo: famous for sports fishing, three days there, went snorkelling

Acapulco: two weeks there, stayed just outside city, did scuba-diving course, 1 week of diving afterwards

Mexico City: there for 3 days, people amazing, visited museums

Veracruz: four days there, visited ancient cities and island with monkeys

New Orleans: last few days there, enjoyed nightlife, went to nature reserves, saw many birds and alligators

6 **Writing a report of an interview: Writing task**

Example article:

The trip of a young lifetime

Twenty-year-old Clara Sanchez has just returned from the trip of a lifetime in Mexico and the southern USA with a group of six friends. I met up with her to find out how it went.

The first six weeks of Clara's trip were spent exploring the Pacific coast of Mexico, with the first stop at La Paz, near the bottom of the peninsula of Baja California. According to Clara, La Paz was a great place, and rather than hitting the beaches and relaxing, she and her friends spent two weeks helping out at the turtle rescue centre there.

From there, it was on by ferry to the mainland city of Mazatlán. The rough journey left Clara feeling sick, but she soon recovered and was happily making the most of the many beaches in the region. The highlight of her stay, though, was the whale-watching trip, on which Clara reported seeing humpback whales and dolphins.

From Mazatlán, a calm crossing took Clara to Manzanillo, famous for its sports fishing. There were no such activities for Clara and her buddies, however, pointing out that they preferred saving wildlife to hunting it! Instead, the stay there was spent snorkelling and marvelling at the amazing marine life in nearby Santiago Bay.

A bus ride from Manzanillo to Acapulco, which, at close to 10 hours, stretched Clara's patience to the limit. The scuba-diving course that she and her friends did nearby, however, more than made up for the hardship. After qualifying, the group spent a week testing their new skills at some of the local dive sites.

Clara admits that big metropolitan areas aren't really her thing, so the friends only lasted three days in Mexico City. The time was put to good use, however, visiting some of the city's many museums.

From Mexico City, a second bus ride took the pals to the Caribbean port city of Veracruz. The bus ride through mountains, forest and all sorts of other terrain made the six hours more bearable. The ancient cities in the region proved the main attraction there, as well as a nearby island, home to hundreds of monkeys.

Then came the biggest adventure of all: sailing a family friend's sailing boat across the Caribbean Sea. An eventful and exhausting four-day trip, on which the temporary crew saw dolphins, flying fish and other marine life, ended up in the amazing city of New Orleans. There, the friends spent the last days of their trip enjoying the nightlife this stunning city is so famous for, and exploring the neighbouring wildlife reserves, spotting numerous species of birds, as well as alligators.

So what are you waiting for? If you're young and have a few weeks to spare, why not set off into the unknown like Clara and her friends.

C A remarkable rescue

1 **Vocabulary check**

a	sheer	d	chase
b	condition	e	stranded
c	convinced	f	initially

2 Language study: Defining relative clauses

Possible answers:

a there is plenty to see and do

b lives in the sea

c daughter was lost at sea

d that helps guide larger boats into and out of ports

e when you came to stay with me

f which can cause an incredible amount of damage

3 Language study: Non-defining relative clauses

a ~~that~~ which increased by 50 percent last year.

b which she really loves ~~them~~.

c The zookeeper, who was . . .

d at the zoo, which ~~it~~ was

e I know you'll enjoy ~~it~~.

4 Language study: Adverbs

Forming adverbs:

a extraordinarily

b suitably

c romantically

d steadily

e extremely

f responsibly, immediately

g simply

h dramatically

Complete the sentences:

Example answers:

a bravely

b aggressively

c conveniently

d environmentally

e fluently

f independently

g narrowly

h seriously

D Reacting to the unexpected

1 Analysing the narrative

The text should be marked with a tick (✓) NB all the rules have been followed.

2 Ways of developing an outline

a Ayesha loves photography

b went with camera to Formray Island

c went on weekly motor boat – 30-minute trip

d spent day on island watching wildlife

e good day for photography

f got great photo of seal family

g forgot to check time

h heard then saw motor boat leaving

i grew more panicky at thought of one week alone on island

j heard another engine

k waved yellow coat at driver of speedboat

l got a lift on speedboat back to mainland

3 Building a story from a dialogue

Example narrative

I have always been an extremely keen photographer, but something happened to me recently that nearly put me off my hobby for good!

Last Sunday, I woke up to a bright morning and decided to do what I like best: taking my camera to Formray Island, an uninhabited island close to where I live. I bought a ticket for the motor boat that makes the 30-minute crossing to the island once weekly. During the short journey, I was too busy checking my rucksack and scanning the horizon for interesting seabirds to talk to the other passengers, who were mostly middle-aged tourists. This proved to be a mistake, as it meant few, if any, of them even noticed me.

We soon arrived and I jumped ashore. I spent a wonderful day wandering over the small island, observing the behaviour of seals and all kinds of birds, including birds with incredible colourful beaks called puffins. The strong, clear light was perfect for taking photographs, and I loved the sea air – I could almost taste the salt in it. To my delight, I managed to get a brilliant photograph of a family of seals. So far, so good!

However, as I was watching a baby bird being given some small fish to eat by its mother, I suddenly heard the chug-chug of a boat engine. To my horror, I saw the motor boat heading off in the direction of the mainland. Stupidly, I had forgotten to check the time and obviously none of the other passengers were aware that I had been left behind!

I grew more and more panicky as I realised that I would have to spend a whole week on the island with no food, fresh water or shelter because no one lived on the island and the motor boat wasn't due back for another week. I must have been sitting on the shore for about an hour feeling increasingly alone and desperate when, amazingly, I heard the sound of another engine. Then I saw a young man passing close to the shore where I was sitting. The speedboat engine was far too loud for him to hear me shouting, so I picked up my bright yellow coat and frantically jumped up and down while waving it about. Miraculously, he glanced over and spotted me. He slowed and turned and came into the shore. I rushed over and told him what had happened, and he kindly offered to take me back to the mainland. I was so grateful, I almost hugged him!

As we sped homewards, I looked back at the island I love so much. It looked absolutely beautiful in the fading light of the day but, despite this, I was so glad I was leaving.

4   **Text correction**

Last October, Mr Bains, our science teacher 1) told us about the Young Explorer competition. He 2) was driving to school listening to the radio when he 3) heard an interview with an explorer. At the end of the programme, the competition was announced. To enter the competition, Mr Bains explained that we had to make a model of equipment that would be useful on an expedition. Our club 4) got really excited about the idea, although we were a bit nervous about it too, as it was the first time we 5) had entered a competition.

We decided to make our model from toy construction bricks, which we could 6) borrow from younger brothers and sisters. First of all, we 7) brainstormed our ideas and after some disagreement, we 8) decided to make a sled for carrying equipment on an Arctic expedition. We wanted the sled to be original, and Finlay Hudson 9) suggested making a sled that could also be used as a life raft. We all liked the sound of that!

We 10) experimented with different approaches and finally we 11) built a model we were happy with. We 12) used very small bricks to make the ice axe, skis and storage boxes.

We 13) packed our model carefully and 14) sent it off. The club then 15) forgot about it, because we were busy with exams. To our delight, Mr Bains got an email last week saying our club 16) had won an award for the most inventive model. We were all so proud as none of us 17) had ever won a prize before. The club will get an Explorer's Survival Kit, which 18) includes sleeping bags, ropes and a compass.

Please let me know if you require further information.

Hugo Yi, Year 11

5   **The interrupted past continuous**

a   Everything was going so well, when suddenly one of the sails on the ship tore in half.

b   As they set off, they both knew their car was going to break down.

c   The four friends were driving along the dark country road when they heard a loud bang on the roof of the car.

d   Harriet was hit by a large wave as she was swimming desperately towards the shore.

e   As he was climbing the staircase in the old house, Oliver heard a door slowly opening behind him.

f   When Jim and Helen opened the door, a strange old man was standing behind it.

Unit 9

1   **Animal vocabulary: Parts of animals**

cat: paws, fur, claws

camel: hump, hooves

horse: hooves, mane

bird: beak, feathers, wings, claws

elephant: tusks, trunk

goat: horns, hooves

fish: fins, scales

2   **Definitions**

True: a, b, f, g, i, k, l

False: c, d, e, h, j

3   **Text completion**

a	historians	g	result
b	empire	h	for
c	private	i	from
d	until	j	active
e	classify	k	Nevertheless
f	it	l	but

B Animal experimentation

1   **Vocabulary check**

a	vaccine	f	asthma
b	ethical	g	antibiotics
c	lungs	h	vitamins
d	blood	i	virus
e	veins	j	laboratory

2   **Pre-listening task**

a	see the back of	g	sophisticated
b	cosmetics	h	go along with
c	simulation	i	ins and outs
d	pharmaceutical	j	uninformative
e	lined up	k	dilemma
f	biased	l	vanity

3   **Listening**

1	B	3	C	5	C
2	A	4	A	6	B

4   **Writing an article for the school blog**

Example blog:

Did you know that many of the cosmetics products, such as make-up and skin cream, that we buy from supermarkets and pharmacies has been tested on animals? 'But why,' I hear you say, 'when these are designed for humans?'

The main reason they're tested on animals is to check that they're absolutely safe for humans to use before they're sold in shops. The thinking is that if animals have no negative reactions to the cosmetic products, then they will be safe for us to use. Makes sense, I guess.

However, there's an increasing body of people who believe it is fundamentally wrong to test products that have no health benefits and are only designed to improve our appearance on animals. I happen to be one of those people. If we want safe beauty products, then we should be brave enough to test them on ourselves rather than inflicting that on innocent creatures.

There are, after all, plenty of alternatives available, including paying humans to take part in trials for new products. Creating computer-based tests to simulate what will happen when a cream, for example, is applied is increasingly possible.

I would like, therefore, to see an immediate ban put on animal testing for cosmetic products and these alternatives brought in to end the suffering of laboratory animals.

5   **Prepositions after verbs**

a	to	d	on	g	with
b	for	e	about	h	from
c	by	f	of		

C Animals in sport and entertainment

1   **People's opinions**

a	4	c	6	e	2	g	7
b	5	d	3	f	1	h	8

2   **Vocabulary: Words for feelings**

a	disgusted	d	distressed
b	uneasy	e	saddened
c	immoral	f	ridiculous

3   **Language study: Adding emphasis**

a	innocent	d	apologetic
b	absurd	e	anxious
c	magical		Passionate not used.

D Animals at work

1 Verb forms

a   have become → became

b   was keeping → kept

c   are feeding → feed

d   had been biting → had bitten

e   has sold → sold

f   is used → has been used / was used

g   often criticise → are often criticised

2 Vocabulary: Young animals

ewe

3 Vocabulary: Collective nouns

foal

4 Vocabulary check: Farming

a	orchard	e	organic
b	poultry	f	free range
c	herds	g	pesticides
d	rear	h	processed

5 Text completion

Missing words:

a	was	m	in
b	be	n	for
c	it	o	is
d	which/that	p	in
e	have	q	so
f	where	r	to
g	where	s	while
h	much/far	t	of/for
i	only	u	which
j	what	v	there
k	say/claim/ argue/protest/ believe/think	w	for
		x	to
l	feel/experience	y	but

Identifying bias:

Use of emotive vocabulary (e.g. awful bacteria, absolutely disgusting)

Use of rhetorical questions (e.g. who wants to go back to the olden days . . . ?)

Clear expression of biased opinions (e.g. I think this is shocking.)

Involvement of readers to support writer's bias (e.g. I urge all readers to write . . .)

Capitalisation to emphasise biased opinion (e.g. It IS worth it!)

E Helping animals in danger

1 Understanding graphs

a	F	c	F	e	T
b	F	d	T	f	F

2 Proofreading a report

Our class visit to the animal sanctuary to see ~~with~~ the giant panda and the newborn twin giant panda cubs was so thrilling. We were all looking ~~very~~ forward to it so much. All of us felt we knew ~~so~~ a lot about the cubs before the visit. In our biology lesson, we had learnt that they ~~had~~ were sleeping in warm cots called incubators and special techniques were needed to care for them.

Mrs Lun had ~~been~~ told us about the way in which in the wild, a mother who has twins may struggle to feed both babies and may abandon one of them. In the zoo, however, staff will take one cub to the incubator while the mother ~~her~~ feeds the other one. It was amazing ~~for~~ to see this happen in real life. The zoo staff ~~they~~ used a stick of sugar cane to distract the mother while a member of staff took one of the cubs away.

We all wanted to take photographs, and everyone was able to get ~~there~~ fantastic pictures of the cubs. We also saw ~~how~~ the cubs trying to move by pushing their legs backwards. We were told they only weighed about 113 grams when they ~~been~~ were born, which is about the same as our phones. We don't know their names yet, because the cubs will not be named until they are 100 days ~~of~~ old.

On the way back to school, we decided to upload ~~on~~ the photos onto the school website. Mrs Lun suggested we also write a fun online quiz based on the notes ~~from~~ the staff gave us.

We all appreciated the experience so much and we are going to treasure ~~it~~ the memories for the rest of our lives.

3 **Improving a report**

a	2	c	1	e	7	g	5
b	6	d	8	f	3	h	4

4 **The past perfect passive**

a When I next went to the zoo, many new trees had been planted in the animals' enclosures.

b We ate fresh fish for dinner that had been caught by locals in the nearby lake.

c If the rabbit had been caught, Martha would have been very upset.

d Tiffany noticed that her new make-up had not been tested on animals.

e What would you have done if the zoo had been forced to close?

Unit 10

A The rewards of work

1 **Skills and qualities for work**

Complete the definitions:

a	dentist	i	nursery teacher
b	novelist	j	labourer
c	interpreter	k	carpenter
d	interior designer	l	miner
e	firefighter	m	chauffeur
f	journalist	n	midwife
g	cellist	o	plumber
h	company director	p	choreographer

Students think of three more occupations and write definitions for them.

2 **More work-related vocabulary**

a	research	e	launch
b	competitive	f	campaign
c	investing	g	brand
d	profitable	h	manufacturing

3 **Idioms**

Match the idioms to the definition:

a the kind of job that you do

b to enter a company at a low level with the hope of being more successful in the future

c to be in charge and make important decisions

d to have less than zero in the bank

e to have all the latest information about something so you can do it well

f to watch someone very closely and check what they're doing

Use the idioms in sentences:

a get (herself) (back) up to speed

b got a/his foot in the door

c been in the red

d line of work

e breathing down my neck

f calling the shots

4 **Understanding visual data**

a False – the most popular choice for males was business

b True

c False – the least popular was fashion design

d True

e True

f False – it decreased in popularity with male students

B Facts and figures

1 **Approximations**

Makes sense: a, b, e

Doesn't make sense: c, d, f

2 **Questioning and criticising statistics**

a	3	c	1	e	5	g	8
b	4	d	2	f	6		

Extra: 7

3 **Rewriting in a more formal style**

Example report:

I have recently completed a very enjoyable period of work experience at a local roller-skate and skateboard shop.

My role there was to speak to customers who came into the store with a view to persuading them to purchase products from the shop. As I have a great deal of experience of skateboarding myself, I have developed a thorough knowledge of the sport, which I was able to pass on effectively to customers.

The manager at the shop was friendly and supportive, and we developed a highly positive working relationship. She was, I believe, pleased with my efforts and commented that I was the best work experience student that she had taken on for a considerable time. I found the praise that she gave me extremely encouraging.

During my time at the shop, I learnt a great deal about running a retail outlet. For example, I became proficient at using the till and in persuading shoppers to buy additional items, for instance, by suggesting that someone who was purchasing a skateboard might also need elbow and knee protectors, and perhaps even a helmet to go with it.

As I had such a positive experience of working at the store, I would greatly like to gain paid, part-time, weekend work at the same establishment.

C Internet marketing

1 **Vocabulary check**

a	niche market	d	credibility
b	engagement	e	target audience
c	promoted	f	followers

2 **Common work-related expressions**

Do the sentences make sense:

Makes sense: b, d, g, i

Doesn't make sense: a, c, e, f, h

Guess the meaning:

a failed / went out of business

b do different kinds of things to make money

c someone who buys from the manufacturer and then sells to the consumer

d shared the running of the business with someone else

D Recruitment with a difference

1 **Vocabulary check**

a just four weeks

b chooses his words carefully

c bought a new suit

d barrier

e bought me anything I wanted

f showed me exactly what to do

2 **Reading for gist**

Jan Benson is employed as a human resources assistant for a big clothing chain in Scotland. The main part of her role is recruiting new staff to work at the company. 'HR work is often stereotyped as lacking in excitement,' says Jan, 'but it can offer a fulfilling career to anyone who has a genuine desire to make organisations more efficient.'

Jan took a degree in economics at Birmingham University before deciding she was interested in working in human resources. 'I started as an assistant to an HR officer last August and have been studying for my qualifications in HR management in the evenings,' explains Jan. 'It's hard work but worth it, as I'm able to go on earning while I'm gaining qualifications.'

The aspect Jan most enjoys about her work is the challenge of gaining the respect of the store managers. 'I'm learning from my boss, Mrs Shah, that it's essential to try to understand the managers' needs in terms of the kind of staff they're looking for, rather than just imposing my views,' she explains.

1 A

2 B

3 B

3 **Language study: Similes**

a oven

b naughty little child

c well-oiled machine

d brick wall

e leaf

f won a million dollars

4 **Phrasal verbs**

a turned down   d put him down

b let down   e drew out

c drew up   f turned up

E Preparing for work

1 **Reading, analysis and writing**

Choose the most suitable word:

a is   k have

b give   l of

c to   m help

d are   n to

e such   o might

f information   p in

g if   q which

h know   r how

i a   s found

j to   t include

Answer the questions about the text:

1 to give advice to young people considering their future careers

2 C

3 B

Complete the text:

Example answer:

. . . work experience placements with local companies. Perhaps you know someone who works in one, or you could try asking around a range of businesses until you find one that's willing to provide you with mentoring and training. Colleges also often offer work experience as part of their vocational training courses.

2 **Correcting a report for the headteacher**

We all really appreciated our work experience at Le Yung Motorcycles. At first, students did not want to do work experience because we had a stereotyped idea of what working in a factory was like. We thought the factory was going to be noisy and dirty, and we would be desperate for the day to end. In fact, we found out that in a modern factory like Le Yung Motorcycles, nothing could be further from the truth. The factory itself was clean and pleasant, and the machines were quiet.

After being shown around the factory, to our surprise, we were told we could operate some of the machines ourselves. We felt proud as we walked through the door marked 'Staff Only' and were given our special work uniforms. I personally loved working with the supervisor, Mr Zu, who operated a large machine used to repair damaged engines, and I know other students had similar good experiences.

Everyone in the company encouraged us to think of engineering as a career with many possibilities. Since doing work experience, I have become interested in doing an engineering degree and others in the group are thinking of jobs in marketing, design or sales for an engineering company.

Fatima Al-Sultana

Year 11

3 **Pre-listening task**

a very surprised

b despite what has been said or what you might think

c relaxed and calm

d   like a person when you first meet them

e   angry about something

f   learn something new

4   **Listening**

Match the ideas with the speakers:

a	Speaker 2	d	Speaker 2
b	Speaker 1	e	Speaker 1
c	Speaker 3	f	Speaker 3

Complete the sentences:

1   A

2   C

3   B

5   Superlatives

a   the most sophisticated

b   the worst

c   the cleverest

d   the most successful

e   the laziest

f   the best

6   **Adverbs of degree**

a   good enough

b   not very realistic

c   This sentence is correct.

d   a little noisy

e   rather bad-tempered

f   have slightly/rather different cultures

> Workbook audioscripts

Unit 1

B4 (Audio 1)

Speaker 1

I think I have a similar sense of humour to most of my friends, especially my best friend. There's nothing better than having a good laugh with someone – you somehow feel so much better afterwards. It occasionally causes problems, though, because for some strange reason, I find some serious situations, like school assemblies, incredibly funny. I can usually control my laughter, but from time to time, I can't hold it in and end up getting into trouble. I'm not quite sure why I find things like that as amusing as funny films, but I do.

Speaker 2

My best friend's a bit of a mystery to me because I've hardly ever seen her laugh. Although I'm always laughing along with the rest of our friends when we're watching a good comedy movie together, she just sits there as though it were a tragedy. We're complete opposites, as I burst into laughter at more or less anything. I'm not quite sure why she's like that, but I'm still hoping that one day I'll find a way of getting her to crack a smile a bit more often.

Speaker 3

I've noticed for a while now that when I go to the cinema with a group of friends to see something funny, they'll laugh at the parts of the film that I just don't find funny, and I'll be roaring with laughter while they're sitting there stony-faced. My best friend's the exception, as he's amused by the same scenes as me. It just goes to show that there's nothing universal about humour – it's as individual as all our other likes and dislikes.

Unit 1

D3 (Audio 2)

Hi everyone, and welcome to my talk about the incredible Mexican artist Frida Kahlo. She came from a family of mixed heritage; her mother's side of the family being a combination of Spanish and Amerindian – the original inhabitants of North, Central and South America – while the other side of the family had arrived in Mexico from Germany several years before.

Frida caught a serious disease called polio when she was just six years old. This made walking very hard for her, at least to begin with, but her father urged her to take up swimming and even soccer to help develop her strength again. Frida later wrote that her relationship with her father was extremely close, so she was keen to follow his advice.

When she was 18, Frida was on her way home from school when the bus she was in crossed in front of a tram, which unfortunately hit the side of the bus. Many passengers climbed from the wrecked bus with minor injuries, but Frida was badly hurt. It was while recovering from the accident that Frida started painting seriously.

Frida got married to a famous artist called Diego Rivera in 1929, and they moved to the United States together in 1931. Even though their political beliefs occasionally got them into trouble with the authorities, they were both successful so had no shortage of money. However, she missed Mexico, so they decided to go back there in 1933.

Frida's striking paintings are often interpreted as products of her imagination. Frida commented, however, that they were actually her way of showing visually the many different feelings she experienced in her life. She saw painting as the best way of expressing them, and her art came to be admired by many. So despite all of her setbacks in life, Frida achieved great success in her lifetime and is often described as one of the most important artists of the 20th century.

Unit 2

C4 (Audio 3)

Speaker 1

I saw the Tour de France Elite advertised in a cycling magazine and just thought, why not? I'd been considering getting a new bike, but winter was approaching, so I decided I'd get one I could use in the warmth and comfort of my own home. Although I've no regrets about my decision now, I seriously thought about sending it back as I just couldn't get it to work to begin with. Several calls to the company's helpline later and it was all sorted out. I'm hoping to begin racing once I'm totally used to riding it.

Speaker 2

I was really excited when the box arrived and was expecting to have a big struggle getting the machine working – several users had commented on this in the reviews on the website I bought it from. Anyway, I had it up and running in a few minutes and was soon cycling along a riverbank in South America, but in the comfort of my own home. The screen's certainly quite big but the simulated countryside looks very unreal. Anyway, a couple of my friends also have Tour de France Elites, and I've beaten them several times already.

Speaker 3

The adverts for the Tour de France Elite emphasised how the machine was almost silent when you were riding it. I must say that I haven't found that to be the case, and the new bike I use on the roads is actually quieter. Other than that, I'm really pleased with it. I have races planned already with several friends but want to get my fitness up first. But I've noticed in just the first two weeks of using it what a difference it's made already. Even the setting up was much less difficult than I imagined, so I'd definitely recommend it to anyone who's interested in cycling.

Speaker 4

I was so excited when my Tour de France Elite arrived, having seen a demonstration of one at a cycling show where the user was taking part in a stage of the real Tour de France bike race. I can't begin to describe how disappointed I was when I first started using it, though. The colours on the display seem totally unnatural, and there's no sense of actually travelling anywhere – I should've used the money on the real thing because I could have got a really good one for the amount that the Tour de France Elite cost me.

Unit 3

B3 (Audio 4)

Interviewer: As part of our modern architecture season, we have Jamila Balicki with us in the studio. Jamila, you live in a house that's partially underground. What gave you the idea for creating a home like that?

Jamila: It's funny, but that's just what the architect I employed to create the designs for the house asked me! I think he was expecting me to say that I'd seen something similar in a posh lifestyle magazine, but the inspiration actually came from a documentary about creatures called badgers, which live partly underground. Their homes looked so cosy and warm that I wanted to live like that too.

Interviewer: And how was it when you first moved in there?

Jamila: Amazing! I'd insisted on having large rooms throughout the house when I was discussing the designs so there's much more space than where I used to live. What took me ages to get used to was the silence, as more or less any sound from outside is cut out by the walls. About as much sun gets in as my old home, though. I'd asked for glass domes in the ceilings, which are great, so I never got the impression I was in a deep, dark tunnel.

Interviewer: So what's the best thing about living there?

Jamila: I really feel like part of the landscape when I'm in it, and therefore connected to everything that lives in that area, which is an amazing feeling. It gives you a sense of solidity and security too, but that's not so important to me. On a practical level, I thought it might prove easier to look after than a more traditional house, but the opposite's actually the case.

Interviewer: So what kinds of problems have you had?

Jamila: By far the most serious was when lots of water came in after a long period of heavy rain a couple of years ago, but I had that issue fixed. In fact, it rained a lot recently and there was no repeat, so it seems to be sorted. I had to get someone in to remove an ants nest a couple of weeks ago. The nest itself was outside but they were all coming into the house looking for food. I thought I might get lots of people walking across the land because they didn't realise the house was there, but it's only happened once or twice.

Unit 4

B2 (Audio 5)

Thank you for coming to my talk today. I'd like to tell you more about an extremely exciting development in environmentally friendly transport that's being developed in many countries around the world as we speak: the use of a gas called hydrogen as a fuel.

Hydrogen is the simplest and most common element in the universe. Stars are actually 90 percent hydrogen, and indeed 75 percent of all matter is made from it, so we certainly have plenty of it! The best thing about it environmentally speaking is that, when it's burnt, instead of getting harmful by-products like greenhouse gases, we get water.

This sounds like the perfect solution to all of our problems, but there's a major drawback. Although production of hydrogen is not a particularly complex process, it's actually quite costly to produce in large quantities. Hopes are that it will become increasingly cheap as technology improves.

The global market value of renewable energy as a whole is approaching 1.5 trillion dollars in total, but that of hydrogen is projected to reach 2.5 trillion by around 2050.

There are lots of ideas for how hydrogen could be used as a fuel. Most interest lies in hydrogen-powered buses and aeroplanes, as well as trucks. Trains are progressively using electricity from renewable sources, and low-emission cars will be far more likely to run on lithium-ion batteries recharged using green power than hydrogen.

European plane manufacturer Airbus has already produced designs for a passenger plane they hope will be the first to run on hydrogen. Unveiled in 2020, they're hoping it'll be in service in or before 2035, helping governments to keep to long-term reduction targets for greenhouse gases, many of which run to 2050. It's designed to seat 200 passengers, so not as many as the average airliner of today which can take around 350 passengers, but pretty good, nonetheless.

Unit 4

D2 (Audio 6)

Laura: What do you think you'll do when you leave school, Martin?

Martin: I'm not sure, Laura. University's definitely an option.

Laura: Yeah, for me too. My parents are expecting me to go, hopefully to study a science of some sort, but I might look to start work straight after instead, probably for an organisation that helps the environment.

Martin: I'm interested in that sort of thing too. There are loads of projects these days that are helping to replant trees, which I wouldn't mind getting involved with. Contrary to what you hear on the news, I'm actually optimistic that the amount of forested land will increase before too long.

Laura: It might, I guess, but it'll take a lot of effort. I'd like to volunteer for a charity of some sort round here that helps the environment.

Martin: Yeah? So what's stopping you?

Laura: Well, schoolwork at the moment. I suppose I'm likely to get less over the summer, so I may do some then.

Martin: Sounds good! I'm going to help raise some money for charity.

Laura: Oh?

Martin: Yeah. A few of my friends did a 30-kilometre hike to make money for a children's hospital a few weeks ago – you know, friends and family promised to pay them a certain amount of money per kilometre. Doing the same sort of thing but with lengths of the swimming pool might be fun, but I think it'd be more appropriate if I did something like not speaking for a whole day.

Laura: Why – because you talk so much normally?

Martin: Exactly! So I'll almost certainly do that.

Laura: Good idea! We've all got to do something to help stop global warming.

Martin: Yeah. A lot of scientists are saying that average temperatures worldwide will go up by over two degrees centigrade.

Laura: I know. And I must say that I agree with them, actually. Hoping that it's less than this is just wishful thinking. If we can limit it to that figure, that would be great, but I have my doubts.

Martin: We'll see.

Unit 5

B6 (Audio 7)

I'd like to tell you about a film called Toy Story today as it's a real milestone in film-making, due to being the first full-length movie made entirely using CGI (computer-generated imagery).

Toy Story wasn't the first film to use CGI, of course. Tron, the 1982 film that tells the story of a man trapped inside a computer, was probably the best-known movie that made extensive use of CGI up to that point. It initially appeared, however, in 1973 sci-fi movie Westworld, although only two-dimensional images were made and just a small part of the film was created in this way. Its sequel, Futureworld, was the first to use 3D CGI effects in 1976.

Newly formed production company Pixar was chosen to put Toy Story together. Long before it began working on the storyline, they had to develop the technology required to actually produce a whole full-length film – it was such a new idea, it hadn't actually been invented yet. Once that was done, the characters and plot could begin to take shape.

Pixar actually ran into some trouble with the central character, a toy cowboy named Woody. The writers decided to make him different to the rather bland cartoon heroes that they felt cinemagoers were getting bored with, so they tried to create a somewhat sarcastic and arrogant character, but they went too far and Woody ended up being more like a verbally violent bully than the hero of a children's film. The scripts and storyboards were quickly rewritten to avoid the negative reception they knew such a character would receive.

There were, however, further issues with the scripts, characters and plots. Toy Story's investors liked the fact there were jokes that adults would enjoy in the film as well as plenty of humour for children, but thought there were insufficient human characters, so put pressure on Pixar to add more. They did, but when a new writer took charge, he pointed out that it was a film about toys, not people, so they were all taken out again. Back to square one!

Once the storyline was agreed on, the production of the animation began in earnest. The previous record for a 100 percent CGI film that Pixar had made was a full 80 minutes shorter than Toy Story was intended to be. Yet just 27 animators were responsible for producing this breakthrough film, which went on to make 356 million dollars at the box office worldwide.

Had the film not been a hit, it's unlikely that the company would have survived, but Pixar made a name for themselves thanks to Toy Story. Up to the film's release, they feared that the picture quality, which to them was far from satisfactory, would put audiences off. No one seemed to notice, however, and soon audiences were lapping up the action-packed 81 minutes of unusual story, moving songs and endearing adventure that together make up Toy Story.

Unit 6

B4 (Audio 8)

I've just finished a hectic summer working as a volunteer at a summer camp near Vancouver in Canada. Some volunteers only stay for four weeks, because that's all the time they have available to give, but I was there for eight, which passed astonishingly quickly.

I must say that it was harder than I expected, and I especially struggled with the long working hours. There were some great kids there, who came from pretty much all over the world, and we had a great deal of fun together doing the activities. I was familiar with most of the things the kids had to do, but there were others that I'd never tried before. I learnt to do some of them in the little free time I had. Windsurfing's definitely something I'll try again, but I wasn't sure at all about horse riding.

Unfortunately, cleaning was also an unavoidable part of the job! I really didn't enjoy doing the dining areas, but it was expected that all the volunteers would help out. It was hard work, and boring too. Fortunately, the kids were responsible for keeping their bedrooms clean, as having to sort out the messes there would've been a nightmare!

All the volunteers had to provide entertainment for the teenagers in the evening. I'm quite a shy person, so going on stage was a bit of a challenge for me. The musical shows we put on weren't too bad, because there'd be loads of us on stage all playing and singing together, so I could hide behind the others, but we took part in some comedy plays and sketches too, and acting has never been my thing, really.

Overall, though, it was a wonderful experience, and I'm going to spend the next few weeks travelling across Canada, from the west coast, where the camp is, to the east, where I catch my flight home from. I'll stay for a few days in any place that takes my fancy. I'll almost certainly feel exhausted by the time I get back to college, but it's definitely going to be worth it.

Unit 7

D2 (Audio 9)

Selena: It must be strange living with people you don't know.

Jack: It certainly is. I'd become so used to living with my parents and sister, so it was quite a shock to suddenly find myself in a shared university flat with five strangers.

Selena: So how has it been?

Jack: Good, generally. As we're all men, I was expecting the flat to become a complete mess within a week of us moving in, but it's actually astonishingly tidy . . . so far, at least. There's a student called Chen, who's organised a rota for all of the chores like cleaning and tidying up the communal areas, and everyone's sticking to it so far.

Selena: That's amazing! Is it easy to study when there are so many people around?

Jack: Well, we're all out at lectures and tutorials during the day, so the flat is pretty quiet then, but it can get quite noisy in the evening, with people having loud conversations and playing music. I haven't had much coursework yet, but I'm sure the essays and assignments will start coming in soon. I just hope we all get deadlines for coursework at the same time because everyone will need to study if that's the case. The difficulties will come if only one or two of us have exams or mock exams we need to revise for while the others just carry on being their usual noisy selves.

Selena: Yeah, you'll have to be very diplomatic if that happens, to try and persuade everyone to be quiet while you're working.

Jack: I guess so. I'd prefer to work in my own room, but I could just go to the library and work there if worse comes to worst.

Selena: Hopefully it won't come to that. Do you all go out socialising together?

Jack: Sometimes, but to be honest, we've all got student loans, so we don't want to spend too much by going out clubbing every night. I'd have to spend the rest of my life paying the money back if I did that.

Selena: And I don't suppose you'd do very well on your course either, would you?

Jack: I guess not.

Unit 8

B5 (Audio 10)

Interviewer: So Clara, I believe you've just returned from an eight-week trip, mostly spent in various places in Mexico. Talk us through the first part of your trip.

Clara: Well, the first six weeks were spent in places along the Pacific coast of Mexico. We got a plane from San Diego, where we all live, to La Paz, which is near the bottom of a long peninsula called Baja California. It was a fairly short journey, so we were there in a couple of hours. La Paz is great – we stayed in an eco-tourist resort and helped out at a turtle rescue centre there for a couple of weeks.

Interviewer: And where did you go to from there?

Clara: We took a ferry across to a city called Mazatlán on the Mexican mainland. The sea was quite rough, so I felt a bit sick. Anyway, we relaxed there for a week and a half after all our efforts at the rescue centre. It's a big tourist city and there are many beaches around there, so we really made the most of them. The best thing we did there was go on a whale-watching trip. We saw humpback whales, and dolphins too.

Interviewer: And after Mazatlán?

Clara: We took another ferry to Manzanillo. Fortunately, this time it was relatively calm so I didn't get ill. It's really famous as a sport fishing destination, but none of us are into that – we all prefer saving wildlife to catching it! We spent three days snorkelling there, at a place called Santiago Bay. The marine life was astonishing! Then we got the bus from Manzanillo to Acapulco – that was a mistake!

Interviewer: Oh? Why was that?

Clara: Well, mainly because it took nine and a half hours! My phone ran out of battery after about four hours, and it was dark outside by then, so I couldn't even look out at the scenery. Anyway, it was worth it when we finally got to Acapulco. We weren't staying in the city itself, but just outside it. We'd booked to do a scuba-diving course, so we spent a week doing that, then another week afterwards going to some of the local dives sites.

Interviewer: And where did you go from there?

Clara: To Mexico City. We got the plane there – it was a really short flight – and only stayed for three days, visiting museums mainly. None of us is into staying in big metropolitan areas like that, and believe me, Mexico City is huge! The people there were amazing, though. In fact, they were great everywhere we went in Mexico. After that, we caught the bus to a port city called Veracruz, which is on the other side of Mexico, on the Caribbean coast. We wanted to take the train there, but they only carry freight on that line, not people.

Interviewer: That's a shame.

Clara: Yeah. Anyway, the bus was fine – just six hours this time, but in daylight, so we could watch the beautiful scenery rolling by. It was so different throughout the journey – mountains, forests and then the flat coastal plain. We spent four days there, mostly visiting sites of ancient cities, but we also visited an island where there were lots of monkeys.

Interviewer: And from Veracruz?

Clara: From there, we headed back to the States, New Orleans to be precise. Some friends of my parents have a large sailing boat, and we'd organised to make the journey with them. They said we could travel for free as long as we acted as crew on the boat. The journey was hard work and took about four and a half days – we saw dolphins and flying fish and loads of other stuff. We spent the last few days enjoying the fantastic nightlife in New Orleans and exploring the nature reserves in the area. There was an amazing variety of birds and lots of alligators too. Then all too soon, we had to fly back to San Diego.

Interviewer: Many thanks for talking to me today about your trip, Clara.

Clara: You're welcome!

Unit 8

D2 (Audio 11)

Youssef: Have you always been interested in photography, Ayesha?

Ayesha: For a long time, Youssef, but something happened recently that nearly put an end to my hobby!

Youssef: Oh?

Ayesha: Yeah, well last Sunday, I woke up to a bright morning and decided to do what I like best: taking my camera to Formray Island.

Youssef: That's the small island off the coast near where you live, isn't it?

Ayesha: That's right – the one that's home to just birds and seals and lots of other wonderful creatures. Anyway, I got a ticket for the motor boat that runs weekly to the island.

Youssef: Does it take long to get there?

Ayesha: No, only about 30 minutes. During the short journey, I was too busy checking my rucksack and scanning the horizon for interesting seabirds to talk to the other passengers, who were mostly middle-aged tourists. We soon arrived and I went ashore.

Youssef: So what did you do there?

Ayesha: I spent a wonderful day wandering over the small island, observing the behaviour of seals and all kinds of birds, including puffins – amazing little seabirds that have really colourful beaks.

Youssef: Was it a good day for taking photos, then?

Ayesha: Absolutely! The light was really strong and clear, so it was perfect for taking pictures. I loved the sea air – I could almost taste the salt in it.

Youssef: It sounds great. I wish I could've been there to share it with you.

Ayesha: That would've been great. Anyway, to my delight, I managed to get a brilliant photograph of a family of seals. I'll show it to you when you next come to my house.

Youssef: This all sounds great! So what happened that nearly caused you to give up photography then?

Ayesha: Well, I was watching a baby bird being given some small fish to eat by its mother when suddenly I heard the chug-chug of a boat engine. To my horror, I saw the motor boat heading off in the direction of the mainland. Stupidly, I had forgotten to check the time, and obviously no one was aware that I had been left behind! I grew more and more panicky as I realised I would probably be stuck on the island without food, drink or shelter for a week, because, of course, there are no houses or people there.

Youssef: Oh no! So, what did you do?

Ayesha: Well, I must have been sitting there for about an hour feeling increasingly alone and desperate when, amazingly, I heard the sound of another engine. Then I saw a young man in a speedboat going past.

Youssef: So did you shout for him to stop?

Ayesha: There was no point because his engine was so loud, but I jumped up and down and waved my coat around, which fortunately was bright yellow.

Youssef: So did he see you?

Ayesha: Thankfully, he did. He slowed and turned and came into the shore. I rushed over and told him what had happened, and he kindly offered to take me back to the mainland. I was so grateful, I almost hugged him!

Youssef: So what were you thinking as you left?

Ayesha: Well, as we were speeding homewards, I looked back at the island I love so much. It looked absolutely beautiful in the fading light of the day, but I was so glad to be leaving.

Youssef: I'm not surprised!

Unit 9

B3 (Audio 12)

Recording 1

Male: That was an interesting class discussion on animal experimentation and testing.

Female: It was. I surprised myself by voting in favour of it in the end, but I did make the point that the type of animals used should be limited.

Male: Oh? What – to rats I suppose?

Female: Well, I don't particularly like them, but my argument was that if it's done for medical research, then scientists should use animals that are as close to humans genetically as possible, so I was thinking more of monkeys. The cats they use for some experiments are just too different to people to be of any use, in my opinion.

Male: Hmm, I'm not sure I go along with your idea, but I see what you mean. What I'd dearly like to see the back of is animal experimentation for non-essential products like make-up and face creams. I can see the point if it's to create effective drugs and medical treatments, but animals shouldn't suffer because of human vanity! Thankfully, the food industry's never thought of using animals to test new food products.

Recording 2

Thanks for coming to my talk today on animal experimentation. Before I go into the ethical dilemmas of animal testing, I'll tell you a little about what I do. I work as a research scientist at a large university. There are lots of research teams there looking into ways of treating and curing a range of diseases – pretty much everything, in fact, from diabetes and heart disease to cancer, which is what the team I'm leading is investigating.

As I'm sure you're aware, animal experimentation is a controversial topic. We have regular protests outside our lab. Despite the noise they make, I'd never suggest that they're thrown out of the university campus as I'm a strong believer in everyone's right to protest. What has struck me when I've spoken to those involved outside our building is how little they actually know about what we do, and why we use animals in our research. If it were me, I'd want to have a pretty strong argument lined up against what I'm protesting about, but that doesn't always seem to be the case.

Anyway, let me move onto the ethical arguments for and against . . .

Recording 3

Female: Do you think we'll still be experimenting on animals to produce new medicines in 20 years' time?

Male: I hope not. There's a strong argument for using humans in all medical trials, but I think the risks are too high with many of them for that to ever happen. The processing power of IT hardware's multiplying rapidly though, and the software's getting ever more sophisticated, so my guess is that these'll be used instead of animals.

Female: What, you mean like a simulation of what effects the new drugs have?

Male: Exactly!

Female: Hmm, great idea. What I find odd is how little you see the ethical questions raised by animal experimentation in the news. I mean, it's a major issue, but the few things I've read about it in the last year or so have all been written by scientists who are all using animal testing in their research. They certainly know the ins and outs of it, but you can imagine which side of the debate they all argue for.

Male: Yeah!

Female: And there never seems to be anything in the news to balance that out.

Unit 10

E4 (Audio 13)

Speaker 1

I started work at an architect's office when I was 18. I'd studied technical drawing in metalwork and woodwork lessons and was a bit taken aback to be asked to use them in my first week there – I thought all I'd be trusted with was some photocopying and filing. What I did wasn't perfect, but they were impressed nonetheless, and I've gradually been given more and more responsibility as time has gone on. What struck me about it to begin with was how exhausted I was, presumably because everything was so new – the working environment, having adult colleagues rather than classmates my own age, and so on. I was really happy at the same time, though.

Speaker 2

I got a weekend job at a bakery while I was still at school. I thought I'd be tired out by the end of the day as I had to start at 5:30 a.m. It was so interesting developing all these new skills, though, that it seemed to provide me with loads of extra energy. One of the bakers there, who'd been around for years, clearly didn't take to having a chatty young bloke like me there and tried to give me a hard time. The manager, who was the complete opposite of the strict, shouty person I was expecting, had a quiet word in his ear, though, and that seemed to sort it out. I've left there now, but I still pop in to see my old workmates if I'm passing by.

Speaker 3

My first job was in a local garage. It's always been my dream to be able to work on racing cars, fixing them and getting them running as fast as possible, and this was the first step on the ladder. I'd pictured it being quite a stressful place to work, with customers coming in and getting all hot under the collar that their cars weren't ready, and so on. It was actually a pretty laid-back place, though, and the boss had a miraculous way of dealing with customers that always ended up with them smiling. I felt like I wasn't picking much up at first, but then I was working on a car one day, replacing the brakes, when I realised I'd done it all myself without even asking for help. That was a good feeling!

> Acknowledgements

The authors and publishers acknowledge the following sources of copyright material and are grateful for the permissions granted. While every effort has been made, it has not always been possible to identify the sources of all the material used, or to trace all copyright holders. If any omissions are brought to our notice, we will be happy to include the appropriate acknowledgements on reprinting.

Unit 1 Reading Test Text adapted and used with permission of author 'Goal setter or problem solver?' by Rick McDaniel, HuffPost, June 2016; *Unit 2 Reading Test 'Healthy work-life balance for teens' by Educating Matters, July 2019; Unit 10 Reading Test Text adapted and used with permission from 'Slashie life: Career freedom or burnout waiting to happen?' by Jess Amy Dixon, May 2019, www.youthemployment.org.uk*

Thanks to the following for permission to reproduce images:

Cover Andriy Onufriyenko/Getty Images; *Writing Test 2* Sorapong Chaipanya/GI; *Listening Tests 2* robynmac/GI; Adam Gault/GI; fcafotodigital/GI; Tetra Images/GI; ronstik/GI; gt29/GI; ermingut/GI; Tanja Esser/GI; baibaz/GI; onurdongel/GI; jurisam/GI; Image Source/GI; samael334/GI; Creative Crop/GI; Ghislain & Marie David de Lossy/GI; RapidEye/GI; Sitade/GI; Thanadol Benyasirisataporn/GI; alanphillips/GI; Luca Sage/GI; AscentXmedia/GI; James O'Neil/GI; *Writing Test 4* Inside Creative House/GI; *Writing Test 6* Carlina Teteris/GI; *Listening Tests 7* Vostok/GI; adventtr/GI; chrisboy2004/GI; rilueda/GI; Fotosearch/GI; Mint Images/GI; opulent images/GI; Minerva Studio/GI; Busà Photography/GI; Jacobs Stock Photography Ltd/GI; Mint Images/GI; Klaus Vedfelt/GI; Anikona/GI; Jasmin Merdan/GI; webphotographeer/GI; Taiyou Nomachi/GI; *Writing Test 8* tdub303/GI; *Writing Test 10* ViewStock/GI

GI = Getty Images